Life-Span Development and Behavior

VOLUME 12

Life-Span Development and Behavior

VOLUME 12

Edited by

David L. Featherman

Social Science Research Council
New York, New York

Richard M. Lerner

Michigan State University
East Lansing, Michigan

Marion Perlmutter

The University of Michigan
Ann Arbor, Michigan

LEA LAWRENCE ERLBAUM ASSOCIATES, PUBLISHERS
1994   Hillsdale, New Jersey   Hove, UK

Lawrence Erlbaum Associates, Inc., Publishers
365 Broadway
Hillsdale, New Jersey 07642

The Library of Congress has cataloged this work as
   follows:

Life-span development and behavior.
v. 1–
   1978–
      v. 24 cm. annual.
   Key title: Life-span development and behavior, ISSN 0161-9454

   1. Developmental psychology—Periodicals.
   BF712.L535   155′.05   78-643797
   ISBN 0-8058-1507-4

Books published by Lawrence Erlbaum Associates are printed on acid-free paper,
and their bindings are chosen for strength and durability.

Printed in the United States of America
10 9 8 7 6 5 4 3 2 1

Contents

Parenting Across the Life Span: The Normative and Nonnormative Cases

Marsha Mailick Seltzer and Carol D. Ryff

The Dynamics Between Dependency and Autonomy: Illustrations Across the Life Span

Margret M. Baltes and Susan B. Silverberg

**Coping During Childhood and Adolescence:
A Motivational Perspective**

Ellen A. Skinner and James G. Wellborn

**Aging, Personality, and Social Change: The Stability of Individual
Differences Over the Adult Life Span**

Duane F. Alwin

**Wholesome Knowledge: Concepts of Wisdom in a Historical and
Cross-Cultural Perspective**

Aleida Assmann

**Log-Linear Modeling of Categorical Data in
Developmental Research**

Alexander von Eye, Kurt Kreppner, and Holger Weßels

**Integrating Scholarship and Outreach in Human Development Research,
Policy, and Service: A Developmental Contextual Perspective**

*Richard M. Lerner, Julia R. Miller, Jack H. Knott,
Kenneth E. Corey, Timothy S. Bynum, Leah Cox Hoopfer,
Marvin H. McKinney, L. Annette Abrams, Richard C. Hula, and
Patterson A. Terry*

Contributors

L. Annette Abrams (249), Institute for Children, Youth, and Families and Institute for Public Policy and Social Research, Michigan State University, East Lansing, MI 48824

Duane F. Alwin (135), Institute for Social Research, University of Michigan, Ann Arbor, MI 48109

Aleida Assmann (187), Im Neulich 5, D-6900 Heidelberg, Federal Republic of Germany

Margret M. Baltes (41), Forschungsgruppe für Psychologische Gerontologie, Freie Universität Berlin, Ulmenallee 32, D-1000 Berlin 19, Federal Republic of Germany

Timothy S. Bynum (249), Institute for Public Policy and Social Research and Department of Criminal Justice, Michigan State University, East Lansing, MI 48824

Kenneth E. Corey (249), College of Social Science, 205 Berkey Hall, Michigan State University, East Lansing, MI 48824

Leah Cox Hoopfer (249), Institute for Children, Youth, and Families and Cooperative Extension Service, Michigan State University, East Lansing, MI 48824

Richard C. Hula (249), Political Science, Urban Affairs, Program in Public Policy and Administration, and Institute for Public Policy and Social Research, Michigan State University, East Lansing, MI 48824

Jack H. Knott (249), Institute for Public Policy and Social Research, 301 Olds Hall, Michigan State University, East Lansing, MI 48824

Kurt Kreppner (225), Max Planck Institut für Bildungsforschung, Lentzeallee 94, D-1000 Berlin 33, Federal Republic of Germany

Richard M. Lerner (249), Institute for Children, Youth, and Families, 2 Paolucci Building, Michigan State University, East Lansing, MI 48824

Marvin H. McKinney (249), Institute for Children, Youth, and Families, 2 Paolucci Building, Michigan State University, East Lansing, MI 48824

Julia R. Miller (249), College of Human Ecology, 101 Human Ecology, Michigan State University, East Lansing, MI 48824

Carol D. Ryff (1), Department of Psychology and Institute on Aging and Adult Life, University of Wisconsin-Madison, 1500 Highland Avenue, Madison, WI 53705

Marsha Mailick Seltzer (1), School of Social Work and Waisman Center, University of Wisconsin-Madison, Madison, WI 53705

Susan B. Silverberg (41), Division of Family Studies, 210 FCR Building, University of Arizona, Tucson, AZ 85721

Ellen A. Skinner (91), Department of Psychology, Portland State University, P.O. Box 751, Portland, OR 97207

Patterson A. Terry (249), Institute for Children, Youth, and Families, 2 Paolucci Building, Michigan State University, East Lansing, MI 48824

Alexander von Eye (225), Michigan State University, East Lansing, MI 48824

James G. Wellborn (91), Department of Psychology and Human Development, Vanderbilt University, Nashville, TN 37203

Holger Weßels (225), Freie Universität Berlin, Institut für Kleinkind, Erwachsenen und Sozialpädagogik, D-1000 Berlin 33, Federal Republic of Germany

Preface

Serial publications, like people, have a finite life course. This parallel seems especially apt for a series devoted to reviewing life-span research and theory in the behavioral and social sciences. The serial publication, *Life-Span Development and Behavior,* began in 1978 with Volume 1 of the series, edited by Paul B. Baltes. It ends 15 years later with Volume 12, edited by David L. Featherman, Richard M. Lerner, and Marion Perlmutter.

There were important intellectual reasons for the initiation of the series, and there are similar bases for its end. *Life-Span Development and Behavior* began in order to crystallize, organize, and thereby further a variety of theoretical and empirical endeavors pertinent to human development across the life span; this scholarly activity was occurring in several disciplines but primarily was focused in psychology and sociology. Because of these disciplinary emphases, it was significant for the healthy life of the series that sociologist Orville G. Brim, Jr. joined psychologist Baltes to edit Volumes 2 through 6.

The current editorial team believes that it was the intellectual vision, energy, and productivity of Baltes and Brim that made the series a vital contribution to the literature. It was their leadership that also nurtured the field of life-span human development, extending its boundaries to other disciplines and, in several respects, making it one of the key perspectives within contemporary social and behavior science. Indeed, we may attribute to their scholarly and professional efforts — efforts that certainly extend far beyond their editorship of this series — the fact that all training programs in human development, both in the United States and internationally, include the life-span perspective (and the work of Baltes and Brim) as core foundations of the field.

The breadth of this influence (which we hope has been facilitated by Volumes 7 through 10, edited by Baltes, Featherman, and Lerner, and by Volumes 11 and 12, edited by the present editorial team) is a key reason that it is appropriate to end the series with this volume. Today, there is broad scientific attention given to ideas and issues associated with the life-span perspective: constancy and change in human development; opportunites for and constraints on plasticity in structure and function across life; the potential for intervention across the entire life course (and thus for the creation of an applied developmental science); individual differences (diversity) in life paths, in contexts (or the ecology) of human development, and in changing relations between people and contexts; interconnections and discontinuities across age levels and developmental periods; and the importance of integrating biological, psychological, social, cultural, and historical levels of organization in order to understand human development.

These issues are addressed in numerous scientific journals and reviewed in dozens of undergraduate and graduate textbooks. Moreover, several scientific journals adopt editorial policies that are life span in orientation either explicitly (e.g., *Developmental Psychology,* the *International Journal of Behavioral Development, Human Development,* and the *Journal of Applied Developmental Psychology*) or implicitly (e.g., *Developmental Review* and the *Journal of Research on Adolescence*). In essence, then, the quality and quantity of scientific outlets for the dissemination of scholarship pertinent to life-span human development has led us to conclude that the field has reached a level of maturity and sustainability that no longer requires facilitation by a series of the current format. On the other hand, precisely because of the exciting fast-moving work in this interdisciplinary and international field, we applaud and encourage initiatives now being discussed for what may emerge as a new format of exchange and commentary on frontier issues.

Over the course of the 12 volumes of *Life-Span Development and Behavior,* the editors have been fortunate to have had the advice of a distinguished panel of Advisory Editors. The contributions of the following colleagues to this group is gratefully acknowledged: Glen H. Elder, Jr., E. Mavis Hetherington, Aletha Huston, Martin Kohli, Gisela Labouvie-Vief, Lewis P. Lipsitt, Bernice L. Neugarten, Matilda W. Riley, Michael Rutter, K. Warner Schaie, and Aage B. Sorensen.

In addition to our Advisory Editors we also wish to acknowledge with gratitude and respect the contributions of many colleagues who assisted as consultants in helping us develop the chapters comprising the present volume. These ad hoc reviewers provided valuable comments and suggestions to the contributors before final chapters were prepared. They are:

Duane F. Alwin	Toni C. Antonucci
Paul B. Baltes	Vern L. Bengtson
James Birren	Rosemary Blieszner
Richard Campbell	Avshalom Caspi
Mihaly Csikszentmihalyi	Jack Dennis
Roger A. Dixon	Gunhild Hagestad
Marty Wyngaarden Krauss	Powell Lawton
Gerald Marwell	Jeylan T. Mortimer
John R. Nesselroade	Luther B. Otto

Carol D. Ryff

Martin E. P. Seligman

Laurence Steinberg

Patricia Sears

Alan Sroufe

Alexander von Eye

Finally, we wish to extend special thanks to Linda K. Chapel, Annette Dieli, and Lynne Woods for their splendid editorial assistance over the course of the last several volumes of the series.

David L. Featherman

Richard M. Lerner

Marion Perlmutter

Contents of Previous Volumes

Parenting Across the Life Span:
The Normative and Nonnormative Cases

Marsha Mailick Seltzer and Carol D. Ryff

UNIVERSITY OF WISCONSIN-MADISON

Abstract

The experience of parenthood is examined from a life-span developmental perspective, and within this framework, normative parenting is contrasted with nonnormative parenting. Our nonnormative example pertains to parenting a child with mental retardation. We emphasize that both normative and nonnormative parenthood are lifelong commitments, with shifting roles, responsibilities, and relationships that emerge as parents and children age. Our focus is on the consequences of these changing experiences for the well-being of parents themselves, and on how such consequences vary depending on whether parenthood is experienced in the typical or atypical case. We argue that, in both cases, there is need to establish the life-course connections across the early, middle, and later years of parenthood. The lack of theoretical and empirical inquiry during the middle years is given particular emphasis. We also discuss the need to consider individual differences in the parental experience, changing patterns of reciprocity in parent–child relationships, and historical and/or cohort influences on the experience of parenthood.

I. Introduction

Normative and nonnormative events have been conceptualized as distinct influences on the course of human development (Baltes, 1987). In the former category are experiences governed largely by biological maturation (e.g., puberty) or sociocultural timetables (e.g., graduation from high school). These events tend to be experienced by most individuals with fairly high predictability. Nonnormative experiences, in contrast, are the unshared, unpredictable events for which individuals receive little prior socialization (Brim & Ryff, 1980). This category includes events typically found on life stress inventories (e.g., physical illness, loss of a job, death of a loved one).

The literature on nonnormative events is quite separate from studies of the more predictable transitions of individual, relationship, or family development. Whereas normative influences have been studied developmentally, there has been very little theoretical or empirical analysis of the developmental sequelae or consequences of nonnormative events. This chapter's premise is that much is gained from examining normative and nonnormative influences and their developmental profiles in tandem. That is, the simultaneous consideration of and contrast between these domains extends the conceptualization and empirical assessment of each.

Our illustration for this dual focus is the experience of parenthood. Because parenthood is an experience with long-term, life-course implications, it provides a particularly useful context for this analysis. More important, parenthood is an experience that can be conceived both normatively and nonnormatively. For many adults in our culture, it is a transition experienced at fairly predictable times and in generally shared ways. For others, parenthood is experienced nonnormatively, either by temporal deviation from the norm (e.g., becoming a parent much earlier or later in the life course than is typical), variation in family structure (e.g., single parenthood), or atypical child characteristics (e.g., having a child with a disability). Our particular nonnormative focus is on the life-course experience of parenting a child with mental retardation.

We note that others have called for a developmental contrast between normative and nonnormative experiences. For example, in their studies of the relationships between the developing person and the changing family, Kreppner and Lerner (1989) emphasized that future developmental family research should include nonnormative events such as early motherhood, incest or child abuse, and exceptional creativity or invulnerability, so that these changes can be contrasted with normative events and changes. Featherman (1985) also noted that although the timing of nonnormative events is not typically related to age, nonnormative events can trigger developmental changes. In a related point, Bandura (1982) pointed out that adult development can be profoundly affected by chance encounters, one category of nonnormative events. Finally, Parke (1988), in evaluating families in life-span perspective, emphasized the need to understand how families cope with normative and nonnormative stressful transitions, even though his examples come primarily from the nonnormative domain (e.g., divorce, job loss, off-time parenting). In summary, there is growing recognition of the need to consider simultaneously normative and nonnormative family experiences and their developmental implications.

There is also the need to conceptualize parenting across the full life course. Life-span research on parenting is a departure from the traditional focus of family research, which has emphasized either the beginning or the end of the parental life course (Hagestad, 1987). A particular challenge faced with the life-span conceptualization of parenting is that each life phase is studied by different groups of researchers — child developmentalists, gerontologists, family sociologists, personality psychologists. This diversity in groups of investigators contributes to the lack of connections across life phases, but offers great potential for the synthesis and extension of theory and findings.

A life-span perspective on parenting recognizes that parenting is a lifelong commitment (Lancaster, Altmann, Rossi, & Sherrod, 1987), that the roles of parent and child continue even after the child has become an adult, and that there are expectable changes across the life span in family functions, composition, stability, and individual impacts. As a result of these changes, patterns of individual and family adaptation, such as levels of cohesion, intimacy, and stress, that are observed during the first decade of the child's life might not be characteristic of how the members of a family function when the child is in his or her 20s, 30s, or 40s and the parents are in their 50s, 60s, or 70s. Little is known about the course of intraindividual development of parents and intrafamilial development over the full life course.

This chapter deals with the life stages through which all parents expect to pass, and the divergent course taken when the unexpected (i.e., the nonnormative) occurs. However, the differentiation of the normative from the nonnormative parenthood experience raises a host of complex issues. First, what is meant by normative? Is it the statistically modal experience, or is it the socially desired case? When the statistically modal experience is the socially desired case, the distinction between normative and nonnormative is not problematic. However, in the case of parenting, contemporary changes in the structure of family life have blurred the once-clear distinction between normative and nonnormative parenthood. For example, at the present time more than half of the first marriages in the United States are expected to end in divorce (Castro-Martin & Bumpass, 1989) and more than half of these divorces involve couples with children (Spanier & Glick, 1981). Although more than 60% of children live with two parents who have been married only to each other (Bumpass, 1984), for certain subgroups of the population (e.g., African Americans), single parenthood is the now modal case. Further, stepparenting is an increasingly common phenomenon and is the major cause of stress on remarried couples (White & Booth, 1985). Even within traditional family structures, the likelihood that an adult child will return to the parental home has increased considerably (Aquilino & Supple, 1991). Thus, the statistically modal experience of once-married two-parent families with children moving out of the home when they reach adulthood is becoming less common. Nevertheless, it remains socially desirable for children to be healthy, to be reared by both of their parents, and, when they reach maturity, to establish an independent household. It is in this context that we conceive of the normative experience of parenthood and contrast it with the nonnormative.

Nonnormative parenthood itself is increasingly heterogeneous. The non-normative parenthood experience can be the result of either an atypical child (as in the case of mental retardation) or an atypical parent (as in the case of parental addiction). The developmental trajectory of nonnormative parenthood when the parent's characteristics define parenthood as atypical would be sharply different for both the parent and the child than when the child's characteristics define parenthood as nonnormative. In this chapter we focus on the latter case, and proceed with the assumption that the parents are not disabled or otherwise markedly atypical in their physical and emotional well-being.

Our plan in this chapter is to first examine parenting across the life course using the normative case. The expansive, complex literature on parenting in the "typical" case exceeds what could be meaningfully reviewed in a single chapter. Thus, our objective is to provide illustrations of parenting studies at different points in the family life cycle (e.g., transition to parenthood, middle years of parenting, parenthood in the later years), rather than a comprehensive account of theories and empirical findings in this literature. Preference was given to illustrative studies that focused on the consequences of the parenting experience for the individual parent.

The discussion of nonnormative parenthood is more narrowly focused than our examination of the normative case, because here we restrict our analysis to one example, namely parenting a child with retardation. The same temporal periods are examined in the nonnormative case, and again, the emphasis is on the consequences of parenting for the parent, rather than for the parent–child dyad or the family as a whole. In the final section of the chapter, we contrast these two literatures to show that each contains important research agendas, but that the two realms point to each other's conceptual and empirical lacunae. We conclude with new directions for research.

II. Parenting Across the Life Span: The Normative Case

A. THE TRANSITION TO PARENTHOOD

The transition to parenthood refers not just to the period immediately before or after the birth of a child, but more generally to the early years of parenthood, when children are young and the parental experience is also in its early years. Parents loom large in the literature surrounding this period, but the vast majority of studies are concerned with the effects of parents on the early development of children, rather than on how the transition to parenthood affects the parent, him or herself. For example, research on childhood attachment (Ainsworth, 1973; Bowlby, 1982; Bretherton & Waters, 1985; Sroufe, 1979) is very much about infants and their parents, particularly mothers. However, the objective in this literature is not to explicate the consequences of this emerging bond for the parent, but rather to provide "a normative account" of the development of attachment of the infant to the mother during the first year of life through observation of the behavior of infants and their mothers (Ainsworth, 1989, p. 709). Life-span extrapolations from early attachments to affectional bonds in adulthood (Lerner & Ryff, 1978) have also focused on the long-term consequences of these early experiences for the child who grows into adolescence or adulthood, rather than for the parent.

The expanding literature on the effects of day care on young children (e.g., Belsky, 1990; Clarke-Stewart, 1989) is also about parent–child relations, and specific characteristics of parents are included in the conceptualization of such relations. But again, the primary focus is on how parents' qualities influence their parenting behaviors, and subsequently, their children's development. Thus, adults who are psychologically healthy, nurturing, and mature provide beneficial care for their offspring. The question of how parenthood contributes to the health or maturity of parents themselves is rarely asked. In short, large domains of developmental research incorporate parents as part of the research design, but they are nearly always conceived as independent, rather than the dependent, variables.

Significant exceptions to this prevailing emphasis must be acknowledged. Bell (1968) and Harper (Bell & Harper, 1977), in reviews of socialization research, explicitly emphasized the effects of children on parents, arguing against the decidedly unidirectional bias in prior studies, where parents were routinely viewed as having influence on their young, but not the reverse. Drawing on evidence from many domains, they showed how the behavior and appearance of the young are a compelling part of the stimulus field for the parent. Children, in fact, were found to initiate the majority of interaction sequences. Behavioral in theory, they offered a control model in which excessive or inappropriate child behavior (e.g., aggression) was seen to induce upper limit control behavior from parental repertoires (e.g., rejection, discipline), whereas child behavior below parental standards was viewed to induce lower limit parent controls that acted to stimulate behavior. Bell and Harper evaluated multiple research strategies (experimental–nonexperimental, molar–specific, short-term–long-term) in terms of their capacity to isolate parent effects on the child and child effects on the parent. Throughout this endeavor the unit of analysis was not the individual child, or the individual parent, but rather the interaction between the two—that is, the parent–child system.

A decade later, Peterson and Rollins' (1987) review of the parent–child socialization literature points to the continuing interest in bidirectional effects, and at the same time, shows that the majority of studies remain focused on how parents influence children. Their review also clarifies that much of the existing work on bidirectionality had been limited to the infancy period. There were few examples of the effects of older children on their parents, with the exception of research on youth movements and how they affect the attitudes of parents (Bengtson & Troll, 1978). The authors, in fact, called for greater attention to the question of how older offspring influence their adult caretakers. Overall, the socialization literature continues to emphasize processes of reciprocity between parent and child, which are frequently studied with microanalyses of interactive behavior. Considerable effort has been devoted to the methodological advances required for the sequential analyses of these complex datasets (Peterson & Rollins, 1987).

Beyond the realm of socialization research, there is also a literature on how children affect the parental marriage and the family itself (e.g., Lerner & Spanier, 1978). These investigations do not have as their focus the question of how parenthood affects the individual parent. Studies of the latter variety are few in number and have been conducted primarily by life-span developmental and/or personality psychologists. Sirignano and Lachman (1985) illustrated this kind of inquiry. Following from a life-events framework (e.g., Brim & Ryff, 1980; Hultsch & Plemons, 1979), they proposed that major life transitions such as parenthood can lead to change in parents' personality characteristics (efficacy and control) and change in their psychological functioning (anxiety and depression). They further proposed that such changes are mediated by parents' perceptions of their infant's temperament. To investigate these ideas, they followed new parents, both mothers and fathers, through the transition to parenthood. Thus, data were collected 4–8 weeks before birth and 8–12 weeks after birth. New parents were also compared with a control group of childless couples. Measures of efficacy, personal control, anxiety, and depression were assessed with global/trait indicators as well as situation-specific, or state indicators. The findings supported the prediction of changes in key personality dimensions during transition to parenthood, which were linked to parent perceptions of infant's temperament. Parents of infants perceived as having an easier temperament generally experienced more positive changes compared to parents of infants perceived as more difficult. Fathers, however, indicated change in more personality dimensions (i.e., global and parental efficacy, global and situation-specific control, and trait anxiety) related to infant temperament than did mothers (who showed change in parental efficacy, global and situation-specific control). Depression levels of both of mothers and fathers did not change over the transition to parenthood.

In addition to research on change in efficacy and control orientations following parenthood, other studies have examined changes in parents' masculinity and femininity across the family life cycle. Abrahams, Feldman, and Nash (1978) compared men and women across four life situations: cohabitation, marriage, the anticipation of first child, and parenthood. They hypothesized that these different life situations are accompanied by changes in sex-role self-concept and attitudes. Because parenthood is so "strongly associated with a reallocation of roles along traditional lines" (p. 396), they predicted that both men and women in the parent group would express more traditional sex-role orientations than their counterparts in the other three situations. Multiple self-rated assessments of masculinity and femininity were obtained. Findings revealed, as predicted, that the parenting situation was accompanied by higher femininity and lower masculinity ratings among women (compared with women in the other situations). Men's scores were in the predicted direction (i.e., higher masculinity and lower femininity in parenting situation), but were not significant. Outcomes for sex-role attitudes revealed the predicted traditional orientation for both mothers and fathers, compared to other groups. Feldman, Biringen, and Nash (1981) expanded this line of inquiry to include a larger sample, more stages of the family life cycle (e.g., empty nesters, grandparents), and a multidimensional assessment of sex-role self-concept. Specific to the stage of parenthood, their findings showed that mothers of young children scored higher on the dimension of tenderness than did other women, whereas fathers of young children scored higher on leadership and somewhat higher on autonomy than did other men. Mature parents (i.e., youngest child was 14–17 years old) also showed sex-specific differences from other life stages. Mature mothers were lower than other women on self-ascribed masculinity, whereas mature fathers rated themselves higher on leadership, autonomy, and assertiveness, and lower on acquiescence than did other men. A subsequent study (Cunningham & Antill, 1984), based on a survey of Australian respondents, suggested that it is adults' employment status, not their family life status, that has greater conse-quences for sex-role attitudes of masculinity and femininity. They con-cluded that previous studies in this area have been "too hasty in identifying the presence or absence of children as the key feature of the family life cycle affecting masculinity and femininity, instead of the employment or educa-tion of the female partner" (p. 1135).

In summary, most research on the early years of parenthood has included parents because of interest in how they affect their children. The socializa-tion literature has, however, been sensitive to bidirectional influences in parent–child interaction. Studies that have focused explicitly on change in individual parents have been in the realm of life-span developmental research, have employed largely self-report methods, and have explored change in personality characteristics, psychological functioning, and sex-role attitudes. Differences between mothers and fathers are recurrent themes in these findings.

B. THE MIDDLE YEARS OF PARENTHOOD

More than 30 years ago, Erikson (1959) postulated that continued development in middle adulthood requires that one express concern for guiding and directing the next generation. He described this concern as the task of "generativity" and stated that it could be achieved in multiple contexts including work and family. Ironically, life-course studies of parenting reveal a prominent omission during the middle years of adult-hood. Hagestad (1987) observed, in fact, that most of the research on parent–child relations can be divided into two phases: the "alpha" phase, which encompasses studies of young children and new parents (as described in the prior section), and the "omega" phase, in which parents are old and their children are middle-age (the focus of the next section). Decidedly absent in this literature are those years when children are growing up, but parents have not yet become aged. Even the work that has followed from Erikson's formulation of generativity (e.g., McAdams, Ruetzel, & Foley, 1986; Peterson & Stewart, 1990; Ryff & Heincke, 1983) has rarely been tied to the experience of parenting, per se.

Again, we focus on the exceptions to this general depiction. For example, Rossi (1980a) conducted an exploratory study of middle-age mothers of early adolescents, noting at the outset that family stage typologies (e.g.,

Hill, 1964) had been defined, not in terms of parental age, but in terms of age of youngest child. Rossi observed, however, that parents of early adolescent children show wide age variation. Thus, of interest was how parental age (explored in relation to physiological changes, the characteristics of the parental cohort, and as a marker of family developmental phase) affected the parental experience. Results suggested that women who wished they were younger reported greater difficulty rearing adolescent children than did women who accepted their age. Further, women who had recently experienced and an elevation of aging symptoms reported less emotional closeness to their early adolescent children. There were also suggestions of possible cohort differences between older and younger mothers.

Despite Rossi's (1980a) intriguing juxtaposition of adolescent development and midlife parental development, little research followed in this vein. A decade later, Silverberg and Steinberg (1990) examined the influence of developing adolescent children on the psychological well-being of midlife parents. Drawing on the perspective that the middle years may be a time of increased life appraisal and introspection, their guiding question addressed the consequences for parents when they are "faced with youngsters who are becoming physically mature, socially active, and psychologically independent" (p. 658). The study was based on intact families with a firstborn child between the ages of 10 and 15 years. Adolescent development was assessed in terms of pubertal maturation, heterosocial involvement, and persuasive reasoning abilities. Parents' well-being was assessed in terms of identity concerns, self-esteem, life satisfaction, and lack of psychological symptoms. Only modest direct relations were found between signs of adolescent development and parental well-being. Such relations were, however, clarified when the strength of the parent's orientation toward his or her work role was taken into consideration. For parents with a weak orientation toward work, adolescent development was negatively associated with well-being; for those with a strong work orientation, the associations were often positive. Specifically, higher levels of youngsters' dating behavior and mixed-sex peer group activities were associated with more intense midlife concerns, lower life satisfaction, or more frequent psychological symptoms on the part of parents, but these effects were found only among parents not strongly invested in a paid-work role (mothers of daughters were the one exception to this pattern). The authors suggested that parents with a low work-role orientation lack a strong sense of self and satisfaction outside the family, and may thus have difficulty dealing with youngsters' maturity and expanding social world outside the family.

Another relevant line of midlife inquiry has emerged from demographic trends, which point to the increasing presence of adult children in the homes of their midlife parents. Data from the 1988 National Survey of Families and Households indicate that, among midlife parents (age 45–54 years) who have adult children, 45% have an adult child living at home (Aquilino, 1990). Of interest has been the causes and consequences of this trend. Children's marital status was found to be the strongest predictor of coresidence: Only parents with unmarried adult children had any appreciable risk of having an adult child at home. Subsequent work (Aquilino, 1991b) pointed to other factors that influence the likelihood of coresidence: When families have not been reconstituted through parental remarriage, when parent–child relations are good, and when parents have favorable attitudes toward the continued support of adult children, coresidence is more probable. With regard to the consequences of coresidence, that is, with how "children's success in grappling with the tasks of young adulthood affects the lives of parents," Aquilino (1991a, p. 14) noted that continued presence of unlaunched adult children has been assumed to create difficulties (e.g., increased parent–child conflict, reduced opportunities for parents' self-development, and decreased parental satisfaction with coresidence). He found, however, that the majority of parents (mothers and fathers) were highly satisfied with the coresident living arrangement and described mostly positive relationships with their adult children. That is, parent–child relations were not dominated by conflict, although conflict remained the strongest single predictor of parents' satisfaction with coresidence. Aquilino noted that the limited evidence of negative effects of coresidence may, in part, be due to selection effects, in which conflicting coresident arrangements are likely to end sooner. Overall, this realm of research is directly pertinent to the life course of parenting, although we noted that most outcomes to date have dealt with the parent–child relationship, rather than the parents' self-development and well-being, despite the purported interest in the latter.

The theme of parent–child relations in the middle years of adulthood is also prominent in a significant new contribution that explores the continuity and change in such relationships over time and across generational dyads in the same lineages (Rossi & Rossi, 1990). Of particular interest was the reciprocity or imbalance in the flow of affection, comfort, and goods between the generations. Among a rich array of findings, the research pointed to the significant influences of early family of origin characteristics on the sentiment and behavior of adults in their relationships with children, parents, or spouses, as well as clarified that types of help between the generations tend to be channeled along traditional gender lines. With regard to the life-course profiles of intergenerational ties, an intriguing finding was that intimacy between parents and adult children actually increases over the adult years, thereby underscoring the importance of affective ties between parents and grown children. Presumably such increments in intimacy have positive consequences for parents' well-being, although such claims have yet to be tested. Personal characteristics of parents were considered in these analyses, but typically were conceptualized as influences on the parent-child relationship, rather than as an outcome of such interaction. An exception pertained to analyses of the determinants of dominance and expressivity, personal characteristics derived from the prior literature on gender differences. The authors hypothesized that the experience of parenthood "may encourage the flowering of tender, nurturant qualities in men" (p. 305), whose prior socialization, unlike that of women, has not emphasized such qualities. As predicted, having children was found to have a significant positive effect on the expressivity levels of men, but not of women.

To summarize, research on the middle years of parenthood has paid little heed to Erikson's (1959) claim that continued development in adulthood requires that one express a concern for guiding and directing the next generation. Promising new lines of inquiry have juxtaposed the development of adolescent children with the continued development of their parents as well as examined the implications for parental well-being of adult children's continued residence in the parental home. The relationship between midlife adults and their grown children remains a more prominent focus of investigation than the effects of such children on the parent, per se.

C. THE LATER YEARS OF PARENTHOOD

The study of aged parents and middle-age children, following from the aforementioned inquiries, is generally referred to as the intergenerational relations literature, or the literature on families in later life (Hagestad, 1987). Much of the omega work is done by family sociologists and gerontologists. This research examines patterns of contact, the intergenerational transmission of values and attitudes, family norms and expectations, and patterns of support. For the most part, scholars in this area do not draw linkages between alpha and omega phases—that is, caregiving for aged parents is rarely linked to the quality of early parent-child relationships. The conventional assumption that aged parents who provided quality care and security for their young children will have their efforts reciprocated when needed receives little empirical attention. As an exception, Spitze and Logan (1989) did investigate whether women's kin-keeping activities at earlier stages of the life cycle pay off in more contact and assistance in old age. Using national data for respondents over age 65 years, they found evidence, albeit weak, of such payoff, in terms of closer proximity to children, more phone calls, and marginally more visits. There was little direct effect of gender on assistance.

Another theme in the intergenerational relations literature is the tension between the forces of social continuity and innovation between the generations—that is, the extent to which parents, children, and grandchildren appear distinctive from or replicate each other in behaviors, attitudes, and orientations (Bengtson, 1987). Researchers in this domain examine the causes of generational contrasts or similarities and delineate the types of solidarity between the generations (Bengtson & Schraeder, 1982). From the parental viewpoint, an assumption is that "parents invest prodigious amounts of time, energy, and material resources in the uncertain hope of producing offspring who will be happy, healthy, and wise, and who will, hopefully, validate at least some of the parents' principles" (Bengtson, 1987, p. 435). Considerable research has explored the actual values and attitudes of the different generations as well as how parents and grown children perceive each others' values and attitudes. Specific assessments of whether parents, in fact, feel "validated" by their children have received less attention. That is, despite the appeal of the "developmental stake" concept (i.e., the idea that the parental generation has a particular investment in socializing their young as a means of ensuring their own immortality and generational continuity; Bengtson & Kuypers, 1971), little is known about the consequences of such stakes, achieved or failed, on the well-being of parents.

In contrast to family sociologists, gerontologists give greater emphasis to the topic of parent care, even to the extent of defining it as a normative family role (Brody, 1985). Brody argued that nowadays adult children provide more care to more parents over much longer periods of time than they did in the past. The stresses associated with such caretaking include financial hardships, possible decline in physical health, and most notably, emotional strains. Despite the pervasiveness, and even predictability of parent care, most adult children do not anticipate parent care as a likely developmental task. Brody emphasized that a central issue in parent care is the dialectic tension of dependence/independence. That is, people differ in the extent to which they have the capacity to meet the dependency needs of others. She emphasized that successful resolution of the filial crisis (i.e., the challenge adult children face in caring for their aged parents) may involve acceptance by adult children of what they cannot do for their aging parents. Interestingly, Brody's thoughtful formulation revolves entirely around the effects of parent care on adult children, not the reverse. Equally compelling questions address the consequences for the mental and physical well-being of aging parents, once they realize their needs for and dependency on their adult children. What factors influence how aged parents negotiate this transition? Beckman's (1981) research suggests that elderly mothers report lower well-being when their adult children do more for them than they do for their children. However, if greater input from children is balanced by past maternal efforts on the children's behalf, this is not the case. Mothers who devoted much effort to being a good parent in the past thus feel more deserving of the benefits they receive from their adult children. This finding is consistent with Antonucci and Jackson's (1990) concept of the support bank, which suggests that earlier life "investments" in a relationship can be legitimately "withdrawn" in later years.

The literature on what elderly parents expect of their adult children in times of need sheds additional light on the aforementioned questions. Mancini and Blieszner's (1989) summary suggests that aged parents think not only in terms of receiving concrete aid and assistance from their children, but also emphasizes the importance of affection, thoughtfulness, and open communication in these relationships. In reflecting on changes in the parenting role over time, aged parents stated that dimensions of caretaking and influence had diminished, and that children were now viewed more as friends than subordinates (Blieszner & Mancini, 1987). This review of aging parents and adult children, as well as other studies (Greenberg & Becker, 1988), also underscored the finding that older parents continue to provide support of various kinds to their adult children and are not only recipients of support.

In summary, the literature on the later years of parenthood addresses primarily the growing needs for care and assistance among aged parents. The effects of these needs for caretaking on adult children receives much more emphasis than do the effects of such emerging dependence on the elderly themselves. Moreover, despite prevailing theoretical claims, little empirical research has addressed the consequences, for parents themselves, of the perception that their children will contribute to their own immortality by adoption and continuance of parental beliefs and values.

D. PARENTHOOD VERSUS NONPARENTHOOD

In addition to the previously discussed literatures on different temporal periods of parenting, a separate realm of inquiry deals primarily with the contrast is between parents and nonparents. Here the central question has been how parenthood influences the well-being of adults, compared to those who do not become parents. Years ago, LeMasters (1957) described the transition to parenthood as a crisis, a claim that became the preoccupation of researchers in this domain. Reviews of this voluminous literature suggest that parenthood does, in fact, have negative consequences for psychological well-being (McLanahan & Adams, 1987). Adults with children at home report they are less happy and less satisfied with their lives than are other groups, although overall differences appear to be small. No single study in their summary found that parents were better off than nonparents on any of the conventional measures of well-being. McLanahan and Adams suggested that the differences between parents and nonparents may stem, in part, from economic and time constraints related to women's increased labor force participation and increasing rates of marital disruption and single parenthood.

Such survey studies have been generally nondevelopmental in their formulations of the effects of parenthood, although considerable debate has centered around the apparent U-shaped curve of marital satisfaction associated with stages of the family life cycle—satisfaction appears to drop with the advent of the first child and continues to decline up until the first child's adolescence, and then begins to increase as children leave home (see McLanahan & Adams, 1987, for reviews of this literature). However, these studies have been criticized on multiple grounds including the use of small, nonrepresentative samples and the confounding of variables (such as duration of marriage with births of children). Recently, Umberson and Gove (1989) argued that children have both positive and negative effects on parents. For example, they found that parents scored better than nonparents on measures of life meaning. Other indicators, such as affective well-being and satisfaction, appeared to be influenced more by the context of parenting (i.e., when children are young, when parents are divorced). They noted benefits of parenting for the affective well-being of parents whose children are adults and have left home, and for parents who are widowed. They also emphasized that divorced parents experience greater costs from parenting that do married or widowed parents.

Underscoring variations in the experience of parenting, Scott and Alwin (1989) documented the recurrent finding of sex differences—namely, that mothers experience more parental role strain than do fathers. Little of this difference seems, however, to be due to differential role experiences between mothers and fathers. Rather, these authors suggested that women bring different expectations with them to the parenting role (such as the view that they are more responsible for relationships) and hence are more affected by the emotional stress in family relationships. Wethington and Kessler (1989) focused on variations in well-being just among mothers, and how their well-being is influenced by change in employment and parenting roles. They concluded that change in parental roles has no significant direct effect on mothers' well-being, although large changes in employment commitment were associated with increases in mothers' well-being. That is, going from full to no employment decreased well-being, but having a baby did not.

The importance of the "normative expectedness" of one's parental experiences has also been investigated in this survey literature. Menaghan (1989) began with the observation that occupying normatively expected social roles is associated with psychological advantages (e.g., social integration, sense of meaning). The well-being of adults occupying normative parental statuses was thus contrasted with that of adults in nonnormative statuses (e.g., over age of 30 years and childless, living apart from minor children, living with adult children who were still at home). Findings showed that parental status effects interacted with gender and extent of economic pressure. Childlessness beyond age 30 years had greater negative impact on women, whereas living apart from minor-age children was more negative for men. The older childless, and both empty nest parents and delayed launchers, were more negatively affected by economic pressures than were other groups.

E. SUMMARY

The normative literature on the transition to parenthood and the early years of parenting revolves largely around how parents influence their children's development, particularly their socioemotional well-being. This work is done primarily by developmental psychologists interested in children, not parents. Life-span developmental and family life-cycle researchers, in contrast, study the early years of parenting with a focus on consequences for personality change in the parent. Select personality characteristics have been studied, such as efficacy, control, anxiety, masculinity, and femininity. Other relevant domains that have yet to be directly linked to parenting include changes in nurturance, patience, flexibility, social responsibility, and purpose in life.

Following the transition to parenthood, there is little direct study of parenting in the middle years. Exceptions to this dearth of research point to the effects of developing adolescents on parents and underscore the continuing salience of parent–child relations even into the adult years of both. Other potentially important transitions for parents' psychological well-being during these years include the departure of children from the home as well as their lack of departure or reemergence in the parental home.

Prominent issues in the later years of parenting include patterns of contact and support, transmission of values, and norms of caretaking. The primary concern here seems to be with what grown children do for their aged parents (in terms of keeping in touch with them, validating their beliefs, or caring for them). Less, but growing, attention is given to what aged parents expect from their children, how they characterize their relationships with adult children, and the ways in which they also do for their adult children (i.e., the reciprocal nature of these exchanges). The question of how aged parents feel about having adult children care for them is rarely asked.

Finally, the separate normative literature that contrasts parenthood with nonparenthood emphasizes the negative psychological consequences associated with becoming a parent. Recent endeavors have focused on the variability among different categories of parents and have broadened the assessment of parental outcomes to include possible gains as well as strains.

III. Parenting Across the Life Span:
The Nonnormative Case

In this section, parenting a child with mental retardation is examined to illustrate the nonnormative case of parenthood. Our purpose is not to treat parenting a child with mental retardation as the prototypic case of nonnormative parenthood, but rather to use this example for heuristic purposes. Mental retardation is one among many nonnormative parenting situations, including having a child with mental illness, physical illness, delinquency, and so forth. The selection of any single child diagnosis or difficulty as the illustration of nonnormative parenthood is problematic, as there are both unique effects associated with each example, as well as common elements that cut across these examples. In particular, parenting a child with mental retardation appears to be less stressful than parenting a child with autism (Holroyd & McArthur, 1976) but more stressful than parenting a child with chronic illness (Cummings, Bayley, & Rie, 1966). However, although diagnostic-specific differences have been reported in some studies, others have found evidence for the common experience of parenting a child with special needs (Kazak, 1987). Mental retardation is a particularly useful case for our purposes, as unlike other nonnormative examples that are more transitory, mental retardation is a lifelong condition and carries with it inherent developmental challenges for the family as well as for the child.

As in the preceding discussion of normative parenthood, a life-span perspective is used to illustrate the impact of a child with mental retardation on the parents. First, however, the definition of mental retardation and a brief discussion of its prevalence are presented.

A. DEFINITION OF MENTAL RETARDATION

Mental retardation is defined by the American Association on Mental Retardation as significantly subaverage general intellectual functioning, existing concurrently with deficits in adaptive behavior, and first manifested during the developmental period (before age 18 years) (Luckasson et al., 1993). Significantly subaverage general intellectual functioning refers to an IQ score of at least two standard deviations below the mean of 100 (i.e., an IQ of approximately 70 or below). The population with mental retardation is often divided into four levels: mild (IQ range of approximately 55 to 70), moderate (IQ range of approximately 40 to 54), severe (IQ range of approximately 25 to 39), and profound (IQ score below 25, approximately), with mild mental retardation accounting for about 80% of this population. According to this psychometric definition, 3% of the U.S. population is considered to have mental retardation.

An alternative approach to the definition of mental retardation is the sociocultural definition, in which mental retardation is conceptualized as a role, not a condition (Mercer, 1973). According to this model, mental retardation is socially and culturally determined. The demands for competence vary considerably from family to family, and from cultural group to cultural group. An individual who is considered to have mild mental retardation in one context may have the same abilities as a nonlabeled person who functions in a less intellectually demanding context. Further, an individual may be labeled and delabeled several times during his or her life. (An example is a mildly retarded man who was labeled as having mental retardation when he was in school, but who functions adequately in a job and no longer bears this label in adulthood, although his IQ score remains unchanged.) According to the sociocultural model, the prevalence of mental retardation is approximately 1%, much lower than the 3% hypothesized by the psychometric model of retardation. The two definitional approaches differ primarily in their classification of adults with mild mental retardation.

The vast majority of persons with mental retardation (however defined) live with their families, many for their entire lives. According to national estimates, fewer than 20% of the U.S. population with mental retardation lives in any form of nonfamily licensed placement, institutional or community-based (Fujiura, Garza, & Braddock, 1989; Lakin, Hill, Bruininks, 1985).

B. THE TRANSITION TO PARENTHOOD

In parenting a child with mental retardation, the normative challenges of the transition to parenthood are compounded by the diagnosis that the child has a disability. In cases in which the child has Down syndrome or another easily identifiable disorder, parents learn of their child's retardation at birth or shortly thereafter. In other cases, the diagnosis is made sometime during the first few years of life, based on an observable developmental delay.

Parental reactions to the diagnosis of their child as having mental retardation have been described as a series of stages that parallel Kubler-Ross' (1969) categorization of the reactions to death and dying. Although noting the controversy regarding the existence of discrete stages, Blacher (1984a) described these stages of parental adjustment to the diagnosis of mental retardation as: (a) initial crisis responses (shock, denial, and disbelief), (b) emotional disorganization (guilt, disappointment, anger, and lowered self-esteem), and finally (c) emotional reorganization (adjustment, acceptance). Although the sequence of stages is not invariant, there is accumulating evidence that the initial period following the diagnosis is the most stressful stage, that adaptation is the dominant response as time passes, and that parents may periodically reexperience their feelings from an earlier stage at later points in the life course (Featherstone, 1980; Solnit & Stark, 1961; Turnbull & Turnbull, 1978; Wikler, Wasow, & Hatfield, 1981). Positive impacts associated with parenting a child with retardation have also been noted, particularly in recent research, with many parents attributing increased family cohesion, newly developed coping skills, and enhanced personal faith to the challenge of parenting a child with mental retardation (Abbott & Meredith, 1986; Noh, Dumas, Wolf, & Fisman, 1989).

However, the persistence of both positive and negative impacts over the life course on parents with differing personality profiles has not been studied. A life-events framework suggests that the nonnormative event of having a child with mental retardation will have developmental consequences for the parent, and that these consequences are heterogeneous, with some parents experiencing persistent negative outcomes whereas others are affected more positively. Sources of this heterogeneity have yet to be delineated in empirical research. However, as is discussed later, such heterogeneity is likely to stem from multiple sources, including the parent's personality profile prior to having the child with retardation, characteristics of the family (e.g., number of other children), and characteristics of the child him or herself (e.g., level of retardation, etiology).

For decades, researchers have investigated the impact of a young child with retardation on the members of his or her family (Blacher, 1984b; Farber, 1959; Gallagher & Vietze, 1986), particularly on the parents. The hypothesis that guided early research on family adjustment was that a child with retardation has a negative impact on family members. Among the hypothesized outcomes in the early studies were the negative adjustment of the parents as individuals, a poor marital relationship, and pathological development of the other children in the family. The child with retardation was thus hypothesized to be the stressor that made the family different from (i.e., worse off than) unaffected families.

It is increasingly recognized that adaptation in parents of a child with retardation is quite varied, with some coping well and others manifesting more serious problems (Ramey, Krauss, & Simeonsson, 1989). Furthermore, specific risk factors and protective mechanisms have been identified that account for variation in parental adaptation, at least during the child's early years. The risk factors include having a child with more severe retardation, poorer health, maladaptive behavior, and older age (Crnic, Friedrich, & Greenberg, 1983; Seltzer & Krauss, 1984b). The protective mechanisms include strong and satisfying parental social support networks (Erickson & Upshur, 1989; Tausig, 1985), effective personal coping skills (Friedrich, Wilturner, & Cohen, 1985), and the quality and strength of the parental relationship with the child (Blacher, 1984b). However, the durability of these risk and protective mechanisms across the life span is presently unknown.

Parenting any child has both stressful and gratifying aspects, and this is also true for parenting a child with retardation. However, the balance of the negative and positive aspects of parenting is not uniform at all stages. In addition to the high level of stress associated with the initial diagnosis, parenting a child with retardation is said to be most stressful at expected times of family transitions, such as when the child enters school, and is least stressful during periods of continuity and stability in family roles (Wikler, 1986). However, the severity of the child's retardation mediates the level of stress at different life stages, with parents of children who have mild mental retardation manifesting improved adjustment as the child grows older, whereas parents of children with moderate or more severe retardation experience a stable level of stress as the child ages (Blacher, Nihira, & Meyers, 1987; Flynt & Wood, 1989).

Although parental adaptation to the task of parenting a young child with mental retardation appears to be the norm rather than the exception, there is an undeniable challenge experienced by these parents, especially those with children with more severe retardation. One consequence of this challenge is the decision made by some parents to place the child in a residential setting other than the home. Such settings include foster homes, group homes, or, in rare instances, in institutions.

Although out-of-home placement is an option selected by only a small minority of families, the likelihood of placement increases as the child gets older, due to the accumulation of stress, the increasing demands of physical care, and the normative loosening of bonds between parents and their older child. At all ages, the likelihood of out-of-home placement is higher for children with severe or profound retardation (Meyers, Borthwick, & Eyman, 1985), when the child has maladaptive behaviors, is medically fragile, when the parents are of higher socioeconomic status, or have marital distress (Seltzer & Krauss, 1984a). The most powerful factors that impede the placement of high-risk children are parents' feelings of attachment to the child and their guilt about the consequences of placement for the child's quality of life (Bromley & Blacher, 1989).

The dynamics of out-of-home placement appear to be different at different stages of the family life course. Tausig (1985) found that for families whose child was under the age of 21 years, the stressful characteristics of the child were most strongly predictive of out-of-home placement, whereas after the age of 21 years, problematic family relations were more predictive of placement than were child characteristics.

A possible explanation for these stage-related differences concerns the extent to which the active parenting role is normative at different stages of life. The routines and demands of parenting a young child with mild mental retardation are not markedly different from the tasks required of families with young normally developing children. However, when the child's characteristics are unusually stressful, the placement option is more likely to be exercised by young families. In contrast, the interactions between parents and their adolescents with mental retardation are very different from the interactions of parents with their normally developing adolescents. As noted earlier in the review of normative parenting, a loosening of the bonds between parent and adolescent is increasingly expected as preparation for the "launching" of the young adult. However, in many families with an adolescent with retardation, particularly those with moderate, severe, or profound retardation, the dependency needs continue. Thus, parenting at this stage becomes increasingly nonnormative (Suelzle & Kennan, 1981), as many decide to parents forego the empty nest years and continue their active parenting responsibilities.

C. THE MIDDLE YEARS OF PARENTHOOD

As in the normative case, the middle years of parenting a child with retardation have received very little attention, perhaps because until recently, the life expectancy of most persons with retardation was considerably shorter than that of the general population. At the present time, however, the life expectancy of those with mild and moderate retardation more closely approximates that of the general population, although those with severe and profound retardation still have a substantially shorter life span (Eyman, Grossman, Chaney, & Call, 1990). Today, most parents of a child with retardation can expect him or her to outlive them by several decades (Janicki & Wisniewski, 1985).

To advance our understanding of parental adaptation to the long-term parenting of an adult son or daughter with retardation, two theoretical models are considered that have been found to account for the impact of caregiving on family members. The first of the two models is what Townsend, Noelker, Deimling, and Bass (1989) referred to as the "wear and tear" hypothesis of caregiving. According to this perspective, the constant demands of care over a long period of time wear down the caregiver's adaptive reserves and deplete his or her mental health (Brody, 1985; George & Gwyther, 1986). This model assumes a pile-up or accumulation of negative effects on the caregiver and also possibly on other family members. Although change over time is inherent to the wear and tear hypothesis, most of the studies that have provided support for this hypothesis are cross-sectional in design (e.g., Morycz, 1985; Zarit, Reever, & Bach-Peterson, 1980). These studies, and scores of others, agree that caregiving is stressful. However, they do not chart the developmental course of the caregiver's response to the demands of caregiving.

The second of the two models, the adaptational hypothesis (Townsend et al., 1989), provides an alternative account for the impact of caregiving on the family caregiver. Consistent with the research on the adjustment of young families with a child with retardation, caregiving for adult or elderly family members is most stressful when it is a new role, but over time some caregivers develop new coping strategies and manifest psychological growth. Towsend et al., in a test of the wear and tear versus the adaptational model, reported that there was a great range in individual differences in response to interhousehold caregiving by adult children for their aged parents. The dominant response, however, was improvement rather than deterioration in subjective caregiving effectiveness and depression during the 14-month study period. Other longitudinal studies have found that adaptational processes develop in many caregivers in response to prolonged periods of caregiving. For example, Zarit, Todd, and Zarit (1986) reported that some caregivers improve their ability to cope with the problem behaviors manifested by the care recipient, even though such behaviors become more extreme over time.

Both the wear and tear hypothesis and the adaptational hypothesis help explain parents' response to long-term parenting responsibilities for a son or daughter with mental retardation. When the nonnormative parenthood experience depletes personal and family resources, parents are more likely to manifest negative personal outcomes and place their son or daughter out of the home, whereas parents who develop adaptational coping strategies are more likely to continue in this role even though it is nonnormative and off-cycle. For parents of adults with mild or moderate retardation, placement is often a positive adaptation, in that many of these adults have the skills to care for themselves and the parents do not need to forgo their empty nest years. Future research is needed to discriminate between the types of parents for whom the wear and tear hypothesis is predictive of parental functioning, the types of parents more correctly characterized by the adaptational model, and how out-of-home placement of the adult with retardation is related to parental adaptation.

A few studies have examined the nature and impacts of the relationships between midlife and older parents and their adult children with mental retardation. Winik, Zetlin, and Kaufman (1985) identified three types of parent–child relationships at this stage of life: (a) supportive, in which the parents promote the growth and development of the child; (b) dependent, in which the parents are overprotective of the child; and (c) conflict-ridden, in which parent–child interaction is discordant. The adults in the supportive relationships were the most well-adjusted and the oldest in the sample, whereas those in the conflict-ridden relationships had the poorest adjustment and were the youngest in the sample. The effect of age on the quality of these parent–adult child relationships is reminiscent of Rossi's

(1980a) study, described earlier in this chapter, which found age to be an important mediator of the relationship between parent and child.

In a study that spans both the middle and latter later years of parenting an adult child with retardation, Seltzer and Krauss (1989) followed 450 mothers between the ages of 55 and 85 years (mean age = 66 years) whose co-residing son or daughter with retardation ranged in age from 15 to 66 years (mean age = 33 years) over a 5-year period of time. Counter to the hypothesized negative outcomes, expected on the basis of the wear and tear model, the mothers in the Seltzer and Krauss study had, on average, favorable well-being. Specifically, a higher proportion of these women viewed their physical health as good or excellent (78%) than did a national probability sample of women their age (60%; Bumpass & Sweet, 1987). Similarly, the Seltzer and Krauss sample members were substantially more satisfied with their lives and reported slightly less caregiving stress and feelings of burden than did other samples of family caregivers (Friedrich, Greenberg, & Crnic, 1983; Gallagher et al., 1985; Zarit et al., 1980).

There are at least two possible explanations for these unexpectedly favorable outcomes. First, selection factors might be responsible, such that parents who experienced high levels of stress had placed their child out of the home before the child reached adulthood, and were not therefore included in the sample. However, because continued in-home living remains the rule rather than the exception until the parents reach the stage when they are no longer able to provide the needed care, selection alone does not account for the positive outcomes observed. A second alternative is that adaptational processes might contribute to the favorable adjustment of these midlife and older mothers who have continued their in-home caregiving responsibilities. That is, for some mothers, the experience of rearing a child with retardation might actually lead to the development of new capacities and strengths that foster adaptational responses.

In an effort to identify characteristics of mothers who manifest favorable outcomes, the correlates of maternal well-being in this sample were examined. It could be expected that the older, more experienced mothers would report the most favorable well-being. However, even with a 30-year age spread in the Seltzer and Krauss (1989) sample, there was no relation between chronological age and maternal well-being. Rather, two factors, in particular, were found to be associated with favorable well-being in the mothers: the etiology of the adult's retardation and the level of involvement of his or her siblings. Mothers of adults with Down syndrome experienced significantly less stress and less burden associated with caregiving than did the mothers of adults whose retardation was due to other factors, even after background factors such as maternal age and family size were controlled (Seltzer, Krauss, & Tsunematsu, 1993). The more favorable well-being of families with a child with Down syndrome is consistent with studies of young families with a child with retardation (Beavers, Hampson, Hulgus, & Beavers, 1986; Holroyd & McArthur, 1976; Krauss, 1989; Van Riper, Ryff, & Pridham, 1992). Possible reasons for the positive outcomes associated with having a child with Down syndrome include the immediacy of the diagnosis (i.e., at birth) and the consequent absence of a period of ambiguity and uncertainty about whether the child has a disability, the greater degree of knowledge available to these families regarding their child's disorder as compared with other forms of retardation, less stigma associated with Down syndrome, and possibly temperamental differences between those with Down syndrome and those with other forms of retardation. Further, these "protective mechanisms" associated with having a child with Down syndrome may actually accumulate over the life course, and thus, are possible developmental sequelae of this nonnormative event.

The second factor particularly associated with positive well-being in the mothers in the Seltzer and Krauss (1989) sample was a high level of sibling involvement with the adult child with retardation. In families where some instrumental or affective support was provided by at least one sibling to the adult with retardation, the mothers had significantly better physical health, greater life satisfaction, and less stress and burden associated with caregiving than mothers who either had no other children, or whose other children who were not involved with their brother or sister with retardation (Seltzer, Begun, Seltzer, & Krauss, 1991). Further, the mother's well-being was more strongly related to the exchange of affective support between these siblings and the child with retardation, than to the amount of affective support provided directly to the mother by her other adult children. Presumably, the involvement of siblings represents to the mother the chance for continuity of her caregiving efforts into the future, beyond the period of her primary responsibility for the child with mental retardation, although this assumption has not yet been tested.

These two factors—the etiology of the child's retardation and the extent of involvement of the siblings with the child with retardation—are powerful (and independent) predictors of maternal well-being among mothers who have reared their child with retardation at home through adulthood. These findings suggest that contextual factors, such as characteristics of the child and family relations, as well as individual characteristics of parents, shape the course of nonnormative parenthood during the middle years.

D. THE LATER YEARS OF PARENTHOOD

A potentially stressful task faced by parents of an adult child with retardation during the later years of parenthood is the need to plan for their son or daughter's future. In most families, the adult with retardation will outlive the parents. Planning for one's child's future is, in essence, a unique developmental task experienced by these parents during the later years of parenthood.

Research on families of persons with mental retardation has consistently found that parents worry about their child's future throughout the life course (Birenbaum, 1971; Turnbull, Brotherson, & Summers, 1985). Nevertheless, many express a strong present, rather than future, orientation in their coping strategies, which does not facilitate the task of long-range planning (Turnbull, Summers, & Brotherson, 1986). Older adults generally have difficulty making plans for their own future (Gold, Dobrof, & Torian, 1987; Heller & Factor, in press), a pattern that is mirrored by aging families with a son or daughter with mental retardation.

The available research indicates that only about a third of aging parents who have been studied make concrete future plans for their family member with retardation (Heller & Factor, 1991; Roberto, 1988). It is more common, however, for families to have a preference for future caregiving arrangements, but not to have acted on their preferences. For example, when asked, most older parents express the wish that a new long-term residential arrangement be put in place before they die (Gold et al., 1987), but considerably fewer take steps to make these arrangements. Parents most likely to make long-range plans have higher socioeconomic status and are more likely to be White (Heller & Factor, 1991). Seltzer and Krauss found that parents who have made long-range plans perceive parenting to be less stressful than do those who have not made future plans, although the direction of effects has not yet been ascertained (Seltzer, 1989).

Although reciprocity is a dominant characteristic of normative parenthood in the later years, in the case of an adult with mental retardation, many parents persist in the active parenting role considerably well beyond the time that they would otherwise relinquish this responsibility. Nevertheless, there are elements of reciprocity in this relationship, and especially when the adult has mild mental retardation, the reciprocity between adult child and aging parent becomes more symmetrical over time. When an aging parent is frail, he or she might be physically dependent on the able-bodied adult with retardation for some household tasks. In such instances, the roles of caregiver and care recipient become blurred, as new elements of the relationship emerge. The involvement of adults with retardation in the caretaking of aged parents warrants greater attention in future empirical studies.

E. SUMMARY

The nonnormative literature on parenthood suggests that the early transition to parenthood is a highly stressful stage, possibly more stressful than those that follow. Subsequent to the initial diagnosis, parental response becomes more highly differentiated, with some manifesting persistent negative effects whereas others become more well-adjusted. Although out-of-home placement is an atypical choice, it becomes more likely as the child ages.

In the middle years, parents whose adult child still lives at home face what would otherwise be the empty nest years with continuing and increasingly nonnormative caregiving responsibilities. There is some evidence that positive adaptational responses might be more common than negative outcomes at this stage, particularly in those parents whose son or daughter has Down syndrome and when siblings are involved with their brother or sister with retardation.

In the later years, planning a secure future for the adult with retardation is an important task. Although most older parents express the wish that a new long-term arrangement is put in place before they die, only a minority implement this transition. It is not surprising that this task is associated with ambivalence and feelings of stress, given that there are no normative analogs in which aged parents have the responsibility of preparing for their adult child's future.

IV. The Normative–Nonnormative Contrast

In this section we evaluate the life-span developmental features of both the normative and nonnormative literatures on parenthood and address how these contrasting domains of theory and research inform each other. We organize this section according to six themes.

A. NEED TO ESTABLISH LIFE-COURSE CONNECTIONS

Normative and nonnormative research on parenthood are equally culpable for the failure to forge explicit connections across the different stages of parenting. In studies of the later years of normative parenthood, for example, it is rare that researchers look back to the characteristics of the parent–child relationship in the early years to understand the dynamics affecting these relationships in old age. Similarly, the literature on the transition to parenthood rarely looks either ahead to future periods that may be influenced by the early years, or back to events of the childhood of the new parent that might influence his or her performance in this new role.

In the literature on parenting a child with mental retardation, most studies have focused only on the early years. Few studies have employed a developmental perspective to compare families at different stages of life, or considered the implications of patterns observed at any given stage for other stages. Instead, the impacts of having a child with retardation have largely been investigated with cross-sectional designs, which compare parents of children with retardation with parents of unaffected children to detect the impact of the disabled child on the parent and the family. The age range of the target child is ordinarily restricted as part of the process of matching the two groups (e.g., Dyson & Fewell, 1986; Wilton & Renaut, 1986). By controlling for age, the differences between families of younger and older children are obscured and the lifelong change processes that are set in motion with the birth of the child cannot be examined.

We underscore here the importance of viewing parenthood in the nonnormative case as a developmental process in its own right. That is, whereas unexpected events are typically viewed as disruptions of the usual developmental trajectories, the birth of a child with a disability is an experience with lifelong implications, many of which may have their own predictable features. There may be, for example, unique developmental tasks that must be confronted by parents of children with retardation. As we have noted, when such a child reaches adulthood, the parents must decide whether to postpone or permanently forego the launching of their child into the adult world, knowing full well that the decision not to launch will result in the loss of their empty nest phase. Later, parents of the adult child with retardation must plan for the child's future after they are no longer able to function as primary caregivers. This may entail the need to activate the involvement of siblings and other relatives in the direct care and/or overseeing of the child with retardation, as preparation for the transition from parent care to care by another family member. However, parents often express a reluctance to burden their children and other relatives. These challenges have only recently been recognized as part of the unfolding developmental processes faced by the aging parents of adult children with disabilities. To understand the timing, duration, and consequences of these parental challenges requires much greater use of longitudinal research designs.

B. NEED TO CONSIDER INDIVIDUAL DIFFERENCES IN THE PARENTING EXPERIENCE

There is the tendency in both the normative and nonnormative literatures to think of parents as a generic group and to contrast them with nonparents to pinpoint the significance of the parenting experience. Thus, investigations of change in parents' psychological characteristics (e.g., efficacy, control) in the transition to parenthood frequently employ control groups of matched individuals who were not becoming parents (e.g., Sirignano & Lachman, 1985). The extensive survey literature on parenthood and psychological well-being also routinely contrasts parents with nonparents (McLanahan & Adams, 1987; Umberson & Gove, 1989). Such an approach detracts from the potentially wide variation within the group of parents. Thus, it is heartening to see considerable movement in large-scale survey studies in the direction of disaggregating the "generic parent" into relevant subcategories (e.g., married vs. divorced vs. single parents, working vs. nonworking parents, older vs. younger parents, stepparents vs. biological parents, etc.). In addition to such sociodemographic variations, important individual differences in parenting have been shown to follow from the personality traits and level of maturity that individuals bring with them to the experience of parenting (Levy-Shiff & Israelashvili, 1988), and these also warrant increased attention in future research. Thus, although we introduced this chapter with the caveat that our review would not address the heterogeneity of the parenting experience, we think it imperative to call for attentiveness to these individual differences in the work that lies ahead.

In the nonnormative case, there has been a parallel tendency to compare parents of children with disabilities with parents of nondisabled children, rather than to probe the variation that exists within the former. An example of the within-group variation is the heterogeneity surrounding the decision of whether to rear a child with retardation at home or place the child in an out-of-home setting. This decision is made not once, but many times during the life of the child and the parent. If families were followed over time to describe the placement process, it would clarify the multitude of factors predictive of placement, such as child characteristics, the availability of social support, and the health of the parent, and hence the wide variation in how parents affect and are affected by having a child with mental retardation (Blacher, Hanneman, & Rousey, 1992).

C. NEED TO INVESTIGATE THE MIDDLE
YEARS OF PARENTING

Both the normative and nonnormative literatures give minimal attention to the longest stretch of parenthood—that is, when children grow into adulthood and parents are not yet in advanced old age. What goes on during these periods? Apart from the discernible transitions, such as when children leave home, become employed or married, or have children themselves, there may be as well a host of hidden, yet powerful, experiences that occupy parents during the middle years. For example, in the normative case, midlife parents face the task of coming to grips with how their children have "turned out"—that is, whether they are well-adjusted (personally and socially) and whether they are making their way in life (e.g., educational and occupational attainment). Presumably, such evaluations have consequences for parents' well-being. It is also during these middle years that parents must work out the roles that they will play in the lives of their adult children. This challenge may include multiple tasks, including learning to accept adult children's life decisions, even when such are viewed as mistaken, becoming friends with one's grown children on an adult-to-adult basis, and learning to relate to the spouses or children of one's children (i.e., how to function as a mother- or father-in-law, or grandparent). Thus, the dearth of research on the middle years of parenthood cannot be explained on grounds that nothing is happening. The challenge rather is to probe beneath the surface of this midlife plateau to capture the issues that give parenthood its salience during these years.

A number of different issues face parents of a child with retardation in the middle years. For example, parents must deal with their child's transition out of school. This is an especially problematic transition because although federal law mandates that all children with disabilities be provided with a school placement, there is no comparable mandate for adults with retardation to attend a day program. Consequently, in cases in which the adult remains at home during the day, there is increased responsibility for the parents to provide daytime supervision. In another example of the critical issues unique to the middle years of parenting, parents of adults with mild mental retardation, in particular, must face and resolve issues of the sexuality and parental striving of the adult child. Also in the middle years, the demands on the parents for active parenting continue, including the physical, financial, and emotional demands that this role carries, and the missed opportunities for freedom and reduced responsibilities during the retirement years. By focusing only on one stage of life, either the early childhood period, or the later years of the parents' lives, past research has failed to explore these issues unique to the middle years of parenthood.

D. GIVING AND GETTING: ISSUES OF RECIPROCITY

Questions about what adults both give and get in their roles as parents have been insufficiently addressed in both normative and nonnormative perspective on parenting. In the normative literature, the early years of parenthood address primarily the experiences of giving, that is, doing for children and the consequences of such efforts for the child's development. The later years of parenthood elevate the theme of getting, that is having adult children assume roles for providing care. Both of these tales need complementary extensions — that is, new parents may also experience gains associated with their new role, such as possible increments in the sense of meaning in life (Umberson & Gove, 1989). To identify what new parents get from their parental experience requires, however, outcome measures that go beyond the monitoring of strains and burdens, into the measurement of meaning, fulfillment, purpose in life and personal growth (Ryff, 1989; Umberson & Gove, 1989), and perhaps the experience of generativity (Ryff & Heincke, 1983). For the later years of parenthood it is also important to remember that even dependent, frail parents may provide significant and needed sources of affection, support, and friendship to their children (Greenberg & Becker, 1988). Thus, what one gives and gets as a parent needs continual, lifelong evaluation.

The nonnormative literature has focused exclusively on the contributions of the parent to the child, with virtually no examination of the child's contributions to the parent. However, there are at least four ways that parenting a child with retardation may have reciprocal benefit for the parent. First, early in their adult life, these parents face a nonnormative challenge. For those who successfully cope with this challenge, the continuing experience of parenting a child with a disability might enable them to develop personal competencies that otherwise would not emerge. A second possible source of benefit for parents, which emerges in later life, is that the adult with retardation may provide a source of companionship to the parent as well as a continuing sense of purpose in life. Third, some adults with retardation are a source of direct assistance to the parent, and when the parent becomes frail, the adult might be the family member who maintains the household beyond the time when the parent can no longer do so. A fourth benefit is that in many cases, the affectional bonds between parent and child nurture the parent at the same time the parent nurtures the child.

Although past research has examined the factors that predict which families will place their child with retardation out of the home, perhaps this is not the central issue. Following from the earlier description of parental benefits, the more important and theoretically interesting question may concern the reasons why parents bond with their child with retardation and persist in their parenting role for the rest of their lives. These reasons undoubtedly have to do with what the parent gets from this nonnormative role as well as what he or she gives. Unfortunately, extant research has been noticeably imbalanced in the direction of explicating only the latter.

E. ASSUMPTIONS REGARDING THE IMPACT OF NORMATIVE AND NONNORMATIVE PARENTHOOD

It is commonly assumed that parenting a typically developing child is a positive experience, whereas parenting a child with a disability is more stressful. This assumption is based on the fact that most adults become parents, that it is a "natural" role, and that there is anticipatory socialization for the role and reference groups to support it. In contrast, parenting a child with a disability is seen as stressful, atypical, and an isolating experience.

The studies we have summarized herein seem to challenge these assumptions regarding normative and nonnormative experiences. For example, the large-scale survey studies of parenting suggest that in the general population, adults with children at home report more distress and less well-being than do nonparents (McLanahan & Adams, 1987; Umberson & Gove, 1989). Many of these parents fit the characterization of normative parenting, in terms of their age, their family structure, and the health and well-being of their children. Why are these parents reporting difficulties or costs associated with this natural role? Economic strains, divorce, and their consequences undoubtedly account for some of the diminished well-being, but it is also possible that inadequate socialization plays a role in these outcomes. Most young parents receive detailed anticipatory socialization for the birth of their children (via the extensive network of childbirth classes offered in communities throughout the country). This well-institutionalized training offers little guidance, however, for the long task that lies ahead, once parents take their bundles home from the hospital. In short, parenthood may be a normative experience in the sense that most people have children and do so at fairly predictable times, but its prevalence and predictability do not guarantee that adults possess the necessary skills to function effectively in this demanding role, nor can it be assumed that all adults embrace the values associated with successful parenting, including self-denial and delay of gratification.

In the nonnormative case, most parents engage in a long process of accommodation and adjustment to the nonnormative aspects of parenting a child with retardation, whereas a minority of parents are not able to cope or choose to place their child out of the home. Although it is assumed that parenting a child with a disability is isolating, in fact there are reference groups (e.g., the Association for Retarded Citizens) that provide support and socialization to these parents across the life course. The heterogeneity of experience at each stage of life and the dynamic nature of parenting has begun to be documented in recent research. However, additional study is needed to fully develop profiles of parents for whom having a child with a disability is overwhelmingly stressful, and to contrast these parents with those who have adjusted to this role and who derive more gratification from the experience.

In a related point, the impact on the parent of having a child with retardation is not the same for all outcomes. A parent might experience feelings of burden at the same time that he or she derives gratification and a sense of accomplishment from the parenting experience. The point here is that there is heterogeneity not only within each group, but within each individual parent, depending on the outcomes examined.

F. COHORT/HISTORICAL ISSUES

Those who study development over the life span are mindful that lives unfold in particular historical eras and that these effects of time and place must be seen as part of the developmental process. Specific to parenthood, Rossi (1980a) argued that parental age must be seen not just as an index of physiological status, but also as a marker of cohort experience. She also clarified that much of what we know about adult development may reflect "cohort particularity" (Rossi, 1980b), that is, the unique experiences of particular cohorts that may render developmental profiles of limited generalizability. How much the existing knowledge of parenthood suffers from such particularity is a question addressed infrequently in this literature.

In the normative case, historical changes in the participation of mothers in the labor force, along with changes in the availability of and attitudes about day care, demonstrate that the background against which parents have and rear their children has shifted to one in which parental employment is an increasingly significant factor in the well-being equation. This shift helps to explicate Silverberg and Steinberg's (1990) finding that the effects of developing adolescents on the well-being of their parents is mediated by the level of parental investment in the work role, and Cunningham and Antill's (1984) finding that it is not just family life status, but also adults' employment status, that has consequences for their sex-role attitudes. Also in the normative realm, we have emphasized the demographic trends in which adult children are increasingly present in the homes of their midlife parents (Aquilino, 1990). These two examples point to the inherent flux in the normative experiences and expectations about the parental life course.

Although cohort and historical influences have an effect on all parents, these effects may be more pronounced for parents of a child with retardation. This is so because such families are more profoundly affected by changes in social policies and social attitudes than are families of typically developing children.

During the past 25 years, there have been major social and policy changes that have affected parents with a child with mental retardation, including new federal laws, new social programs, and increased social acceptance of persons with disabilities. Thus, parents of a child with mental retardation born in 1950, for example, became parents in a markedly different social environment than those whose child was born in 1970, and parents of a child born in 1990 are encountering yet another set of contextual factors. It was the parents of those who were born in the 1950s who created the Association for Retarded Citizens (currently the 14th largest nonprofit organization in the United States) and the other components of the elaborate infrastructure of services and supports for persons with mental retardation and their families. Today, these pioneering parents are in their 60s and 70s. In contrast, the parents of children born in 1970 benefited from PL 94-142, a federal law that guaranteed a free and appropriate public education for all children with disabilities between the ages of 3 and 21 years, which was passed in 1975. These parents, who today are in their 40s and 50s, had considerably fewer opportunities to create new educational programs and social services than did the earlier younger cohort of parents, primarily as a result of the successful efforts of the earlier cohort and the new federal legislation. The youngest group of parents, who today are in their 20s and 30s, have even more legal and social support for their child with retardation and for themselves, and thus, less that they have to do on their own to create the needed social and political structures. An example of a major change affecting this youngest cohort of parents is PL 99-457, passed in 1986, which extends services to infants and toddlers with disabilities and to their families, who previously were not eligible for most services until 3 years of age. For the first time, eligibility begins at birth or at initial diagnosis. Now parents can receive an array of services to help them cope with the transition to nonnormative parenting.

Although no one would argue that the dramatic revolution in services that has characterized the past 40 years is undesirable, one possible unintended consequence was that it changed the opportunities for personal growth and development that accompanied having a child with retardation in the 1950s. There is a similarity here with the findings reported by Elder and Liker (1982) regarding the unanticipated effects of the Depression on the personal development of the cohort of women who came of age in the 1930s. They found that middle-class women who experienced economic hardship had unexpectedly better well-being in later life than either middle-class women who did not experience hardship or working-class women.

To compound the cohort effects produced by changing social policies and climates, there are cohort effects attributable to changes in the role of women in society. Mothers of children who were born in the 1950s had considerably fewer career opportunities than mothers of children who were born more recently. Perhaps having a child with retardation in the 1950s, when career opportunities were more limited and when the need to create an infrastructure of services was acute, gave these mothers a unique opportunity to develop leadership abilities and to feel effective, which would not otherwise been easily available to them at that time and which may not be characteristic of contemporary young mothers with a child with retardation.

V. Conclusions

The task of comparing the normative and nonnormative literatures on parenthood across the life span is daunting. We have covered extensive terrain in this review, and yet we are mindful that much remains unexplored. There are many studies of parenthood in the normative or the nonnormative case that have not been summarized here. In addition, there are a number of important issues that have not been raised. For example, we acknowledge that the fundamental definitions of normative and nonnormative parenthood are continually in flux as a result of changing social values, shifts in personal behavior, and emergent family structures. Although our chapter treats normative and nonnormative parenthood as ideal types, we recognize that changes in what is socially desirable make this distinction relative rather than absolute.

Further, we have discussed parents as if they are the same for all of their children even though parents are inevitably different in their interactions and relationship with each of their children. For example, most parents of children with mental retardation also have nonretarded children. Thus, such parents face both normative and nonnormative challenges, but these dual impacts have not been explored in previous research. Conversely, in many families categorized as normative, there are unexpected crises or events that momentarily or even over the long term create nonnormative circumstances. For example, it is often the case that mental illness is first manifested in young adulthood. Thus, the experience of parents of a young adult with mental illness would have been classified as normative prior to the young adult's diagnosis, but nonnormative subsequently. Thus, the normative experience becomes more heterogeneous as the family matures, with the risk of nonnormative parenthood increasing across the life course. Therefore, because the distinction between normative and nonnormative parenthood is neither simple nor unchanging, there is a need for future studies to take into account both perspectives in the conceptualization and implementation of research agendas.

Despite these complexities, our attempts to synthesize the normative and nonnormative perspectives on parenthood have distilled the following points. First, contrary to the conventional wisdom, normative experiences are not always smooth and easy, and nonnormative experiences are not always burdensome and stressful. To date, research has provided evidence for within-group heterogeneity in this aspect of life. Second, the parent-child relationship at all stages in the life course is characterized by reciprocity. In future research, attention should be given to not only to what the new parent gives to the young child, but also what the child gives to the parent, and in a parallel fashion what the aged parent gives to the adult child as well as what he or she receives. This observation holds true in both the normative and nonnormative cases.

Third, the middle years of parenting are woefully understudied, especially given the rich fabric of the parent-child relationship that endures and becomes elaborated during these years. It may well be that the middle years of parenting are the most meaningful, especially in the normative case, because this is the time when dependency needs of both parent and child are at a minimum. And, in the nonnormative case, these years are characterized by stability and continuity, whereas the earlier and later years of parenting a child with a disability are considerably more unpredictable and stressful. Finally, there is a compelling case that the experience of parenthood can best be understood by looking both forward and backward in time. That is, the early years of the parent–child relationship are inevitably influenced by the parent's own childhood, and they have consequences for the child's future as a parent.

Acknowledgments

This chapter was prepared with support from R01-AG08768-01 from the National Institute on Aging to the first author and The John D. and Catherine T. MacArthur Foundation Research Network on Successful Midlife Development, of which the second author is a member. The authors would like to express their gratitude to Nadine Marks, Alice Rossi, and four anonymous reviewers for their very helpful comments on an earlier draft of this manuscript.

References

Abbott, D. A., & Meredith, W. H. (1986). Strengths of parents with retarded children. *Family Relations, 35*, 371–375.

Abrahams, B., Feldman, S. S., & Nash, S. C. (1978). Sex role self-concept and sex role attitudes: Enduring personality characteristics or adaptations to changing life situations. *Developmental Psychology, 14*, 393–400.

Ainsworth, M. (1973). The development of infant–mother attachment. In B. Caldwell & H. N. Ricciue (Eds.), *Review of child development research* (Vol. 3, pp. 1–94). Chicago: University of Chicago Press.

Ainsworth, M. D. S. (1989). Attachments beyond infancy. *American Psychologist, 44*, 709–716.

Antonucci, T. C., & Jackson, J. S. (1990). The role of reciprocity in social support. In I. G. Sarason, B. R. Sarason, & G. R. Pierce (Eds.), *Social support: An interactional view* (pp. 173–189). New York Wiley.

Aquilino, W. S. (1990). The likelihood of parent–adult child coresidence: Effects of family structure and parental characteristics. *Journal of Marriage and the Family, 52*, 405–419.

Aquilino, W. S. (1991a). Parent–child relations and parents' satisfaction with living arrangements when adult children live at home. *Journal of Marriage and the Family, 53*, 13–27.

Aquilino, W. S. (1991b). Predicting parents' experience with coresident adult children. *Journal of Family Issues, 12*, 323–342.

Aquilino, W. S., & Supple, K. R. (1991). Parent–adult child relations and satisfaction with coresidence. *Journal of Marriage and the Family, 53*, 13–28.

Baltes, P. B. (1987). Theoretical propositions of life-span developmental psychology: On the dynamics between growth and decline. *Developmental Psychology, 23*, 611–626.

Bandura, A. (1982). The psychology of chance encounters and life paths. *American Psychologist, 37*, 747–755.

Beavers, J., Hampson, R. B., Hulgus, Y. F., & Beavers, W. R. (1986). Coping in families with a retarded child. *Family Process, 25*, 365–378.

Beckman, L. J. (1981). Effects of social interaction and children's relative inputs on older women's psychological well-being. *Journal of Personality and Social Psychology, 41,* 1075–1086.

Bell, R. Q. (1968). A reinterpretation of the direction of effects in studies of socialization. *Psychological Review, 75,* 81–95.

Bell, R. Q., & Harper, L. V. (1977). *Child effects on adults.* Hillsdale, NJ: Lawrence Erlbaum Associates.

Belsky, J. (1990). Parental and nonparental child care and children's socioemotional development: A decade in review. *Journal of Marriage and the Family, 52,* 885–903.

Bengtson, V. L. (1987). Parenting, grandparenting, and intergenerational continuity. In J. B. Lancaster, J. Altmann, A. S. Rossi, & L. R. Sherrod (Eds.), *Parenting across the life span: Biosocial dimensions* (pp. 435–456). New York: Aldine de Gruyter.

Bengtson, V. L., & Kuypers, J. A. (1971). Generational differences and the developmental stake. *Aging and Human Development, 2,* 249–260.

Bengtson, V., & Schraeder, S. S. (1982). Parent-child relations. In D. J. Mangen & W. A. Peterson (Eds.), *Research instruments in social gerontology: Vol. 2. Social roles and social participation* (pp. 115–187). Minneapolis: University of Minnesota Press.

Bengtson, V. L., & Troll, L. (1978). Youth and their parents: Feedback and intergenerational influence in socialization. In R. M. Lerner & G. B. Spanier (Eds.), *Child influences on marital and family interaction: A life-span perspective* (pp. 435–456). New York: Academic.

Birenbaum, A. (1971). The mentally retarded child in the home and the family life cycle. *Journal of Health and Social Behavior, 12,* 55–65.

Blacher, J. (1984a). Sequential stages of parental adjustment to the birth of a child with handicaps: Fact or artifact? *Mental Retardation, 22,* 55–68.

Blacher, J. (1984b). *Severely handicapped children and their families: Research in review.* New York: Academic.

Blacher, J., Hanneman, R. A., & Rousey, A. B. (1992). Out-of-home placement of children with severe handicaps: A comparison of approaches. *American Journal on Mental Retardation, 96,* 607–616.

Blacher, J., Nihira, K., & Meyers, C. E. (1987). Characteristics of the home environment of families with mentally retarded children: Comparison across levels of retardation. *American Journal of Mental Deficiency, 91,* 313–320.

Blieszner, R., & Mancini, J. A. (1987). enduring ties: Older adults' parental role and responsibilities. *Family Relations, 36,* 176–180.

Bowlby, J. (1982). *Attachment and loss: vol. 1. Attachment* (2nd ed.). New York: Basic Books.

Bretherton, I., & Waters, E. (Eds.). (1985). Growing points of attachment theory and research. *Monographs for the Society for Research in Child Development, 50*(1-2, Serial No. 209).

Brim, O. G., Jr., & Ryff, C. D. (1980). On the properties of life events. In P. B. Baltes & O. G. Brim, Jr. (Eds.), *Life-span development and behavior* (Vol. 3, pp. 368–388). New York: Academic.

Brody, E. M. (1985). Parent care as a normative family stress. *The Gerontologist, 25,* 19–29.

Bromley, B., & Blacher, J. (1989). Factors delaying out-of-home placement of children with severe handicaps. *American Journal on Mental Retardation, 94,* 284–291.

Bumpass, L. (1984). Some characteristics of children's second families. *American Journal of Sociology, 90,* 608–623.

Bumpass, L., & Sweet, J. (1987). *A national survey of families and households.* Madison: University of Wisconsin-Madison, Center for Demography and Ecology.

Castro Martin, T. & Bumpass, L. L. (1989). Recent trends and differentials in marital disruption. *Demography, 26,* 37–51.

Clarke-Stewart, K. A. (1989). Infant day care: Maligned or malignant? *American Psychologist, 44,* 266–273.

Crnic, K. A., Friedrich, W. N., & Greenberg, M. T. (1983). Adaptation of families with mentally retarded children: A model of stress, coping, and family ecology. *American Journal of Mental Deficiency, 88,* 125–138.

Cummings, S. T., Bayley, H. C., & Rie, H. E. (1966). Effects of the child's deficiency on the mother: A study of mothers of mentally retarded, chronically, ill, and neurotic children. *American Journal of Orthopsychiatry, 36,* 595–608.

Cunningham, J. D., & Antill, J. K. (1984). Changes in masculinity and femininity across the family life cycle: A reexamination. *Developmental Psychology, 20,* 1135–1141.

Dyson, L., & Fewell, R. R. (1986). Stress and adaptation in parents of young handicapped and nonhandicapped children: A comparative study. *Journal of the Division for Early Childhood, 10,* 25–34.

Elder, G., & Liker, J. K. (1982). Hard times in women's lives: Historical influences across forty years. *American Journal of Sociology, 88,* 241–269.

Erickson, M., & Upsher, C. C. (1989). Caretaking burden and social support: Comparison of mothers of infants with and without disabilities. *American Journal on Mental Retardation, 89,* 250–258.

Erikson, E. (1959). Identity and the life cycle. *Psychological Issues, 1,* 18–164.

Eyman, R., Grossman, H., Chaney, R. H., & Call, T. L. (1990). The life expectancy of profoundly handicapped people with mental retardation. *The New England Journal of Medicine, 323,* 584–589.

Farber, B. (1959). Effects of a severely mentally retarded child on family integration. *Monographs of the Society for Research in Child Development, 24*(2, Serial No. 71).

Featherman, D. L. (1985). Individual development and aging as a population process. In J. Nesselroade & A. von Eye (Eds.), *Individual development and social change: Explanatory analyses* (pp. 213–241). New York: Academic.

Featherstone, H. (1980). *A difference in the family: Life with a disabled child.* New York: Basic.

Feldman, S. S., Biringen, Z. C., & Nash, S. C. (1981). Fluctuations of sex-related self-attributions as a function of stage of family life cycle. *Developmental Psychology, 17,* 24–35.

Flynt, S. W., & Wood, T. A. (1989). Stress and coping of mothers of children with moderate mental retardation. *American Journal on Mental Retardation, 94,* 278–283.

Friedrich, W. N., Greenberg, M. T., & Crnic, K. (1983). A short-form of the Questionnaire on Resources and Stress. *American Journal of Mental Deficiency, 88,* 41–48.

Friedrich, W. N., Wilturner, L. T., & Cohen, D. S. (1985). Coping resources and parenting mentally retarded children. *American Journal of Mental Deficiency, 90,* 130–139.

Fujiura, G. T., Garza, J., & Braddock, D. (1989). *National survey of family support services in developmental disabilities.* Mimeo: University of Illinois-Chicago.

Gallagher, D., Rappaport, M., Benedict, A., Lovett, S., Silven, D., & Kramer, H. (1985). *Reliability of selected interview and self-report measures with family caregivers.* Paper presented at the 38th annual meeting of the Gerontological Society of America, New Orleans.

Gallagher, J. J., & Vietze, P. M. (Eds.). (1986). *Families of handicapped persons: Research, programs, and policy issues.* Baltimore: Brookes.

George, L. K., & Gwyther, L. P. (1986). Caregiver well-being: A multidimensional examination of family caregivers of demented adults. *The Gerontologist, 27,* 253–259.

Gold, M., Dobrof, R., & Torian, L. (1987). *Parents of the adult developmentally disabled* (Final report presented to the United Hospital Trust Fund). New York: Brookdale Center on Aging.

Greenberg, J., & Becker, M. (1988). Aging parents as family resources. *The Gerontologist, 28,* 786–791.

Hagestad, G. O. (1987). Parent–child relations in later life: Trends and gaps in past research.

In J. B. Lancaster, J. Altman, A. S. Rossi, & L. R. Sherrod (Eds.), *Parenting across the life span: Biosocial dimensions*. New York: Aldine de Gruyter.

Heller, T., & Factor, A. (1991). Permanency planning for adults with mental retardation living with family caregivers. *American Journal on Mental Retardation, 96,* 163–176.

Hill, R. (1964). Methodological issues in family development research. *Family Process, 3,* 186–206.

Holroyd, J., & McArthur, D. (1976). Mental retardation and stress in the parents: A contrast between Down syndrome and childhood autism. *American Journal of Mental Deficiency, 80,* 431–436.

Hultsch, D. F., & Plemons, J. K. (1979). Life events and life-span development. In P. B. Baltes & O. G. Brim, Jr. (Eds.), *Life-span development and behavior* (Vol. 2, pp. 1–36). New York: Academic.

Janicki, M. P., & Wisniewski, H. M. (Eds.). (1985). *Aging and developmental disabilities: Issues and approaches*. Baltimore: Brookes.

Kazak, A. E. (1987). Families with disabled children: Stress and social networks in three samples. *Journal of Child Abnormal Psychology, 15,* 137–146.

Krauss, M. W. (1989). *Parenting a young child with disabilities: Differences between mothers and fathers*. Paper presented at the 22nd annual Gatlinburg Conference on Research and Theory in Mental Retardation and Developmental Disabilities, Gatlinburg, TN.

Kreppner, K., & Lerner, R. M. (1989). Family systems and life-span development: Issues and perspectives. In K. Kreppner & R. M. Lerner (Eds.), *Family systems and life-span development* (pp. 1–13). Hillsdale, NJ: Lawrence Erlbaum Associates.

Kubler-Ross, E. (1969). *On death and dying*. New York: Macmillan.

Larkin, K. C. Hill, B. & R. Bruininks (Eds.). (1985). *An analysis of Medicaid's ICF-MR program*. Minneapolis: University of Minnesota.

Lancaster, J. B., Altmann, J., Rossi, A. S., & Sherrod, L. R. (Eds.). (1987). *Parenting across the life span: Biosocial dimensions*. New York: Aldine de Gruyter.

LeMasters, E. E. (1957). Parenthood as crisis. *Marriage and Family Living, 19,* 352–355.

Lerner, R. M., & Ryff, C. D. (1978). Implementation of the life-span view of human development: The sample case of attachment. In P. B. Baltes (Ed.), *Life-span development and behavior* (Vol. 1, pp. 2–45). New York: Academic.

Lerner, R. M., & Spanier, G. B. (1978). *Child influences on marital and family interaction* . New York: Academic.

Levy-Shiff, R., & Israelashvili, R. (1988). Antecendents of fathering: Some further exploration. *Developmental Psychology, 24,* 434–440.

Luckasson, R., Coulter, D. L., Polloway, E. A., Reiss, S., Schalock, R. L., Snell, M. E., Spitalnik, D. M., & Stark, J. A. (1993). *Mental retardation: Definition, classification, and systems of supports*. Washington, D.C.: American Association on Mental Retardation.

Mancini, J. A., & Blieszner, R. (1989). Aging parents and adult children: Research themes in intergenerational relations. *Journal of Marriage and the Family, 51,* 275–290.

McAdams, D. P., Ruetzel, K., & Foley, J. M. (1986). Complexity and generativity at mid-life: Relations among social motives, ego development, and adults' plans for the future. *Journal of Personality and Social Psychology, 50,* 800–807.

McLanahan, S., & Adams, J. (1987). Parenthood and psychological well-being. *Annual Review of Sociology, 13,* 237–257.

Menaghan, E. G. (1989). Psychological well-being among parents and nonparents: The importance of normative expectedness. *Journal of Family Issues, 10,* 547–565.

Mercer, J. (1973). The myth of 3% prevalence. In G. Tarjan, R. K. Eyman, & C. E. Meyers (Eds.), *Sociobehavioral studies in mental retardation* (pp. 1–18). Washington, DC: American Association on Mental Deficiency.

Meyers, C. E., Borthwick, S. A., & Eyman, R. (1985). Place of residence by age, ethnicity, and level of retardation of the mentally retarded/developmentally disabled population of California. *American Journal of Mental Deficiency, 90,* 266–270.

Morycz, R. K. (1985). Caregiving strain and the desire to institutionalize family members with Alzheimer's disease. *Research on Aging, 7,* 329–361.

Noh, S., Dumas, J. E., Wolf, L. C., & Fisman, S. N. (1989). Delineating sources of stress in parents of exceptional children. *Family Relations, 38,* 456–461.

Parke, R. D. (1988). Families in life-span perspective. In E. M. Hetherington, R. M. Lerner, & M. Perlmutter (Eds.), *Child development in life-span perspective* (pp. 159–190). Hillsdale, NJ: Lawrence Erlbaum Associates.

Peterson, B. E., & Stewart, A. J. (1990). Using personal and fictional documents to assess psychosocial development: A case study of Vera Brittain's generativity. *Psychology of Aging, 5,* 400–411.

Peterson, G. W., & Rollins, B. C. (1987). Parent–child socialization. In M. B. Sussman & S. K. Steinmetz (Eds.), *Handbook of marriage and the family* (pp. 471–507). New York: Plenum.

Ramey, S., Krauss, M. W., & Simeonsson, R. (1989). Research on families: Current assessment and future opportunities. *American Journal on Mental Retardation, 94,* ii–vi.

Roberto, K. A. (1988). *Caring for aging developmentally disabled adults: Perspectives and needs of older parents* (Final report presented to the Colorado Developmental Disabilities Planning Council). Greeley: University of Northern Colorado, Department of Human Services.

Rossi, A. S. (1980a). Aging and parenthood in the middle years. In P. B. Baltes & O. G. Brim, Jr. (Eds.), *Life-span development and behavior* (Vol. 3, pp. 138–205). New York: Academic.

Rossi, A. S. (1980b). Life-span theories and women's lives. *Signs: Journal of Women in Culture and Society, 6,* 4–32.

Rossi, A. S., & Rossi, P. H. (1990). *Of human bonding: Parent–child relations across the life course.* New York: Aldine de Gruyter.

Ryff, C. D. (1989). Happiness is everything, or is it? Explorations on the meaning of psychological well-being. *Journal of Personality and Social Psychology, 57,* 1069–1081.

Ryff, C. D., & Heincke, S. G. (1983). The subjective organization of personality in adulthood and aging. *Journal of Personality and Social Psychology, 44,* 807–816.

Scott, J., & Alwin, D. F. (1989). Gender differences in parental strain: Parental role or gender role? *Journal of Family Issues, 10,* 482–503.

Seltzer, G. B., Begun, A., Seltzer, M. M., & Krauss, M. W. (1991). The impacts of siblings in the lives of adults with mental retardation and their aging mothers. *Family Relations, 40,* 310–317.

Seltzer, M. M. (1989). *Long-range planning* (Report to the Dane County Association for Retarded Citizens). Madison: University of Wisconsin.

Seltzer, M. M., & Krauss, M. W. (1984a). Family, community residence, and institutional placements of a sample of mentally retarded children. *American Journal of Mental Deficiency, 89,* 257–266.

Seltzer, M. M., & Krauss, M. W. (1984b). Placement alternatives for mentally retarded children and their families. In J. Blacher (Ed.), *Severely handicapped children and their families: Research in review.* (pp. 143–175). New York: Academic.

Seltzer, M. M., & Krauss, M. W. (1989). Aging parents with mentally retarded children: Family risk factors and sources of support. *American Journal on Mental Retardation, 94,* 303–312.

Seltzer, M. M., Krauss, M. W., & Tsunematsu, N. (1993). Adults with Down syndrome and their aging families: Diagnostic group differences. *American Journal on Mental Retardation, 97,* 464–508.

Silverberg, S. B., & Steinberg, L. (1990). Psychological well-being of parents with early adolescent children. *Developmental Psychology, 26,* 658–666.

Sirignano, S. W., & Lachman, M. E. (1985). Personality change during the transition to parenthood: The role of perceived infant temperament. *Developmental Psychology, 21,* 558–567.

Solnit, A. J., & Stark, M. H. (1961). Mourning and birth of a defective child. *Psychoanalytic study of the child, 16.* New York: International Universities Press.

Spanier, G. B., & Glick, P. C. (1981). Marital instability in the U.S.: Some correlates and recent changes. *Family Relations, 30,* 329–338.

Spitze, G., & Logan, J. (1989). Gender differences in family support: Is there a payoff? *The Gerontologist, 29,* 108–113.

Sroufe, L. A. (1979). The coherence of individual development. *American Psychologist, 34,* 834–841.

Suelzle, M., & Keenan, V. (1981). Changes in family support networks over the life cycle of mentally retarded persons. *American Journal of Mental Deficiency, 86,* 267–274.

Tausig, M. (1985). Factors in family decision-making about placement for developmentally disabled individuals. *American Journal of Mental Deficiency, 89,* 352–361.

Townsend, A., Noelker, L., Deimling, G., & Bass, D. (1989). Longitudinal impact of interhousehold caregiving on adult children's mental health. *Psychology and Aging, 4,* 393–401.

Turnbull, A. P., Brotherson, M. J., & Summers, J. A. (1985). The impact of deinstitutionalization on families: A family systems approach. In R. H. Bruininks, & K. C. Lakin (Eds.), *Living and learning in the least restrictive environment* (pp. 115–140). Baltimore: Brookes.

Turnbull, A. P., Summers, J. A., & Brotherson, M. J. (1986). Family life cycle: Theoretical and empirical implications and future directions for families with mentally retarded members. In J. J. Gallagher & P. M. Vietze (Eds.), *Families of handicapped persons: Research, programs, and policy issues* (pp. 45–65). Baltimore: Brookes.

Turnbull, A. P., & Turnbull, H. R. (Eds.). (1978). *Parents speak out.* Columbus, OH: Merrill.

Umberson, D., & Gove, W. R. (1989). Parenthood and psychological well-being: Theory, measurement, and stage in the family life course. *Journal of Family Issues, 10,* 440–462.

Van Riper, M., Ryff, C., & Pridham, K. (1992). Parental and family well-being in families of children with Down Syndrome: A comparative shedy. *Research in Nursing & Health, 15,* 227–235.

Wethington, E., & Kessler, R. C. (1989). Employment, parental responsibility, and psychological distress: A longitudinal study of married women. *Journal of Family Issues, 10,* 527–546.

White, L. K., & Booth, A. (1985). The quality and stability of remarriages: The role of stepchildren. *American Sociological Review, 50,* 689–698.

Wikler, L. M. (1986). Family stress theory and research on families of children with mental retardation. In J. Gallagher & P. Vietze (Eds.), *Families of handicapped persons: Research programs and policy issues* (pp. 167–196). Baltimore: Brookes.

Wikler, L., Wasow, M., & Hatfield, E. (1981). Chronic sorrow revisited: Parent vs. professional depiction of the adjustment of parents of mentally retarded children. *American Journal of Orthopsychiatry, 51,* 63–70.

Wilton, K., & Renaut, J. (1986). Stress levels in families with intellectually handicapped preschool children and families with nonhandicapped preschool children. *Journal of Mental Deficiency Research, 30,* 163–169.

Winik, L., Zetlin, A. G., & Kaufman, S. Z. (1985). Adult mildly retarded persons and their parents: The relationship between involvement and adjustment. *Applied Research in Mental Retardation, 6,* 409–419.

Zarit, S., Reever, K. E., & Bach-Peterson, J. (1980). Relatives of the impaired elderly: Correlates of feelings of burden. *The Gerontologist, 20,* 649–655.

Zarit, S. H., Todd, P. A., & Zarit, J. M. (1986). Subjective burden of husbands and wives as caregivers: A longitudinal study. *The Gerontologist, 26,* 260–266.

The Dynamics Between Dependency and Autonomy: Illustrations Across the Life Span

Margret M. Baltes
FREE UNIVERSITY, BERLIN

Susan B. Silverberg
UNIVERSITY OF ARIZONA

Abstract

In this chapter we examine the dynamic interplay between autonomy and dependency across four phases of the life span: infancy/early childhood, adolescence, middle adulthood, and old age. The concept of *developmental task* is used to emphasize three different sources—physical/

41

organic, social/cultural, and psychological—creating this dynamic by exerting demands, pressures, restrictions, and opportunities differing in number, degree, and scope across the life course. In applying such a framework we highlight the phase-specific mutuality between dependency and autonomy and provide some description of, and explanation for, interindividual differences in patterns of autonomy and dependency across the life span. In accord with contemporary scholarship in this domain, we underscore throughout the chapter that dependency, when considered in its diverse expressions, as there are in attachment, social connection, interdependence, and reciprocity, is not necessarily an obstacle to be hurdled and outgrown—an antagonist to optimal functioning—but is vital to human growth and well-being. We pay special attention to the necessity of observing individuals' competence levels and ensuring multiple environments that provide a match with these competencies and existing needs.

I. Introduction

The aim of this chapter is to examine the dynamics between dependency and independence or autonomy through the life course. Although the interplay between dependency and autonomy is notable during all life phases, we follow an illustrative approach here and concentrate on *infancy/ early childhood, adolescence, middle adulthood,* and *old age.* In popular discussion in Western societies, these concepts are treated as antagonists. Likewise, in scientific discussion, we often find dependency and independence as two extreme poles of the same dimension. In the more recent literature, however, these concepts are seen in a dynamic relationship that plays itself out differently across the different phases of life, across different cultures, across different people, and across different domains within one and the same person. In its strongest sense, dependency connotes a state in which a person is unable to exist or function in any satisfactory manner without the aid or use of another. In a weaker sense, the term *dependency* connotes connectedness, communion, attachment, or solidarity and is manifested in the need of children for adults (Hartup, 1989), in the need of adults for adults (Gilligan, 1986), and in the need of adults for children. *Independence,* in contrast, is associated with terms such as *agency, autonomy, self-reliance, individuation,* and *self-control.* Scholars have often equated competence at each stage of the life course with signs of independence.

Rather than providing an exhaustive review of empirical studies and diverse theoretical conceptions, we intend in this chapter to highlight a common, critical thread that joins together the literatures on independence and dependency across the periods of infancy/childhood, adolescence, adulthood, and old age. This thread marks a shared progression, both in theory and research, that began with the longstanding view of autonomy and dependency as antagonistic characteristics—at odds with one another, with autonomy replacing dependency in healthy, mature development, and well-being (Maccoby & Masters, 1970). As Gilligan (1988), Josselson (1988), and others have reminded us, until quite recently psychology has emphasized the development of autonomy in terms of self-reliance, disconnection, and separateness often to the exclusion of the study of how continued dependencies on others are not only normative, but healthy at all age periods.

Progress in the field has, at once, uncovered the complexity and multidimensionality of autonomy and dependency and recognized the mutuality and interdependence between the two. More and more, scholars maintain the view that we are not rid of relationships and the need for support, security, and assistance from others as we mature, but that we strive for an "embedded self" throughout the life course (Josselson, 1988; Takahashi, 1990). The nature of dependency and autonomy transform over the life span and the balance between the two may shift; nonetheless, simultaneous with increased self-reliance and a sense of agency comes the development of a social sense of self—a realization that the self does not stand alone (Youniss & Smollar, 1985)—as well as the uninterrupted need for social connection, whether that be in the form of attachment, intimacy, interdependence, or generativity (Kahn & Antonucci, 1980; Lerner & Ryff, 1978; Troll, 1986). Indeed, we discuss later how a sense of independence can actually derive from a sense of connection and from specific kinds of dependencies.

Briefly stated, a careful reading of the literature reveals a continuous dialectic between dependency, provided by attending to security and autonomy, provided by fostering identity and individuation, that acts like a life plan in need of continuous modification and adjustment. The balance between dependency and autonomy changes constantly with personal development, environmental contexts, across time, and change in cultural and societal values, expectations, and demands.

In what follows, we proffer the concept of *developmental tasks* as an organizing principle to describe and explain changes in the dynamic between dependency and autonomy across the life course. Developmental tasks, as defined in developmental psychology (Oerter, 1982) and in the literature on aging (Havighurst, 1948), are the result of three interacting sources: biology, sociology, and psychology. The biological source refers to physical growth and biological demands. The sociological source points to the importance of societal demands such as norms and expectations. The psychological antecedents encompass individual preferences, skills, and goals. Interactions among the sources occur when, for example, physical/biological growth influences the timing and nature of societal demands as seems the case quite often in childhood (see toilet training, school entry). Nevertheless, at different stages through the life course, these three components hold differential weight in the determination of developmental tasks. Developmental tasks of infancy and childhood seem more dependent on physical growth and biological demands; developmental tasks in middle adulthood seem to be defined to a greater extent by societal demands and individual goals.

It is important to note that neither biological nor societal nor individual demands are fixed or universal. Much rather, the interplay, the differential weighing, as well as the norms themselves are subject to cultural differences and changes due to factors as diverse as quality of nutrition, values placed on autonomy or intimacy, workplace demands, life expectancy, and so on. It is not surprising, therefore, to find differences with regard to, for example, childrearing practices and values placed on autonomy in childhood and old age across generations, within cultures across socioeconomic classes, and between cultures (e.g., Western vs. Asian cultures).

We see later that concomitant with changes in developmental tasks are changes in the usage of terms, from dependency, independence, and attachment in infancy and early childhood, to autonomy and agency in later childhood, to identity and individuality in adolescence, to interdependence, reciprocity, cooperation, and mutuality in adulthood, and back to dependency, autonomy and independence in old age.

Our focus on whether developmental tasks require more independence or dependence not only traces general developmental trajectories with respect to dependency and autonomy, but also provides some description and explanation of interindividual differences and intraindividual change, that is, continuity versus discontinuity across the life span. One obvious way in which people differ is with respect to their unique balance between dependency and agency (reliance on the self); the nature of this balance differs across individuals and within each individual across time. Differences are also apparent in the pace or timing of having to cope with developmental tasks, which in turn may result in the expression of more agency at certain times and more dependency at others. Moreover, one can detect both intra- and interindividual differences in the specific life domains in which persons might show more agency or more dependency. There might be stability in the patterns of dependency/independence over time because individuals act upon their own development by selecting environments that reinforce their behaviors, expectations, values, and so forth. At the same time, there might be discontinuity because both societal as well as biological demands are subject to change over time. As a consequence, individuals show quite diverse patterns of dependency and agency and, although they may experience similar developmental tasks, may easily switch between behavioral patterns of dependency and independence. These intra- and interindividual differences likely reflect differences in preferences, competencies, resources, social, and cultural contexts in terms of opportunity as well as demand structures.

In using the developmental task perspective with its three determining components we focus our discussion about autonomy/dependency largely on the "person" rather than on "relationships." In this perspective, autonomy and dependency are behavioral characteristics suited differentially to coping with developmental tasks. The perspective also permits the possibility of change in the meaning of or the developmental transformations in dependency and autonomy across life phases (Kagan, 1982).

II. Infancy and Childhood

A. DEVELOPMENTAL TASKS OF EARLY CHILDHOOD: ATTACHMENT AND AUTONOMY

Western definitions of competence for infants, toddlers, and young children invariably—regardless of theoretical origin or terminology—include reference to object-mastery skills, autonomous functioning, and progress in the separation-individuation process vis-à-vis primary caregivers (Ainsworth, Blehar, Waters, & Wall, 1978; Erikson, 1963; Heathers, 1955; Mahler, 1968). This strong emphasis on an early start toward self-reliance and self-assertion, notable in the views of both theorists and parents in present day United States and many Western European countries, contrasts with the greater encouragement of early emotional dependence in cultures such as Japan (Caudill & Weinstein, 1969; Mikaye, Chen, & Campos, 1985), where adult qualities including interdependence, mutual obligation, and conformity are held in higher esteem (see Spence, 1985).

The attainment of greater self-reliance in the early years of life is, of course, driven in part by maturational forces shared by all healthy children. Increasing muscular development and control make possible children's attempts at doing things on their own—walking, dressing, and feeding themselves. Likewise, cognitive advances permit more sophisticated manipulation of objects toward the child's desired ends. Emerging language skills allow the child to express his or her wishes and thus to make added gains in power and independence. According to Western definitions, however, the autonomy of children considered to be well-functioning is also expressed in their healthy sense of effectance or personal agency (Ford & Thompson, 1985; White, 1959) and in their eagerness to invest their energy in active and independent exploration of their immediate physical and social environment (Matas, Arend, & Sroufe, 1978).

Researchers have debated over the issue of how young children reach these ends (see Baltes & Reisenzein, 1986; Maccoby & Masters, 1970; Sroufe, Fox, & Pancake, 1983). Does the increasingly autonomous functioning of children merely replace the close parent–infant ties and signs of emotional and instrumental dependency that seem quite evident during the first years of life? Should infant behaviors such as crying, clinging, and seeking caregiver comfort, help, attention, or proximity be understood merely as signs of immature dependency, as behaviors characteristic of some infants and toddlers and not others, as something to be overcome? The most widely cited theoretical and empirical outlook on this issue — the study of infant-caregiver attachment — would say no. Indeed, the work of attachment scholars has led to a reconceptualization and reevaluation of many of the same behaviors that in previous years were subsumed under the very global, and often pejorative, concept of dependency (Grusec & Lytton, 1988). Their work has shed new light on the possible linkage between the development of autonomous functioning and child-caregiver affective bonds (e.g., Ainsworth et al., 1978; Bowlby, 1969; Bretherton, 1987; Sroufe & Waters, 1977), but has probably raised as many questions as it has answered (Waters, Hay, & Richters, 1986). (For a detailed discussion of this perspective and its potential shortcomings, see Bretherton & Waters, 1985; Lamb, Thompson, Gardner, Charnov, & Estes, 1984.) In brief, the attachment concept moved the study of infant-adult ties beyond a focus on the simple frequency or duration of discrete behaviors (e.g., cry, cling, approach, look) toward a conceptualization of qualitative differences in the way such behaviors are adaptively organized and timed to meet a goal of felt security, which in turn is assumed to permit independent exploration of the environment (Sroufe & Waters, 1977).

Attachment, as presented by Bowlby (1969) and Ainsworth et al. (1978), seemed to provide a mechanism to make sense of infants' simultaneous needs for safety and security, on the one hand, and for exploration and varied learning experiences on the other. Attachment theorists have concentrated on the child's development of a secure, confident, and enduring affective relationship with one or a few primary caregivers as the basis for the development of a sense of competence (Ford & Thompson, 1985) and relaxed autonomous functioning in infancy and later years (e.g., Ainsworth et al., 1978; Sroufe et al., 1983; cf. Takahashi, 1990). In this sense, the attachment view parallels Erikson's (1963) emphasis on the development of a sense of basic trust in infancy — a sense that the world is dependable and safe — as a critical foundation for autonomy and initiative during toddlerhood and the preschool years. The actual extent to which an early secure attachment relationship plays a formative (causal) role in the development of later autonomous functioning is a question that is still under debate, however (Lamb et al., 1984; Waters et al., 1986), and is discussed at a later point in this chapter. In any event, one would conclude that the developmental task of the early years of life, from the attachment perspective, entails reaching a dynamic equilibrium between two interacting behavioral-motivational systems — the need for security provided by the child-caregiver relationship alongside the need for self-initiated functioning of the child within his or her physical and social environment (see Cicchetti, 1989).

B. PATTERNS OF ATTACHMENT

According to Bowlby (1969), Ainsworth et al. (1978), and other attachment theorists, infants are preadapted to form a close affective bond with a caregiver who responds to their bids for comfort, soothing, and protection but who "also permits and supports autonomous action and exploration" (Bretherton, 1990, p. 61). Attachment, in its full sense, does not emerge suddenly in the newborn's relations with his or her caregiver, however; it develops gradually over the course of the first year of life (Ainsworth et al., 1978; Damon, 1983). Near the end of the first year, a time when the infant develops locomotive abilities and object permanence, transactions with the environment are increasingly based on the infant's inner representations, or internal working models, of the self and caregiver in the attachment relationship (Bretherton, 1990).

Although virtually all infants form an attachment relationship with at least one caregiver — typically their mother — there are apparent differences in the quality of attachments across infant–caregiver pairs. The most critical way in which attachment differ is the degree to which infants are able to depend on their caregiver to meet their emotional needs, particularly in times of stress, but also in low-stress situations (Waters, Wippman, & Sroufe, 1979).

Many researchers have used Ainsworth's classic *strange situation* research paradigm to observe and assess differential patterns of infant–caregiver attachment relationships (Ainsworth et al., 1978). Assessments, typically made when the infant is 12 or 18 months of age, are aimed at the classification of the patterning or organization of infant behavior in response to the brief (maximum 3-min) separations from and reunions with the caregiver in the unfamiliar playroom setting. The most global distinction between secure and insecure or anxious attachment relationships is especially significant for the present chapter because of the apparent differential *sequelae* of secure and insecure attachment relationships in infancy for later autonomous functioning and levels of dependency.[1]

One-year-olds whose attachment to their primary caregiver is labeled *secure* are those who appear confident about their caregiver's availability

---

[1] It is important to note here that a number of researchers, even some sympathetic with the attachment perspective, have raised concerns over the use of the Strange Situation procedure as a valid assessment of the quality of infant–caregiver attachment (see Lamb et al., 1984; see also footnotes 2 and 3). The procedure is very brief (20 min) and somewhat artificial. The caregiver and stranger come and go at appointed times and refrain from interacting with the infant at times when interaction might be typical or expected.

and responsiveness; they are easily able to use their caregiver both as a secure base from which to explore novel objects and places and as a safe haven of comfort in the face of distress due to fear, discomfort, or separation (Ainsworth et al., 1978). Although infants with a secure attachment relationship are active in seeking and maintaining contact with their caregiver when distressed in the strange situation (through crying, clinging, and other comfort-seeking behavior; Sroufe et al., 1983), the attachment relationship seems effective in quickly meeting the infant's emotional needs and the infant is free to expend energy on play and independent exploration of the novel environment (see Belsky, Garduque, & Hrncir, 1984). These infants are thought to carry with them a secure psychological contact with their caregiver that enables them this physical independence; tolerance of physical distance will be even greater at 18 months than it is at 1 year (Sroufe & Waters, 1977).

Infants whose attachment relationships are classified as *insecure* or anxious in the strange situation follow one of two general patterns (see Main & Solomon, 1986, for a discussion of a third insecure attachment pattern — disorganized/disoriented). Those infants with an *anxious-resistant* attachment have difficulty in distancing themselves from the caregiver to explore the novel playroom and often require clingy, physical contact with their caregiver even prior to separation. Upon their caregiver's brief departure these infants become quite distressed. In contrast to infants whose attachment is considered secure, these infants are not easily settled upon reunion with their caregiver. Their approach to their caregiver appears ambivalent — alternating between contact seeking (e.g., arms stretched out as a bid for closeness) and comfort resistance (e.g., angrily pushing away, squirming, rejecting toys offered, and/or continuing to cry). In short, these infants do not easily focus their energies on active exploration in the Strange Situation context, but instead are likely to keep a watchful eye on their caregiver.

Finally, 12-month-old infants whose attachment to their caregiver is classified as *anxious-avoidant* readily distance themselves from their caregiver in the Strange Situation and are unlikely either to check visually on their caregiver's whereabouts or to share their play with the caregiver. These infants typically show little or no sign of distress upon their caregiver's temporary departure. Most striking, is that upon reunion these infants may actively avoid and ignore the caregiver by turning, looking, and/or moving away. Interpretation of this pattern of behavior in the context of a discussion of autonomy and dependency is challenging. Attachment theorists would suggest that although this pattern of behavior might be interpreted as "precocious independence, . . . from the developmental/ organizational view . . . these infants are also failing to develop the base they need for autonomous functioning" (Sroufe et al., 1983, p. 1617). This conclusion is somewhat controversial especially in light of the slightly elevated rates of so-called anxious-avoidant attachments in certain samples. It raises many questions including those concerning alternative adaptive pathways in development and the ecological validity of the Strange Situation procedure as a measure of attachment quality across all populations.[2,3]

[2]Some scholars argue that the Strange Situation procedure may be a valid assessment of attachment quality among most U. S. samples but may not be among samples from other cultures (e.g., Lamb et al., 1984). Most U. S. samples include approximately 65%–70% secure, 15% anxious-resistant, and 15%–20% anxious-avoidant attachments when assessed in the Strange Situation. Infants raised in other cultures exhibit apparently higher rates of anxious-resistant attachments (e.g., in Japan) or anxious-avoidant attachments (e.g., in northern Germany) relative to typical U.S. samples. These differences may be attributable to the fact that many Japanese and northern German infants have caregiving histories sufficiently different from most U. S. infants, that the infants experience the brief separations from their mothers as well as the presence of an unfamiliar adult in the Strange Situation in qualitatively different ways. On the one hand, the separations may be overly demanding and stressful for many Japanese infants, whose mothers stress close physical contact and infrequent separations (Caudill & Weinstein, 1969; Mikaye et al., 1985). In contrast, the strong emphasis on early self-reliance and greater interpersonal distance in the childrearing practices of many mothers in northern Germany may cause their infants to experience the temporary separations as nonthreatening, and thus as no cause for proximity- and comfort-seeking (Grossmann, Grossman, Spangler, Suess, & Unzner, 1985). Two additional points should be considered, however (van IJzendoorn, 1990). First, meta-analysis of attachment research studies indicate the intracultural differences in attachment classification distributions are larger than intercultural differences. Second, "the cross-cultural debate on attachment has often been based on fragmentary, limited evidence, with the risk of capitalizing on unreliable data from small samples isolated from other attachment studies done in the same culture" (van Ijzendoorn, 1990, p. 6).

[3]Like other U. S. samples, the majority of U. S. infants who have experienced extensive early day care have a secure attachment with their mothers as assessed in the Strange Situation. Nonetheless, research—though mixed in its results—suggests that extensive substitute care in the first year of life is associated with slightly higher rates of insecure (anxious-avoidant) attachments (see, for reviews, Clarke-Stewart, 1989; Hoffman, 1989). This slight elevation is open to a number of interpretations (Clarke-Stewart, 1989). One possibility is that these children may indeed be "at risk" for an insecure attachment relationship especially if other risk factors are present (Belsky & Rovine, 1988). It is also possible that the Strange Situation procedure is not a valid assessment of the quality of infant–mother attachment for infants who, as a result of their day-care experience, do not experience the Strange Situation setting or procedure as particularly stressful; consequently, they do not need to seek proximity or comfort from their mothers. Third, the meaning or significance of attachment quality (as assessed in the Strange Situation) may be different for home-reared versus day-care infants (especially for those day-care infants who entered nonparental day care prior to 12 months of age). Preliminary evidence for the latter view stems from a recent study that found that although infant–mother attachment security was a good predictor of social-emotional functioning at 24 months for home-reared infants, it was not a good predictor for infants who experienced nonparental day-care rearing during the first year of life (Vaughn, Deane, & Waters, 1985).

One of the most intriguing questions in this area of research concerns the possible underlying causes for individual differences in patterns of attachment during infancy. Some researchers have argued that attachment classifications merely reflect variations in infant temperamental disposition (Kagan, 1982). This view has been strongly questioned, however, in light of infants' differing attachments with different caregivers, changes in attachment classification associated with significant changes in family life circumstances, and inconsistent findings (see Sroufe, 1985). Other researchers have argued that attachment quality is largely a result of the quality of caregiver behavior (Ainsworth et al., 1978). Although empirical findings to support this view are equivocal (Lamb et al., 1984), a number of studies suggest that caregiving that is sensitive to the infant's needs and goals and promptly responsive to the infant's signals—both contact-seeking signals such as crying and autonomy-seeking signals such as engrossed play—is associated with the development of a secure attachment pattern (e.g., Ainsworth et al., 1978; Belsky, Rovine, & Taylor, 1984; Egeland & Farber, 1984; Grossmann et al., 1985).

Most researchers would now agree that a number of factors including neonatal behavior, infant disposition, and the nature of caregiving (which is influenced by family living conditions, stress and support, cultural expectations for early self-reliance, and cultural attitudes toward optimal caregiving) interact to produce individual differences observed in both quality of attachment and its specific expression (e.g., Belsky & Rovine, 1987; Crockenberg, 1981; Egeland & Farber, 1984; Grossmann et al., 1985; Mikaye et al., 1985; Waters, Vaughn, & Egeland, 1980; see footnote 2). It ought to be added here that although attachment classifications based on the Strange Situation have been found to be fairly stable over the second year of life in most middle-class families (especially where there is stability in paternal employment, residence, and marital status) and in the majority of low-income families, quality of attachment relationships can change from secure to anxious (or from anxious to secure) in response to changes in caregiving arrangements and to stressful events that affect the mother's daily life (Thompson, Lamb, & Estes, 1982; Vaughn, Egeland, Sroufe, & Waters, 1979; Waters, 1978).

C. SECURE ATTACHMENTS AND AUTONOMOUS FUNCTIONING BEYOND THE FIRST YEAR OF LIFE

Both neo-analytic (Erikson, 1963) and attachment (Ainsworth et al., 1978) theories predict that a child's inner sense of security and confidence in the physical and emotional availability of an attachment figure serve as a crucial foundation for concurrent and later psychosocial competence, including mastery motivation and autonomous exploration. Quite a large body of short-term longitudinal research confirms that quality of attachment at 12 and 18 months predicts level of psychosocial competence — including indices of autonomous functioning — during toddlerhood and the preschool years in most samples (see Bretherton, 1985; Waters et al., 1986, for reviews). In general, young children who have a stable history of secure attachment are capable of greater instrumental independence, show greater enthusiasm for problem solving even in the face of difficulties, and use external assistance more age appropriately (i.e., in a nondemanding, nondependent way) than those whose attachments have been insecure (see, however, footnote 3).

For example, Matas et al. (1978) found that 2-year-olds whose attachments had been rated secure in infancy were more self-directed and less prone to frustration in a laboratory problem-solving situation with their mothers than were those whose attachments had been rated insecure. When faced with a tool-using problem difficult enough to require adult help, the secure toddlers were more likely to attempt first to solve the task on their own and then to turn to their mothers for help. In contrast, toddlers classified as having had an insecure attachment in infancy were less enthusiastic in approaching the problems and were less persistent once they did. They were more easily frustrated and negativistic in the face of both the easy and more difficult tasks, and were more likely to become engaged in noncompliance and conflict with their mothers.

In this same study, Matas et al. (1978) found that it was the securely attached 2-year-olds who, in the context of a toy clean-up task following free-play, were more likely to say "no" to their mother's clean-up requests. Although this may appear inconsistent with attachment theory predictions upon first consideration, researchers have argued that one indication of a 2-year-old's growing autonomy comes in the form of self-assertion — the ability and willingness to say "no" to parents' directions or requests (Crockenberg & Litman, 1990). Self-assertion is both conceptually and practically distinguishable from defiance, however. In being self-assertive, the child's primary attempt is to persist in his or her own present goals — in this case, engaged play activity. In being defiant, the child's primary attempt is to resist the adult, for example, by taking out additional toys upon a clean-up request (Crockenberg & Litman, 1990). Vaughn, Kopp, and Krakow's (1984) finding that toddlers who say "no" more often in a clean-up task situation are more developmentally advanced (based on Gesell schedules) than other children of their age provides further support that this form of self-assertion is a sign of competent autonomy among very young children (see also Mahler, Pine, & Bergman, 1975).

Other research indicates that children who had been classified as securely attached in infancy are more competent and curious (Arend, Gove, & Sroufe, 1979) and less dependent on emotional and instrumental assistance

(Sroufe, 1983) than their insecurely attached peers in the preschool and kindergarten years (at ages 4, 5, and 6 years). For example, based on teacher ratings, Sroufe found that preschool children who were securely attached as infants were more socially competent, autonomous, and resourceful in initiating activities. Children who had been classified as insecurely attached as infants were, in contrast, rated as overly dependent by their teachers for both instrumental and emotional support. They were more likely to demand teacher attention unnecessarily and in negative ways and to seek physical contact with their teacher at times that were situationally inappropriate (e.g., during group circle activities). Moreover, they were less effective in interacting with other children and in initiating independent activity. In a later part of the chapter, we discuss the long-term trajectories of dependency with a review of research on adults who were considered dependent as young children.

Additional evidence for the predictive value of attachment security for later autonomous functioning derives from a study of Israeli 5-year-old children who grew up on traditional kibbutzim (Oppenheim, Sagi, & Lamb, 1988). As infants, these children formed attachments to their mother, father, and metapelet (the designated caregiver for a small group of infants with whom the children spend the majority of their time; see Sagi et al., 1985, for a detailed description of caregiving in the Kibbutzim). Interestingly, although there was no clear relationship between infant–mother or infant–father attachment quality as assessed in the Strange Situation and measures of socioemotional development administered at age 5 years, infant–metapelet attachment quality was a good predictor of later development—including indices of autonomous functioning. Grossmann and Grossmann's (1990) research with German children also points to the predictive value of attachment classification. In their sample, 5-year-old preschoolers who were securely attached at 12 months exhibited more concentrated play and were rated as more organized, planful, and relaxed when compared to their peers whose attachments were classified as anxious-avoidant in infancy.

The longitudinal findings just described are quite impressive but can be interpreted in a number of competing ways (Denenberg, 1984; Lamb et al., 1984; Waters et al., 1986). One might hypothesize that there is a causal link between secure attachments in infancy and autonomous and competent functioning in the preschool years—that adjustment in the preschool years is the inevitable outcome of an early secure attachment relationship and that an early secure attachment is a prerequisite for later adjustment. Alternatively, one might propose that the correlation between secure attachment in infancy and later childhood adjustment emerges not because of the enduring effects of early experiences per se, but because both early attachment and later adjustment are influenced by contemporaneous patterns of caregiver–child interaction, "and it is the continuity of . . . care taking that explains the prediction" (Lamb et al., 1984, p. 166).[4] Indirect support for this alternative interpretation derives from research that suggests that the predictive value of attachment at 12 months obtains only among samples where there appears to be general "continuity in the quality of care or in the security of attachment relationships" over time (Lamb et al., 1984, p. 138). Among samples (or subsamples) were attachment classification or quality of parent–child interaction change markedly over time, attachment at age 12 months is generally not a good predictor of subsequent adjustment (see Lamb et al., 1984, for a review).

The latter findings could imply that only current quality of care is significant for the child's adjustment and autonomous functioning and that the import of earlier experiences and attachment patterns is simply erased once children reach toddlerhood and the preschool years. A number of scholars argue, however, that it is possible that early experiences (and their meaning for the self) are not completely lost to later experiences (e.g., Denenberg, 1984; Erickson, Sroufe, & Egeland, 1985; Lamb et al., 1984; Waters et al., 1986), but instead "must be viewed in the context of later experiences in a statistical interaction framework" (Denenberg, 1984, p. 151). That is, the lack of a significant (or strong) correlation between early attachment and later adjustment among some samples may indicate either that there is no longlasting relationship or that a relationship exists, but intervening events in the child's life "have generated interactional effects that mask the underlying relationship" (Denenberg, 1984, p. 151). Even Lamb and his colleagues, who have taken a rather critical stance on much of the attachment literature, noted that:

> an alternative probably more realistic, hypothesis is that early experiences, like constitutional differences, shape children's reactions to subsequent experiences and also influence the types of experiences they encounter. In this way, early experiences interact with later experiences to shape behavior . . . The challenge is to specify these interactions more systematically and to conduct hypothesis-testing studies. (p. 166)

It appears that improvements in the quality of care after infancy may support increased autonomy and adjustment in the preschool years among children with a history of early insecure attachment and that disruptions in the quality of care may undermine autonomy and adjustment in the preschool years among children with a history of early secure attachment. It is possible, however, that the former children may remain "differentially vulnerable" to later stresses or worsened conditions, whereas the latter children may "rebound more quickly should life supports again improve"

---

[4]It is also possible that early secure attachment and later adjustment are spuriously associated due to third variables such as parental adjustment.

(Erickson et al., 1985, p. 166). To date, we do not have the longitudinal studies designed in such a way to test these alternative interpretations of the specific role of secure and insecure attachment in long-term adjustment.

D. BASIC DEVELOPMENTAL TRENDS THROUGH MIDDLE CHILDHOOD

Although individual differences are apparent, most children make a good deal of progress toward increased autonomous functioning during the preschool years. More specifically, most children exhibit a notable shift in the balance between their need for contact with their primary caregiver and their ability to interact on their own within the physical and social world. This general developmental trend toward greater autonomous functioning is nicely illustrated in Maccoby and Feldman's (1972) longitudinal study of young children's behavior in the Strange Situation. Between the ages of 2 and 3 years, for example, nearly all children increased in their ability to recover from separations from their mother and quickly resume independent play. Moreover, by 3 years of age, most children no longer required the presence of their mother in order to engage in a sustained and friendly interaction with the unfamiliar adult. The means with which these young children maintained contact with their caregivers also exhibited change with age. For example, whereas most of the 2-year-olds relied largely on physical contact as means to feel secure after a brief separation, by age 3 years the children increasingly used "distal" contact-maintaining behaviors such as speaking, smiling, and showing objects. There also appeared to be marked developmental growth in attention span from age 2 years to 3 years as evidenced in longer manipulations of a single toy before moving on to something else; attention span increases will undoubtedly support greater autonomous functioning.

Cross-cultural researchers who use naturalistic observational methods have produced a wealth of information on the apparently universal change in the degree of independence and responsibility that adults expect of children once they reach age 5 or 7 years (Whiting & Whiting, 1975). By looking at the day-to-day lives of children during middle childhood, researchers reveal the higher degrees of responsible, autonomous functioning both expected and possible at this age. For example, during the course of middle childhood, youngsters spend substantially more time unsupervised by adults whether they live in rural or urban settings (e.g., Ellis, Rogoff, & Cromer, 1981; Wright, 1956). At this age children are also increasingly able to carry out tasks with just a preliminary set of instructions from an adult. These growing capacities for autonomous functioning stem from a variety of sources, including improvements in fine-motor coordination, memory performance, goal formulation skills, and self-control.

Children across cultures also begin to receive some form of systematic instruction from adults or older children at the start of middle childhood, either under informal conditions or in formal, school settings (Erikson, 1963). The goals of the more formal educational settings include not only children's increased knowledge and skills, but also their increased "capacity to be self-regulating or autonomous with respect to the learning process and to [their] own behavior" (Grolnick & Ryan, 1989, p. 143). Thus, although school-age children are expected to conform to rules of conduct in the classroom, adults are often encouraged when they see signs of self-initiative.

The degree to which children's self-direction and independence are valued by adults appears to vary, however, across diverse cultures (Hoffmann, 1988) and within cultures across both historical eras and socioeconomic classes (Alwin, 1988; Kohn, 1977). Indeed, in a series of articles that focus on the United States from the 1920s to the 1980s, Alwin (1984, 1988) argued convincingly that, on the whole, parental preferences for autonomy and self-regulation in children have systematically increased, whereas emphases on obedience and conformity to external authority have declined. These changes in parents' ideals seem to parallel the greater demands of a more technologically modern society within which increasing numbers of individuals are called on to take self-initiative and act autonomously in their occupational roles (Coleman, 1990).

Variation exists within today's more modern society as well. Kohn's (1977) research, for example, indicates that contemporary middle-class parents — parents who hold white-collar managerial or professional jobs — are more likely than working-class parents to encourage their children's self-direction and independence. Working-class parents, in contrast, tend to place a higher value on obedience to rules and authority — qualities that may be more critical to the working-class occupations that these parents may imagine their children taking on as adults (see also Alwin, 1988).

Regardless of their societal environment, children seem to thrive when acquiring skills that increase their sense of autonomy during middle childhood (Erikson, 1963). Nonetheless, there are many elements that comprise responsible autonomous functioning (e.g., mature decision-making skills) that do not begin to emerge until the adolescent years (Lewis, 1981). Likewise, there are many transformations in the nature of parent–child connections that only begin to appear at the transition to adolescence.

Comment. Bakan (1966) proposed that human beings possess two basic but antagonistic senses. On the one hand, there is a sense of self or *agency* manifested in self-assertion and autonomous functioning; on the other hand, there is a sense of *communion* — the desire to become or remain unified with others. The challenge for individuals, according to this scheme, is to reconcile and to balance these competing tendencies. Although, as we have discussed, these two senses and the attempt to balance them are apparent from very early on in a child's life, the research reviewed here leads one to question whether these senses are fully antagonistic. The relationship context in which a healthy sense of autonomy develops (e.g., the parent-child relationship) is one that not only permits independence, but also provides the security of emotional support (Bretherton, 1987). In short, meeting the needs of communion in an age-appropriate way may actually allow greater agency—independence and exploration—to blossom.

III. Adolescence

A. DEVELOPMENTAL TASKS OF AUTONOMY AND IDENTITY

The developmental task of adolescence, in Western cultures, has been popularly and historically seen as synonymous with gains in autonomy and self-identity (Erikson, 1963; Freud, 1958; see also Baumeister & Tice, 1986, for a historical perspective on self-definition and adolescence). The general expectation today is that by the time individuals reach the stage of early adulthood they have developed both "a coherent and positive sense of self and the ability to make informed decisions, exercise judgment, and regulate [their] own behavior appropriately" (Steinberg, 1991). In other words, although most scholars in Western cultures would agree that development of identity and self-governance continues past the age of 20 years, they expect that during the course of adolescence young people have gained a sense of self-reliance and have developed basic skills needed to begin to meet the challenges they will face once they leave their families of origin.

However, the long-held proposition that autonomy—whether conceived of as disengagement from parental ties and control (e.g., Freud, 1958), resistance to peer or parental pressure (e.g., Berndt, 1979), confidence in self-governance (e.g., Greenberger, 1984), a subjective sense of identity or independence (e.g., Blos, 1967; Douvan & Adelson, 1966; Erikson, 1963; Kandel & Lesser, 1972), or mature decision making (Lewis, 1981)—is the sole and primary developmental task of adolescence, does not fully capture the nature of the psychosocial challenges with which adolescents must grapple. Indeed, the classic view of adolescent autonomy as independence and self-reliance—free of emotional attachments—has come under criticism by a number of contemporary scholars (e.g., Gilligan, 1988; Greene & Boxer, 1986; Josselson, 1988; see also, Sampson, 1985; Spence, 1985). One concern is that "psychologists in characterizing adolescence as a 'second individuation' (Blos, 1967) and in celebrating an identity that is 'self-wrought'

(Erikson, 1962), have encouraged a way of thinking in which the interdependence of human life and the reliance of people on one another becomes either problematic or tacit" (Gilligan, 1988, p. xii.)

By emphasizing exclusively independence and self-reliance during adolescence, psychologists, until recently, have accorded minimal significance to relational ties, support, and interpersonal competence at this period of the life span (Powers, Hauser, & Kilner, 1989). Moreover, true gains in autonomy at adolescence have often been misunderstood. For example, when family relationships are considered, rebelliousness and parent–child detachment have sometimes been confused with the development of a healthy sense of autonomy (Freud, 1958). In fact, rebellion is most likely an indicator of problems in the development of autonomy rather than its equivalent; and the majority of teens maintain fairly close relationships with their parents over the course of adolescence (Collins, 1990; Montemayor, 1983). Moreover, youngsters who appear most competent at late adolescence in terms of ego development and identity exploration are those who have maintained close, supportive—albeit transformed—relationships with their parents (Grotevant & Cooper, 1986; Powers et al., 1989; Ryan & Lynch, 1989).

Thus, the developmental task of adolescence seems to be a complicated one that calls for a negotiated balance between an emerging sense of self as a competent individual on the one hand, and a transformed, but continued, feeling of connection with significant others on the other (Josselson, 1988; Quintana & Lapsley,1990). Internal and external processes seem to work together to initiate this complex developmental task (Sessa & Steinberg, 1991). Internal processes include physiological, social-cognitive, and intrapsychic changes of the child; external processes include the social expectations of the larger culture, school, and community as well as changes in the particular child's family relationships and role responsibilities. Josselson (1988) captured the more contemporary view of the task of adolescence by using Mahler's (Mahler et al., 1975) concept of rapprochement initially used to describe development during toddlerhood. She stated, "Rapprochement is about preserving bonds of relationship in the presence of increasing autonomy. . . . The adolescent, as much as the toddler, brings his new ideas and his new ways of being home, to be recognized in the context of ongoing connection, to bring the relationship up to date" (pp. 94–95).

B. FROM PSYCHOANALYTICAL ROOTS TO CONTEMPORARY VIEWS

The shift in the literature on adolescent psychosocial development toward a more integrative view of autonomy and social connection was largely in response to the lack of empirical support for predictions deriving from the psychoanalytic perspective on adolescence. The classic psychoanalytic view stresses the severance of emotional attachments and dependencies on parents during adolescence (Freud, 1958). Indeed, the psychosocial goal of adolescence, from the psychoanalytic perspective, is detachment from parental ties which, in turn, makes possible mature autonomy and later attachment to extrafamilial objects (Freud, 1958). Pubertal development is considered the driving force behind the process of detachment. According to Anna Freud, the physiological changes of puberty cause a reawakening of sexual impulses toward parents. These impulses lead inevitably to severe intrapsychic turmoil and anxiety for young adolescents and make continued emotional attachment to parents extremely difficult. The inner emotional turmoil is not dealt with by adolescents consciously; instead, it is expressed in rebelliousness toward parents, severe arguments in the home, and, finally, emotional detachment from parents. In essence, from this view-point, there is virtually no room for the maintenance of calm, supportive emotional ties with parents at this stage of development, if development of autonomous functioning is to occur. From the psychoanalytic perspective, autonomy necessarily involves the repudiation of parents as well as an initial overzealous dependence on, and orientation toward, peers (Freud, 1958).

Research that has accumulated over the past 20 years on large, nonclinical samples of adolescents reveals that parent–child emotional bonds and long-term attachments are not threatened at this point in the child's life (Collins, 1990; Steinberg, 1990). The vast majority of adolescents feel close to and respect their parents, even as the adolescents make increasingly more independent decisions, direct and manage more of their practical affairs, and spend less time in the home (Offer, 1969; Rutter, Graham, Chadwick, & Yule, 1976; Steinberg, 1990); that is, even as adolescents develop a greater functional independence (Hoffman, 1984). The somewhat diminished positive interactions found between children and parents at early adolescence (Montemayor, 1986) and the temporary increases in parent–child bickering, especially at the apex of pubertal development (Steinberg, 1989b), should not be mistaken for detachment in the service of autonomy. They might instead be con-sidered moderate levels of distancing behavior that provide the impetus for healthy transformations in the parent–child relationship—includ-ing the move toward more egalitarianism. In brief, for most teens, the striving for independence and the concern over autonomy from parents take "place within the context of a close, cooperative, and even somewhat dependent relationship" (Damon, 1983, p. 310) and are balanced by youngsters' continued reliance on parents for emotional support and guidance.

C. DEPENDENCE ON PARENTS

Findings from a number of studies lead to the conclusion that healthy adolescents continue to depend on their parents, but are not dependent on them in the sense of being unable to function without them. Most adolescents, for instance, consider their parents to be supportive and guiding influences (Rutter et al., 1976; Weiss, 1982) and continue to rely on their parents' advice, but the domains and centrality of this reliance have changed from the early childhood years. Adolescents seem somewhat more selective in their reliance on parents. When it comes to long-term questions concerning educational or occupational plans, or questions of values, for example, adolescents seem to follow parental advice even over peer advice (e.g., Brittain, 1963; Kandel & Lesser, 1972; Young & Ferguson, 1979). In fact, careful research has shown that the core values of youth activists of the 1960s very much reflected those of their parents (see Troll & Bengtson, 1979). Moreover, adolescents today seem to follow their parents' lead on social-political issues even more than they did in the 1970s (Sebald, 1986). Adolescents do rely on their peers' views and opinions, especially during early and middle adolescence, when it comes to short-term, social matters such as style of dress, taste in music, language, and dating and leisure practices (Brittain, 1963; Brown, 1982).

Lewis' (1981) laboratory research on adolescent advice giving when faced with more "weighty" decisions (e.g., elective medical treatments) suggests that over the course of adolescence youngsters become no more or less likely to recommend parent advice seeking to a hypothetical peer, but do become increasingly likely to recommend independent, expert professional advice seeking. They also become more likely to consider possible future risks and long-term consequences of decisions, at least in this advice-giving situation. Thus, although adolescents gradually develop the capabilities to arrive at important decisions on their own (an indicator of autonomous functioning), many use parents and other adults as an emotional or informational resource (Kenny, 1987; Lewis, 1981), just as securely attached infants and toddlers use caregivers as a resource when they are confronted with more difficult challenges (e.g., Matas et al., 1978). Part of the development of responsible autonomy during adolescence, then, appears to include a sense of when it is appropriate to turn to others—including parents, peers, and nonfamilial adults (see Ryan & Lynch, 1989). Such a portrayal is quite different from one that equates rebellion against parental wishes as a sign of healthy autonomy.

D. PSYCHOLOGICAL SEPARATION

Youngsters do, however, begin to deidealize their image of their parents during the early adolescent years as Blos' (1967) neo-analytic theory of adolescent individuation would predict (Steinberg & Silverberg, 1986). For example, Smollar and Youniss' (1989) interviews with adolescents indicate that, by middle adolescence, most youngsters have disengaged somewhat from an inner representation of their parents as "all-knowing" and "all-powerful"—a representation held by younger children. When asked to describe changes in their relationships with their parents over the past 5 years, one 15-year-old in the Smollar and Youniss study said, "I used to listen to everything [he said]. I thought he was always right. Now I have my own opinions. They may be wrong, but they're mine and I like to say them" (p. 77).

Thus, although emotional ties to parents are maintained throughout adolescence for most individuals (Kenny, 1987), there seems to be a degree of psychological separation vis-à-vis parents as youngsters attempt to differentiate some aspects of self from significant others (Blos, 1967; Hill & Holmbeck, 1986; Josselson, 1980). Although, from the neo-analytic perspective, youngsters are likely to experience a feeling of loss as this process begins, the sharpening of psychological boundaries between parent and adolescent is thought to lay the groundwork for the development of a stable and integrated sense of self at late adolescence and early adulthood (Josselson, 1980). Indeed, Frank and her colleagues found that young adults who experience so little separation that their relationship with their parents could be described as enmeshed, often are troubled by their inability to cope with day-to-day challenges and responsibilities without parental assistance (Frank, Avery, & Laman, 1988).

Youniss and Smollar's (1985) program of research on youngsters and their relationships from middle childhood through adolescence provides convincing evidence that alongside this gradual but clear progression toward greater individuality including greater self-agency and self-awareness come "the simultaneous development of a social sense of self . . . realizing what is owed to others for the self's development and . . . recognizing that others are needed for the self's current functioning" (p. 168). One thus finds that older adolescents (college sophomores) tend to report an increased sense of responsibility toward their parents compared to previous years (Pipp, Shaver, Jennings, Lamborn, & Fischer, 1985).

Feelings of emotional detachment from parents, on the other hand, are related to a sense of parental rejection among older adolescents and, notably, to a perceived lack of family support for independence among college students (Ryan & Lynch, 1989). This latter finding is of particular interest because it underscores the role that secure and supportive relationships are likely to play in facilitating adolescent self-regulation and self-definition (Baumrind, 1989; Kobak & Sceery, 1988).

E. AUTONOMY GROWING FROM CONNECTION

Much of the recent empirical literature on adolescent development and family relationships examines the hypothesis that encouragement of adolescent individuality (permitting disagreement and the expression of alternative views) within a context of familial affective support and connectedness provides an optimal environment for the development of responsible autonomy, a sense of identity, and psychological well-being among adolescents (e.g., Baumrind, 1989; Grotevant & Cooper, 1986; Hauser, Powers, Noam, & Bowlds, 1987; Kobak & Sceery, 1988; Powers, Hauser, Schwartz, Noam, & Jacobson, 1983; Quintana & Lapsley, 1990).

One study of structured interactions of 14- to 15-year-old adolescents and their parents indicated that adolescent ego development was most advanced when families exhibited a high amount of noncompetitive sharing of perspectives or challenging behavior within a context of high affective support and low affective conflict (Powers et al., 1983). In related research, Grotevant and Cooper (1986) outlined a model of adolescent development that highlights the facilitative role of individuation in family dyadic relationships. According to their model, an individuated relationship is one that displays a balance between individuality and connectedness in communication patterns; individuality is reflected by *separateness* (expressing differentness of self from others) and *self-assertion* (expressing one's own point of view clearly), whereas connectedness is reflected by *mutuality* (expressing sensitivity to and respect for others' ideas) and *permeability* (expressing openness and responsiveness to others' views; Cooper, Grotevant, & Condon, 1983). The results from Grotevant and Cooper's observational study of high school seniors and their families provide some support for the view that an effective combination of cohesion and separation in family relationships is associated with adolescent identity exploration and perspective-taking skills (Cooper et al., 1983; Grotevant & Cooper, 1985). In general, "adolescents rated highest in both identity exploration and role-taking skill were found to have participated with at least one parent in an individuated relationship . . . examining their differences, but within the context of connectedness" (Grotevant & Cooper, 1986, p. 92).

The similarity to the work on infant attachment relationships and competence is clearly apparent. Although the nature of attachment during adolescence must differ from that of early childhood in light of changes in youngsters' cognition, identity, and sexuality (Chapman, 1991; Gilligan, 1988; for further discussion, see Armsden & Greenberg, 1987; Kobak & Sceery, 1988), adolescents still require confidence in their parents' commitment to them (Weiss, 1982). They still require a secure psychological base from which to explore options outside the family; and they flourish when parents acknowledge, respect, and support their youngsters' developing sense of self-reliance and individuality (Harter, 1990; Quintana & Lapsley, 1990; Rice, 1991).

Baumrind's (1978, 1989) oft-cited notion of authoritative parenting also becomes relevant in this discussion about the value of supportive relationships for the development of healthy autonomy. Indeed, a number of large-scale studies have found that youngsters who score highest on a constellation of domains that might be labeled *healthy autonomy* — self-confidence, academic competence, impulse control, positive work attitudes, leadership, and social responsibility — are likely to have parents who rely on authoritative parenting practices (e.g., Dornbusch, Ritter, Leiderman, Roberts, & Fraleigh, 1987; Lamborn, Mounts, Steinberg, & Dornbusch, 1991; Steinberg, Elmen, & Mounts, 1989). That is, their parents strike an effective balance — they encourage warm parent–child relationships, permit their children to take part in decision making and to express their opinions and individuality, and, at the same time, set age-appropriate rules, standards, and limits for their youngsters' behavior. These parents are also those most likely to provide rational explanations for family rules and to engage in verbal give-and-take with their children especially around issues of discipline. In short, parents who use authoritative parenting provide a supportive base from which adolescents can develop both positive feelings about themselves and the capabilities for responsible, independent action.

Authoritarian parents, a second subgroup in the Baumrindian (1978, 1989) model, also set limits and rules for their youngsters' behavior. When compared to other parents, however, they tend to be less warm, accepting, and supportive of their children and are more likely to restrict their youngsters' autonomy, self-expression, and involvement in decision making (Baumrind, 1978; Lamborn et al., 1991). Their underlying belief seems to be that children should accept rules and standards set by parents without question or explanation. Interestingly, adolescents raised in such households often appear to be obedient and conform to the behavioral standards held by adults, but they suffer from a lack of self-confidence and are generally more depressed and somatically distressed than their peers (Lamborn et al., 1991). In contrast to their peers, these youngsters then are less likely to exhibit healthy autonomy or a positive sense of self.

F. CULTURE-BOUND GOALS OF IDENTITY AND MUTUALITY IN THE TRANSITION TO ADULTHOOD

In modern, Western cultures, the transition from late adolescence to early adulthood marks an important time for establishing an integrated sense of identity — a coherent sense of oneself, one's life and work goals, one's belief-systems, and one's place in society (Erikson, 1963; Waterman, 1985

Waterman & Archer, 1990). Marcia (1980) wrote, for example, that at minimum, young people should make a "commitment to a sexual orientation, an ideological stance, and a vocational direction" (p. 160). According to Erikson (1963) and many researchers, the healthiest way to reach this goal is to experience a period of moratorium–a time during which one explores the wide variety of possibilities "eliciting information about oneself or one's environment in order to make a decision about . . . important life choice[s]" (Grotevant, 1987, p. 204). Many young people do reach this sense of identity through a gradual process of exploration and consideration of the choices before them. The process and even the notion of identity formation, however, is not a universal one, but is culture bound: "It is based on the assumption that individuals have choices about careers, ideologies, values, and relationships" (Grotevant, 1987, p. 215), and is probably confined to cultures where the individual is valued highly. Even within modern Western cultures there are young people who do not have the economic freedom to delay the taking on of adult responsibilities to explore possibilities for the definition of self (Steinberg, 1989a).

Researchers have also pointed out that the transition from adolescence to adulthood marks an important time for changes in relationships with parents. One group of investigators, for example, has laid out a series of stages in quality of parent–child relationships (White, Speisman, & Costos, 1983). What is worth noting in this stage model is the suggestion that a partner- or peerlike relationship with parents – a relationship that is open and egalitarian and in which there is a mutual recognition of the other's perspective – is the goal once young people reach early adulthood. Although this may be possible and desired in some cultures and subcultures, it is unlikely to be even considered in others. Individuals living in cultures and subcultures where parental authority, respect, and standing in the familial hierarchy are traditionally held in strict observance, regardless of child age, are unlikely to share this goal.

Comment.   There is no question that adolescence is a period of increased autonomy, a period during which youngsters desire greater freedom to live according to personal preferences rather than family rules and conventions (Smetana, 1988). Nevertheless, like early childhood, adolescence is also a time when relationships, connections, and a sense of emotional support and belongingness with respect to family and peers are vital to growth rather than obstacles to be hurdled. There is a growing awareness, on the part of both researchers who have begun to cast their questions on adolescent development in new ways, and among social commentators on Western – and specifically American – society, that maturity and success ought not be measured in terms of independence or individualism at any cost (see Allen, 1987; Bellah, Madsen, Sullivan,

Swindler, & Tipton, 1985; Sampson, 1985; Spence, 1985). Social connection to family and community are equally central to mature development.

IV. Adulthood

The usage of concepts like *dependency, independence, autonomy,* and *loss of autonomy* is rare when it comes to normal developmental psychology of adulthood. The concepts do not seem to represent typical developmental issues any longer; they have been left behind, outgrown, outlived, or adapted to as such. In developmental theories of adulthood, the struggle toward personal autonomy is no longer a primary developmental task. Autonomy, when related to finding one's identity in one's work career, life goals, and belief systems, is assumed to require *stabilization* in adulthood rather than *initiation*. Erikson (1963), for example, postulated the task of identity for the adolescent, but intimacy for the young adult and generativity for the middle-age adult. Successful coping with the developmental tasks of adolescence launches and establishes a healthy sense of autonomy in the adult. If the developmental process has fallen short,the consequences are dealt with in psychiatry, clinical psychology, or medicine, not developmental psychology. We see later, however, that the dialectic dynamism between autonomy, affiliation, and generativity is played out in adulthood, too.

A. DEVELOPMENTAL TASKS OF INTIMACY AND GENERATIVITY: INTERDEPENDENCE

The terms that closely describe the developmental tasks of intimacy and generativity in Erikson's (1963) language are *interdependence, reciprocity, affiliation,* or *cooperation* incorporating the terms *dependency* and *autonomy*. Freud's notion of "love and work" (cited by Hazan & Shaver, 1990) aptly describes the developmental tasks identified for adulthood, such as finding a partner, adjusting to and rearing children, and/or establishing and stabilizing one's work or professional career. These themes have found empirical support in the work by Vaillant (1977) and by Levenson (1978; see also Michaels & Goldberg, 1988, for a review on parenthood, and Main, Kaplan, & Cassidy, 1985, work on attachment in adulthood).

Current theorists have leveled criticism at both the psychoanalytically oriented theories and the empirical work, arguing either that the theories cannot explain how a striving for agency from infancy on allows for the development of connectedness, intimacy, reciprocity, and generativity in adulthood (Clark & Reis, 1988; Franz & White, 1985) or that undue emphasis is put on agency and independence as the goal of development

(Gilligan, 1982, 1988). Different solutions are offered. Gilligan argued that male-oriented theories and findings of development have little explanatory power for the developmental career of women. She proposed a separate developmental career for women noting that women's identity and self are intricately related to relationships and cannot develop outside of relationships, a prerequisite of Erikson's (1963) theory. Clark (see, e.g., Clark & Reis, 1988) and Franz and White (1985) asserted that any marked imbalance between independence and connectedness in both men or women will cause problems and thus proposed that Erikson's theory needs to be expanded to include both the development of agency and of connectedness. Similarly, Hazan and Shaver (1990) argued that the theme "love and work" is intimately tied to both modalities: agency and communion, instrumentality and expressiveness, individuation and connectedness, or individuation and attachment. An unmitigated agency and unmitigated attachment are both equally immature and selfish.

Such a view is very much in contrast to the argument by Waterman (1981, 1985) or Bowlby (1969) that a highly developed individuality (autonomy) automatically encompasses a highly developed sense of caring and respect for others. In other words, attachment does not present an earlier stage in development that is then transformed into individuality at a later stage in development.

In sum, the need for autonomy and individuation or agency and the need for communion and interpersonal connectedness, jointly, should be taken into account in the developmental career of both men and women (see also Bryant, 1989; Frank, Avery, & Laman, 1988; White, Speisman, Costos, & Smith, 1987). A new label to encompass both agency and attachment or independence and dependency is found in the term *interdependence*.

B. INTERDEPENDENCE IN ADULTHOOD

How then does interdependence function? Empirical answers to this question derive largely from social psychology laboratory studies on relationships and relationship change. Descriptive work from family sociology and intergenerational studies seems to echo the findings from social psychology.

Kelley et al. (1983) conceptualized interdependence very broadly in terms of ongoing chains of mutual influence between two people. Interdependence, in their model, represents a balance between dependency and independence. Being dependent here means that one has an effect on others as do others on oneself; it does not imply being helpless, powerless, or without control. In this sense, interdependence—the willingness to help and to care and be helped and cared for—empowers both the self and the other (Gilligan, 1988).

Different norms, of which the most widely studied and acclaimed is the equity norm, have been proffered to regulate when and how people benefit each other. Hatfield and Traupmann (1981) claimed that the equity norm determines individuals' satisfaction level in relationships including close relationships. Interestingly, for our life-span view of dependency and independence, they found that underbenefit (giving more than receiving) distresses men more than women, overbenefit (receiving more than giving) women more than men. One might expect the opposite to hold if agentic development is socialized more strongly in men and communal development more strongly in women. Also, as we see later, men seem to experience more conflict about dependency, whereas women feel more comfortable about dependency.

Deutsch (1985) took a more differentiated view of relationship norms and argued that the equity norm predominates adult relationships when maximizing economic productivity is the goal. He was able to demonstrate that, in contrast, when cooperation or positive socioemotional bonds are salient, the norms of equality or need-based rules tend to prevail. Deutsch, therefore, differentiated between exchange relationships and communal relationships. The essential developmental tasks of adulthood, intimacy and generativity, are best realized in communal relationships that are based on reciprocity and mutuality. True reciprocal and mutual relationships require both mature agency or individuality and attachment (Franz & White, 1985) and, in turn, allow further growth in both attachment and agency. Thus, interdependence is a multidimensional concept encompassing aiding others (agency) and receiving aid and contact from others (attachment) (Gilligan, 1982, 1988; Walker, Thompson, & Morgan, 1987).

This joint emphasis on attachment and autonomy plays a central role in building a social convoy (Kahn & Antonucci, 1980), which guarantees social support throughout life. Family sociologists have used the term solidarity to describe the ongoing exchanges that come in the form of contact, interaction, warmth and closeness, instrumental help, provision of goods, and the sharing of common beliefs and orientations (Bengtson & Black, 1973; Marshall & Bengtson, 1983). The same literature also supports the notion that, in general, interdependence and attachment are more often and more easily expressed by women than by men thus reflecting Gilligan's (1988) view discussed earlier. These capabilities (or tendencies) are seen as a prerequisite for women to maintain family and kinship. Fu, Hinkle, and Hanna (1986) demonstrated that dependency tends to be a female characteristic and establishing family interdependence a female task. Hagestad (1981, 1985) and Troll (1986) expressed similar thoughts when they described the functions and structure of grandparenthood, specifically of grandmothers as kin-keepers and as the "minister of the interior" (Hagestad, 1985, p. 39).

Rossi and Rossi, in their book *Of Human Bonding* (1990), provided a detailed account of the interactions between family members throughout life. They emphasized the highly structured character of kin obligations, the perceptions of these obligations held by different members of kin, the generally strong affectional ties between children and parents throughout the life course, and the lifelong impact disruptions in the structure (e.g., divorce of parents, emotional discord between children and parents) can have for the nature and extent of family interaction. In general, one is impressed by the number and reciprocity of interchanges particularly in moments of "crises of celebrations" (Riley, 1983). It is, however, the mother–daughter relationship that stands out in its degree of interchanges throughout the life course. Relationships between mothers and daughters and, to a lesser extent, between fathers and daughters are considered and experienced as closer and more important relationships than those between mothers and sons or fathers and sons. Such data are well stated in an old proverb: "Sons stay sons till they take a wife, daughters stay daughters for life."

Being dependent in the adult context, thus, takes on quite a different meaning from dependency in childhood. In the adult context, dependency and independence seem to have melted into interdependence requiring agency and autonomy. Nevertheless, an intriguing question remains: What becomes of dependent children over the course of their developmental career? Could it be that dependency in childhood breeds dependency in adulthood or will early dependency just grow into later interdependence?

C. DEVELOPMENTAL TRAJECTORIES OF DEPENDENT INFANTS

In the context of the Fels Study with its longitudinal follow-ups, Kagan and Moss (1960) examined the stability of dependency from childhood to adulthood. They concluded that there is differential stability for women and men. They argued that higher stability in women is due to societal encouragement of passivity and dependency in the face of frustration in women but not in men. On the personal level, they found that men were more conflicted about dependent behavior than were women. Dependency seemed less accepted by men, which Kagan and Moss perceived as the reason for a greater turnaround in men from high dependency in childhood to low dependency in adulthood than in women.

Caspi and colleagues (Caspi, Bem, & Elder, 1989; Caspi, Elder, & Herbener, 1990) also suggested quite diverse developmental courses for dependent versus independent children, but more important perhaps, they outlined diverse trajectories for dependent boys versus dependent girls. They regarded dependency, and independence for that matter, as interactional styles that may be self-perpetuating for two reasons. First, individuals are reinforced for the behavior they exhibit and will create and select environments that tend to sustain dependency or independence. Second, individuals become increasingly skilled at evoking from others those nurturing responses that reinforce dependency. Thus, one might predict that developmental careers of dependency and independence are rather stable.

Caspi et al.'s (1989) longitudinal data show, however, differential patterns as a function of gender. Dependent boys tended to grow up into warm, insightful, undefensive, and socially poised men who are on time in their role transitions (completion of schooling, initiation of a career, marriage, fatherhood) and who are more likely to have intact marriages at midlife than same-cohort men with no history of childhood dependency. For women with childhood dependency, development was far less positive. They tended to have quite a negative profile as adults: low aspiration level, unassertive, moody, self-pitying, and so forth, with an early entrance into marriage and parenthood. Many of these women had no educational career beyond high school and their marriages were not more stable or harmonious than those of other women in the same cohort. Caspi and his colleagues suggested that childhood dependency has grown into dependability and nurturance in men, but into defensiveness and unhappiness in women.

In contrast, using the Fels data as well, Skolnik (1986) demonstrated that developmental trajectories are not set in infancy: Security of attachment in infancy had little impact on adult well-being. Instead, according to her analyses, it is relationship quality during adolescence, specifically peer relationship quality in adolescence, that correlates highly with both peer relations during childhood and health, sociability, and marital satisfaction in adulthood. These data, however, do not negate the possibility of early behavioral patterns or interactional styles developing and becoming the pattern of choice. Hazan and Shaver (1987), for instance, argued for a predictive relationship between early attachment styles and later love relationships between adults (see also Main et al., 1985).

Comment. The nature of developmental tasks in adulthood seems to require interdependence in the sense of cooperation and attachment combined with agency and autonomy. Relying on Caspi et al.'s (1989, 1990) data, it is difficult to envision a person who is highly dependent on others for care and happiness who is at the same time capable of true generativity and intimacy. Both independence and dependency need to mature in order to allow for an interdependent adult. Whether there is a shift toward more dependency for women to fulfill their social roles and a shift toward more autonomy and agency for men to fulfill theirs is related to how social roles are distributed and socialized.

V. Aging

In contrast to adulthood, the concepts of dependency, independence, autonomy, and loss of autonomy surface again in the study of aging and take on renewed importance potentially delegating second place to interdependence.

Given the vast interindividual differences in aging, antecedents for this change differ in timing, intensity, and scope and, therefore, create individually different backgrounds for the developmental tasks of old age. In general, however, there are three domains to consider. First, there is an increase in physical losses and in experiences with biological impairments. Health becomes more of a problem for more people (Brody, Brock, & Williams, 1987). Second, social stresses and losses also seem to accumulate for most older adults. Demographic data show, for instance, that major life changes both in terms of numbers and accumulations continue into the aging years (Bumpass, 1991). There is a rise from the rather low percentages of loss of spouse, child, or sibling for individuals in their 40s, to over 50% for over-60-year-olds, to 70% for over-70-year-olds. In addition, retirement and losses in social roles have an impact on the extent and intensity of the elderly's social network. Western societies typically provide few opportunities for new social roles for older adults. Third, older adults are confronted with adjusting to the idea of time running out, thus creating new tasks for their understanding of self and sense of life.

A. DEVELOPMENTAL TASKS: EGO INTEGRITY

Developmental tasks in the fourth phase of life can be subsumed under Erikson's (1963) concept of ego integrity. Adjusting to retirement and role loss, to increasing health problems and impairments, and to the realization of one's own finitude prove major tasks and reorientations. In contrast to the "other-oriented" tasks of midlife, the elderly, similarly to the adolescent, are confronted largely with "self-oriented" tasks. It is no wonder that the importance of interdependence pales in light of the growing salience of personal autonomy and agency in coping with the demands of the later years (Cohler, 1983; Cohler & Boxer, 1984). Indeed, studies support complaints by the elderly, particularly by elderly women, regarding continued family responsibility (for a review, see Cohler, 1983). In this same context, Rosenmayr and Köckeis (1965) have coined the expression "intimacy at a distance."

This is not to negate the continued importance of social integration for the well-being of the elderly and the need for social contact in old age. The need for support, however, often seems overemphasized at the cost of the need for autonomy. The social environment of the elderly, still very much under the influence of negative aging stereotypes, is all too ready to step in and take over for the elderly. Physical impairment is all too easily equated with psychological impairment (Collopy, 1988). Looking at demographic data (Bumpass, 1991), it is surprising how many elderly are still engaged in economic transfer to their children (about 10% of White parents over 70 years of age provide financial assistance to their adult children). About 80% of the elderly are able to live independently in the community. With regard to weekly contacts with children and siblings, percentages hover around 50%. Thus, many elderly have an intact, albeit reduced, social network (see also Rossi & Rossi, 1990).

This reduction in social contact with age has been, however, frequently deplored in the aging literature and has been considered a pressing problem in need of intervention or as a sign of disengagement (Arnett, Eyre, & Theorell, 1982; Bennett, 1980). Quite a different and rather positive view was presented by Carstensen (1991; for a few earlier attempts see Kalish & Knudtson, 1976; Larson, 1978). Carstensen (1991) argued that social contacts for the elderly or, more specifically, for individuals closer to death take on a different meaning. The elderly become very selective about which contacts to engage in and which ones to avoid or give up. Carstensen's (1991) socioemotional selectivity theory claims that emotional and affective benefits are the driving force for contacts in aging, whereas information-seeking purposes more frequently underly the contacts chosen by young adults (Fredrickson & Carstensen, 1989).

Into this line of reasoning, we can also fit the extended notion of attachment to old age (Antonucci, 1976; Lerner & Ryff, 1978; Troll, 1986; Troll & Smith, 1976). Inherent in this literature is the suggestion that successful adjustment across adulthood and old age depends on the existence of mutually supportive social networks, such as confidants. Thus, intimate and affective bonds rather than large social networks serve as a buffering system in moments of stressful life events.

In sum, when we speak of a shift toward autonomy with old age it continues to be a question of balance between dependency and autonomy. Given the increasing negative balance between gains and losses (Baltes, 1987), increasing biological vulnerability, and the major developmental task involving the acceptance of one's finality, both social integration and personal autonomy seem of utmost importance. In other words, both security provided by a supportive environment and autonomy fostered by a stimulating environment are necessary for the elderly person's well-being (we remind you of the notion of secure attachment in infancy). How much security and how much autonomy is provided for by the environment should be determined foremost by the person's competency and resources, for there is no doubt that autonomy is challenged by physical, social, psychological, and economic limitations imposed on a body more vulnerable and more easily exhausted.

From the perspective just discussed, the dependencies of old age are both the result of biological changes as well as changes in societal demands. Often, however, the latter seem to predate the former. The major dependencies of old age, structured dependency, physical dependency, and behavioral dependency, illustrate the interplay between biology and environment.

B. STRUCTURED DEPENDENCY

The intellectual origins of structured dependency are the functionalist social control theories. As a term, it implies that human worth is determined primarily by participation in the productive process. Loss of work and/or retirement create structured dependency (Townsend, 1981; Walker, 1980). Thus, in essence, culture lays the groundwork for dependency and its societal structure even requires dependency from certain subgroups in the population in order to function. Although this position has been criticized (Johnson, 1989), it has stood its ground and is used, for instance, in the determination of the dependency ratio defined as the proportion of the working population that is available to support those who are out of the labor force (for a full discussion, see Hauser, 1976).

Most recently, but from a rather different vantage point, Guillemard (1992) also focused on societal responsibilities in creating dependencies in old age. After analyzing the delivery systems of social services whose purported aim is to maintain autonomy and independent living among the elderly, Guillemard claimed that just the opposite is achieved. The fact that these services are highly fragmented, Guillemard agued, leads automatically to less autonomy and choice by the elderly. Guillemard argued that the autonomy of the elderly person is extinguished by the dependency of the elderly upon the service system.

C. PHYSICAL DEPENDENCY

Physical dependency is defined as "functional incapacity" (e.g., Akhtar, Broe, Crombie, McLean, & Andrews, 1973; Shanas et al., 1968; Wan, Odell, & Lewis, 1982) or as "practical helplessness" (van den Heuvel, 1976), or as the individual's incapacity to carry out the essential activities of daily living (Gallagher, Thompson, & Levy, 1980). There are, however, many different nuances or degrees of functional dependency related to which and how many incapacities to include in the assessment of dependency. Assessment strategies vary and, thus, produce different results regarding the prevalence of functional dependency in old age and its relationship to other variables such as age (e.g., Svanborg, Landahl, & Mellström, 1984), sex, social class (Sosna & Wahl, 1983; Wan et al., 1982), and psychiatric impairment (Wahl, 1987).

Physical dependency can become most prominent when an elderly person is subject to a degenerative brain disease, such as Alzheimer's, or has suffered a stroke or some other debilitating impairment. It should be noted, however, that an organic impairment is neither a necessary nor a sufficient condition for dependency. Despite this disclaimer, within the dynamics of social interactions and social perception, physical dependency is frequently interpreted as a sign of general incompetence leading to an expectation of general dependency. In this vein, Collopy (1988) asked the question: Within the dynamics of care, is physical dependency interpreted as a sign of decisional dependency? Unfortunately, there seems to be a direct link between competence and autonomy, on the one hand, and incompetence and dependency, on the other hand, without any variation in between.

D. BEHAVIORAL DEPENDENCY

Behavioral dependency is one of the dependencies most feared by the elderly. Fear of becoming dependent on others for self-care, for instance, is frequently used to legitimize one's own death. Often, physical dependency is a precursor of behavioral dependency.

To date, there exist two major explanatory paradigms for behavioral dependency in the aged. First, there is dependency as the result of learned helplessness; second, there is dependency as an instrument of passive control. In contrast to physical dependency that is physically induced and is the consequence of a true physical incompetence of the person, both types of behavioral dependency are socially induced regardless of the competence level of the elderly person. The environment either expects incompetence and provides help even if not needed or wanted, or is unresponsive and neglectful. The unresponsive and neglectful environment has been characterized by Seligman (1975) as a noncontingent environment leading to helplessness and ensuing dependency. In contrast, the low-demanding environment is a contingent environment characterized by overcare, which also results in dependency. The empirical work of Baltes and her colleagues (for review see Baltes, 1988) has demonstrated that some behavioral dependencies or dependent behaviors are the result of the presence of specific contingencies and competencies rather than the presence of non-contingency and incompetence. In this context, dependency is instrumental in maintaining personal control. Let us look at these two different explanatory paradigms in more detail.

Dependency as the Product of Learned Helplessness or Loss of Control.
Over the last decade one can witness in psychology a growing interest in the
importance of mastery and personal control for human development across
the life span. Examples are the models of self-efficacy (Bandura, 1977,
1982), agency (Kuhl, 1986; 1986; Skinner, 1985; Skinner & Connell, 1986),
personal control (Lefcourt, 1976), illusion of control (Langer, 1979, 1983),
and learned helplessness (Seligman, 1975). Despite the differences in the
theoretical focus of these models–ranging from a social learning to an
action-theoretical orientation–the major link between autonomy and control or mastery is assumed to be based on two major cognitions, namely two
expectations or beliefs on the part of the individual actor: (a) "I am in
command of behaviors or skills producing specific outcomes and consequences that are required by the situation at hand," and (b) "The world in
which I live is a contingent one and I am dealing with a responsive
environment." Lack or loss of control in a specific situation will result,
therefore, from either not expecting a contingent and responsive environment or not expecting to be competent, that is, to have the skills to cope
with the situation in question. According to these theoretical approaches,
dependency is considered the product of experiences with either lack of
competence or lack of contingency.

More recently, the assumed association between dependency and
incompetence or loss of control has been moderated by introducing finer
differentiations within the area of personal control, such as the differentiation between primary and secondary control (Azuma, 1984; Schulz,
1986; Schulz, Heckhausen, & Locher, 1991) and similarly between
assimilative and accommodative coping (Brandtstädter & Renner, 1990).
By distinguishing between primary and secondary control, the assumption
is made that in the case of loss of competencies and the incurrence of
dependencies, compensations can be made by the use of secondary control.
The individual changes his or her goals to adjust to environmental givens
and/or defers his or her primary control to someone else and thereby stays
in control of events. Discriminating between assimilative and accommodative coping, the elderly person is aware that in the face of irreversible and
irrevocable events, losses are inevitable. Successful coping can no longer be
achieved by changing the environment, that is by patching up the loss, but
only by accepting the loss and changing oneself, that is one's goals or
desires.

This perspective comes very close to the explanation of dependency as
being the product of the existence of environmental contingencies in
contrast to the existence of noncontingencies.

Dependency as Instrument of Passive Control. The main aspect of
Baltes' research (see Baltes, 1988, in press, for review) is an account of the

existence of environmental conditions involved in the maintenance and development of dependent behaviors of the elderly. Specifically, to analyze the behavioral system producing dependency three methodological strategies — experimental, sequential observational, and ecological intervention — were employed to answer the following research questions: (a) Is behavioral dependency plastic or reversible? (b) What are the natural environmental conditions fostering dependent behaviors in the elderly? (c) Can we modify these "natural" conditions and, if yes, can we thereby produce a change in dependent behavior?

With respect to the first question, experiments were designed (for reviews, see Baltes & Barton, 1979; Mosher-Ashley, 1986–1987) in which a specific dependent behavior, such as not dressing oneself, was targeted for change by either changing discriminative stimuli (e.g., providing clothes that have a zipper instead of buttons; providing verbal cues) or reinforcing stimuli (e.g., walking out of the bedroom to the breakfast room as soon as dressing is completed). We found great plasticity and reversibility of even chronic dependent behaviors in the elderly. This suggests that it is not always true incompetence due to physical or mental impairment that is at the root of behavioral dependency. Rather, such findings point to environmental factors that are at least coresponsible in the development and maintenance of dependency.

This hypothesis is supported by the second major body of findings. Using sequential observations we demonstrated that the microsocial system of institutions supports dependency and tends to ignore independence of the elderly. This observed behavioral system linking older persons and their social partners can best be described as a *dependency-support script*; that is, dependent behaviors, of the elderly are expected and, more than any other behavior, experience immediate and positive reactions from the social environment. They initiate and provide social contact.

The dependency-support script is the dominant dyadic interaction pattern in long-term care institutions (for review see Baltes, 1988; Baltes & Reisenzein, 1986; Baltes & Wahl, 1987); it is still dominant though less exclusive in interactions between the elderly and their partners in private dwellings (Baltes & Wahl, 1992) and seems to be age-specific (Baltes, Reisenzein, & Kindermann, 1985; Kindermann, 1993).

What does the dependency-support script mean and what are its implications? First, evidence for differential contingencies for dependent behaviors of the elderly speak against the model of learned helplessness. The institutional environment as well as the community environment are not ones in which helplessness prevails, but are worlds in which dependent behaviors generate specific consequences. It is the dependent, rather than the independent behaviors, that are instrumental in securing social consequences, attention, and contact. They are an instrument for control, albeit passive control.[5] It is the task of empirical research to show whether passive control in the long run has the same consequences as no control (according to the use it or lose it paradigm) or whether it is more in line with secondary control (Schulz et al., 1992).

Second, in selecting or preferring one interaction pattern over others and thereby creating a social script, dependent behavior is treated as appropriate and expected. This suggests a perception of the elderly by their partners as incompetent or at least dependent-prone (Baltes, Wahl, & Reichert, 1991). Reichert (1990) confirmed this suggestion empirically. When comparing nurses and educators interacting with elderly people in problem-solving situations, nurses appear to provide, on average, more verbal and direct help than do educators. The perception of incompetence of elderly persons, quite prevalent among nurses, can be regarded as a consequence of their helping model. Karuza, Rabinowitz, and Zevon (1986) titled this helping model the medical model, in which neither responsibility for the occurrence nor for the solution of a problem is ascribed to the elderly person. Responsibilities are taken over by the nurse. This leads to an environment that provides overcare and is insensitive to a person's remaining strengths. This is particularly troublesome in the light of experimental findings (see previous discussion) that have attested over and over again that the elderly are quite often capable of performing required behaviors and that dependent behaviors can be reversed by appropriate management of environmental contingencies (Baltes, 1988).

[5]To prevent a possible misunderstanding, three observations are made. First, whereas in the present research it has been shown that dependent behavior in the elderly is associated with positive consequences, such as predictable control and social contact, this does not imply that dependent behavior as a whole is desirable. The consequences of dependent behavior also include potential negative consequences, such as a trajectory toward less competence and less autonomy. Second it is occasionally argued that the instrumental control of dependent self-care displayed in our data implies a "manipulative" and therefore undesirable strategy on the part of the elderly. On the one hand, we do not have the data (such as indicators of cognitive measures) to support this conclusion of conscious and instrumental goal orientation. On the other hand, we need to acknowledge that attributing a negative evaluation to instrumental control characteristic of dependent behavior is somewhat cynical. Any sense of psychological control dealing with the social environment in whatever age group involves predictable impact of one's behavior on one's environment. Third, it is also suggested that having to resort to dependent behavior as the focus of social control is undesirable, because it would be more appropriate to connect social control with independent, autonomous behavior. In our view, this seems meaningful, in principle. However, because of the factual existence of failing resources in the elderly, this expectation is idealistic. What appears more beneficial is to offer the elderly a sense of control on both realms: dependency and independence. Achieving a good balance between social control in situations of dependence as well as independence is the challenge of the future. Until such a balance is achieved, the fact that the elderly display a sense of social control following their dependent behavior must be considered a desirable though incomplete characteristic of their social world.

Third, when confronting elderly and their partners with the dependency-support script, Wahl (1991) found that staff members make the elderly responsible in that they attribute dependency to personality characteristics of the elderly. In contrast, staff members attribute independence of the elderly to their own (the staff's) encouraging behavior. The elderly themselves ascribe independence to their own personality characteristics, dependency in case of incompetence to illness or physical or mental impairment, and dependency in case of nonuse of competence to staff behavior.

In sum, in both instances of behavioral dependency — as the product of noncontingencies or as the result of existing contingencies — the elderly person is, in principle, competent. In both instances of behavioral dependency, thus, it seems plausible to require changes in the environmental conditions in the direction of fostering competencies rather than discouraging them or fostering dependency. This can be done, for instance, by teaching staff to increase independence-related interaction patterns (Baltes, Neumann, & Zank, 1991, in press). Environments can be structured to be stimulating and demanding and thereby fostering strengths and competencies of the elderly.

This conclusion is not intended to give green light to interventionism in aging. In fact, given the increase in losses and impairments it is only too true that the elderly will experience weaknesses that need to be compensated for or if possible deleted or avoided altogether. Compensation of losses very often can mean permitting others to do things for you and selectively distributing your energy and competencies. Thus, Baltes and Baltes (1990) recently made the argument for a third explanatory paradigm for behavioral dependency, namely, *person-induced dependency* (see also Baltes & Carstensen, in press; Baltes, Wahl, & Reichert, 1991). We venture that, due to increasing loss in reserves and strengths, the elderly person is faced with the possibility (a) of giving up the domains and activities hampered by loss, (b) of compensating for them,or (c) of becoming dependent in those domains in order to free energy for the pursuit of other domains and activities. Baltes and Baltes, in putting forth the model of selective optimization with compensation, argued for a concerted interplay between three components — *selection, compensation,* and *optimization* — to ensure successful aging despite the many losses encountered and the diminution in reserve capacities.

Selection is based on the argument that a reduced reserve capacity and the age-associated increase in losses mandates both a reduction of activities and domains and a concentration on fewer domains. These latter domains take on high priority and involve a convergence of environmental demands, individual motivations, skills, and biological capacity. The component optimization is derived from the argument that it is possible to maintain high levels of functioning in some domains via practice and the acquisition of new bodies of knowledge and technology. The third component, compensation, becomes operative when life tasks require a level of capacity beyond the current level of performance potential. We experience loss or reduction of behavioral capacities, particularly in situations and goals demanding high mental or physical levels for adequate functioning.

Comment.   Dependency is often socially induced in old age and does do injustice to the still remaining competencies of the elderly. The other side of the coin of dependency, however, is its association with successful aging. The developmental tasks of old age — adjustment to retirement and social loss, to increasing health impairments, and to one's own finitude — require an adaptation to an increasing negative balance between losses and gains. On the one hand, autonomy and agency are required to deal with these tasks. On the other hand, the elderly person has to be able to transform agency, when and where needed, into behavioral dependency and secondary control in order to adapt successfully.

VI. Conclusions

The aim of this chapter was to demonstrate the dynamics between dependency and independence throughout the life course and to highlight the shifting balance between the two depending on life stage. Birth and growth are typically thought to constitute processes in which dependency continually decreases whereas independence increases. Dependency is intended to be outgrown. The assumption is that this can be achieved more readily and efficiently by cultivating autonomy. Fostering autonomy, however, includes at times support of an infant's, child's, or adult's dependency. In Western cultures, such a posture is felt justified because it is always directed toward autonomy. It is assumed that the natural course of events (i.e., developmental advances, overcoming an illness, etc.) undermines in the end this kind of paternalism. Furthermore, it is assumed that the process of individuation and autonomy, most pronounced at adolescence, is a necessary precursor of and will find its mature expression in the balance between personal autonomy and social connectedness, namely in interdependence. Interdependence is the goal of mature adulthood and the basis of personal adjustment, life satisfaction, and generativity.

Such a normative developmental course from dependency to independence and interdependence promising full personal adjustment in adulthood has been extended to the fourth phase of life as well — old age. This perhaps logical extension is questionable, however, in view of what we know about the nature of aging. The fairly organized and predictable process of becoming an interdependent adult does not apply to the changes during the aging years. Typically, autonomy has been established by then and the risk is that of losing it; normally interdependence exists and the risk is that it will be overextended.

Thus, in old age the task of balancing autonomy and interdependence seems to tip more toward autonomy, as it does in adolescence. The emphasis on autonomy seems to be more in step with the developmental tasks at hand, namely ego integrity and finding meaning of life and death. This is not to say that interdependence and social connectedness become unimportant in old age. Instead, connectedness takes on a different role, function, and breadth and does not outweigh autonomy. As is the case during adolescence, connectedness and attachment are a necessary base of security facilitating the development and maintenance of autonomy.

Both the lack of autonomy and the risk of losing autonomy can arise from either intrinsic or extrinsic causes or a combination of the two. Intrinsic causes relate mostly to a lack of, or losses in, physical and mental competencies. Intrinsic causes, such as physical immaturity, are inherent in development during infancy and childhood. Physical decline is often considered a necessary corollary of aging. Extrinsic or social causes, such as socialization, seem to be at the root of different developmental trajectories for men and women with regard to values put on dependency and independence. With aging, extrinsic causes such as the negative aging stereotype as well as economic decline come into play. The most frequent social or extrinsic cause mentioned in the aging literature is economic. When such dependencies exist, the spouse, the family or kin members, social services or the state often assume the role of a parent. Those who manage these social services and provide assistance or care (e.g., nursing homes) come to assume a degree of control and power over the elderly person that normally only parents have over their children. Despite the legal status of most nursing home residents or elderly people needing support, they share much with young children. The control of individual life in long-term care institutions for the elderly is pervasive. This kind of surrogate paternalism is allowed, because it is assumed that the interest of the client is the interest of the caretaker (Glasser, 1981). Thus, particularly in aging, the ease with which physical dependency is all too often equated with decisional dependency followed by the implementation of societal paternalism is a dangerous shortcut. It justifies taking over for the elderly and denying freedom, choice, and autonomy.

These negative connotations of dependency, particularly in old age, however, should not detract from the positive side of dependency as the facilitator of connectedness, interdependence, and indeed autonomy. Dependency can allow, for example, the elderly to compensate for losses in competencies and still experience a feeling of mastery and personal control. It is worthwhile to speculate whether this function of compensating for losses or lack in competencies and thus producing gains is not inherent in dependency at all life stages. Obviously, this positive and compensatory function applies to infancy and childhood. In adulthood, the fact that dependency is considered a necessary ingredient for the maintenance of family and generational ties also confirms this positive function of dependency.

Most of the time, most people behave in ways that are compatible with or adaptive to the settings they occupy and the conceptions of their future they entertain. Typically there is a fit between competencies of the person and demands of the environmental setting. A loss or gain in competencies or an increase or decrease in environmental demand characteristics will disturb the existing adaptive level, however (Lawton, 1987). Both in old age, where there exists increasing biological vulnerability, and in infancy/early childhood with its inherent physical and mental limitations, the environment may exert a particularly strong influence both in optimizing and in hindering behavioral outcomes, such as autonomy or dependency. It is at those times that the social environment may have a particularly critical responsibility for accurately assessing the competence level of the person and providing a fitting match of support and stimulation. The person-environment fit idea does not suggest that an individual plays no active part in his or her own development and is only reactive; according to this view, the individual may proactively search for environmental niches best suited to his or her competence level and needs (Lawton, 1987). The person-environment fit idea as discussed earlier also does not preclude the importance of person–environment fit at other age periods, that is, adolescence and adulthood. The loss of mastery over one's environment can have significant negative consequences for physical and psychological health at all ages (Rodin, 1986). Mastery must be seen within a social context, however. For, from the perspective of a diverse range of personality and developmental models (Erikson, 1963; Gilligan, 1988; Maslow, 1954), autonomy and security are universal, basic needs.

Acknowledgments

During the writing of this chapter M. M. Baltes spent a sabbatical in the Department of Psychology at Stanford University supported by a research stipend from the Volkswagen-stiftung.

References

Ainsworth, M. D. S., Blehar, M. C., Waters, E., & Wall, S. (1978). *Patterns of attachment: A psychological study of the strange situation.* Hillsdale, NJ: Lawrence Erlbaum Associates.

Akhtar, A. M., Broe, G. A., Crombie, A., McLean, W. M., & Andrews, G. R. (1973). Disability and dependence in the elderly at home. *Age and Ageing, 2,* 102–111.

Allen, K. R. (1987). Forgotten streams in the family life course: Utilization of qualitative retrospective interviews in the analysis of lifelong single women's family careers. *Journal of Marriage and the Family, 49,* 517–526.

Alwin, D. (1984). Trends in parental socialization: Detroit 1958–1983. *American Journal of Sociology, 90,* 359–382.

Alwin, D. (1988). From obedience to autonomy: Changes in desired traits in children, 1924–1978. *Public Opinion Quarterly, 52,* 33–52.

Antonucci, T. (1976). Attachment: A life-span concept. *Human Development, 19,* (3), 135–142.

Arend, R., Grove, F. L., & Sroufe, L. A. (1979). Continuity of individual adaptation from infancy to kindergarten: A predictive study of ego-resiliency and curiosity in preschoolers. *Child Development, 50,* 950–959.

Armsden, G., & Greenberg, M. (1987). The inventory of parent and peer attachment: Individual differences and their relationship to psychological well-being in adolescence. *Journal of Youth and Adolescence, 16,* 427–454.

Arnett, B. B., Eyre, M., & Theorell, T. (1982). Social activation of the elderly: A social experiment. *Social Science and Medicine, 16,* 1685–1690.

Azuma, H. (1984). Secondary control as a heterogeneous category. *American Psychologist, 39,* 970–971.

Bakan, D. (1966). *The duality of human existence.* Chicago: Rand McNally.

Baltes, M. M. (1988). The etiology and maintenance of dependency in the elderly: Three phases of operant research. *Behavior Therapy, 19,* 301–319.

Baltes, M. M. (in press). Dependencies in old age: Gains and losses. *Current Directions in Psychological Science.*

Baltes, M. M., & Barton, E. M. (1979). Behavioral analysis of aging: A review of the operant model and research. *International Journal of Behavioral Development, 2,* 297–320.

Baltes, M. M., & Carstensen, L. L. (in press). *The process of successful aging.*

Baltes, M. M., Neumann, E.-M., & Zank, S. (1991). *Independence-supportive vs. dependence-supportive script in institutions: An intervention program for staff: Final project report* (Research Project No. 07017659). Berlin: Free University of Berlin, Research Unit of Psychological Gerontology.

Baltes, M. M., Neumann, E.-M., & Zank, S. (in press). Maintenance and rehabilitation of independence in old age: An intervention program for staff. *Psychology and Aging.*

Baltes, M. M., & Reisenzein, R. (1986). The social world of long-term care institutions: Psychological control toward dependency? In M. M. Baltes & P. B. Baltes (Eds.), *The psychology of control and aging* (pp. 316–343). Hillsdale, NJ: Lawrence Erlbaum Associates.

Baltes, M. M., Reisenzein, R., & Kindermann, T. (1985, July). Dependence in institutionalized children: an age-comparative analysis. Poster presented at *the 8th Biennial Meeting of the International Society for the Study of Behavioral Development,* Tours, France.

Baltes, M. M., & Wahl, H. W. (1987). Dependency in aging. In L. L. Carstensen & B. A. Edelstein (Eds.), *Handbook of clinical gerontology* (pp. 204–221). New York: Pergamon.

Baltes, M. M., & Wahl, H. W. (1992). The behavior system of dependency in the elderly: Interactions with the social environment. In M. Ory, R. P. Abeles, & L. Lipman (Eds.), *Aging, health, and behavior* (pp. 83–106). Beverly Hills, CA: Sage.

Baltes, M. M., Wahl, H.W., & Reichert, M. (1991). Successful aging in long-term care institutions. In K. W. Schaie (Ed.), *Annual review of gerontology and geriatrics* (Vol. 11, pp. 311–337). New York: Springer-Verlag.

Baltes, P. B. (1987). Theoretical propositions of life-span developmental psychology: On the dynamics between growth and decline.*Developmental Psychology, 23,* 611–626.

Baltes, P. B., & Baltes, M. M. (1990). Psychological perspectives on successful aging: The model of selective optimization with compensation. In P. B. Baltes & M. M. Baltes

(Eds.), *Successful aging: Perspectives from the behavioral sciences* (pp. 1-34). New York: Cambridge University Press.

Bandura, A. (1977). Self-efficacy: Toward a unifying theory of behavioral change. *Psychological Review, 84*, 191-215.

Bandura, A. (1982). Self-efficacy mechanism in human agency. *American Psychologist, 37*, 122-147.

Baumeister, R., & Tice, D. (1986). How adolescence became the struggle for self: A historical transformation of psychological development. In J. Suls & A. G. Greenwald (Eds.), *Psychological perspectives on the self* (Vol. 3, pp. 183-201). Hillsdale, NJ: Lawrence Erlbaum Associates.

Baumrind, D. (1978). Parental disciplinary patterns and social competence in children. *Youth and Society, 9*, 239-276.

Baumrind, D. (1989, August). *The influence of parenting style on adolescent competence and problem behavior*. Paper presented at the American Psychological Association's Science Weekend, New Orleans.

Bellah, R., Madsen, R., Sullivan, W., Swindler, A., & Tipton, S. (1985). *Habits of the heart: Individualism and commitment in American life*. Berkeley: University of California Press.

Belsky, J., Garduque, L., & Hrncir, E. (1984). Assessing performance, competence, and executive capacity in infant play: Relations to home environment and security of attachment. *Developmental Psychology, 20*, 406-417.

Belsky, J., & Rovine, M. (1987). Temperament and attachment security in the strange situation: An empirical rapprochement. *Child Development, 58*, 787-795.

Belsky, J., & Rovine, M. (1988). Non-maternal care in the first year of life and the security of infant-parent attachment. *Child Development, 59*, 157-167.

Belsky, J., Rovine, M., & Taylor, D. G. (1984). The Pennsylvania Infant and Family Development Project: 3. The origins of individual differences in infant-mother attachment: Maternal and infant contributions. *Child Development*, 706-717.

Bengtson, V. L., & Black, K. D. (1973). Intergenerational relations and continuities in socialization. In P. Baltes & K. W. Schaie (Eds.), *Life-span developmental psychology: Personality and socialization* (pp. 208-234). New York: Academic.

Bennett, R. (1980). *Aging, isolation, and resocialization*. New York: Van Nostrand Reinhold.

Berndt, T. (1979). Developmental changes in conformity to peers and parents. *Developmental Psychology, 15*, 608-615.

Blos, P. (1967). The second individuation process. *Psychoanalytic Study of the Child, 22*, 162-186.

Bowlby, J. (1969). *Attachment and loss* (Vol. 1). New York: Basic Books.

Brandtstädter, J., & Renner, G. (1990). Tenacious goal pursuit and flexible goal adjustment: Explication and age-related analysis of assimilative and accommodative strategies of coping. *Psychology and Aging, 5*, 58-67.

Bretherton, I. (1985). Attachment theory: Retrospect and prospect. *Monographs of the Society for Research in Child Development, 50* (1-2, Serial No. 209), 3-35.

Bretherton, I. (1987). New perspectives on attachment relations: Security, communication, and internal working models. In J. D. Osofsky (Ed.), *Handbook of infant development* (pp. 1061-1100). New York: Wiley.

Bretherton, I. (1990). Open communication and internal working models: Their role in the development of attachment relationships. In R. Thompson (Ed.), *Nebraska symposium on motivation 1988: Socioemotional development* (pp. 57-113). Lincoln: University of Nebraska Press.

Bretherton, I., & Waters, E. (Eds.). (1985). Growing points of attachment theory and research. *Monographs of the Society for Research in Child Development, 50* (1-2, Serial No. 209).

Brittain, C. V. (1963). Adolescent choices and parent/peer cross-pressures. *American Sociological Review, 28*, 385-391.

Brody, J. A., Brock, D. B., & Williams, T. F. (1987). Trends in the health of the elderly population. *Annual Review of Public Health, 8*, 211–234.

Brown, B. B. (1982). The extent and effects of peer pressure among high school students: A retrospective analysis. *Journal of Youth and Adolescence, 11*, 121–133.

Bryant, B. K. (1989). The need for support in relation to the need for autonomy. In D. Belle (Ed.), *Children's social networks and social supports* (pp. 332–351). New York: Wiley.

Bumpass, L., (1991, April). *Demographic data for middle aged and elderly persons in the U. S.* Paper presented at the Mac Arthur Meeting on Midlife, Stanford, CA.

Carstensen, L. L. (1991). Socioemotional selectivity theory: Social activity in life-span context. *Annual Review of Gerontology and Geriatrics, 11*, 195–217.

Caspi, A., Bem, D. J., & Elder, G. (1989). Continuities and consequences of interactional styles across the life course. *Journal of Personality, 57*, 377–399.

Caspi, A., Elder, G. H., & Herbener, E. S. (1990). Childhood personality and the prediction of life-course patterns. In L. N. Robins & M. Rutter (Eds.), *Straight and devious pathways from childhood to adulthood* (pp. 13–35). New York: Cambridge University Press.

Caudill, W., & Weinstein, S. (1969). Maternal care and infant behavior in Japan and America. *Psychiatry, 32*, 12–43.

Chapman, S. (1991). Attachment and adolescent adjustment to parental remarriage. *Family Relations, 40*, 232–237.

Cicchetti, D. (1989). How research on child maltreatment has informed the study of child development: Perspectives from developmental psychopathology. In D.Cicchetti & V. Carlson (Eds.), *Child maltreatment: Theory and research on the causes and conse-quences of child abuse and neglect* (pp. 377–431). New York: Cambridge University Press.

Clark, M. S., & Reis, H. T. (1988). Interpersonal processes in close relationships. *Annual Review of Psychology, 36*, 609–672.

Clarke-Stewart, K. A. (1989). Infant day care: Maligned or malignant? *American Psycholo-gist, 44*, 266–273.

Cohler, B. J. (1983). Autonomy and interdependence in the family of adulthood: A psychological perspective. *The Gerontologist, 23*, 33–39.

Cohler, B. J., & Boxer, A. M. (1984). Personal adjustment, well-being, and life events. In C. Zander Malatesta & C. E. Izard (Eds.), *Emotion in adult development* (pp. 85–100). Beverly Hills, CA: Sage.

Coleman, J. (1990). *Foundations of social theory.* Cambridge, MA: Harvard University Press.

Collins, W. A. (1990). Parent–child relationships in the transition to adolescence: Continuity and change in interaction, affect, and cognition. In R. Montemayor, G. R. Adams, & T. P. Gullotta (Eds.), *From childhood to adolescence: A transitional period?* (pp. 85–106). Newbury Park, CA: Sage.

Collopy, B. J. (1988). Autonomy in long-term care: Some crucial distinctions. *The Gerontol-ogist, 28*, 10–27.

Cooper, C. R., Grotevant, H. D., & Condon, S. M. (1983). Individuality and connectedness in the family as a context for adolescent identity formation and role-taking skill. In H. D. Grotevant & C. R. Cooper (Eds.), *Adolescent development in the family: New directions of child development* (pp. 43–59). San Francisco: Jossey-Bass.

Crockenberg, S. (1981). Infant irritability, mother responsiveness, and social support influ-ences on the security of infant–mother attachment. *Child Development, 52*, 857–865.

Crockenberg, S., & Litman, C. (1990). Autonomy as competence in 2-year-olds: Maternal correlates of child defiance, compliance, and self-assertion. *Developmental Psychology, 26*, 961–971.

Damon, W. (1983). *Social and personality development: Infancy through adolescence.* New York: Norton.

Denenberg, V. (1984). Stranger in a strange situation: Comments by a comparative psychologist. *Behavioral and Brain Sciences, 7,* 150–152.

Dornbusch, S., Ritter, P., Leiderman, P., Roberts, D., & Fraleigh, M. (1987). The relation of parenting style to adolescent school performance. *Child Development, 58,* 1244–1257.

Douvan, E., & Adelson, J. (1966). *The adolescent experience.* New York: Wiley.

Deutsch, M. (1985). *Distributive justice: a social psychological perspective.* New Haven: Yale University Press.

Egeland, B., & Farber, E. (1984). Infant–mother attachment: Factors related to development and changes over time. *Child Development, 55,* 753–771.

Ellis, S., Rogoff, B., Cromer, C. (1981). Age segregation in children's social interactions. *Developmental Psychology, 17,* 399–407.

Erickson, M. F., Sroufe, L. A., & Egeland, B. (1985). The relationship between quality of attachment and behavior problems in preschool in a high-risk sample. *Monographs of the Society for Research in Child Development, 50* (1–2, Serial No. 209), 147–166.

Erikson, E. (1963). *Childhood and society* (2nd ed.). New York: Norton.

Ford, M. E., & Thompson, R. A. (1985). Perceptions of personal agency and infant attachment: Toward a life-span perspective on competence development. *International Journal of Behavioral Development, 8,* 377–406.

Frank, S., Avery, C., & Laman, M. (1988). Young adults' perceptions of their relationships with their parents: Individual differences in connectedness, competence, and emotional autonomy. *Developmental Psychology, 24,* 729–737.

Franz, C. E., & White, K. M. (1985). Individuation and attachment in personality development: Extending Erikson's theory. *Journal of Personality, 53,* 224–256.

Freud, A. (1958). Adolescence. *Psychoanalytic Study of the Child, 13,* 255–278.

Fu, V. R., Hinkle, D. E., & Hanna, M. A. K. (1986). A three-generational study of the development of individual dependency and family interdependence. *Genetic, Social, and General Psychology Monographs, 112,* 153–171.

Gallagher, D., Thompson, L. W., & Levy, S. M. (1980). Clinical psychological assessment of older adults. In L. W. Poon (Ed.), *Aging in the 1980s* (pp. 19–40). New York: American Psychological Association.

Gilligan, C. (1982). Adult development and women's development: Arrangements for a marriage. In T. Z. Giele (Ed.), *Women in the middle years: Current knowledge and directions for future research and policy* (pp. 89–114). New York: Wiley.

Gilligan, C. (1986). Remapping the moral domain: New images of the self in relationship. In T. C. Heller, M. Sosna, & D. E. Wellbery (Eds.), *Reconstructing individualism: Autonomy, individuality, and the self in Western thought* (pp. 237–252). Stanford, CA: Stanford University Press.

Gilligan, C. (1988). Adolescent development reconsidered. In C. Gilligan, J. Ward, & J. Taylor (Eds.), *Mapping the moral domain* (pp. vii–xxxix). Cambridge, MA: Harvard University Press.

Glasser, I. (1981). Prisoners of benevolence: Power versus liberty in the welfare state. In W. Gaylin, I. Glasser, S. Marcus, & D. Rothman (Eds.), *Doing good. The limits of benevolence* (pp. 99–170). New York: Pantheon Books.

Greenberg, E. (1984). Defining psychosocial maturity in adolescence. In P. Karoly & J. Steffen (Eds.), *Adolescent behavior disorders: Foundations and contemporary concerns* (pp. 54–81). Lexington, MA: Heath.

Greene, A. L., & Boxer, A. M. (1986). Daughters and sons as young adults: Restructuring the ties that bind. In N. Datan, A. L. Greene, & H. W. Reese (Eds.), *Life-span developmental psychology: Intergenerational relations* (pp. 125–149). Hillsdale, NJ: Lawrence Erlbaum Associates.

Grolnick, W., & Ryan, R. (1989). Parent styles associated with children's self-regulation and competence in school. *Journal of Educational Psychology, 81,* 143–154.

Grossmann, K. E., & Grossmann, K. (1990). The wider concept of attachment in cross-cultural research. *Human Development, 33*, 31-47.

Grossmann, K. E., Grossmann, K., Spangler, G., Suess, G., & Unzner, L. (1985). Maternal sensitivity and newborns' orientation responses as related to quality of attachment in northern Germany. *Monographs of the Society for Research in Child Development, 50* (1-2, Serial No. 209), 233-256.

Grotevant, H. D. (1987). Toward a process model of identity formation. *Journal of Adolescent Research, 2*, 203-222.

Grotevant, H. D., & Cooper, C. R. (1985). Patterns of interaction in family relationships and the development of identity exploration in adolescence. *Child Development, 56*, 415-428.

Grotevant, H. D., & Cooper, C. R. (1986). Individuation in family relationships: A perspective on individual differences in the development of identity and role-taking skill in adolescence. *Human Development, 29*, 82-100.

Grusec, J., & Lytton, H. (1988). *Social development: History, theory, and research.* New York: Springer-Verlag.

Guillemard, A. M. (1992). Europäische Perspektiven der Alternspolitik [European perspectives of politics in aging]. In P. B. Baltes & J. Mittelstrass (Eds.), *Zukunft des Alterns und gesellschaftliche Entwicklung* (pp. 614-639). Berlin: De Gruyter.

Hagestad, G. O. (1981). Problems and promises in the social psychology of intergenerational relations. In R. W. Fogel, E. Hatfield, S. B. Kiesler, & E. Shanas (Eds.), *Aging* (pp. 11-46). New York: Academic.

Hagestad, G. O. (1985). Continuity and connectedness. In V. L. Bengtson & J. F. Robertson (Eds.), *Grandparenthood* (pp. 31-48). Beverly Hills, CA: Sage.

Harter, S. (1990). Self and identity development. In S. Feldman & G. Elliot (Eds.), *At the threshold: The developing adolescent* (pp. 352-387). Cambridge, MA: Harvard University Press.

Hartup, W. (1989). Social relationships and their developmental significance. *American Psychologist, 44*, 120-126.

Hatfield, E., & Traupmann, J. (1981). Intimate relationships: A perspective from equity theory. In S. Duck & R. Gilmour (Eds.), *Personal relationships 1: Studying personal relationships* (pp. 165-178). London: Academic.

Hauser, P. B. (1976). Aging and world-wide population change. In R. H. Binstock & E. Shanas (Eds.), *Handbook of aging and the social sciences* (pp. 58-86). New York: Van Nostrand Reinhold.

Hauser, S. T., Powers, S. I., Noam, G., & Bowlds, M. K. (1987). Family interiors of adolescent ego development trajectories. *Family Perspective, 21*, 263-282.

Havighurst, R. J. (1948). *Developmental tasks and education* (3rd ed.). New York: McKay.

Hazan, C., & Shaver, P. R. (1987). Romantic love conceptualized as an attachment process. *Journal of Personality and Social Psychology, 52*, 511-524.

Hazan, C., & Shaver, P. R. (1990). Love and work: An attachment-theoretical perspective. *Journal of Personality and Social Psychology, 59*, 270-280.

Heathers, G. (1955). Acquiring dependence and independence: A theoretical orientation. *Journal of Genetic Psychology, 87*, 277-291.

Hill, J. P., & Holmbeck, G. N. (1986). Attachment and autonomy during adolescence. In G. Whitehurst (Ed.), *Annals of child development* (Vol. 3, pp. 145-189). Greenwich, CT: JAI.

Hoffman, J. (1984). Psychological separation of late adolescents from their partners. *Journal of Consulting Psychology, 31*, 170-178.

Hoffman, L. W. (1988). Cross-cultural differences in child-rearing goals. In R. LeVine, P.

Miller, & M. West (Eds.), *Parental behavior in diverse societies: New directions in child development* (pp. 99–122). San Francisco: Jossey-Bass.

Hoffman, L. W. (1989). Effects of maternal employment in the two-parent family. *American Psychologist, 44,* 283–292.

Johnson, P. (1989). The structured dependency of the elderly: A critical note. In M. Jeffers (Ed.), *Growing old in the twentieth century* (pp. 62–72). London: Routledge.

Josselson, R. (1980). Ego development in adolescence. In J. Adelson (Ed.), *Handbook of adolescent psychology* (pp. 188–210). New York: Wiley.

Josselson, R. (1988). The embedded self: I and thou revisited. In D. K. Lapsley & F. C. Power (Eds.), *Self, ego, and identity: Integrative approaches* (pp. 91–106). New York: Springer.

Kagan, J. (1982). *Psychological research on the human infant: An evaluative summary.* New York: Grant.

Kagan, J., & Moss, H. A. (1960). The stability of passive and dependent behavior from childhood through adulthood. *Child Development, 31,* 577–591.

Kahn, R. L., & Antonucci, T. C. (1980). Convoys over the life course: Attachment, roles, and social support. In P. B. Baltes & O. G. Brim, Jr. (Eds.), *Life-span development and behavior* (Vol. 3, pp. 253–286). New York: Academic.

Kalish, R. A., & Knudtson, F. W. (1976). Attachment versus disengagement: A life-span conceptualization. *Human Development, 19,* 171–181.

Kandel, D., & Lesser, G. (1972). *Youth in two worlds.* San Francisco: Jossey-Bass.

Karuza, J., Rabinowitz, V. D., & Zevon, M. A. (1986). Implications of control and responsibility on helping the aged. In M. M. Baltes & P. B. Baltes (Eds.), *The psychology of control and aging* (pp. 373–396). Hillsdale, NJ: Lawrence Erlbaum Associates.

Kelley, H. H., Berscheid, E., Christensen, H., Harvey, J. H., Huston, T. C., Levinger, G., McClintock, E., Peplau, A., & Peterson, D. (1983). *Close relationships.* New York: Freeman.

Kenny, M. (1987). The extent and function of parental attachment among first-year college students. *Journal of Youth and Adolescence, 16,* 17–29.

Kindermann, T. (1993). Fostering independence in everyday mother-child interaction: Intra-dyad changes in contingency patterns as children grow competent in developmental tasks. *International Journal of Behavioral Development, 16,* in press.

Kobak, R., & Sceery, A. (1988). Attachment in late adolescence: Working models, affect regulation, and representations of self and others. *Child Development, 59,* 135–146.

Kohn, M. (1977). *Class and conformity: A study of values.* Chicago: University of Chicago Press.

Kuhl, J. (1986). Aging and models of control: The hidden costs of wisdom. In M. M. Baltes & P. B. Baltes (Eds.), *The psychology of control and aging,* (pp. 1–33). Hillsdale, NJ: Lawrence Erlbaum Associates.

Lamb, M. E., Thompson, R. A., Gardner, W. P., Charnov, E. L., & Estes, D. (1984). Security of infantile attachment as assessed in the "strange situation": Its study and biological interpretation. *Behavioral and Brain Sciences, 7,* 127–171.

Lamborn, S., Mounts, N., Steinberg, L., & Dornbusch, S. (1991). Patterns of competence and adjustment among adolescents from authoritative, authoritarian, indulgent, and neglectful families. *Child Development, 62,* 1049–1065.

Langer, E. J. (1979). The illusion of incompetence. In L. C. Perlmuter & R. A. Monty (Eds.), *Choice and perceived control* (pp. 301–313). Hillsdale, NJ: Lawrence Erlbaum Associates.

Langer, E. J. (1983). *The psychology of control.* New York: Sage.

Larson, R. (1978). Thirty years of research on the subjective well-being of older Americans. *Journal of Gerontology, 33,* 109–125.

Lawton, M. P. (1987). Environment and the need satisfaction of the aging. In L. L. Carstensen

& B. A. Edelstein (Eds.), *Handbook of clinical gerontology* (pp. 33–40). New York: Pergamon.

Lefcourt, M. M. (1976). *Locus of control: Current trends in theory and research*. Hillsdale, NJ: Lawrence Erlbaum Associates.

Lerner, R. M., & Ryff, C. D. (1978). Implementation of the life-span view of human development: The sample case of attachment. In P. B. Baltes & O. G. Brim, Jr. (Eds.), *Life-span development and behavior* (Vol. 1, pp. 1–44). New York: Academic.

Levenson, D. J. (1978). *The seasons of a man's life*. New York: Ballantine.

Lewis, C. (1981). How adolescents approach decisions: Changes over grades seven through twelve and policy implications. *Child Development, 52*, 538–544.

Maccoby, E., & Feldman, S. (1972). Mother-attachment and stranger reactions in the third year of life. *Monographs of the Society for Research in Child Development, 37* (1, Serial No. 146), 1–85.

Maccoby, E. E., & Masters, J. C. (1970). Attachment and dependency. In P. H. Mussen (Ed.), *Carmichael's manual of child psychology* (3rd ed., Vol. 2, pp. 73–157). New York: Wiley.

Mahler, M. (1968). *On human symbiosis and the vicissitudes of individuation*. New York: International University Press.

Mahler, M., Pine, F., & Bergman, A. (1975). *The psychological birth of the human infant*. New York: Basic.

Main, M., Kaplan, N., & Cassidy, J. (1985). Security in infancy, childhood, and adulthood: A move to the level of representation. *Monographs of the Society for Research in Child Development, 50* (1–2, Serial No. 209), 66–104.

Main, M., & Solomon, J. (1986). Discovery of an insecure-disorganized/-disoriented attachment pattern. In T. B. Brazelton & M. W. Yogman (Eds.), *Affective development in infancy* (pp. 95–124). Norwood, NJ: Albex.

Marcia, J. (1980). Identity in adolescence. In J. Adelson (Ed.), *Handbook of adolescent psychology* (pp. 159–177). New York: Wiley.

Marshall, V. W., & Bengtson, V. L. (1983). Generations: Conflict and cooperation. In M. Bergener, U. Lehr, E. Lang, & R. Schmitz-Scherzer (Eds.), *Aging in the eighties and beyond* (pp. 298–310). New York: Springer.

Maslow, A. H. (1954). *Personality and motivation*. New York: Harper & Row.

Matas, L., Arend, R., & Sroufe, L. A. (1978). Continuity of adaptation in the second year: The relationship between quality of attachment and later competence. *Child Development, 49*, 547–556.

Michaels, G. Y., & Goldberg, W. A. (1988). *The transition to parenthood*. New York: Cambridge University Press.

Mikaye, K., Chen, S., & Campos, J. (1985). Infant temperament, mother's mode of interaction, and attachment in Japan: An interim report. *Monographs of the Society for Research in Child Development, 50* (1–2, Serial No. 209), 276–297.

Montemayor, R. (1983). Parents and adolescents in conflict: All of the families, some of the time, and some families most of the time. *Journal of Early Adolescence, 3*, 83–103.

Montemayor, R. (1986). Family variation in storm and stress. *Journal of Adolescent Research, 1*, 15–31.

Mosher-Ashley, P. M. (1986–1987). Procedural and methodological parameters in behavioral-gerontological research: A review. *International Journal of Aging and Human Development, 24*, 189–229.

Oerter, R. (Ed.). (1978). *Entwicklung als lebenslanger Prozess*. Hamburg: Hoffman & Campe.

Offer, D. (1969). *The psychological world of the teenager*. New York: Basic.

Oppenheim, D., Sagi, A., & Lamb, M. E. (1988). Infant–adult attachments on the kibbutz and their relation to socioemotional development 4 years later. *Developmental Psychology*, *24*, 427–433.

Pipp, S., Shaver, P., Jennings, S., Lamborn, S., & Fischer, K. (1985).Adolescents' theories about the development of the relationships with parents. *Journal of Personality and Social Psychology*, *48*, 991–1001.

Powers, S. I., Hauser, S. T., & Kilner, L. (1989). Adolescent mental health. *American Psychologist*, *44*, 200–208.

Powers, S. I., Hauser, S. T., Schwartz, J. M., Noam, G. C., & Jacobson, A. M. (1983). Adolescent ego development and family interaction: A structural-development perspective. In H. D. Grotevant & C. R. Cooper (Eds.), *Adolescent development in the family: New directions of child development* (pp. 5–24). San Francisco, CA: Jossey-Bass.

Quintana, S. M., & Lapsley, D. K. (1990). Rapprochement in late adolescent separation-individuation: A structural equations approach. *Journal of Adolescence*, *13*, 371–385.

Reichert, M. (1990). *Hilfeverhalten gegenüber alten Menschen: Eine experimentelle Überprüfung der Rolle von Erwartungen* [Helping behavior toward the elderly: An experimental examination of the role of expectations]. Unpublished doctoral thesis, Free University of Berlin.

Rice, K. (1991, July). *Attachment, separation-individuation, and adjustment to college.* Poster presented at the biennial meetings of the International Society for the Study of Behavioural Development, Minneapolis.

Riley, M. (1983). The family in an aging society: A matrix of latent relationships. *Journal of Family Issues*, *4*, 439–454.

Rodin, J. (1986). Health, control, and aging. In M. M. Baltes & P. B. Baltes (Eds.), *The psychology of control and aging* (pp. 139–165). Hillsdale, NJ: Lawrence Erlbaum Associates.

Rosenmayr, L., & Köckeis, R. (1965). *Der alte Mensch in Familie und Gesellschaft* [The old person in family and society]. Neuwied, Germany: Luchterhand.

Rossi, A., & Rossi, P. (1990). *On human bonding.* New York: Aldine de Gruyter.

Rutter, M., Graham, M., Chadwick, O., & Yule, W. (1976). Adolescent turmoil: Fact or fiction? *Journal of Child Psychology and Psychiatry*, *17*, 35–56.

Ryan, R. M., & Lynch, J. H. (1989). Emotional autonomy versus detachment: Revisiting the vicissitudes of adolescence and young adulthood. *Child Development*, *60*, 340–356.

Sagi, A., Lamb, M. E., Lewkowicz, K. S., Shoham, R., Dvir, R., & Estes, D. (1985). Security of infant-mother, -father, and -metapelet attachments among kibbutz-reared Israeli children. *Monographs of the Society for Research in Child Development*, *50* (1–2, Serial No. 209), 257–275.

Sampson, E. E. (1985). The decentralization of identity: Toward a revised concept of personal and social order. *American Psychologist*, *40*, 1203–1211.

Schulz, R. (1986). Successful aging: Balancing primary and secondary control. *Adult Development and Aging News*, *13*, 2–4.

Schulz, R., Heckhausen, J., & Locher, J. L. (1992). Coping with problems related to health and aging: Matching control strategies with developmental trajectories. *Journal of Social Issues*, *47*, 177–196.

Sebald, H. (1986). Adolescents' shifting orientations toward parents and peers: A curvilinear trend over recent decades. *Journal of Marriage and the Family*, *48*, 5–13.

Seligman, M. E. (1975). *Helplessness: On depression, development, and death.* San Francisco: Freeman.

Sessa, F. M., & Steinberg, L. (1991). Family structure and the development of autonomy during adolescence. *Journal of Early Adolescence*, *11*, 38–55.

Shanas, E. P., Townsend, P., Wederburn, D., Friis, H., Miloj, J., & Stehouwer, J. (Eds.). (1968). *Old people in three industrial societies.* New York: Atherton.

Skinner, E. A. (1985). Action, control judgments, and the structure of control experience. *Psychological Review, 92,* 39–58.

Skinner, E. A., & Connell, J. P. (1986). Control understanding: Suggestions for a developmental framework. In M. M. Baltes & P. B. Baltes (Eds.), *The psychology of control and aging* (pp. 35–70). Hillsdale, NJ: Lawrence Erlbaum Associates.

Skolnik, A. (1986). Early attachment and personal relationships across the life course. In P. B. Baltes, D. L. Featherman, & R. M. Lerner (Eds.), *Life-span development and behavior* (Vol. 7, pp. 174–206). Hillsdale, NJ: Lawrence Erlbaum Associates.

Smetana, J. G. (1988). Concepts of self and social convention: Adolescents' and parents' reasoning about hypothetical and actual family conflicts. In M. G. Gunnar & W. A. Collins (Eds.), *Development during the transition to adolescence: Minnesota symposium on child development* (Vol. 21, pp. 79–122). Hillsdale, NJ: Lawrence Erlbaum Associates.

Smollar, J., & Youniss, J. (1989). Transformations in adolescents' perceptions of parents. *International Journal of Behavioural Development, 12,* 71–84.

Sosna, U., & Wahl, H. W. (1983). Soziale Belastung, psychische Erkrankung und körperliche Beeinterächtigung im Alter: Ergebnisse einer Felduntersuchung [Social stress, mental illness, and physical impairment in old age: Results from an epidemiological study]. *Zeitschrift für Gerontologie, 16,* 107–114.

Spence, J. (1985). Achievement American style: The rewards and costs of individualism. *American Psychologist, 40,* 1285–1295.

Sroufe, L. A. (1983). Infant–caregiver attachment and patterns of adaptation in preschool: The roots of maladaptation and competence. In M. Perlmutter (Ed.), *Minnesota symposium on child psychology* (Vol. 16, pp. 41–81). Hillsdale, NJ: Lawrence Erlbaum Associates.

Sroufe, L. A. (1985). Attachment classification from the perspective of infant–caregiver relationships and infant temperament. *Child Development, 56,* 1–14.

Sroufe, L. A., Fox, N. E., & Pancake, V. R. (1983). Attachment and dependency in developmental perspective. *Child Development, 54,* 1615–1627.

Sroufe, L. A., & Waters, E. (1977). Attachment as an organizational construct. *Child Development, 48,* 1184–1199.

Steinberg, L. (1989a). *Adolescence.* New York: Knopf.

Steinberg, L. (1989b). Pubertal maturation and parent–adolescent distance: An evolutionary perspective. In G. R. Adams, R. Montemayor, & R. P. Gullotta (Eds.), *Biology of adolescent behavior and development* (pp. 71–97). Newbury Park, CA: Sage.

Steinberg, L. (1990). Autonomy, conflict, and harmony in the family relationship. In S. Feldman & G. Elliot (Eds.), *At the threshold: The developing adolescent* (pp. 255–276). Cambridge, MA: Harvard University Press.

Steinberg, L. (1991). The logic of adolescence. In P. Edelman & J. Ladner (Eds.), *Adolescence and poverty: Challenge for the 1990s* (pp. 19–36). Washington, DC: Center for National Policy Press.

Steinberg, L., Elmen, J., & Mounts, N. (1989). Authoritative parenting, psychosocial maturity, and academic success among adolescents. *Child Development, 60,* 1424–1436.

Steinberg, L., & Silverberg, S. B. (1986). The vicissitudes of autonomy in early adolescence. *Child Development, 57,* 841–851.

Svanborg, A., Landhal, S., & Mellström, D. (1984). Basic issues of health care. In H. Thoma & G. Maddox (Eds.), *New perspectives on old age* (pp. 31–52). New York: Springer.

Takahashi, K. (1990). Affective relationships and their life-long development. In P. B. Baltes, D. L. Featherman, & R. M. Lerner (Eds.), *Life-span development and behavior* (Vol. 10, pp. 1–27). Hillsdale, NJ: Lawrence Erlbaum Associates.

Thompson, R., Lamb, M., & Estes, D. (1982). Stability of infant–mother attachment and its relationship to changing life circumstances in an unselected middle-class sample. *Child Development, 53,* 144–148.

Townsend, P. (1981). The structured dependency of the elderly: A creation of social policy in the twentieth century. *Aging and Society, 1,* 5–28.

Troll, L. (Ed.). (1986). *Family issues in current gerontology.* New York: Springer-Verlag.

Troll, L., & Bengtson, V. (1979). Generations in the family. In W. Burr, R. Hill, F. I. Nye, & L. Reiss (Eds.), *Contemporary theories about the family: Research-based theories* (pp. 127–161). New York: Free Press.

Troll, L. & Smith, J. (1976). Attachment through the life span: Some questions about dyadic bonds among adults. *Human Development, 19,* 156–170.

Vaillant, G. E. (1977). *Adaptation to life.* Boston: Little, Brown.

van den Heuvel, W. (1976). The meaning of dependency. In J. M. A. Munnichs & W. van den Heuvel (Eds.), *Dependency or interdependency in old age* (pp. 162–173). The Hague, Netherlands: Martinus Nijhoff.

van IJzendoorn, M. H. (1990). Developments in cross-cultural research on attachment: Some methodological notes. *Human Development, 33,* 3–9.

Vaughn, B., Deane, K., & Waters, E. (1985). The impact of out-of-home care on child–mother attachment quality: Another look at some enduring questions. *Monographs of the Society for Research in Child Development, 50* (1–2, Serial No. 209), 110–135.

Vaughn, B., Egeland, B., Sroufe, L. A., & Waters, E. (1979). Individual differences in infant–mother attachment at twelve and eighteen months: Stability and change in families under stress. *Child Development, 50,* 971–975.

Vaughn, B., Kopp, C., & Krakow, J. (1984). The emergence and consolidation of self-control from eighteen to thirty months of age: Normative trends and individual differences. *Child Development, 55,* 990–1004.

Wahl, H. W. (1987). Behinderung in der Altenbevölkerung: Ergebnisse einer Feldstudie [Impairment in the aged population: Results of a field study]. *Zeitschrift für Gerontologie, 20,* 66–73.

Wahl, H. W. (1991). Dependence in the elderly from an interactional point of view: Verbal and observational data. *Psychology and Aging, 6,* 238–246.

Walker, A. (1980). The social creation of poverty and dependency in old age. *Journal of Social Policy, 9,* 172–188.

Walker, A. J., Thompson, L., & Morgan, C. S. (1987). Two generations of mothers and daughters: Role position and interdependence. *Psychology of Women Quarterly, 11,* 195–208.

Wan, T. T. H., Odell, B. G., & Lewis, D. T. (1982). *Promoting the well-being of the elderly: A community diagnosis.* New York: Haworth.

Waterman, A. S. (1981). Individualism and interdependence. *American Psychologist, 36,* 762–773.

Waterman, A. S. (1985). Identity in the context of adolescent psychology. In A. S. Waterman (Ed.), *Identity in adolescence: Progress and contents. New directions for child development* (No. 30, p. 5–24). San Francisco: Jossey-Bass.

Waterman, A. S., & Archer, S. L. (1990). A life-span perspective on identity formation: Developments in form, function, and process. In P. B. Baltes, D. L. Featherman, & R. M. Lerner (Eds.), *Life-span development and behavior* (Vol. 10, pp. 29–57). Hillsdale, NJ: Lawrence Erlbaum Associates.

Waters, E. (1978). The reliability and stability of individual differences in infant–mother attachment. *Child Development, 49,* 483–494.

Waters, E., Hay, D., & Richters, J. (1986). Infant–parent attachment and the origins of prosocial and antisocial behavior. In D. Olweus, J. Block, & M. Radke-Yarrow (Eds.), *Development of antisocial and prosocial behavior: Research, theories, and issues* (pp. 97–125). New York: Academic.

Waters, E., Vaughn, B., & Egeland, B. (1980). Individual differences in infant mother attachment relationship at age one: Antecedents in neonatal behavior in an urban, economically disadvantaged sample. *Child Development*, *51*, 208–216.

Waters, E., Wippman, J., & Sroufe, L. A. (1979). Attachment, positive affect, and competence in the peer group: Two studies in construct validation. *Child Development*, *50*, 821–829.

Weiss, R. S. (1982). Attachment in adult life. In C. M. Parkes & J. Stevenson-Hinde (Eds.), *The place of attachment in human behavior* (pp. 171–184). New York: Basic.

White, K. M., Speisman, J. C., & Costos, D. (1983). Young adults and their parents: Individuation to mutuality. In H. D. Grotevant & C. R. Cooper (Eds.), *Adolescent development in the family: New directions for child development* (pp. 61–76). San Francisco: Jossey-Bass.

White, K. M., Speisman, J. C., Costos, D., & Smith, A. (1987). Relationship maturity: A conceptual and empirical approach. In J. Meachem (Ed.), *Contributions to human development* (Vol. 18, pp. 81–101). New York: Karger.

White, R. (1959). Motivation reconsidered: The concept of competence. *Psychological Review*, *66*, 297–333.

Whiting, B. B., & Whiting, J. W. (1975). *Children of six cultures: A psycho-cultural analysis*. Cambridge, MA: Harvard University Press.

Wright, H. (1956). Psychological development in Midwest. *Child Development*, *27*, 265–286.

Young, H., & Ferguson, L. (1979). Developmental changes through adolescence in the spontaneous nomination of reference groups as a function of decision context. *Journal of Youth and Adolescence*, *8*, 239–252.

Youniss, J., & Smollar, J. (1985). *Adolescent relations with mothers, fathers, and friends*. Chicago: University of Chicago Press.

Coping During Childhood and Adolescence: A Motivational Perspective

Ellen A. Skinner and James G. Wellborn

UNIVERSITY OF ROCHESTER

Abstract

A new theory of coping across the life span is presented that departs radically from dominant perspectives in the field. It is based on the assumption that all people have basic needs for relatedness to others, for competence, and for autonomy or self-determination. Based on this assumption about human commitments, it is possible to derive dimensions of universal stress, namely, events that threaten or damage the three basic psychological needs. Hence, three universal stressors are posited: (a) neglect, because it threatens relatedness; (b) chaos, because it undermines competence; and (c) coercion, because it impinges on autonomy. In general, coping itself encompasses peoples struggles to maintain, restore, replenish, and repair the fulfillment of basic psychological needs in the face of experienced assaults on those needs. Hence, coping is an organizational construct, which describes how people regulate their own behavior, emotion, and motivational orientation under conditions of psychological distress. Close relationships are seen as critical to whether children's needs are met and hence to the development of their coping. Three self-system processes are psychological resources for coping; they correspond to secure internal working models (which buffer threats to related-ness), perceived control (which protects competence against threats), and autonomy orienta-tions (which minimize damage to autonomy). The way in which a child copes should predict whether the child will engage or withdraw from further encounters with challenging situations. This engagement or disaffection should in turn influence long-term outcomes for the child, viewed in general terms as developmental gains or losses.

I. Introduction

"Children are not strangers to stress" (Garmezy, 1983, p. 49). Chronic stressors as well as day-to-day problems are a feature of all children's lives. Optimal challenges are opportunities for children to exercise their compe-tencies and so provide grist for developmental advancements. When children are overwhelmed, however, stress forestalls development and increases the likelihood of psychopathology. The study of stress and coping has a long tradition in the psychological, sociological, and medical sciences (Freud, 1927; Selye, 1951; see Moos & Billings, 1982, for a review). Its history in the developmental disciplines is as deep, although discussed under many different construct names (Compas, 1987; Garmezy & Rutter, 1983). Many factors influence the way a child copes with stress, including the social context of the event, the child's personal resources, and the way the child frames and responds to the event. The purpose of this chapter is to specify and integrate these elements of the coping process into a general theory of how children cope with psychological stress. As a context for evaluating the utility of the new theory, we present a selective overview and critique of current work on coping.

II. Stress, Coping, and Development

Views about what constitutes "stress" evolved long before the field of coping developed. Theories and research have examined biological, physi-ological, medical, interpersonal, and societal stresses, ranging in intensity from daily hassles to natural catastrophes, terminal illness, and wartime experiences. As many theorists have pointed out, "Stress seems to apply equally to a form of stimulus (or stressor), a force requiring change of adaptation (strain), a mental state (distress), and a bodily reaction or response (that is, Selye's general adaptation syndrome of stress)" (Rutter, 1983, p. 1).

A. STRESS

A thorny problem in any conceptualization of coping is to disentangle these facets of stress, and then to define them independently and specify their interrelations. Two general approaches to this problem have been to define stress as (a) an internal subjective phenomenon or (b) an external objective phenomenon. Prominent theories in adulthood view stress as within the experience of the individual or in the individual-context interaction (Lazarus & Folkman, 1984). In contrast, developmental theories of coping tend to focus more on identifying objective events in the environment that are stressful (see Garmezy, 1983; Rutter, 1983, for a historical review). A wide range of specific life events and experiences in childhood have been considered, including war, maternal deprivation, divorce, birth of a sibling, relocation, chronic illness, and medical treatments.

The central problem with defining stress subjectively as a person-environment interaction is the difficulty of identifying the target of study. Do differences between people in distress experiences reflect people's differential *vulnerability* to the effects of similar events or the fact that people are dealing with differentially stressful objective *events*? These sources of distress could be separated if a definition of objective stress could be formulated. But it has proven very difficult to catalog events that are universally stressful or even to construct a metric to index the potential stressfulness of events. Indeed, a few events have been identified that seem to be universally stressful, such as maternal deprivation or loss of control. However, without a theoretical framework, it is very difficult to discover other stressors or even to explain why these particular events should be so stressful. In sum, in a theory of coping, it would be useful to include definitions of both objective stress and subjective distress.

B. COPING

Almost from the beginning of the study of stress, researchers have been impressed by the broad range of individual differences in physiological and psychological reactions to the same objective stressor. One approach to the study of these individual differences has been coping. Given the importance of the topic and the burgeoning literature devoted to it over the last 50 years, it is surprising to discover "the confusions as to what is meant by coping and how it functions in the process of adaptation" (Lazarus & Folkman, 1984, p. 117). A summary of definitions of coping in adulthood and childhood appear in Tables I and II, respectively (see Skinner, Altman, & Sherwood, in prep., for a review). As can be seen, at one end of the spectrum, definitions of coping are very broad and general. For example, Rutter (1983) defined coping at its most general as "individual differences in children's responses to all manner of stressful events, happenings, and circumstances" (p. 2). Silver and Wortman (1980) defined coping as "any and all responses made by an individual who encounters a potentially harmful outcome" (p. 281). Compas (1987) summarized this viewpoint by describing

TABLE I
Definitions of Coping in Adulthood

Author	Definition
Billings & Moos (1987)	"cognitive and behavioral responses to specific [stressful] events" (p. 952)
Carver, Scheier, & Weintraub (1989)	"the process of executing a perceived potential response to threat"
Endler & Parker (1990)	"a response to environmental and psychological demands in particular stressful situations" (p. 844)
Fleishman (1984)	"overt and covert behaviors that are taken to reduce or eliminate psychological distress or stressful conditions" (p. 2)
Lazarus & Folkman (1984)	"constantly changing cognitive and behavioral efforts to manage specific external and/or internal demands that are appraised as taxing or exceeding the resources of the person" (p. 141)
McCrae (1982)	"behavior designed to relieve emotional distress or to solve the troubling problem or both" (p. 455)
Pearlin & Schooler (1978)	"things people do to avoid being harmed by life strains" (p.2) "any response to external life strains that serves to prevent, avoid, or control emotional distress" (p.3) "the behaviors, cognitions, and perceptions in which people engage when actually contending with their life problems" (p. 5)
Rosenbaum (1980)	use of cognitions and self statements to control emotional and physiological responses
Silver & Wortman (1980)	"any and all responses made by an individual who encounters a potentially harmful outcome" (p. 31)

the definition of coping as "all responses to stressful events or episodes" (p. 393).

Attempts to delimit this definition have led theorists to distinguish among aspects of the coping process. For example, coping responses can be differentiated from coping resources (Moos & Billings, 1982; Pearlin & Schooler, 1978). "Resources refer not to what people do, but to what is available to them in developing their coping repertoires" (Pearlin & Schooler, 1978, p. 5). More subtle is the distinction between initial *reactions* to potentially stressful events and coping *responses*. Reactions refer to the subjective experience of stress, and would include initial appraisals and psychological distress. Also important is the distinction between coping and its *consequences*. Early theories of coping tended to define coping by its outcomes. Coping was regarded as anything individuals did that reduced the objective stressor or reduced the individual's psychological distress. However, current theories of coping have argued that coping attempts must be defined independently of their effects (e.g., Lazarus & Folkman, 1984). As a result, responses to stress can be referred to as coping regardless of whether they are effective in reducing distress or eliminating the stressor.

Such distinctions are useful in identifying aspects of the coping process that should be excluded from the definition of coping responses per se. When discussing what definitions of coping responses should include, however, attempts to further delimit coping definitions have their own

TABLE II
Definitions of Coping in Childhood

Author	Definition
Ayers, Sandler, West, & Roosa (1990)	cognitive and behavioral processes
Band & Weisz (1988)	"internal response to stressful circumstances" (p. 248)
Compas (1987)	"all purposeful attempts to manage stress regardless of their effectiveness" (p. 394)
	"a subset of adaptational actions involving effort" (p. 399)
Elias, Gara, Rothbaum, Reese, & Ubriaco (1987)	"thought processes believed both to accompany and to direct behavioral performance" (p. 308)
Miller, Danaher, & Forbes (1986)	behavioral strategies used in situations where there is "a competition of viewpoints" (p. 543) or "an occasion that threatens to produce negative affect in either one's . . . partners or oneself" (p. 544)
Rutter (1983)	"What the person does about the stress situation. Coping mechanisms include individual's attempts to directly alter the threatening conditions themselves, and the attempts to change only their appraisal of them so that they need not feel so threatened" (p. 27)
Spirito, Overholser, Ashworth, Morgan, & Benedict-Drew (1988)	"cognitive and behavioral . . . strategies" (p. 706)
Tero & Connell (1984)	"the processes people use to deal with various forms of stress and threat" (p. 3)

drawbacks. One criterion upon which current theories have uneasily converged requires closer examination, namely, the notion of coping as purposeful, conscious, intentional, or strategic. In his review of coping in children and adolescents, Compas (1987) ended the section on conceptualizations of coping with the conclusion that it "seems necessary to limit the use of the term to a subset of adaptational actions involving effort" (p. 399). Endler and Parker (1990) defined coping as a "response to external stressful or negative events" (p. 844), noting that "these responses are usually conscious strategies or styles on the part of the individual" (p. 844). They conclude that "individuals actively and consciously select and engage in particular coping behaviors" (p. 846). Use of the terms *coping strategies*, *coping efforts*, and *coping attempts* also imply that coping is a purposeful, intentional, volitional, and effortful process.[1]

The focus on purpose and effort creates two problems. First, it excludes phenomena that most researchers would agree are interesting facets of

---

[1]It can be difficult to discern what theorists mean by *effortful*. For example, if by effortful responses, Lazarus and Folkman (1984) meant all responses a person shows "when demands are appraised as taxing or exceeding a person's resources" (p. 142), then the only defining characteristic of effortful responses seems to be that they follow appraisals of stress. Few coping theorists would disagree that coping follows such appraisals, although some (ourselves included) would disagree that *effortful* is an appropriate term to describe this.

coping, especially, but not exclusively, in children. For example, in Compas' (1987) review of coping in childhood, he cites learned helplessness as a form of coping. A helpless style of responding to the stress of failure includes passivity, self-derogation, pessimism, and discouragement (Dweck & Leggett, 1987). Although this form of catastrophizing would not be considered intentional, it captures an important pattern of coping responses (Dweck & Wortman, 1982). To exclude such reactions from definitions of coping robs conceptualizations of richness and complexity.

The second problem with defining coping as intentional and effortful stems from developmental considerations. Perhaps one of the most interesting developmental questions is how early coping responses are transformed with development into purposeful attempts to deal with challenges (Maccoby, 1983) and why some people never seem to accomplish this transformation. From this perspective, purposeful, reflective, self-guided attempts to manage stress are seen as only one kind of coping, and a very mature and unusual form of coping at that (see Pearlin & Schooler, 1978, for empirical support for this conclusion in adults). One of the key developmental issues is the epigenesis of such coping. This issue cannot be studied, of course, if all coping is defined a priori as intentional and purposeful. In sum, a clear definition of coping is needed that (a) distinguishes coping from its antecedents and consequences, (b) is not so global that it includes all reactions to stress, but at the same time (c) does not use criteria of purposefulness to exclude a range of interesting coping responses.

C. WAYS OF COPING

The identification of the ways that people cope is the bridge between relatively general conceptual definitions of coping and the specific responses that people show in situations of psychological distress. Given the heterogeneity in definitions of coping, it is not surprising that a range of category systems have been developed to identify kinds or ways of coping. A number of coping categories considered during adulthood and childhood are summarized in Tables III and IV, respectively (see Skinner et al., in prep., for a review).

Typically, these systems are based only loosely on corresponding definitions of coping. Instead, the overarching categories are typically the result of theoretical analyses of the functions of coping; whereas specific categories are usually identified using empirical analyses of coping responses (Carver, Scheier, & Weintraub, 1989). The difficulty with using functions of coping as a basis for identifying categories is that overarching functions, such as problem- or emotion-focused coping, cannot be used to derive specific lower order categories; functions can only be used to classify categories after they have been identified. Hence, almost all theories of coping rely on empirical analyses of open-ended responses to generate specific coping categories.

Factor analyses of individuals' responses to open-ended questions about the "things you did and thought" during a recent specific stressful episode and of people's ratings of the responses generated by others have produced a wide array of dimensionalizations (Carver et al., 1989; see Skinner et al., in prep, for a review). The first drawback of this approach is the lack of consensus about the number and kinds of coping categories that should be used (Carver et al., 1989). Second is the interpretability of the dimensions so identified. The questions used to generate responses imply that coping is everything a person does, thinks, and feels following stress, a definition that has been explicitly rejected by current theories of coping. The critical measurement problem this creates is that the distinctions mentioned earlier, such as between distress reactions and coping responses, become empirically indistinguishable. In measurement terms, it is impossible to determine how the items that mark one factor are conceptually related: Are they parts of the same construct (as has been assumed) or are they distress reactions, causes, antecedents, or correlates of coping categories? In sum, a category system is needed that is derived from a definition of coping, that includes only coping responses (and not coping reactions, resources, or consequences), and that is comprehensive with respect to identifiable criteria.

D. COPING RESOURCES

Central to any theory of coping is the question: What are the resources that allow individuals to cope effectively with stress? The answer has important implications for efforts to intervene in stressful situations. On the one hand, theories of coping have been unanimous in asserting that a wide range of factors support and constrain coping responses. On the other, however, few theories have addressed the nature and effects of coping resources. Indeed, Lazarus and Folkman (1984) assert that "it would be impossible to catalogue all the resources upon which people draw in order to cope with the myriad demands of living" (p. 159).

In the adult literature, theorists typically distinguish between two major classes of resources, psychological and social (Pearlin & Schooler, 1978) or personal and environmental (Lazarus & Folkman, 1984). The spectrum of intrapsychic resources suggested by researchers is broad, ranging from optimism versus pessimism (Carver et al., 1989) to health and energy (Lazarus & Folkman, 1984) to ego development (Moos & Billings, 1982). The list of social resources is equally long. Research focuses on objective and subjective properties of social networks as well as the quantity and quality of different relationships.

TABLE III
Coping Categories in Adults

Carver et al. (1989)	Endler & Parker (1990)	McCrae (1982)
Active Coping	Task-Oriented Coping	Hostile Reaction — Humor
Planning	Emotion-Oriented Coping	Rational Action — Passivity
Suppression of Competing Activities	Avoidance-Oriented Coping	Seeking Help — Indecisiveness
Restraint Coping		Isolation — Faith
Seeking Instrumental Social Support	*Holohan & Moos (1987)*	Fatalism
Seeking Emotional Social Support	Active-Cognitive Strategies	Expression of Feelings
Positive Reinterpretation	Active-Behavioral Strategies	Positive Thinking
Acceptance	Avoidance Strategies	Distraction
Turning to Religion		Escapist Fantasy
Emotional Venting	*Moos & Billings (1982)*	Intellectual Denial
Denial	Problem-Focused	Self-Blame
Behavioral Disengagement	Seek Information or Advice	Taking One Step at a Time
Mental Disengagement	Take Problem-Solving Action	Social Comparison
Alcohol-Drug Disengagement	Develop Alternative Rewards	Sedation
	Appraisal-Focused	Substitution
Lazarus & Folkman (1984)	Logical Analysis	Restraint
Information seeking	Cognitive Redefinition	Drawing Strength from Adversity
Problem-Solving	Cognitive Avoidance	Avoidance
Wishful Thinking	Emotion-Focused	Withdrawal
Interpretation	Affective Regulation	Self-Adaptation
Minimizing threat	Resigned Acceptance	Wishful Thinking
Seeking Social Support	Emotional Discharge	Active Forgetting
Blaming Self		Humor
Avoidance		

Pearlin & Schooler (1978)	Rohde et al. (1990)	Rosenbaum (1980)
Psychological Resources	Cognitive Self-control	
Self-Denigration	Ineffective Escapism	
Mastery	Solace Seeking	
Self-Esteem		
Marriage Coping Responses		Cognitions to Control Emotional
Self-Reliance versus		or Physiological Sensations
Advice Seeking		Problem-Solving Strategies
Controlled Reflectiveness		Delay Gratification
versus Emotional Discharge		Perceived Self-Efficacy
Positive Comparisons		
Negotiations		
Self-Assertion versus		
Passive Forebearance		
Selective Ignoring		
Parental Coping Responses		
Exercise of Parental Potency		
Nonpunitiveness versus		
Reliance on Discipline		
Household Economic Coping		
Responses		
Devaluation of Money		
Optimistic Faith		
Occupational Coping Responses		
Substitution of Rewards		

TABLE IV

Coping Categories in Childhood

Band & Weisz (1988)	Elias et al. (1987)	Spirito et al. (1988)	Ayers et al. (1990)
Primary Control	Stop and Think	Distraction	Problem-Focused Strategies
Direct Problem Solving	Mutual Compromise	Social Withdrawal	Cognitive Decision Making
Problem-Focused Crying	Direct Discussion	Cognitive Restructuring	Direct Problem Solving
Problem-Focused Aggression	Support Seeking	Self-Criticism	Emotion-Focused Strategies
Problem-Focused Avoidance	Nonconfrontation	Blaming Others	Positive Cognitive Restructuring
Secondary Control	Give Up	Problem Solving	Seeking Understanding
Social/Spiritual Support	Wishful Resolution	Emotional Regulation	Expressing Feelings
Emotion-Focused Crying	Pestering	Wishful Thinking	Distraction Strategies
Emotion-Focused Aggression	Aggression	Social Support	Physical Release of Emotions
Cognitive Avoidance	Uncertainty	Resignation	Distracting Actions
Pure Cognition			Avoidant Strategies
Relinquished Control			Avoidant Actions
Doing Nothing			Cognitive Avoidance
			Support Strategies
			Problem Focused Support
			Emotion Focused Support
			Not Indicative of Coping
			Problem Behavior

Miller et al. (1986)		Tero & Connell (1984)
Persuasion Tactics	Conflict Mitigation	Positive Coping
Heavy-Handed	Clarification of Others' Feelings	Projection
Physical Force	Changing the Topic	Denial
Threat	Peaceful Acquiescence	Anxiety Amplification
Moderate	Proposal of Compromise	
Simple Proposition	Indirect Display of Anger	*Spaulding (1978)*
Check Desire	Avoidance	
Check Ability		Aggressive Behavior
Give Directions		Negative (Inappropriate),
Entreaty		Attention-Getting Behavior
Appeal to Situational Constraints		Manipulating, Controlling, and-
Appeal to Social Norms		Directing Others
Effusion of Affect		Resisting
Appeal to Social Norms		Self-Directed Activity
Co-Opting		Paying Close Attention;
Justification by Appropriateness		Thinking, Pondering
Justification by Desire Outcome		Integrative Sharing and Helping
Offers Exchange		Integrative Social Interactions
Deescalation of Request		Integrative Seeking and
Clarification of Social Intent		Receiving Support, Assistance,
Clarification of Reference		and Information
		Following Directions Passively
		and Submissively
		Observing Passively
		Responding to Internal Stimuli
		Physical Withdrawal

In research with children, the primary literature from which insights about coping resources have been gained involves the study of *resilience*. In this research, individual differences in reactions to stress are the target phenomenon and a variety of individual and relationship characteristics are used to predict these (Rutter, 1983). These predictors can be thought of as analogous to coping resources; in fact, overlap exists in the factors that have been examined in childhood and adulthood. In childhood, individual factors include age, sex, genetic factors, temperament, intelligence, and other skills. Interpersonal resources are thought to be especially important during childhood, and they include social networks, close relationships with family members, teachers, and peers, social groups, and the social context (Rutter, 1983).

Although research has provided many insights into the social and psychological contexts of coping, three major problems remain: (a) The number of possible resources suggested is virtually limitless; (b) empirical support for the connection between resources and coping has been surprisingly inconsistent and difficult to uncover (Carver et al., 1989); and (c) little is understood about the mechanisms by which these resources support or undermine coping (Rutter, 1983). A serious attempt must be made to formulate a theory of the intrapsychic and interpersonal antecedents of coping that is comprehensive, that specifies the sets of resources that will support (or undermine) coping with particular classes of stressors, and that suggests the mechanisms by which these resources make coping easier or more difficult.

E. DEVELOPMENT

Theories have emphasized the importance of coping by focusing on its broad and pervasive impact on physical and mental health. For example, Lazarus and Folkman (1984) assert that "the three basic kinds of outcomes are functioning in work and social living, morale and life satisfaction, and somatic health" (p. 181). Likewise, in childhood, general outcomes are emphasized: functioning in school and with peers, personal adjustment, and developmental psychopathology (Rutter, 1983). Coping researchers have begun to recognize the problems created by using such global aggregated outcomes. Empirically, it has proven difficult to find strong relations between specific coping responses in specific stressful encounters and these general outcomes. Even when using diathesis-stress models in which connections between coping and outcomes are only expected to obtain under conditions of stress, robust relations are the exception and not the rule. In retrospect, this lack of consistent findings makes some sense. It is difficult to explain how specific coping responses accrue in their effects to produce outcomes of the magnitude that are considered.

It makes sense that coping should have important global effects on children's development as well as on the development of psychopathology. To understand this connection, however, a theory is needed that distinguishes between the short- and long-term outcomes of coping and then explains how different kinds of coping result in short-term outcomes and how these short-term outcomes in turn result in long-term outcomes.

In short, a theory of coping is proposed that is organized according to a series of questions that are central to a developmental approach to understanding the process of coping: (a) What constitute objectively stressful events? (b) What constitute subjectively stressful experiences? (c) What are initial reactions to stressful experiences? (d) What is coping? (e) What are the qualities or kinds of coping? Along what dimensions can coping responses be arrayed? (f) What are the predictors, both individual and interpersonal, of coping? (g) What are the short- and long-term outcomes of different kinds of coping? and (h) Do the answers to these questions differ depending on the developmental level of the target individuals? This theory of coping is embedded within a motivational model of psychological needs and so we begin by describing the basics of that model.

III. A Motivational Theory of Psychological Needs

There are two central questions that guide the study of motivation: (a) What energizes behavior? and (b) What directs behavior? One bold and newly rediscovered answer (see McClelland, 1951; White, 1959) is that individuals' behaviors are energized and directed by basic psychological needs (Connell, 1990; Connell & Wellborn, 1991; Deci & Ryan, 1985; Harter, 1983). Theories of psychological needs, derived from organismic or dialectic meta-theories, assign a central role to the individual in shaping his or her development. The value of a motivational needs model as a framework for the theory of coping comes from its strong assumptions about universal human commitments. These commitments provide the foundation for deriving a theory of coping that can then be judged on its own merits.

A. NEEDS

The motivational model upon which the coping theory is based postulates three basic psychological needs: the need for *relatedness*, or the need to have close relationships with other people; the need for *competence*, or the need to be effective in interactions with the environment; and the need for *autonomy*, or the need to freely determine one's own course of action. (For a detailed presentation, see Connell, 1990, or Connell & Wellborn, 1991; see Fig. 1.) One of the basic, and most controversial, postulates of this theory

Relatedness: Need to feel securely
                     connected to others <u>and</u>
                     the need to experience oneself
                     as worthy and capable of love
                     (i.e., self-esteem).

Competence: Need for effective interactions
                     with the environment (i.e.,
                     achieve positive outcomes and
                     avoid negative ones).

Autonomy: Need for self-determined (i.e.,
                     choiceful) interactions with the
                     environment.

Fig. 1. A definition of three fundamental, psychological needs.

is that the three psychological needs are universal and innate (Connell, 1990).

From an evolutionary perspective, the value of each need can be postulated. Infants who desire proximity with their caregivers, and who, under stress, use whatever behavioral repertoire is available to them in achieving it, are more likely to survive the vulnerable early years (Bowlby, 1969, 1973). As to the need for competence, individuals who innately seek to interact effectively with the environment will attempt to manipulate physical and social events until they discover how to produce and reproduce desired outcomes. Learning of great instrumental value would accumulate about contingencies in the environment and about repertoires of one's own effective behaviors (White, 1959). Finally, autonomy can be seen as a counterforce to the needs for relatedness and competence. It would provide a mechanism whereby individuals organize and channel personal development according to their unique talents and proclivities (Deci & Ryan, 1991).

Long and rich traditions of research that focus on each of the three needs can be identified. The need for relatedness has been identified and elaborated under the umbrella term *attachment* (Ainsworth, 1979; Bowlby, 1969, 1973), a dominant theme in infancy research and research on social development for decades. The study of the need for competence was organized by White (1959) in his seminal paper on effectance motivation. It has been elaborated by those studying perceived control in all its formulations (Abramson, Seligman, & Teasdale, 1978; Bandura, 1977; Connell, 1985; Crandall, Katkovsky, & Crandall, 1965; Rotter, 1966; Skinner, Chapman, & Baltes, 1988; Weiner, 1979). The need for autonomy has been studied under the rubrics of intrinsic motivation, effectance motivation, or self-determination (deCharms, 1968; Deci & Ryan, 1985; Harter, 1983). Taken together, research on attachment, on perceived control, and on self-determination represent large theoretical and empirical commitments in developmental, social, personality, clinical, and motivational psychology.

B. ENGAGEMENT AND DISAFFECTION

The three needs can be used to organize a model of context, self, action, and developmental outcomes (Fig. 2). According to this model, the extent to which basic psychological needs are met determines whether individuals will be "engaged versus disaffected." Engagement versus disaffection includes three components: energized versus enervated *behavior* (initiation, effort, concentrated attention, persistence, and continued attempts in the face of failure vs. avoidance, passivity, resistance, giving up, fleeing); positive versus negative *emotion* (enthusiasm, happiness, curiosity, interest vs. boredom, anger, anxiety, fear); and *orientation* (commitment to vs. alienation from the goals of developing relatedness, competence, and autonomy). (For an integration of this perspective with major theories of motivation, see Wellborn, 1991.)

C. SELF-SYSTEM PROCESSES

According to the motivational model, individuals appraise the extent to which the context is meeting each of their psychological needs. In their most elaborated form, these appraisals, called *self-system processes*, have been conceptualized and studied for relatedness as internal working models of attachment figures (e.g., Main et al., 1985); for the competence need, as perceived control (e.g., Skinner, 1991); and for the need for self-determination, as autonomy orientations (e.g., Deci & Ryan, 1985). The components of self-system processes as well as their developmental course are a matter of vigorous theoretical and empirical debate.

D. SOCIAL CONTEXT

According to the motivational model, individuals construct their self-system processes based on their interactions with the environment. How the social context fulfills the three basic psychological needs has been studied by

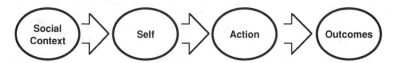

Fig. 2. A model of the relationship between the social context, the self, action, and outcomes.

motivational theorists (e.g., Connell & Wellborn, 1991; Deci & Ryan, 1985; Grolnick, Ryan, & Deci, 1989; Skinner, 1991) and is based in many other literatures as well. The activities of the social context that facilitate the experience of relatedness have been grouped under the construct *involvement*. The aspects of social contexts that promote the experience of competence are examined under the construct of *structure*. Finally, contextual features that allow children to experience themselves as self-determining are included in the construct of *autonomy support*. (More specific descriptions follow.) According to this motivational model, involvement, structure, and autonomy support, taken together, are the backbone for any context wishing to promote psychological development of the individual.

E. DEVELOPMENTAL OUTCOMES

From a motivational perspective, one of the primary mechanisms for development across the life span is engagement. Children (and adults) who show active, flexible, interested involvement in activities and relationships are hypothesized to derive maximum pleasure as well as maximum learning about the self and the activity. If environments are structured such that the three needs are fulfilled or optimally challenged, then learning and development will be optimal and adaptive. In contrast, children who are rigid or pressured in their involvement, or who are fearful, passive, and withdrawn will forego opportunities to exercise their own capacities or to learn about the context. Three kinds of developmental gains, broadly defined, are postulated to accrue from engagement with other people and the physical environment: social, cognitive, and personality development (see Fig. 3).

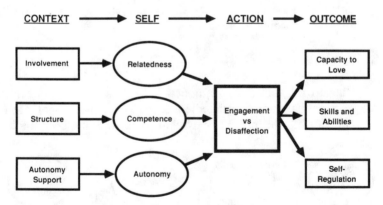

Fig. 3. A simple process model of the relationship between the social context, self, action, and outcomes.

IV. A Motivational Theory of Coping

The working definition of coping includes children's regulation of their behavior, emotion, and motivational orientation during psychological stress. When children's psychological needs are met, they will cope with stresses in more active, flexible, and positive ways. In contrast, when children feel that their needs are ignored or insulted, they will react to challenges in ways that are passive, rigid, and punitive. Close relationships are seen as the key to whether children's needs are met and, hence are central to the development of their coping. The general developmental trend is for coping to become more reflective, self-regulated, and internalized with age over middle childhood to adolescence, as well as more stable in either the adaptive or maladaptive direction. Furthermore, the ways in which a child copes should predict the child's emotional, behavioral, and orientational reaction to stress, and whether the child will engage or withdraw from further encounters with challenging situations. This engagement or disaffection should in turn influence long-term outcomes for the child, viewed in general terms as developmental gains or losses. The outline of the theory is presented in Fig. 4. The questions a developmental theory of coping should answer are used to organize the following sections.

A. WHAT ARE PSYCHOLOGICALLY STRESSFUL EVENTS?

According to the motivational perspective, objectively stressful events are those that threaten or damage the three basic psychological needs. Definitions of stress can be derived directly from the three kinds of social contextual elements that fulfill needs by considering the opposites of these

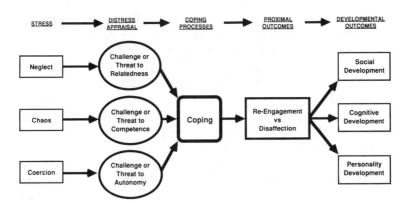

Fig. 4. A simple, process model of the relationship between the social context, self, coping, and developmental outcomes.

supports. If involvement, structure, and autonomy-support nurture children, then neglect, chaos, and coercion are the categories of major objective psychological stress. A brief review is presented to corroborate this argument.

Neglect

Neglect is defined as a lack of involvement from important social partners. The construct of *involvement* denotes the expression of affection and caring. It includes dedicating energy and resources, spending time, and listening, as well as being warm, dependable, and emotionally available, and expressing affection, interest, pleasure in and enjoyment of the child (Connell & Wellborn, 1991; Grolnick et al., 1989). The opposite of involvement is negligence and rejection. Neglect ranges from social partners who are physically or emotionally unavailable, who are cold and distant, and who do not like or enjoy the child to social partners who actively reject or hate the child. Neglect has been shown to predict developmental outcomes such as low self-esteem, depression, and withdrawal (Lipsitt, 1983; Sroufe, 1979). In developmental psychology, involvement versus neglect is the central feature of every theory of parenting, and is included as a basic requirement in major theories of adult–child socialization (Maccoby & Martin, 1983).

Chaos

Chaos is defined as a lack of structure in the social context. Structure denotes information about pathways for interactions with the environment that lead to desired outcomes. Aspects of structure include the provision of clear expectations for behaviors, consistency, contingent responsiveness, challenges geared to the level of competence of the child, information about how to reach desired outcomes (e.g., strategies), and support in developing competencies to enact those strategies (Connell & Wellborn, 1991; Grolnick et al., 1989; Skinner, 1991).

Chaos is the opposite of structure, and refers to social contexts and relations characterized by inconsistency, unpredictability, noncontingency, normlessness, and vague or inconsistent expectations. Understimulation or challenges that are overwhelming, as well as lack of information and lack of support for trying out strategies and building competencies are also aspects of chaos. In stress research, unpredictability and loss of control have emerged as major themes, especially in experimental studies of animals (Weinberg & Levine, 1980). The aspect of chaos that has received the most intense empirical scrutiny in humans is noncontingency (Alloy & Abramson, 1979). Its devastating psychological consequences (emotional, behavioral, and motivational) as well as immunological effects have been documented in laboratory and field settings, from infancy to old age (Abramson et al., 1978; Baltes & Baltes, 1986; Gunnar, 1980; Levine, 1983; Seligman, 1975; Watson, 1979). Like involvement, structure is featured prominently in every theory of parenting and socialization (Maccoby & Martin, 1983).

Coercion

The third source of psychological stress is lack of support for autonomy. Autonomy support consists of allowing actual freedom of expression, through means such as choice, respect, and minimum constraints or rules. Autonomy support also involves facilitating the internalization of nonintrinsically motivated activities through means such as providing rationales, acknowledging conflicting feelings, and pointing out the relevance of the activities for the child's own goals (Deci & Ryan, 1985; Ryan, 1982).

The opposite of autonomy support is coercion. Coercion involves contexts that constrain, manipulate, or control the child. These ends can be accomplished through means that also appear coercive (such as verbal or physical threats or punishment) but they can also be achieved through more subtle means, such as love withdrawal, guilt induction, competition and comparison, or rewards and bribes (Ryan, 1982). The developmental effects of coercion have been widely documented, ranging from undermining intrinsic motivation, to failure to internalize norms and attitudes, to inability to regulate one's own behavior, to failure to develop an integrated self (Deci & Ryan, 1985). This dimension can be seen in theories of adult–child socialization as critical to the internalization of values, attitudes, and the regulation of behavior; it is an important aspect of discipline and rule setting (e.g., Baumrind, 1977; deCharms, 1968).

In sum, the motivational theory specifies three dimensions of social context that are hypothesized to be psychologically stressful; this assertion is consistent with evidence from major research traditions. The theory grounds the potency of these three dimensions to cause stress in an explanatory theory: Distress directly results from assaults on the three basic needs. The theory can organize a variety of components of stress under each dimension, arguing that they have in common the potential to undermine the respective need. Further, the theory asserts that it is reasonably comprehensive in terms of major categories of psychological stress. Finally, it points to the dynamics among the needs as a major source of stress. Maximally stressful would be a situation in which all three needs are threatened or a social context that makes the fulfillment of one need contingent on the denial of another.

B. WHAT IS THE EXPERIENCE OF
PSYCHOLOGICAL DISTRESS?

Life events would be experienced as stressful when the individual feels that his or her basic psychological needs are not being met, or are being actively attacked. From a motivational perspective, infants are born with a "hard-wired" predisposition to react to contextual events that are relevant to their basic psychological needs. Reactions to opportunities to fulfill needs are coded in energized behaviors (active movement), positive emotions (enthusiasm, joy, satisfaction), and attentive orientations (toward the event, such as interest). Need-irrelevant events would result in a lack of attention and energy directed at the events. Events that impinge on the needs would result in distress reactions.

Distress Reactions

The set of reactions that are relevant to coping processes are those in which needs are impinged upon. Following Lazarus and Folkman (1984), appraisals are divided into irrelevant, challenge, threat, and loss. Consistent with the motivational theory, distress reactions are conceptualized as a complex of behavior, emotion, and orientation. During distress reactions, behavior can be either active or passive, emotions either positive or negative, and orientation either toward or away from the event. In general, responses to *challenges* to needs are active, positive, and oriented toward the event or activity. Challenge responses are energetic and optimistic, aimed at restoring or reestablishing need fulfillment. In general, *threat* responses are emotionally negative, are oriented toward the event or activity, and can be passive or active. Responses to threat are aimed at fighting for the needs and differ from responses to challenge in their tone of anxiety and deprivation. Responses to *loss* are, in general, passive, negative, and oriented away from the event or activity. Loss responses are aimed at protecting the self from the impact of the assault to the needs. Loss responses differ from threat responses in their tone of hopelessness and despair. Finally, as pointed out by Lazarus (Lazarus & Folkman, 1984), some events, those that do not impinge on commitments, lead to disinterest. These differ from disaffection in that the tone is emotionally benign or neutral (cf. Roth & Cohen, 1986).

Reactions to Impingement of the Needs

According to the motivational perspective, all individuals begin with a commitment to the fulfillment of the three needs.[2] However, based on the

[2]According to the motivational theory, it is possible for an individual, after prolonged periods of deprivation from a basic need, to eventually "detach" from that need and relinquish a commitment to that need. This would result in severe psychopathology and so is not considered part of this general theory. It is important to distinguish between *detachment* from

	Appraisals	Coping Reactions	Behavior	Emotion	Orientation
RELATEDNESS	Challenge	Seek Proximity	Active (Move)	Positive (Love)	Away (Safety)
	Threat	Freeze	Passive (Don't Move)	Negative (Sadness)	Toward (Disappear)
COMPETENCE	Challenge	Observe	Passive (Look & Listen)	Positive (Wonder)	Toward (Attend)
	Threat	Flee	Active (Move)	Negative (Fear)	Away (Escape)
AUTONOMY	Challenge	Test	Active (Move)	Positive (Interest)	Toward (Choose)
	Threat	Fight	Active (Move)	Negative (Anger)	Toward (Attack)

Fig. 5. Reactions to psychological stress.

contexts in which they have developed, individuals will differ dramatically on the extent to which they currently experience themselves as related, competent, and autonomous. These individual differences act as filters for experience, rendering children vulnerable, for example, to feeling coerced when they have low perceived autonomy, or protecting them from feeling neglected when they have high perceived relatedness.

According to this theory, three simple sets of intuitive, nonreflective appraisals, corresponding to the needs, determine how easy it is for the social context to "push a child's buttons" and hence produce a distress reaction. Experienced impingement of each of the needs is predicted to produce a different stress reaction (see Fig. 5). Challenges to relatedness would produce a "seek contact" reaction, threats a "freeze" reaction. Challenges to competence would produce an "observe" reaction, threats a "flight" reaction. Challenges to autonomy would produce a "test" reaction, threats a "fight" reaction. Those familiar with the infancy literature will note that these reactions are present in normal infants: They will bid for physical proximity and comfort if separated from the caregiver (neglect), will protest physical constraint (coercion), and will react with fear and escape to unpredictable events (chaos). (See Levine, 1983; Lipsitt, 1983.)

These behavior-emotion-orientation patterns are seen as the developmental primitives out of which self-system processes, coping, and engagement are differentiated. These appraisals are prerequisites for the appearance of differential interpretations of (and hence, individual differences in distress responses to) ambiguous events. Although these filters are not intentional, reflective, or rational, they become more accessible to reflec-

---

a basic need and *disaffection or disengagement* from an activity, context, relationship, or enterprise in which it is impossible to have a need fulfilled. The latter allows for reengagement in alternative activities and relations that are more likely to fulfill needs whereas the former is a form of psychological suicide.

tion and self-regulation with age. With development, children's distress reactions may become more differentiated, reflecting the specific need being threatened by events. These differentiations can be expressed through emotions, behaviors, or orientations that imply the needs. For example, emotions would include loneliness (relatedness), embarrassment (competence), and shame (autonomy). Reflective indications of attacks on the needs would move from vague feelings of misgiving and panic ("Danger. Something's wrong.") to more differentiated feelings or reflections, such as "I feel alone. The world is cold" (relatedness), "I feel helpless. The world is unpredictable" (competence), or "I don't know what I want. The world is hostile" (autonomy). The advent of these changes makes it possible to assess children's appraisals independently from their stress reactions.

C. WHAT IS COPING?

From a motivational perspective, coping encompasses peoples' struggles to maintain, restore, replenish, and repair the fulfillment of basic psychological needs in the face of experienced assaults on those needs. Coping is energized by an individual's commitments to relatedness, competence, and autonomy, and is directed by the self-system processes associated with each need. More specifically, responses available to individuals are aimed at managing their engagement with (vs. disaffection from) the stressful situation, that is, managing their behavior, emotion, and outlook. Hence, *coping* is an organizational construct that describes how people regulate their own behavior, emotion, and motivational orientation under conditions of psychological distress.

The notion of coping as management and the notion of coping as aimed at changing problems, emotions, and appraisals appears as a theme in many definitions of coping. Both Carver et al. (1989) and Rohde, Tilson, Lewinson, and Seeley (1990) construct their theories of coping on theories of self-regulation. Maccoby (1983) specifically addresses the developmental importance to coping of maintaining behavioral organization. Lazarus and Folkman (1984) define coping as "efforts to manage specific external and/or internal demands" (p. 141), and Compas (1987) includes "all purposeful attempts to manage stress" (p. 394). In addition to its role in dealing with problems, management surfaces in discussions of the function of coping in regulating emotion (e.g., Lazarus & Folkman, 1984; Pearlin & Schooler, 1978). Finally, some theorists mention ways of coping that serve to transform meaning. For example, Billings and Moos (1984) identify one kind of coping, active-cognitive strategies, that are "efforts to manage the appraisal of the stressfulness of the event" (p. 878). Pearlin and Schooler (1978) include in coping responses those that control the meaning of the strainful experience.

In general, regulation refers to how people mobilize, guide, manage, energize, and direct their behavior, emotion, and orientation, or how they fail to do so. From this definition, it can be concluded that coping has two poles: underregulation and overregulation, with flexible regulation falling in the middle (Block & Block, 1979). Underregulation occurs when behavior, emotion, and orientation are uncoordinated; underregulation includes impulsive behavior, emotional outbursts, or a confused non-goal-directed orientation. Over-regulated coping occurs when behavior, emotion, and orientation become rigid, pressured, repetitive, and unresponsive to internal or external feedback; overregulation includes rigid behavior, suppressed emotions, or perseverating at an outcome. With flexibly regulated coping, behavior, emotion, and orientation are coordinated; behavior is active and intentional, emotion is channeled, and orientation is goal directed. This conceptualization provides a scheme for organizing ways of coping according to the definition of coping (e.g., ways of regulating behavior, emotion, and orientation) rather than according to its functions (e.g., emotion-focused or problem-focused) or consequences (e.g., effectiveness in reducing stress).

In sum, the current definition of coping, in addition to the fact that it is part of a larger theory of motivation, has several strengths. It narrows extremely broad definitions of coping without excluding a range of interesting coping responses. It also includes and integrates many current theories of coping with psychological stress (psychodynamic theories are the exception). In addition, it can then use the literature on self-regulation, ego resilience and ego control, and the development of behavioral, emotional, and motivational regulation as a basis for forming a theory of the epigenesis of regulated coping (Maccoby, 1983).

D. WHAT ARE THE WAYS OF COPING?

Within the current theory, it was seen as desirable to construct a category system that could be derived from the definition of coping, that could be described along a specifiable number of dimensions, that was general enough to be applied to a wide range of stressors but could also be further specified to fit each context, and that could be expanded to incorporate developmental changes in the categories. The system upon which our work converged is pictured in Fig. 6. The specific categories included are the result of a review of all major category systems used for children and adults (Skinner et al., in prep.) as well open-ended interviews with children about their reactions to a variety of stresses (absence, conflict, loss) in the domains of academics and friendship (Mellor-Crummey, 1989; Skinner, Altman, & Sherwood, 1991). This system, or a close variation of it, is currently undergoing empirical scrutiny (Skinner & Wellborn, 1991).

COPING RESPONSES

COPING REACTIONS		APPRAISALS		Regulation of Behavior	Regulation of Emotion	Regulation of Orientation
RELATEDNESS	SELF	CHALLENGE	"I will love."	Cooperate	Appreciate	Support
		THREAT	"I am alone."	Delegation	Self-pity	Abandonment
	CONTEXT	CHALLENGE	"I will reduce neglect."	Contact-seeking	Comfort-seeking	Help-seeking
		THREAT	"The world is cold."	Concealment	Detachment	Avoidance
COMPETENCE	SELF	CHALLENGE	"I will learn."	Strategize	Encouragement	Determination
		THREAT	"I am helpless."	Confusion	Self-doubt	Discouragement
	CONTEXT	CHALLENGE	"I will reduce chaos."	Information-seeking	Optimism	Prevention
		THREAT	"The world is unpredictable."	Escape	Pessimism	Procrastination
AUTONOMY	SELF	CHALLENGE	"I will decide."	Flexibility	Accept Responsibility	Reevaluation
		THREAT	"I don't know what I want."	Perseveration	Self-blame	Obsession
	CONTEXT	CHALLENGE	"I will reduce coercion."	Negotiation	Blamelessness	Rededication
		THREAT	"The world is hostile."	Aggression	Projection	Devaluation

Fig. 6. Motivational coping categories.

The matrix of coping categories was derived by crossing the source of the distress with the targets of regulation. Twelve kinds of distress were considered, depending on which need was impinged upon (competence, autonomy, or relatedness), whether the impingement was experienced as a challenge or a threat, and whether the source of the distress was the self or the context. The other axis of the coping matrix distinguishes the target of the regulation, namely, the three components of engagement: behavior, emotion, and orientation. The current system is able to accomodate almost all of the categories proposed by other researchers (see III and IV). The system also suggests some categories not previously discussed as coping, such as "confusion," "abandonment," and "rededication."

The specific embodiment of each category of coping responses will depend on the developmental level of the target individuals and the domain of stress. Especially important in this regard are the power relationships in the context. When power relations are reciprocal (such as with siblings or peers), children can more directly express their coping responses. However, when relationships are complementary (such as in parent–child or teacher–child relations), children are more constrained. For example, when a competence need is threatened by a peer, a child would be predicted to cope by literally leaving the scene of the interaction; when an autonomy need is threatened, the child would aggress. However, in the classroom, under conditions of threat to competence or autonomy, the child is not allowed to leave or aggress against the teacher. In this context, the child is predicted to regulate behavior to "flee" as much as constraints will allow (wishing it were over) or "fight" as much as possible (e.g., opposition).

The current system makes explicit an issue suggested but not systematically considered in most category systems, namely, the notion that individuals do not have "styles" of coping but instead show patterns or profiles of coping responses. What has been left unspecified by these theories is whether any combinations of coping categories are possible, whether some forms of coping are mutually exclusive, or whether some are more likely to co-occur. As can be seen in Fig. 6, several general predictions can be made about profiles of coping. First, the three large blocks of coping categories organized under each need are independent of each other. Hence, at the very least, an individual could vary on the extent to which each of the three systems are activated. According to the current theory, this would be predicted from the appraisal of which need(s) have been impinged upon.

Second, the two kinds of appraisals within each need (challenge vs. threat) would determine which rows of coping responses would be activated within each block. In general, at any point in time these two appraisals are hypothesized to be mutually exclusive, and as a result, the coping categories they contain should in general be negatively related to each other. Third, whether individuals appraise the source of the impingement as the self and/or the context determines which rows within challenge and threat would be activated. Self and context appraisals are not mutually exclusive; hence, multiple rows can be activated simultaneously. Fourth, because each row is hypothesized to be underlain by the same appraisal, the ways of coping in each row are seen as behavior-emotion-orientation patterns and so are predicted to be positively correlated with each other.

In sum, in addition to organizing existing categories of coping and suggesting new ones, the present dimensions of coping responses can be used to derive predictions about the relations among coping responses, suggesting both profiles of responses and underlying psychological processes that account for them.

E. WHAT ARE THE ANTECEDENTS, BOTH INDIVIDUAL AND INTERPERSONAL, OF COPING?

In the motivational model, intrapsychic and interpersonal resources are studied under the constructs labels *self-system processes* and *social context*, respectively. Three self-system processes are viewed as proximal predictors of coping responses: those associated with relatedness, competence, and autonomy. Three dimensions of the social context are equally important: involvement, structure, and autonomy support (see Fig. 7).

Self-System Processes as Personal Coping Resources

According to the motivational perspective, individual differences in the extent to which children's needs are fulfilled produce individual differences in children's beliefs about their relatedness, competence, and autonomy. These perceptions predict the extent to which potentially stressful environmental events produce psychological distress and how children will regulate

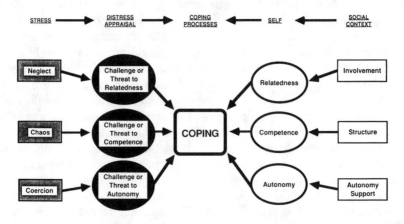

Fig. 7. Context and self as coping resources.

their behavior, emotion, and orientation during stressful encounters. Research and theory about internal working models of attachment figures, perceived control, and autonomy orientations provide support for the proposition that these beliefs buffer or exacerbate children's reactions to potentially stressful events.

Attachment. The potential stress examined in attachment research is codified in "the strange situation" in which an infant is separated from and reunited with its mother as well as left alone in the presence of a stranger. Decades of research have shown that infants with secure attachments to their caregivers respond to this stress with much less distress than do insecurely attached infants, who respond with anxiety, anger, and disruption of their exploratory and play behavior (Ainsworth, 1979). Evidence that internal working models of attachment figures serve the same function at older ages is only inferential. Early attachment status (secure vs. insecure) predicts both the quality of the internal working model that will be formed and the child's resilience to social stress (Sroufe, 1979). Current research is only beginning to catch up to conceptualizations of working models; when measurement issues are resolved, the direct link will be subject to empirical test (Ainsworth, 1989).

Research with the social support construct can be seen as providing evidence that internal working models of relationships buffer the effects of stressful life events in adults. One of the most robust (and unexpected) findings in the stress and social support literature is that the amount of support actually received predicts negative coping and increases in distress; whereas the amount of social support perceived to be available predicts positive coping and decreases in distress (Cohen, McGowan, Fooskas, & Rose, 1984). A central dimension of internal working models of relationships is the perceived emotional and physical availability of the attachment figure.

Internal working models should act as psychological buffers during events that could otherwise threaten relatedness. First, they filter ambiguous potentially threatening events, preventing them from being interpreted as assaults to relatedness. For example, children with secure working models should not interpret events such as separation from a friend, a teacher's refusal of a request, or a group's exclusion as evidence that "they don't like me." In addition to reducing initial psychological distress, these relatedness self-system processes support a range of coping responses to threats of any kind that utilize interpersonal resources, through seeking of help, advice, contact, and comfort.

Perceived Control. One of the most robust findings in the stress literature is that when subjects believe that they can control (usually terminate) a noxious event, they will experience the event as less stressful, even when they never exercise that control. With perceived control in children, the potentially stressful events most often studied are failure and noncontingency (Levine, 1983). Research with the constructs of learned helplessness, attribution theory, locus of control, and self-efficacy have shown that children's beliefs about whether they can control outcomes directly influences their responses to these stressful events (Skinner, 1991). In terms of emotional reactions to failure, for example, research on helplessness has shown that children who do not expect to be able to control outcomes become more upset, anxious, and discouraged in the face of failure than do children with higher perceived control (Dweck & Leggett, 1988). (For a review of research on coping and control in adulthood, see Folkman, 1984.)

As with other self-system processes, perceived control influences coping in two ways. First, it protects children from interpreting potentially distressing events as threats to competence. For example, when children with high perceived control cannot solve a problem or fail in an attempt to achieve something, they should be less likely to "feel stupid" or to feel pessimistic about the eventual outcome. Second, perceived control should support coping attempts that are aimed at discovering new strategies and developing new capacities, such as planning, problem solving, and information gathering.

Autonomy Versus Control Orientation. Within theories of intrinsic motivation and self-determination, researchers have become interested in individual differences in the ways in which people interpret events, as captured by their causality orientations (Deci & Ryan, 1985). Researchers propose that individuals with an *autonomy orientation* tend to interpret events as informational, that is, as providing them with information about conditions and contingencies in the environment upon which they can base their unpressured free choices of behavior. Individuals with a *control orientation*, in contrast, interpret events as controlling and pressuring them to behave in certain ways.

Research has shown that the hallmark of an autonomy orientation is a relaxed, unpressured response to environmental events (even those in which the context intends to control the individual), whereas the hallmark of a control orientation is subjective pressure and emotional distress, either anxiety or anger, in the face of events (even those in which social partners are not attempting to coerce the individual). Research with children has shown that high levels of anger and anxiety characterize children with control orientations (Ryan & Connell, 1989). No direct evidence exists that specifically examines whether the experience of stressful life events is mediated by causality orientations in children.

According to the motivational theory, high perceived autonomy should buffer stress in two ways. First, individuals with an autonomy orientation are less likely to feel coerced, even by coercive circumstances. They are more likely to feel that they can make their own independent decisions and can exercise freely their own choice of actions. Second, in situations that are perceived as coercive, individuals with high perceived autonomy are more likely to cope in more flexible and self-determined ways, such as through negotiation and compromise, rather than in ways that are controlled, such as perseverence and aggression.

Social Contexts as Interpersonal Coping Resources

Theories of coping are unanimous in emphasizing the importance of close relationships, both during childhood and adulthood. The functions of these relationships have been studied most extensively under the rubric of social support. Not surprising to anyone who has studied close relationships is the finding that social support has both positive and negative features (Suls, 1982). In general, research has shown that an absence of social connections makes an individual more vulnerable to stress. However, the presence of dense social networks seem to have both advantages and disadvantages (Belle, 1982). Recent research has attempted to analyze the components of social support and to study them separately. The motivational model suggests that three dimensions will be especially important as buffers against stress. They are involvement, structure, and autonomy support. As described earlier, involvement includes the expression of affection and love, as well as dedication of time and resources; structure includes provision of clear expectations, consistent contigencies and help; and autonomy support includes provision of choice, minimal coercion, and rationales for disciplinary rules.

Just like self-system processes, social contextual supports would be expected to influence coping through two channels. First, they would buffer the effects of stress and by so doing they would reduce the individual's experience of psychological distress. For example, when a child moves to a new neighborhood, the absence of friends would be a potentially stressful event. The motivational theory would posit that the more involvement provided by parents and siblings, the less this event would be experienced as distressful by the child. Likewise, the more attention provided by the father following the birth of a new sibling, the less distress the older child would experience as a result of decreased time spent with the mother.

The second way in which the social context could act as a resource is by influencing the way in which a child copes. The more involved the social partners, the more likely the child will be to turn to the partners for help and comfort. The more structure the context provides, the more the child will respond to distress with active attempts at problem solving. The more autonomy supportive the social context, the more flexible and self-determined children's coping will be. As can be inferred from the foregoing, the mechanism through which the context can have an impact on children's distress reactions and coping is through their effects on the child: by influencing the distress appraisals on the one hand and the self-system processes that direct coping on the other.

The use of involvement, structure, and autonomy support as environmental resources may seem confusing when at the same time their opposites (neglect, chaos, and coercion) are posited to be the three major classes of psychological stress. However, because of the complexity of most social situations, these constructs do not usually form single dimensions. Consider the case of divorce, which is a potentially stressful event involving the loss of proximity to one parent (usually the father). The construct of *neglect* can be used to analyze the severity of the potential impact of paternal separation on the target child (e.g., how often the father visits, the quality of the time spent, the father's availability and dependability). Then the construct of *involvement* can be used to assess the compensatory efforts of other social partners in the context, such as the mother, older brothers and sisters, uncles and aunts, or grandparents. The usefulness of distinguishing the role of the context in stressing children and its role in supporting them is clearest in cases in which the sources of the distress and support inhabit separate social systems. For example, it is a well-documented finding that, when families are marked by chaos and discord, a child's close relationship with a loving and consistent adult outside of the immediate family (often a grandparent or teacher) can provide a buffer against the effects of family stresses (Garmezy, 1983).

The Interaction of Stressors and Coping Resources

The motivational model can be used to specify the interaction of stressors and protective/risk factors. Personal and interpersonal resources should have their most notable effects in mediating stressors that impinge on corresponding needs. More specifically, the study of self-system processes for relatedness and the involvement dimension of social support would be important in coping with stresses that involve interpersonal loss or separation, such as divorce, separation from parents due to illness, relocation, adjustment to birth of a sibling (which usually includes subsequently less involvement from the mother), adjustment to alternative child care, or adjustment to school. Secure internal working models and the availability of other closely attached relationships should reduce children's experience of these events as distressing and should predict to their active attempts to establish new relationships.

According to this line of thinking, perceived control and provision of structure would be especially important psychological and social resources in events involving failure, noncontingency, unpredictability, and novelty. Children with high perceived control and those whose social contexts provide structure are more likely to experience such events as challenges to be overcome rather than as threats to competence, and so evince less distress. Likewise they are likely to cope with these events in ways that involve active problem solving and result in increased learning. In the same vein, an autonomy orientation and contexts high in autonomy support would be expected to mitigate the effects of coercive contexts. For example, many parents find that schools and peer groups are contexts that demand excessive conformity from their children. According to this motivational theory, children who have high perceived autonomy and whose families support autonomy should be able to negotiate these demands using more flexible and independent coping strategies.

Three implications of this view of intrapsychic and social resources should be noted. First, it implies a differentiated picture of the positive and negative effects of certain coping resources. In some stressful encounters, certain self-system processes will be called upon and in others, they will be irrelevant. Likewise, certain social partners may be a great deal of help in specific stressful situations and a detriment in others. The present scheme allows these interactions and matches to be postulated a priori. This may augment empirical attempts to document the influences of social and psychological resources. Second, this view implies that the social context can almost totally ameliorate the long-term effects of any stressor, by compensating for the loss. Consider one of the single most stressful events imaginable, namely, the loss of a child's primary caregiver. If the child is immediately adopted by a loving set of parents who already have an attachment with the child (such as relatives), then the long-term effects would be expected to be minimized, despite the short-term severe distress that would accompany the loss.

Finally, this perspective identifies the mechanisms through which social and personal resources mediate the effects of stressors on children. On the one hand, they influence distress appraisals. Children are less likely to experience negative events as impinging on their basic psychological needs. Second, they influence the kinds of coping children actually show. With higher levels of personal and social resources, children are more likely to maintain the organization of their behavior, emotion, and orientation under conditions of psychological distress. Because many childhood stressors involve some combination of neglect, chaos, and coercion, the three self-system processes and the three social contextual dimensions are expected to facilitate more adaptive coping across a wide range of potentially stressful encounters.

F. WHAT ARE THE OUTCOMES OF COPING?

According to the motivational model, the route by which coping influences children's development is through their reengagement. *Reengagement* refers to the quality and intensity of involvement in the face of obstacles and setbacks; it consists of the same three components as ongoing engagement, namely, behavior, emotion, and orientation. Every coping category can be analyzed for its effects on behavior, emotion, and orientation. This approach solves a recurring problem in discussions of coping effectiveness. It has been difficult to make predictions about the short-term effects of specific coping responses. Most researchers have decided that the adaptiveness or maladaptiveness of a coping response simply cannot be determined; it depends on a myriad of contextual factors. The current theory argues that the short-term outcomes of coping responses are not "effectiveness" or "ineffectiveness" but the multiple effects of the coping response(s) on the intensity and quality of engagement in the face of stress.

The most straightforward hypotheses about the short-term effects of different kinds of coping can be derived directly from Fig. 6. That is, coping responses that regulate behavior are hypothesized to have behavioral effects, those that regulate emotion to have effects on emotion, and those that regulate orientation to have effects on orientation. More interesting predictions result from the general proposition that, although each kind of regulation has its primary effects on the target of that regulation (e.g., behavioral regulation on behavior), each kind nevertheless has an effect on the other two short-term outcomes as well (i.e., behavioral regulation also has an effect on emotion and orientation). In other words, a regulation aimed at a specific aspect of engagement can be effective in regulating that aspect and still impede the regulation of other aspects of engagement. For example, one effective way of regulating behavior to be active is perseverance. At the same time, however, perseverence has negative consequences for regulating emotion (i.e., anxiety) and orientation (i.e., loss of focus on learning).

According to this perspective, optimal coping consists of ways of regulating the target aspect of engagement without impeding any of the other aspects. An example can illustrate this point. Two coping responses that both involve behaviorally disengaging from the stressful activity are *escape* (running away from or avoiding an activity) and *reevaluation* (actively deciding that an activity cannot be pursued at the present time). However, the two differ in that escape involves both a negative emotion (fear) and an orientation that is away from the stressful activity. Both of these features make it less likely that the individual will actively reengage with the stressful activity in the future. In contrast, reevaluation involves less negative emotions (relief, regret) and a flexible orientation toward the event, both of which increase the likelihood that the individual will reengage with the stressful activity in the future. Other examples would include contrasting "accepting responsibility" with "self-blame" or contrasting "help seeking" with "delegation." In each case, the same basic regulation is either accompanied by or free from other short-term outcomes that interfere with reengagement.

A consideration of these three components opens up a wider range of potential outcomes than those typically considered. Effective coping outcomes are assumed to be either changing the stressor or adjusting to it. According to the motivational theory, attempts to change the context can be energetic, coordinated, and goal directed (see the "challenge" rows under "context" in Fig. 6) or they can be uncoordinated, confused, and affectively charged (fearful, aggressive, or despairing) (see the "threat" rows under "context"). Likewise, attempts to change the self can be active, enthusiastic attempts to cooperate, learn, and accept responsibility (see the "challenge" rows under "self" in Fig. 6) or they can be self-destructive, obsessive, and self-pitying (see the "threat" rows under "self").

For example, the row corresponding to a threat to competence due to the self contains confusion, self-doubt, and discouragement, a combination that has been studied under the rubric "learned helplessness" (e.g., Dweck & Wortman, 1982). The row corresponding to a threat to autonomy due to the context includes aggression, projection, and an oppositional orientation, studied under the rubric "externalizing behavior." In addition, patterns of coping can be activated that include a progression of mutually exclusive schemes of behavior, emotion, and orientation. Especially when multiple needs have been impinged upon, uncoordinated patterns of coping would be expected to emerge. For example, if all three needs are compromised, individuals may become aggressive, then flee, then freeze, then become aggressive again.

Development

In addition to facilitating analysis of the short-term outcomes of specific coping responses, the focus on reengagement provides a bridge to predictions about the long-term and global outcomes of different ways of coping. At the simplest level, one can select a long-term outcome and then consider the patterns of engagement that are most likely to produce it. For example, if the long-term outcome were school performance, then coping that facilitates a pattern of sustained behavioral involvement would be the most likely predictor. If one were interested in well-being, then patterns of coping that lead to positive short-term emotional outcomes would be likely candidates. If one were interested in somatic outcomes, one needs a theory of the antecedents of objective health. For example, if health is thought to be the result of prevention, behavioral compliance to medical procedures, and low emotional distress, then the primary predictors of health would be the coping responses that predict these short-term outcomes.

The long-term outcomes of coping can also be painted with broader brushstrokes. In the motivational theory, long-term outcomes correspond to the development promoted by the three needs: social development, cognitive development, and personality development. Corresponding to relatedness, social development is defined as the capacity to love and be loved. Corresponding to competence, cognitive development is defined as the ability to discover and understand how to produce desired outcomes and the capacities to execute those strategies. Corresponding to autonomy, personality development is defined as the construction of a coherent self that integrates one's unique talents and proclivities with the demands internalized from society.

All three kinds of development involve transformation of the context and transformation of the self. Both of these transformations are hypothesized to occur as a result of active, sustained, attentive interactions with the social and physical world. In other words, taken together with engagement, reengagement in the face of obstacles and setbacks is hypothesized to be a major mechanism for cognitive, personality, and social development. By the same token, children who never encounter challenges and stresses are robbed of opportunities to exercise and develop their skills and capacities. This also explains the "steeling" effects of encounters with stress. When stressful encounters are successfully negotiated, they produce developmental resources that are useful in subsequent encounters. As Rutter (1983) points out, "the long-term outcomes will be determined by how the stressors are dealt with at the time, and perhaps especially on whether the outcome of the stress encounter was successful adaptation or humiliating failure" (p. 31).

From this perspective, maladaptive long-term outcomes involve both stasis and the development of patterns of interaction that actively work against the fulfillment of the needs (psychopathology). Ways of coping that forestall development would include (a) coping responses that prevent, avoid, or curtail interactions with the social and physical environment (such as escape or procrastination); (b) coping responses that do not prevent interactions but burden them with so much negative affect that it is impossible for the individual to learn from or enjoy them (such as perseverence or obsession); and (c) coping responses that direct such interactions away from the fulfillment of needs (and toward other targets such as appearing autonomous (through aggression) or appearing related (through delegation)). Fleshing out the long-term adaptive and maladaptive developmental outcomes of coping responses will itself be a long-term proposition. However, specifying the short-term mediational links (i.e., behavioral, emotional, and orientational reengagement) may illuminate the mechanisms by which coping influences broad adaptational outcomes.

Effects of Coping on Objective Stress

The stresses children experience influence the way in which they cope. At the same time, children's responses to stressful events seem likely to influence the stressors they subsequently encounter (Rutter, 1983). On the most general level, the effects of coping on future stressful events are unmediated. If one studies, one is less likely to fail; if one does not plan ahead, one is more likely to run into trouble. Research shows that adults who cope ineffectively are more likely to experience stressful life events (Moos & Billings, 1982).

The effects of coping on stress can also be mediated by the response of the social context. Two models have been suggested for the ways in which contexts respond to individuals (Kindermann & Skinner, 1992). The first, and more optimistic, is the *compensatory model* in which social partners respond to children's maladaptive coping with increased involvement, structure, and autonomy support. Over time, such contexts help "repair" children's self-system processes and so encourage them to use new coping strategies. The second model is the *exacerbatory model* or "the rich get richer model" in which the social context responds to children's poor coping in ways that undermine coping further. It is easy to imagine how, in the academic domain, coping responses such as passivity and confusion would lead teachers to lower their expectations of children's competence and provide them with less challenging activities, thus undermining children's already low competence beliefs. Or, in the domain of family relations, it is easy to see how aggression, projection, and opposition could produce parental coercion, again exacerbating children's feelings of low autonomy. Finally, in the friendship domain, it is possible to see how children who are isolating and self-pitying could lead peers to ignore or actively reject them.

G. COPING AND DEVELOPMENT

Although the theory presented in this chapter was derived from a developmental perspective, it is far from being a developmental theory. In this section, we outline a developmental agenda, identifying issues that will need to be addressed theoretically and empirically before a developmental theory of coping processes can take shape (Maccoby, 1983).

Developmental Changes in Vulnerability to Stress

In her discussion of developmental changes in response to stress, Maccoby (1983) pointed out that although "it is unlikely that there is any linear increase or decrease with age in vulnerability to stress, . . . the nature of the events which are capable of producing stress reactions, and the nature of the coping responses that can be mobilized, do change drastically with age" (p. 219). The first challenge to a motivational perspective would be to identify the nature of events that constitute threats and challenges to relatedness, competence, and autonomy at different ages.

Three strategies may be useful in accomplishing this task. An analysis of the kinds of events that evoke protest and distress reactions at certain ages is one source of information. A second strategy would be to select a need and then to analyze how children's cognitive, social, and emotional capacities at certain ages would allow them to experience impingement of that need. A third source of age-related stressors can be found in the concept of developmental tasks. According to the current perspective, stressors include normative developmental tasks, such as learning to walk, eat, and dress alone, interacting with siblings, learning to follow rules and inhibit behavior, going to school, dealing with academic challenges, and venturing into peer relations. Whether children's navigation through these tasks leads to successful development or to psychopathology depends on how they view these events (appraisals) and how they cope with the inevitable setbacks and difficulties inherent in them.

Viewing developmental tasks as stressors sensitizes researchers to the potential for both challenge and threat in developmental tasks as well as the multiple directions in which these tasks can be resolved (Erikson, 1968). It takes a position in debates about whether increasingly normative life events such as divorce, full-time day care, moving, or self-care after school are stressors (Levine, 1983). According to this perspective, they are. How children experience and deal with them (i.e., whether they are distressing or are opportunities for developing new competencies) depends on a host of factors, including those described in this chapter. In addition, the focus on developmental tasks as potential stressors points out the importance of both coping responses and coping resources (personal and social) in predicting how these tasks will be resolved.

Finally, the domains in which children's needs for competence, autonomy, and relatedness are played out may also change with age. At the youngest ages, much of these take place within the family context. As children reach middle childhood, they are successively challenged in extra-familial domains, such as school, friendship, sports, and so on. Developmentally, domains may be differentially important as sources of need impingement. Rejection by peers is much less distressing to a preschooler than a middle-aged child. During adolescence, some children may give up their commitment to experiencing competence through participation in school and instead seek its fulfillment in peer networks.

Development of Coping

A descriptive theory of the development of coping is needed. It would begin with coping reactions at birth, taking seriously the defensive and aversive capabilities of infants (Lipsitt, 1983). The theory would describe the transformations by which these reactions become action patterns, and how these are in turn differentiated into coping appraisals, coping reactions, coping responses, and coping outcomes. Work will also need to focus on the emergence and transformation of self-regulated coping; discussions will be grounded in the rich literature on the development of behavioral and emotional self-regulation (Kopp, 1982, 1989) as well as on ego resilience and ego control (Block & Block, 1980).

At the core of these discussions will be a consideration of developmental changes and individual differences in the mechanisms of self-regulation. The present conceptualization can be used to generate an outline. At birth, distress reactions are regulated by hard-wired appraisals. Based on early interactions with challenges, infants would develop action patterns (complexes of behavior, emotion, and orientation). External structures would be essential in supporting coping responses at this age (Maccoby, 1983). With the onset of representational capacities, toddlers would develop rudimentary self-system processes in which the role of the self would be differentiated from the role of others. Individual differences in coping would begin to be based on interactions with the social context as mediated by these appraisals. As capacities to self-regulate emerge, regulation may first be mediated by other people, then by verbal means, and subsequently by cognitive reflection. At this point coping as self-regulation (as distinct from coping appraisals, reactions, and outcomes) would emerge.

One important developmental accomplishment would be the extent to which children are accurate in reporting which need(s) is being challenged or threatened by stressful events. Developmentally, children should become more capable of differentiating the dimensions of stressful contexts (neglect, chaos, coercion) with age. However, children may never develop the ability to accurately diagnose the source of the distress, especially if contexts have attempted to deny or distort the stresses to which they subject individuals. If differentiation of stress according to the needs does not occur, children will continue to experience a vague and uninformative generalized distress reaction to all stressful events (e.g., anxiety, fear, anger). On the other hand, differentiation may occur, but the mappings between contextual stressors and needs may not be accurate. For example, if relatedness and autonomy needs are crossed, coercion may be interpreted as a challenge to relatedness and result in proximity seeking. Such confusion or lack of differentiation among the needs cuts off information essential for shaping effective coping strategies.

Children's coping is expected to have effects on their social, cognitive, and personality development. These developments can themselves be seen as important "protective" factors that in turn influence how children cope. They buffer children against the actual occurence of stressful events by making it more likely that children will be able to get along well with parents, teachers, and peers, that they will succeed in school, and that they will be able to control their impulses. At the same time, the accomplishments produced by development in these three domains should promote children's self-system processes. These should, in turn, buffer children against the experience of psychological distress. Finally, developmental competencies should help children cope more effectively when confronting stress. Social development will increase the likelihood that children will have close relationships that they can use for help and comfort. Cognitive development ensures that children will be better able to problem solve and may have more strategies and solutions at their disposal. And personality development will allow children to use strategies that are more intentional and self-regulated.

Families and the Development of Coping

A developmental theory will have to consider carefully the role of the family in the shaping and support of children's coping. Although theories of coping are unanimous about the importance of close relationships, especially families and primary caregivers (Robins, 1983; Rutter, 1983), the current motivational model provides a differentiated explanation for this phenomenon. Specifically, the many functions close relationships serve in the process of coping can be distinguished.

First, they can be a source of objective stress for children. Glossaries of "stressful life events" often involve family members: drinking, drug use, child abuse, loss of a parent, divorce, and so forth. Second, families are the first line of defense in preventing stress from reaching children. Parents shield children from overwhelming stimulation, "childproof" the home, prevent others (e.g., siblings or peers) from coercing them, and in general structure challenges so that they are appropriate to the child's developmental level. Third, interactions with family members are the grist from which children's coping appraisals and coping responses are constructed. Especially at younger ages, families will influence how vulnerable children become to stress (threshold for and intensity of distress reactions) as well as shape their repertoire of coping responses. Fourth, these same interactions serve as the basis from which children's personal resources are formed (perceived control, security of relatedness, and autonomy orientation). Finally, parents act as social resources while children attempt to cope with challenges and threat.

V. Conclusions

Taken as a whole, this chapter can be seen as both a rationale for the importance of developing effective coping and as a blueprint for how to promote this development. Coping is posited to be important both for its effects on individual development and on interpersonal relationships. Effective coping, in addition to relieving children's short-term distress, is hypothesized to be an integral mechanism for their long-term social, cognitive, and personality development.

In terms of interventions aimed at facilitating coping, this theory makes clear that methods in which children are taught coping strategies or coping skills will be of limited use. Instead, the role of the social context is emphasized: in presenting challenges that are developmentally appropriate, in helping children develop personal resources that aid in effective coping, and in supporting children while they are coping. The concerted efforts of the child and of the child's social partners are needed to support the development of flexible, self-regulated, and adaptive repertoires of coping.

Acknowledgments

The authors wish to express their appreciation to James Connell, Edward Deci, and Richard Ryan, their colleagues in the Motivational Research Group, for their valuable contributions to the ideas contained in this chapter. The work of James Connell as a starting point for this chapter is especially appreciated. They also wish to thank the members of their research groups for their continuing challenges and support: Thomas Kindermann, Jeffery Altman, Hayley Sherwood, Michael Belmont, Cara Regan, and Marianne Miserandino. This work was supported by grant HD-19914 from the NICHHD. The authors would like to gratefully acknowledge the support of the W. T. Grant Foundation, which has encouraged research on stress and coping in children for many years, and we dedicate this chapter to its former president, Dr. Robert Haggerty.

References

Abramson, L. Y., Seligman, M. E. P., & Teasdale, J. D. (1978). Learned helplessness in humans: Critique and reformulation. *Journal of Abnormal Psychology, 87*, 49–74.

Ainsworth, M. D. S. (1979). Infant—mother attachment. *American Psychologist, 34*(10), 932–937.

Ainsworth, M. D. S. (1989). Attachments beyond infancy. *American Psychologist, 44*, 709–716.

Alloy, L. B., & Abramson, L. Y. (1979). Judgement of contingency in depressed and non-depressed students: Sadder but wiser? *Journal of Experimental Psychology: General, 108*(4), 441–485.

Ayers, T. S., Sandler, I. N., West, S. G., & Roosa, M. W. (1990). *Assessment of children's coping behaviors: Testing alternative models of coping.* Unpublished manuscript, Arizona State University.

Baltes, M. M., & Baltes, P. B. (Eds.). (1986). *Aging and the psychology of control.* Hillsdale, NJ: Lawrence Erlbaum Associates.

Band, E., & Weisz, J. R. (1988). How to feel better when it feels bad: Children's perspectives on coping with everyday stress. *Developmental Psychology, 24*, 247–253.

Bandura, A. (1977). Self-efficacy: Toward a unified theory of behavioral change. *Psychological Review, 84*, 191-215.

Baumrind, D. 91977). Current patterns of parental authority. *Developmental Psychology Monographs, 4*, 1-102.

Belle, D. (1982). The stress of caring: Women as providers of social support. In L. Goldberger & S. Breznitz (Eds.), *Handbook of stress: Theoretical and practical aspects* (pp. 496-505). New York: Free Press.

Billings, A. G., & Moos, R. H. (1984). Coping, stress, and social resources among adults with unipolar depression. *Journal of Personality and Social Psychology, 46*, 877-891.

Block, J. H., & Block, J. (1980). The role of ego-control and ego-resiliency in the organization of behavior. In W. A. Collins (Ed.), *Minnesota symposium on child psychology* (Vol. 13, pp. 39-101). Hillsdale, NJ: Lawrence Erlbaum Associates.

Bowlby, J. (1969). *Attachment and loss* (Vol. 1). New York: Basic.

Bowlby, J. (1973). *Attachment and loss* (Vol. 2). New York: Basic.

Carver, C. S., Scheier, M. F., & Weintraub, J. K. (1989) Assessing coping strategies: A theoretically based approach. *Journal of Personality and Social Psychology, 56*(2), 267-283.

Cohen, L. H., McGowan, J. Fooskas, S., & Rose, S. (1984). Positive life events and social support and the relationship between life stress and psychological disorder. *American Journal of Community Psychology, 12*, 564-587.

Compas, B. E. (1987). Coping with stress during childhood and adolescence. *Psychological Bulletin, 101*, 393-403.

Connell, J. P. (1985). A new multidimensional measure of children's perceptions of control. *Child Development, 56*, 1018-1041.

Connell, J. P. (1990). Context, self and action: A motivational analysis of self-system processes across the life-span. In D. Cicchetti (Ed.), *The self in transition: From infancy to childhood* (pp. 61-97). Chicago: University of Chicago Press.

Connell, J. P., & Wellborn, J. G. (1991). Competence, autonomy, and relatedness: A motivational analysis of self-system processes. In M. R. Gunnar & L. A. Sroufe (Eds.), *Minnesota symposium on child psychology: Vol. 23. Self processes in development* (pp. 43-77). Hillsdale, NJ: Lawrence Erlbaum Associates.

Crandall, V. C., Katkovsky, W., & Crandall, V. J. (1965). Children's beliefs in their control of reinforcement in intellectual academic achievement behaviors. *Child Development, 36*, 91-109.

deCharms, R. (1968). *Personal causation: The internal affective determinants of behavior*. New York: Academic.

Deci, E. L., & Ryan, R. M. (1985). *Intrinsic motivation and self-determination in human behavior*. New York: Plenum.

Deci, E. L., & Ryan, R. M. (1991). A motivational approach to self: Integration in personality. In R. Dienstbier (Ed.), *Nebraska symposium on motivation: Vol. 38. Perspectives on motivation* (pp. 237-288). Lincoln: University of Nebraska Press.

Dweck, C. S., & Leggett, E. L. (1988). A social-cognitive approach to motivation and personality. *Psychological Review, 95*, 256-273.

Dweck, C. S., & Wortman, C. B. (1982). Learned helplessness, anxiety and achievement motivation: Neglected parallels in cognitive, affective, and coping responses. In H. W. Krohne & L. Laux (Eds.), *Achievement, stress, and anxiety* (pp. 93-125). Washington, DC: Hemisphere.

Elias, M. J., Gara, M., Rothbaum, P. A., Reese, A. M., & Ubriaco, M. (1987). A multivariate analysis of factors differentiating behaviorally and emotionally dysfunctional children from other groups in school. *Journal of Clinical and Child Psychology, 16*, 307-312.

Endler, N. S., & Parker, J. D. A. (1990). Multidimensional assessment of coping: A critical evaluation. *Journal of Personality and Social Psychology, 58*, 844-854.

Erikson, E. H. (1968). *Identity: Youth and crisis.* New York: Norton.

Fleischman, J. A. (1984). Personality characteristics and coping patterns. *Journal of Health and Social Behavior, 25,* 229–244.

Folkman, S. (1984). Personal control and stress and coping processes: A theoretical analysis. *Journal of Personality and Social Psychology, 46,* 839–852.

Freud, S. (1927). *The ego and the id.* London: Hogarth.

Garmezy, N. (1983). Stressors of childhood. In N. Garmezy & M. Rutter (Eds.), *Stress, coping and development in children* (pp. 43–84). New York: McGraw-Hill.

Garmezy, N., & Rutter, M. (Eds.). (1983). *Stress, coping and development in children.* New York: McGraw-Hill.

Grolnick, W. S., Ryan, R. M., & Deci, E. L. (1989). Parent styles associated with children's self-regulation and competence in school. *Journal of Educational Psychology, 81,* 143–154.

Gunnar, M. R. (1980). Contingent stimulation: A review of its role in early development. In S. Levine & H. Ursin (Eds.), *Coping and health* (pp. 101–119). New York: Plenum.

Harter, S. (1983). Developmental perspectives on the self system. In E. M. Hetherington (Ed.), *Handbook of child psychology: Vol. 4. Socialization, personality, and social development* (4th ed., pp. 103–196). New York: Wiley.

Holahan, C. J., & Moos, R. H. (1987). Personal and contextual determinants of coping strategies. *Journal of Personality and Social Psychology, 52*(5), 946–955.

Kagan, J. (1983). Stress and coping in early development. In N. Garmezy & M. Rutter (Eds.), *Stress, coping and development in children* (pp. 191–215). New York: McGraw-Hill.

Kindermann, T. A., & Skinner, E. A. (1992). Modeling environmental development: Individual and contextual trajectories. In J. B. Asendorpf & J. Valsiner (Eds.), *Framing stability and change: An investigation into methodological reasoning* (pp. 155–190). Newbury Park, CA: Sage.

Kopp, C. (1982), Antecedents of self-regulation: A developmental perspective. *Developmental Psychology, 18*(2), 199–214.

Kopp, C. (1989). Regulation of distress and negative emotions: A developmental view. *Developmental Psychology, 25,* 343–354.

Lazarus, R. S., & Folkman, S. (1984). *Stress, appraisal, and coping.* New York: Springer.

Levine, S. (1983). A psychobiological approach to the study of coping. In N. Garmezy & M. Rutter (Eds.), *Stress, coping and development in children* (pp. 107–131). New York: McGraw-Hill.

Lipsitt, L. P. (1983). Stress in infancy: Toward understanding the origins of coping behavior. In N. Garmezy & M. Rutter (Eds.), *Stress, coping and development in children* (pp. 161–189). New York: McGraw-Hill.

Main, M., Kaplan, N., & Cassidy, J. C. (1985). Security in infancy, childhood and adulthood: A move to the level of representation. In I. Bretherton & E. Waters (Eds), *Growing points of attachment theory and research. Monographs of the SRCD, 50*(1–2, Serial No. 209), pp. 66–104.

Maccoby, E. E. (1983). Social-emotional development and response to stressors. In N. Garmezy & M. Rutter (Eds.), *Stress, coping and development in children* (pp. 217–234). New York: McGraw-Hill.

Maccoby, E. E., & Martin, J. A. (1983). Socialization in the context of the family: Parent–child interaction. In P. H. Mussen (Ed.), *Handbook of child psychology: Vol. 4. Socialization, personality, and social development* (pp. 1–101). New York: Wiley.

McClelland, D. C. (1951). *Personality.* New York: Sloane.

McCrae, R. R. (1982). Age differences in the use of coping mechanisms. *Journal of Gerontology, 37,* 454–560.

Mellor-Crummey, C. A. (1989). *Children's coping in social situations.* Unpublished doctoral dissertation, University of Rochester, Rochester, NY.

Miller, P. M., Danaher, D. L., & Forbes, D. (1986). Sex-related strategies for coping with interpersonal conflict in children aged five and seven. *Developmental Psychology* , *22*, 543-548.

Moos, R. H., & Billings, A. G. (1982). Conceptualizing and measuring coping resources and coping processes. In L. Goldberger & S. Breznitz (Eds.), *Handbook of stress: Theoretical and clinical aspects* (pp. 212-230). New York: Free Press.

Pearlin, L. I., & Schooler, C. (1978). The structure of coping. *Journal of Health and Social Behavior*, *19*, 2-21.

Robins, L. E. (1963). Some methodological problems and research directions in the study of the effects of stress on children. In N. Garmezy & M. Rutter (Eds.), *Stress, coping and development in children* (pp. 335-346). New York: McGraw-Hill.

Rohde, P., Tilson, M., Lewinson, P. M., & Seeley, J. R. (1990). Dimensionality of coping and its relation to depression. *Journal of Personality and Social Psychology*, *58*(3), 499-511.

Rosenbaum, M. (1980). A schedule for assessing self-control behavior: Preliminary findings. *Behavior Therapy*, *11*, 109-121.

Roth, S., & Cohen, L. J. (1986). Approach, avoidance, and coping with stress. *American Psychologist*, *41*, 813-819.

Rotter, J. B. (1966). Generalized expectancies for internal versus external control of reinforcement. *Psychological Monographs: General and Applied* , *80* (Whole No. 609).

Rutter, M. (1983). Stress, coping, and development: Some issues and some questions. In N. Garmezy & M. Rutter (Eds.), *Stress, coping and development in children* (pp. 1-41). New York: McGraw-Hill.

Ryan, R. M. (1982). Control and information in the intrapersonal sphere: An extension of cognitive evaluation theory. *Journal of Personality and Social Psychology*, *43*, 450-461.

Ryan, R. M., & Connell, J. P. (1989). Perceived locus of causality and internalization: Examining reasons for acting in two domains. *Journal of Personality and Social Psychology*, *57*, 749-761.

Seligman, M. E. P. (1975). *Helplessness: On depression, development, and death*. San Francisco: Freeman.

Selye, H. (1951). *Stress*. Montreal: Acta.

Silver, R. L., & Wortman, C. B. (1980). Coping with undesirable life events. In J. Garber & M. E. P. Seligman (Eds.), *Human helplessness: Theory and applications* (pp. 279-340). New York: Academic.

Skinner, E. A. (1991). Development and perceived control: A dynamic model of action in context. In M. R. Gunnar & L. A. Sroufe (Eds.) *Minnesota symposium on child psychology: Vol. 23. Self processes in development* (pp. 167-216). Hillsdale, NJ: Lawrence Erlbaum Associates.

Skinner, E. A., Altman, J., & Sherwood, H. (1991, July). *An analysis of open-ended interviews of children's coping in the domains of academics and friendship*. Paper presented at the biennial meetings of the International Society for the Study of Behavioral Development, Minneapolis.

Skinner, E. A., Altman, J., & Sherwood, H. (in preparation). *A catalogue of coping categories* Unpublished manuscript, University of Rochester, Rochester, NY.

Skinner, E. A., Chapman, M., & Baltes, P. B. (1988). Beliefs about control, means-ends, and agency: A new conceptualization and its measurement during childhood. *Journal of Personality and Social Psychology*, *54*, 117-133.

Skinner, E. A., & Wellborn, J. G. (1991, April). *How do children cope with challenges and failures during middle childhood and adolescence? The impact of perceived control*. Paper presented at the biennial meetings of the Society for Research in Child Development, Seattle.

Spirito, A., Overholser, J., Ashworth, S., Morgan, J., & Benedict-Drew, C. (1988). Evaluation of a suicide awareness curriculum for high school students. *Journal of the*

American Academy of Child and Adolescent Psychiatry, 27, 705-711.

Sroufe, L. A (1979). The coherence of individual development: Early care attachment and subsequent developmental issues. *American Psychologist, 34,* 834-841.

Suls, J. (1982). Social support, interpersonal relations, and health: Benefits and liabilities. In G. Sanders & J. Suls (Eds.), *Social psychology of health and illness.* Hillsdale, NJ: Lawrence Erlbaum Associates.

Tero, P. F., & Connell, J. P. (1984, April). *When children think they've failed: An academic coping inventory.* Paper presented at the annual meetings of the American Educational Research Association, New Orleans.

Watson, J. S. (1979). Perception of contingency as a determinant of social responsiveness. In E. B. Truman (Ed.), *Origins of the infant's social responsiveness* (pp. 33-64). Hillsdale, NJ: Lawrence Erlbaum Associates.

Weinberg, J., & Levine, S. (1980). Psychobiology of coping in animals: The effects of predictability. In S. Levine & H. Ursin (Eds.), *Coping and health* (pp. 39-59). New York: Plenum.

Weiner, B. (1979). A theory of motivation for some classroom experiences. *Journal of Educational Psychology, 71,* 3-25.

Wellborn, J. G. (1991). *Engagement versus disaffection: Motivated patterns of action in the academic domain.* Unpublished doctoral dissertation, University of Rochester, Rochester, NY.

White, R. W. (1959). Motivation reconsidered: The concept of competence. *Psychological Review, 66,* 297-333.

Aging, Personality, and Social Change: The Stability of Individual Differences Over the Adult Life Span

Duane F. Alwin

UNIVERSITY OF MICHIGAN

Abstract

The multidisciplinary Zeitgeist of American social science has witnessed numerous efforts to integrate psychological and sociological conceptions of human life-span development. The conceptual sweep of these efforts is often impressive, but seldom do these incorporate a commitment to verify existing hypotheses regarding various aspects of constancy and change in the empirical record. Taking the investigation of *human stability* as theoretically and empirically problematic, this article proposes a framework for integrating what is known about patterns of stability over the life span. This framework focuses explicitly on the introduction of the concept of *molar stability*, the persistence of a behavior or behavioral orientation as expressed in age-homogenous rates of change over specified periods of time, as a means of organizing empirical information on human constancy and change. The approach taken to the estimation of molar stability solves three problems that have plagued past researches on the question of lifespan trajectories of stability. First, using a latent variable model, the approach insists on the unconfounding of measurement errors and true change. Second, this model can be used to assess differences in stability between occasions of measurement in longitudinal studies of the same individuals, or within age groups of reinterview studies of shorter duration in order to ascertain life-span trajectories of stability. The model is extremely useful in conjuction with a *synthetic-cohort* approach, as stability estimates can be generated across several groups of cohorts varying in age, with an eye toward estimating different trajectories of human stability within panels that have considerable heterogeneity in age. Third, this approach allows us a method by which one can not only compare estimates of stability across cohorts differing in age, but also compare molar stability estimates across concepts, or content domains of personality, as well as across different studies using different remeasurement designs. Using this approach, six different prototypic models of human stability are introduced—the *persistence, lifelong openness, increasing persistence, impressionable years, mid-life stability*, and *decreasing persistence* models—and their descriptive applicability to several relevant domains is considered. Longitudinal assessments of intelligence and personality traits reveal relatively high levels of stability from early adulthood to old age, whereas extant evidence on the stability of identities, self-image, and attitudes appear to follow either the impressionable years or mid-life stability models, in which constancies in behavioral orientations are substantially lowest in young adulthood, but reach a peak in midlife, and from there either persist or decline in stability through the mature years.

I. Introduction

Humans are usually assumed to be susceptible to influence in their early years, but are thought to become increasingly stable in important respects with age, remaining resistant to change throughout most of the adult life course. This assumption is rooted in the ideas, first, that the personalities of humans by their nature are malleable mainly early in life and grow increasingly "persistent," "rigid," or "conservative" with age, and second, that opportunities for change are linked to the life cycle, generally declining with age.[1] Assumptions about the *stability* of individuals can often be seen to underlie theories of social change, where change is posited to occur at least in part via processes of cohort replacement. Such *cohort succession* models of social change frequently assume highly stable development of individuals (see, e.g., Inglehart, 1990).

Despite the pervasiveness of such theoretical assumptions of human stability, not everyone agrees. Another, contrasting perspective that has emerged over the past few decades, one that stresses the inherent potential in humans for change and adaptation to new circumstances, assumes considerably less stability. The very concept of stability seems anathema

---

[1]As becomes clear later, I prefer the term *stability* rather than other less precise terms, such as *persistence, rigidity*, or *conservative*. Many such terms convey essentially the same meaning as stability, but frequently connote human agency, as in the case of persistence, suggest negative traits or qualities in the case of rigidity, or suggest political ideology in the case of conservative.

from the point of view of human development, which implies continual change (see Wohlwill, 1980). Human experience is thought to be character- ized by a *lifelong openness to change*, rather than growing stability (e.g., Brim & Kagan,1980; Lerner, 1984). According to this view, individuals are inherently *plastic* throughout virtually the entire adult life course, and given the potential for social influences on individuals over the life span, human development is essentially"open-ended," with little predictability of human characteristics over time. This perspective suggests that human development is *aleatoric* in the sense that early influences on behavioral tendencies may be just as likely to dissipate as to hold firm (Gergen, 1980; Gergen & Gergen, 1987). Thus, distinct cohort experiences may exist and distinguish a "generation" for a time, but such intercohort differences may not persist through historical time. From this perspective social change is more likely to occur via individual-level changes within cohorts rather than being due to systematic differences between them. Although this view is increasingly prevalent among life-span developmentalists, the evidence supporting it is not at all clear-cut.

Each of the aforementioned contrasting images of social change make different assumptions about the nature of human beings, and each of these images of patterns of human development make different assumptions about the nature of society's influence upon the individual.[2] This chapter focuses on the question of the stability of individual differences over the life span, seeking empirical verification of the hypotheses outlined at the be- ginning, which refer to lifespan variations in the stability of human dispo- sitions. Each of these perspectives may be true to some extent, and depending on the particular domains of human functioning considered, the evidence may point to differing conclusions. As a point of departure, I assume that both perspectives are valid and worthy of scientific scrutiny – the essential questions concern the stability of relevant dimensions of personality/ individual differences, that is, the relation between different aspects of personality/individual differences and their trajectories of stability.[3]

[2]This work is part of a larger program of research, the goal of which is to integrate what is known, both empirically and in terms of theoretical development, about the stability and change of individuals, cohorts and society, and to develop a unified perspective on issues of life-span stability and change within a framework for considering macrolevel social stability and change (see Alwin, 1993b).

[3]Although I take a risk in doing so, I here use the term *personality* as essentially "boundaryless" in the sense that I would like to bring potentially *all* human dispositions and behavioral orientations into the discussion (see, e.g., Gilligan, Brown, & Rogers, 1990; House, 1981). However, the implicit interdisciplinary nature of this campaign may prove to be more all-encompassing than what is justified on the basis of cross-disciplinary agreement on concepts, methods, and procedures. Further, and perhaps more devastating, are the limitations and inconsistencies in longitudinal data for addressing questions of stability across such diverse domains implied by this definition of personality. Still, I think it is short-sighted to limit any

II. Conceptions of Human Stability

The idea that individuals are predictable beings, capable of a high degree of consistency of behavior across situations, is a deeply held belief in most cultures. But it is also a question of considerable theoretical interest, given the possibility of situational determinants of behavior. Even as there is little diversity in the nature of cultural beliefs about the constancy of personality, there is debate among psychologists about the extent to which"personality dispositions" are indeed constant over time and across situations (Epstein & O'Brien, 1985). Hypotheses about personality stability over the life span have stimulated considerable research and several excellent reviews are available, although there is a wide array of opinion and judgment on these matters (see Bengtson, Reedy, & Gordon, 1985; Caspi, 1987; Caspi & Bem, 1990; Costa, McCrae, & Arenberg, 1983; Gergen, 1980; Gergen & Gergen, 1987; Moss & Susman, 1980; Sears, 1981, 1990; Stewart & Healy, 1989; Wells & Stryker, 1988).

A. VARIETIES OF STABILITY IN INDIVIDUAL DIFFERENCES

What is meant by stability in relation to human development? As noted, development implies change, so what can be meant by the concept of stability? Consider Jerome Kagan's (1980) discussion of the definition of stability and continuity with respect to psychological development. Kagan maintained a distinction between *stability* and *continuity*, the former referring to "persistence of psychological structures and behavior" and the latter referring to the"maintenance of psychological processes or functions" (pp. 31–32). Asendorph (1992) suggested that if the particular personality continuum has the same meaning at different points in the life span, this suggests continuity of process and function, whereas the question of stability refers to preservation of the rank order of members of a population over time. In other words, stability and continuity are confounded. For the present purposes I assume there is individual-level continuity in the main, but I take the question of stability as problematic. Based on Kagan's (1980) discussion of the various meanings of stability, I suggest there are four possible meanings of stability, each of which is associated with a unique empirical research strategy:

discussion of personality to just those concepts that have heretofore been considered by personality researchers, and because the issues span a much broader terrain, it is my strong preference to include, rather than exclude, dimensions of human orientations. Thus, lacking a better designation for the conceptual domain of focus, I simply equate the term *personality* with *individual differences*.

1. *Normative stability:*[4] The preservation of a set of individual ranks on a quality within a constant population over a specified amount of time.
2. *Ipsative stability:* The persistence of a hierarchical relation between complementary dispositions within an individual over a specified amount of time.
3. *Molar stability:* The persistence of a behavior or behavioral orientation as expressed in the rate of rate of change in that quality for an age-homogenous cohort over a specified period of time.
4. *Structural stability:* The necessary and contingent relation between distinct structures or functions at two points in time as expressed in constancies in relationships among measured qualities.

These types of stability have also been identified by others, although they are often given different names (see, e.g., Caspi & Bem, 1990; Costa & McCrae, 1980; Kagan, 1980; Mortimer, Finch, & Kumka, 1982). Social and behavioral scientists studying these processes typically rely on what I here refer to as normative stability or the persistence of individual differences over time in some population of interest. This is the approach followed by a number of researchers, whose purpose it is to gauge the amount of aggregate stability, in a trait for that population during some period of time (e.g., Converse & Markus, 1979; Costa & McCrae, 1980; de Graaf, Hagenaars, & Luijkx, 1989; Inglehart, 1985; Kohn & Schooler, 1983; Kohn & Slomcynski, 1990)). Estimating the aggregate amount of stability does not explicitly take into account the levels of stability that might be associated with aging, and for that reason, this approach to defining stability is of little use for our present purposes. Obviously, any of these types of stability may be of interest and any of them may be operationalized within longitudinal research designs, but the use of such designs may require greater thought and imagination than has been the case in the past. Rogosa (1988) presented a compelling set of arguments against the ways in which most social and behavioral scientists approach longitudinal research, and although not all of his criticisms apply to many uses of longitudinal designs, some of them do. For example, Rogosa discussed the limitations of the two-wave design for analysis of rates of change representing individual growth, arguing that they may give deceptive information regarding the amount of individual change and its relation to growth and development. In Rogosa's words, "designs with only two observations are usually inadequate for the study of individual growth

---

[4]The terms used here to identify these aspects of stability are mine, not Kagan's (1980). He used the term *normative stability* for what I call *molar stability*, and I use the term *normative* to refer to *molar stability* in the aggregate.

and individual differences in growth" (p. 177). If one focuses purely on normative stability, this observation is potentially correct, but the use of the concept of molar stability as an approach to defining differential rates of change over the life course may have fewer problems. Certainly, Rogosa's argument is valid for those who are inferring something about life-span trajectories of stability from estimates of normative or aggregate stability.

In this chapter I focus only on the concept of *molar stability*, the rate of change in a characteristic within a specific age-homogeneous cohort. As is pointed out later, it is highly desirable to talk about age-linked (or life-cycle driven) rates of change for specific historical periods (see Alwin, Cohen, & Newcomb, 1991; Nesselroade, 1990), but social scientists are rarely able to collect such data. The point is: In the best of all worlds it would be desirable to estimate time-specific/cohort-specific rates of change in relevant characteristics, over enough time periods to be able to subject estimates of molar stability rates to a kind of "age, period, and cohort" analysis (see Mason & Fienberg, 1985), but as it is, this happens so rarely that we are left in a position where it is advantageous to ignore time period (but see Alwin & Krosnick, 1991a; Alwin et al., 1991).

Most discussions of the extent of stability in human ideation, emotion, and behavioral orientations take the view that the level of stability falls somewhere on a continuum subtended by two extremes. On the one hand, human characteristics may be only randomly linked over time—following Gergen's (1980) aleatoric image that developmental trajectories are traceable to the "accidental composite of existing circumstances" (p. 37). On the other hand, after some early period of vulnerability to change, human tendencies become highly stabilized patterns of consistent responses to the environment, often characterized in terms of selective exposure and resistence to change (e.g., Caspi & Elder, 1988). According to this view, the individual's orientations exhibit a great degree of stability in the face of experiences that stimulate reevaluation and change. For any given dimension (trait, disposition, state, etc.) either of these models may accurately describe the level of stability at a given point in the life cycle. Thus, it is important for our present purposes to phrase this issue from a life-span developmental perspective—that is, individual differences may vary in their stability at different "stages" in the life cycle and it may be futile to order such traits as tending either toward stability or instability. Rather, the question I address is one of degrees of stability, in the sense of a rate of change across all periods of the life cycle. I use the concept of *molar stability* to refer to age-specific rates of change in human characteristics.

B. AGING, COHORTS, AND HUMAN STABILITY

The understanding of stability and change in human development is difficult because the factors shaping it are a complex mixture of events that occur along two time lines, *biographical time*, events involving biological/ maturational changes over the life span of the individual, as well as changes in social roles and experiences, and *historical time*, the occurrence of events in time affecting large numbers of persons, but unrelated, in theory, to individuals' positions with respect to their own biographies (Riley, 1973). If one notices changes over the lifetime of an individual, or over a group of individuals, the understanding of these changes is complicated by the confounding of events in biographical and historical time. Because of this confounding it is difficult to separate aging or life-stage explanations of change from historical explanations — those referring to the period in which particular biographies are embedded.

Furthermore, the study of human development is even more complicated because of the intersection of historical and biographical time in people's lives. The fact that people pass through certain stages in their development at a specific point in historical time, the events of which have unique influences on the course of individual development, presents an even more complex picture of the factors shaping experience through time. Some have referred to these unique influences of the intersection of historical and biographical time as "generational" (Mannheim, 1952) or "cohort" effects (Ryder, 1965; Carlsson & Karlsson, 1970). Aging/life-stage explanations are, thus, confounded not only with historical or period explanations, but also with explanations referring to unique cohort experiences. Therefore, the inexorable processes inherent in individual movement through the life cycle in the context of a particular set of social circumstances, themselves continually changing, reflect the intertwining of processes of social change and processes of individual change. Their separate influences on human development are extremely difficult, if possible at all, to disentangle, and this means that several plausible explanations potentially exist for any one set of observations regarding human stability (Alwin et al., 1991).

I, like others, undertake this discussion with the assumption that social change occurs via one or both of two major mechanisms — sets of factors that influence intercohort differences and those that affect intracohort change. As can be shown, this is an algebraic equivalence, because social change can be mathematically partitioned into two orthogonal components, one representing *intracohort change* and one *intercohort change* (see Firebaugh, 1989; Rodgers, 1991). If "pure" cohort differences exist for individual differences in the realm of behavioral predispositions, it is important to inquire about how processes of human development impinge thereupon. Does the existence of "cohort effects" presume a high degree of individual stability after some early point in the life cycle? If individuals, however, are not stable creatures, are cohort differences any more (or less) likely to exhibit stability? If individuals are unstable in their orientations to social objects, situations, and actors over time, is there anything to be gained in hypothesizing that cohort differences might account for social change via processes of cohort replacement? In the following section of the chapter I review several different patterns of molar stability over the life span.

C. TRAJECTORIES OF STABILITY OVER THE LIFE SPAN

The relationship between aging and human stability is not very well understood. There is considerable theory on this subject, as indicated previously, but the necessary empirical database is lacking in a number of ways. Obviously, the stability patterns of individuals are capable of following any number of different trajectories. In Fig. 1 I present six different "pictures" of human stability in adulthood. In each depiction the magnitude of stability is charted with respect to age in adulthood. These models refer to preadult periods only with respect to the issue of whether or not habits and dispositions are carried forward in stable fashion from the end of the preadult period. What is depicted is the expected level of stability in a particular period, that is, how stable a characteristic is expected to be during a given segment of the life span under a particular stability regime. Thus, in Model A, which I refer to as the *persistence model,* a uniformly high level of stability is depicted over each period in the adult life cycle. For convenience I am here using a set of 8-year periods to gauge the level of stability. In this first model the expected magnitude, on a scale ranging from 0 to 1, over each such 8-year period is seen to be at a relatively high level (.9) throughout the life span. This model, thus, depicts a high level of

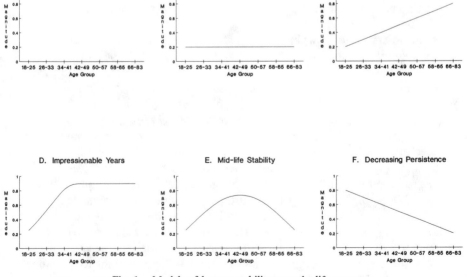

Fig. 1. Models of human stability over the life span.

stability that is uniform with respect to age. Traits for which such patterns are observed would seemingly represent a very high level of stability.[5] According to such a persistence view (see also Block, 1971, 1977, 1981; Moss & Susman, 1980), individual cognitive, emotional, interpersonal, political, ideological, moral and other aspects of human functioning are quite stable throughout the adult years (see Model A).

Citing the lack of evidence for high degrees of continuity in early life, Gergen (1980) proposed an aleatoric account of human constancy–a perspective on development that calls attention to the inherent potential for adjustment and adaptation to changes in the social environment. In his words, "existing (developmental) patterns appear potentially evanescent, the unstable result of the particular juxtaposition of contemporary historical events. For any individual the life course seems fundamentally open-ended. Even with full knowledge of the individual's past experience, one can render little more than a probabalistic account of the broad contours of future development" (pp. 34–35). The entire life span, thus, represents a period of intensity of influence and change. This view on development defines one end of the continuum of theoretical positions that are commonly taken with regard to human development, namely that "human developmental trajectories may be virtually infinite in their variegation" (Gergen, 1980, p. 37). The depiction of stability in Model B similarly reveals a great degree of uniformity in stability with respect to age, but a much lower magnitude of such stability (.2). This model conforms to one version of the lifelong openness view of developmental change, where considerable individual change occurs over time, but it is just as likely in old age as it is in young adulthood.[6] This model is compatible with "state" concepts, as opposed to "traits," those aspects of human behavior that may not be trans-situational, or stable for long periods of time (see Nesselroade, 1988b). I agree with Nesselroade, who argued that the joint focus on traits and states enriches the understanding of human behavior and behavior change. The purpose of the present undertaking is primarily to advance knowledge about the nature of the dimensions of human behavior and orientation that operate as states and that operate as traits. Or, to put it more precisely, where on the continuum

---

[5]Note that if the "average" or "typical" level of stability over an 8-year period (say age 18–25 years inclusive) is .9, the year-to-year stability on average is .987. Subsequently, I discuss the problem of gauging stability. This is an especially important methodological issue, given the variety of time spans used in research on human stability, and the variety of different quantities calculated to indicate levels of stability.

[6]Note that the average 1-year stability corresponding to an 8-year stability of .2 is .818, which may seem relatively high as a 1-year stability, but projected over 8 years at this rate of change, the level of stability is quite low. One thing that is learned from dealing with such stability coefficients is that 1-year stabilities need to be extremely high in order to project out as highly stable over much longer periods.

between these extremes do various dimensions of human orientation fall with respect to issues of stability? For example, if a behavioral orientation has a strong trait component, this would presumably render it highly stable, whereas if there were also a state component, this would tend to make it less so. Differences in stability can be viewed in terms of the relative balance of the trait and state components to a behavior.

For still others, the establishment of personality or "character" is not fully accomplished until early adulthood and vulnerability to influence or change persists through early adulthood. But after that stage, many scholars argue, stability or constancy in human behavior and functioning is characteristic. Figure 1 depicts two models (Models D and E) that portray high levels of change in young adulthood, but a growth in stability reaching a high level thereafter, and then leveling off (Model D), or returning to "youthful" levels of stability in old age (Model E). In these two instances the youngest adult years are viewed as ones in which individuals are particularly vulnerable to change, but reach high levels of stability during middle adulthood or soon thereafter. In Model D—the *impressionable years* model—the level of stability remains high throughout the remainder of the life span, a model that is perhaps most similar to the persistence view of human development, but that posits the development of high degrees of stability much later. This model converges with what I take to be the most prominent view of the relationship between individual development and macro social change, which, as stated at the outset, contains three distinct elements: (a) the impressionable years hypothesis, which holds that youth or young adulthood are periods of greatest mutability, (b) the stability hypothesis, which states that after some early point in adult life most human characteristics become relatively stable, remaining so throughout the adult life span, and (c) the hypothesis that social change occurs via the turnover in cohorts, with each cohort potentially bearing different traits and/or world views, and thus, changing the aggregate nature of society through cohort succession and replacement.

In Model E, by contrast, levels of stability in old age return to those experienced in youth. I refer to this as the *mid-life stability* model, in that it is most compatible with theoretical arguments asserting that there are greater opportunities for change in both early and late adulthood, owing to the greater likelihood of experiencing life events or life-cycle changes during those two periods (Wilensky, 1981).[7] Thus, there may be more than one critical period of vulnerability to changes across the life span.

Two additional models of age-graded human stability portray processes

---

[7]In earlier publications (e.g., Alwin, 1993c; Alwin et al., 1991), I referred to this as the "life-stage change" model to reflect the assumed causal factors involved in this pattern of stability. On the advice of a reviewer, I now use the more descriptive term, *mid-life stability*.

of more or less regular or linear (or at least monotonically increasing/ decreasing) increases/decreases in human stability over time. The *aging-stability* or *increasing persistence* model (Model C in Fig. 1) is critically different from the preceding two models, in that it posits continued changes over time in the nature of human stability. This model is quite common in many discussions of age and stability (see Glenn, 1980; Lorence & Mortimer, 1985; Mortimer, Finch, & Murayama, 1988; Mortimer et al., 1982). Writing about attitude development Sears (1981), for example, suggested that with time an "affective mass" is developed in the attitude structure, making "change progressively more difficult with age" (pp. 186–187). According to this aging-stability model, human traits are least stable among more youthful cohorts, and tend to be increasingly stable in older ones. This model provides a useful baseline against which to compare other models of stability.[8] A final model (F) reverses the process of change, by positing a process of or *aging-instability* or *decreasing persistence*, a loosening up of behavioral tendencies over time, the opposite of a growing conservatism or rigidity with age.

Concepts of Stability in Theories of Human Development.   As several reviewers of previous versions of this chapter pointed out, the aforementioned conceptual apparatus does not appear to take developmental conceptions of continuity and change into account. The classical literatures from biology and psychology are often organized by attention to qualitative and quantitative shifts in the organizing and processual principles of the entity under study. The most obvious, if also the most egregiously overgeneralized, pattern of development is the theoretical view consisting of progressive sequences along one or more axes of differentiation, for example, Eriksonian differentiation, or Piagetian/Kohlbergian stages of development. From this perspective development connotes more than a technical property of constancy/change; it implies more than the issue of duration dependence, even though every pattern of development necessarily involves some potential linkage involving duration dependence with respect to some prior qualitative or quantitative state. This progressive epigenetic unfolding of sequences of stages of development is not captured by the aforementioned concept of molar stability, nor is there any intention to supplant such developmental conceptions with an empirically derived set of stability trajectories.

---

[8]Although we describe such a model as linear, it need not be so. The model might be best thought of as having a variety of forms, all showing essentially a monotonic relationship between attitude stability and age. Sears and his colleagues (Sears & Weber, 1988) suggested that political socialization may actually proceed in "fits and starts," reflecting a more jagged, or steplike relationship with time, but the net relationship with age would be monotonically increasing.

However, little, if any, large-scale empirical work has tried to capture the constancy of personality as seen from such developmental conceptions, so we are left primarily with theories rather than facts. I would assert, however, that if developmentalists were to attend to the empirical issues of stability assessment, greater confidence could be placed in such notions of life-span development and change. For these purposes one might return to the distinction drawn by Asendorpf (1992) between continuity and stability (see earlier discussion) and consider the possibility that the issue of developmental sequences may be best viewed as an issue of continuity, whereas the issue of stability refers to constancies that occur within the framework of overarching consistencies in developmental stage and sequence. And from this point of view the developmental issues may be best considered to be matters involving structural stability.

D. INDIVIDUAL DIFFERENCES IN THE POTENTIAL FOR CHANGE VERSUS DIFFERENCES IN OPPORTUNITIES FOR CHANGE

Theoretical conceptions of human development differ in their specification of the nature of the individual, the influences of the social environment on the individual, the timing of those influences, and the persistence of these influences. Sears (1981) recounted the story told about the Jesuits, who believed that they could control a person's thinking for life if they were able to control their education up to the age of 5 years. This view is compatible with theoretical perspectives that assume there are "critical" stages in which the environment has an impact on the individual and that the "earliest" experiences are the most powerful in terms of their lasting influences on human tendencies. As suggested in the foregoing, other perspectives also stress critical stages, but place the molding of human tendencies to be later in life. A picture of human development is frequently drawn that establishes some aspects of the individual's personality rather later in life, not until age 30 or 35 years, but then set "like plaster" throughout the remainder of the life span (James, 1950/1890, p. 121). It is interesting to note that, despite strong theoretical claims regarding the permanency of attitude orientations after early "generational" socialization experiences (e.g., Mannheim, 1952), some have argued that attitudes may in fact be the least stable of all human traits (e.g., Moss & Susman, 1980).

Theories concerning life-span development of personality can be grouped into three distinct categories. One regards personality as a set of stable predispositions, acquired relatively early in life, and reflected in a number of consistencies or regularities in identities and behavior. Another views personality in terms of systematic changes that result from traversing an ordered sequence of epigenetic stages. A third is one that views personality as having some constancies, but also as inherently flexible and able to take on a variety of different forms over the span of life (see Gergen, 1980). These theories are not necessarily incompatible. There is a general sense in which it is possible that there are both constancies in behavior and changes in personality, due either to epigenetic changes or to changes in the social structuring of behavior (or both), and thus, these various theories can be viewed in terms of degrees of emphasis on life-cycle differences in susceptibility versus opportunity for change. One approach is to consider personality as by definition those behavioral orientations of the person that are stable. As Moss and Susman (1980) put it, "the very concept of personality implies a differentiated and organized hierarchy of psychological sets and behavioral dispositions that are manifested as consistent and enduring patterns in denoting the uniqueness of the individual" (p. 73). Another approach is to define the constancies in personality in terms of the stability of the person's interpersonal environment (Sullivan, 1953).

In order to bring some clarity to this theoretical variegation in views of the stability of personality, elsewhere (see Alwin et al., 1991) we have introduced a theoretical distinction between two complementary sources of stability and change of individuals over time. We noted that factors leading to stability of behavioral orientations may reside both in the person and in the environment. Individuals, we argued, may differ in their *susceptibility* to change, that is, something inherently different among individuals in their predispositions to stability and change. Or, individuals may differ in the *opportunities* for change presented by the social environment. We contrasted explanations of human stability and change that rely on *personological* factors that might implicate differential tendencies of individuals to resist or incorporate change with those *sociological* explanations that target differences in environmentally based experiences in accounting for change and stability (see Elder & Caspi, 1990; Wells & Stryker, 1988).

E. PERSONOLOGICAL EXPLANATIONS OF STABILITY

Psychologists have argued for many years that, despite individual growth and development, continuity exists in personality development, although there is considerable diversity in theoretical perspectives on the nature of this continuity. Some empirical data exist on the stability of aspects of personality from early childhood (e.g., Bloom, 1964; Kagan & Moss, 1962), and other data exist on the stability of aspects of personality in adult life (e.g., Caspi, Bem, & Elder, 1989; Caspi, Elder, & Bem, 1987, 1988; Costa & McCrae, 1980); however as I point out in greater detail later on, the available studies do not always provide consistent results. Nonetheless, the question of whether there are individual differences in susceptibility to change, which relate to personality differences in stability, presents an interesting theoretical explanation of findings concerning the extent of stability and change in behavioral orientations (see, e.g., Feather, 1979; Rokeach, 1960; Wilson, 1973).

Some psychologists have argued that personality differences in openness to change may be linked to the nature of cognitive organization. With regard to attitudes, for example, Rokeach (1968) used the concept of *centrality of attitudes* as a way of thinking about the nature and organization of attitudes and their likelihood of change. This theory hypothesizes that some attitude issues or domains of ideation are more central to the individual than others because of their salience or importance.[9] As such, central attitudes form the basis of the nature and organization of other attitudes and opinions, and because of their central role in attitude organization, they are more resistent to change. Elsewhere (Alwin et al., 1991) we considered the possibility that there are personality differences in openness to change and that levels of change may be more likely among some persons than others. In this regard, we considered Rokeach's concept of the centrality of attitudes as a way of conceptualizing the nature and organization of attitudes. However, in several different operationalizations of the concept of attitude centrality, we found little support for this theory as an explanation of patterns of stability of attitudes (see Alwin et al., 1991, chapter 8).[10]

Similar to theories of stability relying on the conception of enduring personality orientations that govern behavioral orientations over the life span, symbolic interaction conceptions of the "self" and "identities" have suggested that constancies in the self over the life span create a set of organizing principles that endure in behavioral orientations. Wells and Stryker (1988) suggested that *identity theory*, as derived from "structural symbolic interactionism," may be used to help understand the subjective changes in age-linked identities attendant to age-linked transitions between social roles and statuses. Individual selves and biographies are viewed as reflecting general sequences of identity transitions over the life span, but identity theory argues that constancies and/or change in the self reflects constancies/change in social relationships linked to a person's social

---

[9]To an extent, this is a tautology. On the one hand, "central attitudes" are defined as those attitudes that do not change. On the other hand, if one finds attitudes that do not change, it is commonly concluded that they do not change because of their greater centrality to cognitive organization. Despite this ambiguity in defining centrality independently of attitude change, this is nonetheless an important theoretical possibility.

[10]There is some evidence based on the National Election Study panel data collected during the 1980 and 1984 American presidential election campaigns that "important" attitudes change less than "unimportant" ones (Krosnick, 1988). Unfortunately, these results were based on relatively short periods of time (4 months), and are consequently of less interest to us here. We are interested in differences in stability over major periods of the life course.

locations. At the same time, this theory argues that "salient identities" lead to perceptual and other selective cognitive processes that reinforce stability of the self (see Caspi & Elder, 1988). Although the potential for change may be endemic, realities of various socially structured constraints impede and may largely prevent (or make highly improbable) actual change. The relevance of the self for consistency in behavioral orientations is clear, and identity theory can assist in understanding tendencies toward both stability and instability. The question for the present investigation is whether the empirical research literature on the self and identities can support one or another hypothesized trajectory of stability suggested earlier.

F. OPPORTUNITIES FOR HUMAN STABILITY AND CHANGE

As our previous conceptualization suggests, factors leading to stability of habits, traits, and orientations over time may reside either in the person or in the environment, or both. Thus, individual differences in predispositions to stability, or differences in one's social environment that form and sustain behavior and human functioning, each contribute to change and stability of orientations. An example of the distinctions we are making may be useful. On the one hand, persons may be more susceptible to change when they are young, during the impressionable years, or because of personality factors, or other aspects of individual differences. On the other hand, differential exposure to certain events and experiences — such as exposure to a new educational reforms, or such as hearing public speeches in favor of a particular political viewpoint, or such as being exposed to a changing network of social support — may bring about change independent of factors linked to age-related susceptibility to change on the part of the individual. At least one prominent theory of personality actually defines its stability in terms of enduring properties of the interpersonal environment (Sullivan, 1953; see also Wells & Stryker, 1988).

Several theoretical statements have been made about the key ordered changes involving role transitions across the life cycle. Neugarten and Peterson (1957) identified four major adult life stages, each involving differing developmental tasks and life-course issues — young adulthood, maturity, middle age, and old age. The first is, of course, the stage in which most scholars agree contains the most instability in behavioral orientations. This period is characterized by a number of unique circumstances — the transition to adulthood, the completion of schooling, the beginning of a work career, the likelihood of marriage, children, and family-related life events — that all promote great opportunity for change. These circumstances impinge on people at a time in their lives when they may be the most vulnerable to change and otherwise impressionable. The second adult life stage (see Fig. 1) is one in which, according to the *generational persistence* model, a high level of stability is achieved. As indicated by the name given it — maturity — the individual reaches a level of commitment to a set of activities and values. Middle age and old age can also be characterized in terms of continuity rather than change, but there is actually little known about the degree of stability in old age (e.g., Riley, 1987). One hypothesis is that among those experiencing the most numerous and frequent role transitions, stability will be estimated to be lower as a consequence (Glenn, 1980; Steckenrider & Cutler, 1989). If this hypothesis is supported, then a role-transition explanation might be plausible for the life-cycle patterns of stability sometimes found (e.g. Alwin & Krosnick, 1991a; Alwin et al., 1991).

Opportunities for change may vary over the life course, but they also vary over historical time (see, e.g., Elder & Caspi, 1988b, 1990). In going even further, Gergen (1973, 1980) argued that life-cycle theories of development may simply be "contemporary" theories of social behavior, primarily a reflection of contemporary history. Unlike the natural sciences, Gergen argued, principles of human interaction "cannot readily be developed because the facts on which they are based do not generally remain stable" (p. 310). This perspective is also shared by Looft (1973), who concluded that "developmental psychologists [no longer] should focus so exclusively on ontogenetic age functions; each new generation will manifest age trends that are different from those that preceed it, and thus, previous empirical endeavors are reduced to exercises of futility" (p. 51).

But is there no basis in the available research evidence for transhistorical generalizations? It is not possible to generate any lawlike principles of life-course development, specifically in our present case with respect to stability? In answering this question, it should perhaps be noted first that Gergen (1973) made an important qualification regarding the scope of his assertions (a qualification not also found in the 1980 version of this argument). He noted that social phenomena "vary considerably in the extent to which they are subject to historical change" (p. 318). Some phenomena may be "closely tied to physiological givens," and therefore resist the effects of historical change. He gave examples of research on emotional states that appear to depend strongly on physiological propensities for behavior and acquired dispositions that are "sufficiently powerful that neither enlightenment nor historical change" are likely to have a major influence on the behavior in question. On the other hand, some phenomena may be vastly more open to environmental influences, and thus, may show less historical durability. Gergen suggested thinking in terms of a "*continuum of historical durability* with phenomena highly susceptible to historical influence at one extreme and the more stable processes at the other" (p. 318).

Gergen (1973, 1980) has not been explicit regarding where various categories of human orientations would fall along a continuum of historical durability, although others have advanced strong hypotheses about lifelong stability of various human traits. It is clear that some identities stabilize relatively early and never change (e.g., Wells & Stryker, 1988). Personality orientations are often thought to be relatively stable (e.g., Block, 1977, 1981; Costa & McCrae, 1980; Moss & Susman, 1980), although there are clearly dissenting views (Gergen, 1980; Gergen & Gergen, 1987; Mischel, 1969). Glenn (1980) suggested that more basic values, acquired in early childhood and tied to the basic structure of personality, are theoretically more durable over biographical time. Attitudes toward contemporary issues may be less persistent, suggested Glenn (1980), and Moss and Susman (1980) claimed that attitudes may be the least stable of human characteristics. Attitudes are probably more stable than these discussions would suggest (see, e.g., Alwin & Krosnick, 1991; Alwin et al., 1991), but theoretically, one would expect more "surface" dispositions to be somewhat less stable overall. Sears (1983) suggested that some types of attitudes — what he called *symbolic* attitudes — are highly persistent over the life course. Such attitudes are affectively laden dispositions acquired early, and therefore presumably more stable. This "primacy principle," as Searing, Wright, and Rabinowitz (1976) called it, has been seriously questioned, and little support actually exists for Sears' thesis that the "symbolic versus nonsymbolic" distinction is related to stability (see Alwin, 1992a; Alwin & Krosnick, 1991a).

But to argue that a trait is stable versus unstable is to ignore the central point of this chapter — we should be interested in trajectories of stability. That is, as the various models discussed in the previous section indicate, stability of a particular trait may not follow the same degree of stability through all periods of the life course. Thus, rather than characterizing various human traits as existing somewhere along a "continuum of historical durability," we should be asking a different question — namely, what is the level of stability in a given trait at a specific period of the life cycle? Then, once attention is focused on the issue of life-span trajectories of stability, it is possible to ask whether the observed patterns are generalizeable across time periods. There clearly may be variations in life-span trajectories of particular human orientations depending on the historical period in which the observations are embedded (see Nesselroade, 1990). But this does not negate the effort to establish some lawlike principles that describe life-span patterns of behavioral orientations. Clearly, the variation that does exist in patterns of stability may be interpretable in terms of aging/life cycle, cohort or generational differences, in terms of the historical period studied, or socially organized patterns of relations to others.

In the following section I describe an approach to studying human stability, which is intended to bring us closer to an understanding of the life-span variations in human characteristics. This approach, which relies on the calculation of molar stability coefficients, can be formulated within the context of a design that could ultimately decide some of these issues of historical, cohort, and aging factors in patterns of stability. At this point, however, the empirical record is nonexistent to sparse, and little can be done to interpret patterns of stability except from the position of making strong assumptions.

III. The Conceptualization and Measurement of Molar Stability

There are many different types of evidence supportive of the tenet that some individual differences, that is, aspects of personality and patterns of human functioning, are highly stable after some relatively early point in the life span. Typical studies of stability follow one of two patterns. A sample or cohort is reinterviewed at a later time, typically only once, and the responses are compared between the occasions of measurement. Then, one or more of three types of information are often compared: distributions or average levels of characteristics, overtime correlations, or estimates of stability. Or, if a sample or cohort cannot be reinterviewed, some investigators observe mean levels for individual birth cohorts or sets of birth cohorts as a way of establishing levels of stability (e.g., Glenn, 1980). Although such designs are potentially very useful for gauging the stability of cohorts, for the present set of theoretical concerns — the stability of individuals — the most valuable data lie in longitudinal studies of individual lives. The use of intra-cohort trend studies of the type summarized by Glenn can provide excellent results on net levels of change. But such data do not allow one to study the processes of change for individuals; that is, they do not permit the study of the individual-level components of macrolevel cohort change, or *gross change* (Duncan & Kalton, 1987). So, although they represent highly valid data from the point of view of cohort stability, they are not useful in terms of providing evidence of individual-level processes of change.

Thus, for the purpose of studying human stability in the sense of gross change, which corresponds to the concept of stability discussed earlier, it is essential to develop longitudinal panel designs. And although panel studies of cohorts over time do permit a more precise assessment of the components of stability and change, the typical study is lacking in a number of ways. In general there is considerable variability in the nature of the reinterview design. With differing reinterview intervals, with subjects at different ages, and with studies conducted at different times it is very difficult to standardize the notion of stability across studies. There are estimates of stability across various ages, using a variety of methods and measures, and using a variety of remeasurement intervals. Typically, there is no periodic measurement in such panel studies, and rather than explicitly sampling stages of the life course, the few measurements that do exist (usually two or three time points) are also convenience-based rather than uniform and representative of critical stages of the life cycle. Samples are generally very small and typically rely on purposive nonrepresentative samples of "available" cohorts. Thus, there is often little or no attention to issues of representativeness and selectivity (see Nesselroade, 1988a). Finally, there is virtually no attention to the problem of measurement error and the confounding of change with errors of measurement (Alwin, 1988b; Hertzog, 1990). Thus, on the basis of the existing literature, it is extremely difficult to arrive at a well-integrated view of the evidence of human stability over the life span. Next I suggest an approach to assessing patterns of differential stability that has been applied to some degree in the existing research literature.[11] This approach, discussed in the following section, is vastly superior to most examples in the literature that attempt to deal with the issue of stability.

A. A SYNTHETIC COHORT APPROACH

There is an emerging literature that has relied on a type of research design that combines the best qualities of the repeated cross-section and panel approaches. This is the set of studies relying on measurements of panels from large representative samples of populations of interest. The first such study that I am aware of is Sears' (1981, 1983) analysis of the National Election Study (NES) 1970s (1972–1974–1976) panel, which was a large representative 4-year, three-wave panel study. Unfortunately, because of the limited number of such national panel studies, and because they typically cover no more than 4-year periods of time, there are serious limitations to what one can generalize from this type of data. There are certain parallels between these studies of large representative panel studies (Sears, 1981, 1983) and the repeated cross-sectional data sets relied upon by Glenn (1980) and others. In both cases the researchers must rely on what are known as *synthetic cohort* models of persistence and change.[12] Because in neither case is the same cohort followed over a long period of time, data from the cohorts studied are (implicitly or explicitly) arrayed along an age continuum, and levels of change or persistence are attributed to the age

[11]Stability coefficients have been used in one form or another in studying human growth and development for some time (see Baltes & Nesselroade, 1973; Bloom, 1964; Kagan & Moss, 1962; Nesselroade & Baltes, 1974), but unfortunately there is little consensus on how to define stability (see, e.g., Wheaton et al., 1977).

[12]Developmental methodologists refer to these as "cross-sequential" designs (see Baltes & Schaie, 1973).

differences in the cohorts studied. Rarely is it possible to separate aging, cohort, and period influences on levels of persistence and change.

B. GAUGING STABILITY AND CHANGE

One of the enormous difficulties in summarizing the evidence regarding stability is that there is no "common currency" with which to evaluate levels of stability. This problem has two critical features. First, there is no agreed-upon "coefficient" used as an indicator of stability, and second, there is no agreed-upon time unit over which to calculate stability. Obviously, the magnitude of assessed stability will depend intimately on the amount of time elapsed in longitudinal studies. There are many studies in which a sample (or some other aggregation) of persons is measured at multiple time points (the typical study involves no more than two occasions of measurement) and responses overtime are correlated. These correlations are frequently used to draw inferences about the stability of human dispositions. I here refer to such calculations as *normative stability coefficients*. They purport to tell us something about the stability of human traits, but they are ultimately not very useful. As suggested in the preceding discussion, what is needed in the analysis of human stability is the estimation of levels of stability during multiple time periods over the life span, even if one must rely on "synthetic" arrays of how levels of stability might look over time.

As noted, there are two important problems with such normative stability calculations. The first is that there is never any effort to standardize such coefficients for the fact that they represent different remeasurement intervals—that is, across studies such stability estimates reflect potentially widely varying amounts of time. Thus, there is no agreed-upon common currency for the analysis of differential levels of stability. The second problem such estimates of normative stability present is that rarely is there any effort taken to "correct" such overtime correlations for unreliability of measurement. This is particularly tricky matter, in that reliability of measurement is known to vary with age (see, e.g., Alwin & Krosnick, 1991a, 1991b; Andrews & Herzog, 1986).[13] However, even if researchers take

[13]Bloom (1964) and Block (1971) were among the first to draw attention to the difficulties of measuring stability in the presence of unreliability of measurement. However, the issue is not simply one of correcting continuity correlations for unreliability of measurement; the problem is one of specifying a model that allows both instaility and unreliability to vary as a function of age and obtaining estimates of age-specific stability that are unconfounded with measurement error. Several methodological articles have been written on the confounding of unreliability of measurement with true change in attitudes in the intertemporal correlations observed in overtime data (see Heise, 1969; Kessler & Greenberg, 1981; Wheaton et al., 1977; Wiley & Wiley, 1970). I discuss an approach later that confronts this set of problems.

measurement error into account, they often focus on magnitudes of normative stability for cross-sectional samples as a whole, without taking age into account.

C. ESTIMATING AGE-SPECIFIC STABILITIES

It is not necessarily a simple task to estimate age-specific levels of human stability over time. As noted in the foregoing, the simple correlation of measures replicated over time confounds attenuation due to unreliability of measurement and true change. And because age is related to the reliability of measurement (see Alwin, 1989; Alwin & Krosnick, 1991a, 1991b; Andrews & Herzog, 1986), some method must be employed to attempt to separate unreliability from attitude change (see Alwin, 1988b, 1989). Furthermore, in order to assess stability from a life-course approach, it is important to take age into account in calculating levels of stability.

Presumably period factors will be constant over the duration of national panel studies of relatively short duration, so that it is possible to interpret cohort differences in stability in terms of both aging and cohort factors (I discuss the issue of this confounding later). However, in longitudinal research carried out over much longer time periods, it is possible that cohort differences in stability interact with period factors, and if this is the case it may be difficult to determine the role of aging in levels of estimated stability. Thus, it is very desirable to be able to assess the stabilities of measures for cohorts in more than one period. I provide an example of this approach later.

Stability itself could be a cohort phenomenon and not just a matter of where in the life cycle it is assessed. Indeed, the cohort experiences of some young persons may inculcate differing personality orientations that reflect fundamental differences in orientation along the dimension of stability or rigidity (see Mannheim, 1952). Although it will not be possible to completely clarify the role of aging (or life-cycle) explanations of stability differences among cohorts, we expect that aging factors will operate in a gradual fashion, whereas cohort effects on stabilities may be more "lumpy." Although there is no elegant solution to this confounding of interpretations of such stability coefficients, there is some purchase on this issue by the comparison of cohort stabilities across multiple panel studies, as described later. This can give us some idea of whether the most stable cohorts at a given time are always the most stable.

D. LATENT VARIABLE MODELS

It is possible to use linear structural equation models incorporating latent unobserved variables (see Alwin, 1988b; Hertzog, 1990; Jöreskog, 1974,

1979; Wheaton, Muthén, Alwin, & Summers, 1977) to assess the stability of human characteristics free of the effects of unreliability of measurement. There are at least two ways of representing change and stability within the context of these models: as a simple correlation or regression of "true scores" at different points in time or in terms of measures of lack of change in true scores (see Kessler & Greenberg, 1981; Werts et al., 1971). Either approach overcomes many of the problems associated with the analysis of change via simple observed change (or stability) scores, multiple regression, or cross-lagged correlation techniques, principally because they deal with the problems of measurement unreliability.

Both of these approaches to dealing with stability may be phrased in the context of a discussion of the structural equation models proposed for modeling the role of measurement error in panel data. These models are referred to as *simplex* models by Jöreskog (1974). Such models are characterized by a series of measures of the same variable separated in time, positing a Markovian (lag-1) restriction to account for change and stability in the underlying latent or "true" variable. This type of model has been useful in analyzing individual development or change with respect to a single variable measured at several time points, taking unreliability of measurement into account.

Using this type of model for studying the extent of gross change or stability in human characteristics, in the context of a model that incorporates controls for unreliability of measurement, it is possible to achieve a number of objectives. The first is the unconfounding of random errors of measurement from true change. This is essential for understanding life-span patterns in stability estimates. This also, however, discourages one from making such interpretations on the basis of simple overtime correlation coefficients (what Converse & Markus, 1979, called "continuity correlations"). But, to the extent one can achieve estimates of "true stability" free of unreliability, this represents a marked improvement. Second, this model can be used to assess differences in stability between occasions of measurement (or waves) in longitudinal studies of the same individuals, or within age groups of reinterview studies of shorter duration. The model is extremely useful in conjunction with the synthetic cohort approach outlined earlier, as stability estimates can be generated across several groups of cohorts varying in age, with an eye toward estimating different trajectories of human stability within panel studies that have considerable heterogeneity in age. Third, this approach allows us a method by which we can compare estimates of stability across cohorts differing in age, compare estimates of stability trajectories across concepts, or content domains of personality, as well as across different studies using different remeasurement designs. For example, longitudinal studies suggest that IQ is more stable than many other features of personality. We do not know why, but one possibility is that intellective functions are measured more reliably at every age than are other domains. The proposed framework can help us address such questions and direct inquiries about sources of stability and change in human development.

Given the existence of measures of different domains of content within the context of the same longitudinal design, the comparison of stabilities is relatively straightforward given allowance for differing levels of measurement precision. What is perhaps less clear is the possibility of comparisons of levels of stability across studies in which differing lengths of time are represented in the remeasurement designs of various studies. Clearly, estimates of the magnitudes of stability are in part a function of the amount of time elapsed between occasions of measurement. Thus, what is needed is a concept of molar stability, which reflects the estimated stability per unit of time. Molar stability in essence holds constant whatever time differences are inherent in the designs used in different studies. For convenience, and for no other reason, I use a time period of 8 years as the chosen unit of time in which to express molar stability.[14]

In Table I, I illustrate how molar stability estimates can be used to examine (a) age differences in a synthetic cohort array of stabilities, (b) intracohort patterns of stability over time, and (c) the combination of panel designs to potentially approach the separation of aging, period, and cohort differences in stability. In this table are presented hypothetical levels of stability for a single hypothetical variable. One can imagine another dimension to this table (or several tables) that distinguishes different types of content in the personality domain. Indeed, an important goal of the following review of empirical studies of stability is to array available estimates of molar stability within the same framework in order to assess the extent to which different trajectories of life-span stability may be said to exist.[15]

At this point it is important that one understand the nature of the hypothetical molar stability estimates presented in Table I. This table assumes that several three-wave panel studies exist for measuring a particular domain of content, each panel study separated in historical time by a constant interval of time. In this particular example, the hypothetical panel

---

[14]*Molar stability* is calculated as follows. Let k be the number of years over which stability is assessed, let j be the number of years selected to express molar stability, and let β be the cohort-specific or age-homogeneous stability observed over that amount of time. *Molar stability* is then defined as $\beta^{j/k}$. In this analysis I have chosen j equal to 8.

[15]In order to compare stability coefficients across variables, I rely exclusively upon standardized estimates of the β parameters in the aforementioned model (see Alwin, 1988a). This approach is also advocated in a recent article by Asendorp (1992). The main difference is that in the present model unreliability of measurement is unconfounded with change/stability, whereas in the Asendorpf approach the two are confounded.

TABLE I
Hypothetical Estimates of 8-year Stability Coefficients

Years of Age in			Panel Study		
1956	1972	1988	1956–1958–1960	1972–1974–1976	1990–1992–1994
		18–25			.50
		26–33			.65
	18–25	34–41		.50	.80
	26–33	42–49		.65	1.00
18–25	34–41	50–57	.50	.80	1.00
26–33	42–49	58–65	.65	1.00	1.00
34–41	50–57	66–83	.80	1.00	.85
42–49	58–65		1.00	1.00	
50–57	66–83		1.00	.85	
58–65			1.00		
66–83			.85		

studies are separated by 16 years, a multiple of the 8-year unit selected to express molar stability.[16] In this example, it is thus possible to array estimates of molar stability across cohort categories (age groups) within a particular panel study, as well as across time within the same cohort category. The hypothetical estimates of stability given in the table are consistent with the mid-life stability model (Model E) given in Fig. 1 earlier, depicted here as revealed in both within-time estimates for synthetic cohorts and between-time estimates for actual age-homogeneous cohort categories.

IV. Estimates of Molar Stability

In assessing the evidence for patterns of stability of human characteristics, I rely on a broad-based definition of the concept of personality. For present purposes I refer to virtually any conceptually defensible aspect of human functioning in which individual differences, whatever the source of these differences, can be said to exist. As noted previously, I ignore the possibility of sequences or stages of development in the sense that more complex epigenetic structures emerge from preexisting ones. Here I am concerned with differences between individuals regarding which change is possible and measurable. There is no need to restrict the domain of interest to those human characteristics studied in "personality" research, and in fact, there is every reason to broaden the search for human constancy and change to many different types of behavioral orientations, including the exercise of differential abilities, differences in self-concept and identity, differences in motivational qualities, reports of behavioral characteristics

[16]Part of this table actually can be constructed from real data, as is demonstrated later in the chapter (see results for political party identification).

(both by self and others), and expressions of attitude and affect with respect to various social and interpersonal "objects" (see Brim & Kagan, 1980). In this review, however, I restrict primary attention to (a) available research evidence that permits control for unreliability, (b) stability estimates that are based on age-homogeneous cohort categories, and (c) stability estimates that permit the calculation of molar stability estimates. I rely on both cohort and synthetic cohort data, and although the scope of available data with these characteristics is somewhat limited, there is sufficient breadth of content in the available studies to warrant the serious consideration of these results.

A. THE STABILITY OF PERSONALITY TRAITS

When one considers the domains of personality and interpersonal behavior, the evidence of consistency is hard to establish. Mischel (1969) argued that with respect to character traits, such as rigidity, social conformity, aggression, attitudes toward authority, and on virtually any other nonintellective personality dimension, a great deal of trans-situational "behavioral specificity has been found regularly" (p. 1014). This point of view, in other words, suggests that considerable flexibility or potential for change exists in many aspects of personality. Mischel's argument is pertinent because behavioral orientations will not be likely to endure over time if they do not endure from situation to situation. On the other hand, one might argue that the lack of consistency pointed out by Mischel and others reflects not a state of nature, but the state of measurement imprecision. Some have gone even further in stating that Mischel's arguments are overdrawn and based on a selective review of the literature (see Block, 1977; Moss & Susman,1980). Another, perhaps more balanced view gives greater emphasis to possibilities of human constancy. Moss and Susman, for example, argued that empirical consistency over time is "most obvious for personality characteristics that are endowed with positive cultural and societal valences" (p. 590). They indicated that such things as achievement motivation, sex-role behaviors, and interests are found to be stable from middle childhood.

The general conclusion in the literature is that personality traits increase in relative stability in young adulthood (see Nesselroade & Baltes, 1974), and grow to high levels of stability in adulthood, with little increase in stability over most of the adult life span (see Costa et al., 1983).[17] One can

---

[17]Although I do not review the Costa et al. (1983) research in detail, it should be noted that they reported high levels of stability of personality traits over a 14-year period. I should also note that the Costa et al. work embodies most of the methodological requirements posed here, including the estimation of latent variable models that take random measurement error into account.

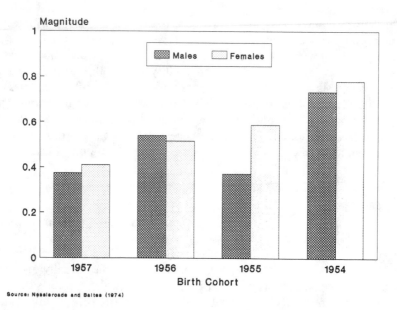

Fig. 2. Stability of personality trait. From Nesselroade and Baltes (1974). Adapted by permission. Copyright 1974 by The University of Chicago Press.

see the gradual increase in stability in figures based on the Nesselroade and Baltes data, in which their model is more precisely parameterized and more refined statistical estimates are given (see Alwin, 1993d).[18] These figures, given in Fig. 2, are entirely consistent with the Nesselroade and Baltes conclusions. In virtually all possible comparisons, the hypothesis of a gradual increase in stability of personality in adolescence is strongly supported.

Considering these estimates within a synthetic cohort framework, they show systematic growth in stability with increasing age, consistent with the

---

[18]This analysis is based on the work of Nesselroade and Baltes (1974) in which a random sample of 1,849 students was selected from three West Virginia counties (ages 12.5 to 17.5 years of cohorts born from 1954 to 1957) in 1970, 1971, and 1972. Subsamples of the four cohorts were studied longitudinally ($N=$ 816) over the three occasions of measurement. Thirty-four measures of personality were obtained using Catell and Catell's High School Personality Questionnaire (HSPQ) and Jackson's Personality Research Form (PRF) self-administered personality inventories. Ten higher order constructs were obtained through factor analysis and correlations were computed for these 10 scores—2 of which were specific to the HSPQ—*anxiety* and *social-emotional anxiety*—3 of which were specific to the PRF—*independence, achievement,* and *aggression*—and 4 of which were common to the HSPQ and PRF—*extraversion ascendence, superego strength/impulse control, tough-mindedness/autonomy,* and *independence/social avoidance.* Nesselroade and Baltes also administered Thurstone's *primary mental abilities* providing six measures of intellectual ability (see later discussion).

conclusions of Nesselroade and Baltes (1974). What is interesting about these results is the relatively low level of stability observed during this period of the life course. When coupled with the best available evidence on stability of personality in adulthood (e.g., Caspi et al., 1987, 1988, 1989; Costa et al., 1983), this suggests that in adulthood personality becomes highly stable. This would point toward support for the impressionable years model (see Fig.1). Further work, however, is required before we will know more about the trajectory of stability in self-reported personality traits.

B. THE STABILITY OF INTELLECTUAL ABILITIES

In addition to personality characteristics, one of the most stable components of human behavior seems to be the domain of intellectual abilities or cognitive skills. Considerable evidence exists that many cognitive and intellective variables tend to stabilize in early adulthood (Wohlwill, 1980). Bloom's (1964) pioneering work demonstrated a high degree of stability in intelligence scores even before early adulthood. There has been some debate about the deterioration of cognitive skills in old age (e.g., Baltes & Schaie, 1976; Botwinick, 1977; Horn & Donaldson, 1976, 1977, 1980) especially with respect to mean levels; however, with respect to the issue of molar stability, the main focus of the present review, the evidence is relatively clear.[19] Measures of intellective variables are highly stable over most of the adult life span, with changes due to differential aging setting in only very late in the adult years. For example, Schaie (1983) concluded that "reliably replicable age changes in psychometric abilities of more than trivial magnitude cannot be demonstrated prior to age 60" (p. 127). He went on to say that, if anything, a decrement is shown in old age, noting that a "reliable decrement can be shown to have occurred for all abilities by age 74" (p. 127). His results are based on a 21-year longitudinal study of Seattle adults, and his conclusions are supported by other longitudinal studies (e.g., Cunningham & Owens, 1983).

The Nesselroade and Baltes (1974) study referred to earlier with respect to the stability of personality, as indicated, also investigated the stability of scores on the Thurstone and Thurstone (1962) *primary mental abilities* battery. Those test scores contain measures of six primary factors: verbal meaning, number facility, letter series (reasoning), work grouping (reasoning), number series (reasoning), and spatial relations (Nesselroade & Baltes,

[19]It should be noted that there is a vast literature dealing with mean levels of cognitive capacities with respect to age, which I essentially ignore in this review (see Horn & Donaldson, 1980). I agree with Hertzog and Schaie (1986), who stated that "the attention paid to stability of mean levels of intelligence has perhaps diverted the field from focusing on a different, critical—and in some cases more critical–type of stability: *stability of individual differences* in intelligence" (p. 159).

1974). Their examination of correlational data for these measures of ability indicates two sets of conclusions. First, they found that the 1-year versus 2-year correlations are only trivially different, suggesting that "interindividual differences in cognitive abilities, contrary to many of the personality dimensions considered, are established prior to age 12" (pp. 54–55). Second, they found that levels of correlation in ability measures are generally higher in the oldest cohorts of students compared to those younger.

As previously done, it is possible to reanalyze the Nesselroade and Baltes (1974) data on measured ability using the simplex models developed by Heise (1969) and others. These results for the total average scores over these subtests are presented in Fig. 2. They provide considerable support for the conclusions that (a) the stability of intelligence test scores increases with age during adolescence, and (b) that very high levels of stability of such individual differences are reached by late adolescence (see also Fig. 3).

Stability estimates in adulthood bear out these conclusions. Based on the Seattle study of Schaie (1983), in which Thurstone and Thurstone's (1962) primary mental abilities battery was employed, Hertzog and Schaie (1986) reported an analysis of stability over a 14-year period for three age groups: young, middle-age, and old.[20] These results, converted into my molar stability units are presented in Fig.4. These results show (a) very high levels of stability from young adulthood through old age, and (b) some growth in the level of stability with age, despite the very high levels already in existence. Thus, both cross-sectionally and longitudinally there is growth in stability with respect to age, despite the fact that the magnitudes of stability are quite close to the ceiling of stability. Based on these data, which are admittedly limited in representation, there is little question that intellectual abilities are highly stable from early adulthood.

These results may seem to pose a serious threat to sociological interpretations arguing that socialization or learning affecting basic intellectual abilities continues well into adulthood. On the other hand, if one argues (see, e.g., Wells & Stryker, 1988) that stability is a function of constancies of person-situation or person-structural linkages, then continuities over time may be viewed as reflections of the stability of human locations in social structure and interpersonal ties. If one argues that such demonstrated stabilities reflects (at least in part) the stability of socially structured experience, then the proper adjudication of the issue of whether a sociological interpretation exists for the stability of intellectual abilities would have to focus on the segment of populations who experience change in social locations at different points in the life cycle, so that life-course

---

[20]Hertzog and Schaie (1986) indicated that the average ages for these groups at the first occasion of measurement in their samples are as follows: young (25–32 years), middle (39–46 years), and old (53–67 years).

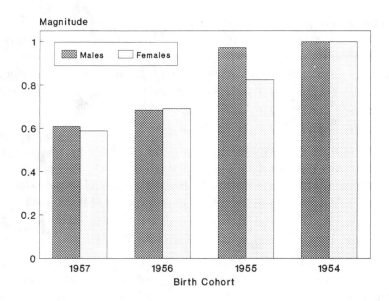

Fig. 3. Stability of intelligence. From Nesselroade and Baltes. Adapted by permission. (1974). Copyright 1974 by The University of Chicago Press.

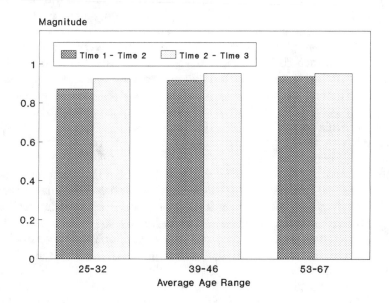

Fig. 4. Stability of intelligence. From Hertzog and Schaie (1986). Copyright 1986 by The American Psychological Association, Inc. Adapted by permission.

linkages to changes in socially structured experiences could be determined. Schooler's (1987) analysis of the development of intellectual flexibility over the life span through exposure to changes in the complexity of the environment represents one attempt to apply theories of social structure and personality to human development (see Kohn & Schooler, 1983; Kohn & Slomczynski, 1990; Schooler & Schaie, 1987), but data from this research program have not been adequately organized to reflect life-span variations in stability. On the other hand, other sociological investigations aimed at the examination of cohort differences in verbal skills, have explicitly incorporated the assumption that "aging" or "life-cycle" contributions to verbal skills beyond early adulthood are negligible (see Alwin, 1991). On the basis of the present evidence that assumption appears to be justified.

C. THE STABILITY OF IDENTITIES AND THE SELF-IMAGE

Social identities are "the fundamental bases upon which society, independent of the special and unique features of each individual, orders and arranges its members . . . scarcely has the infant entered the world than he or she is immediately classified according to race, sex, religion, nationality and so forth" (Rosenberg, 1981, p. 601). It is, of course, a basic tenet of interactionist social psychology that individuals take on such "identities," which then become salient within particular social contexts (Stryker, 1981). Most identities that develop in early childhood, such as gender-role identities or ethnic identities, are in all probability highly stable over individual biographies (see Wells & Stryker, 1988). Very rarely do individuals change such complex, early developmental aspects of the self. Later identities, which are less ascribed and more achieved, may be just as deeply held, and therefore may also be quite stable over time. Here I have in mind such things as family and work identities, such as spouse, parent, worker, and particular career identities. It is important to recognize, however, that although these identities may achieve a high degree of stability within particular periods of the life cycle, they may change quite dramatically and abruptly. Other aspects of the self, such as relational identities, that is, identities that establish themselves in relation to other individuals or groups (e.g., political parties or social institutions), may be somewhat less stable than those connected to gender, ethnicity, family, and work. Identification with geographic areas, nations, political parties, or voluntary associations may be the least stable of all identities. Still, based on the assumption that most identities may be highly salient, one would expect that they are quite stable over most of the adult life course (see, e.g., Wells & Stryker, 1988). In addition, other dimensions of the self may be quite stable over the life span. Indeed, drawing upon social psychological theory regarding the development of the self, Bengtson et al. (1985) argued that a focus on "self-conceptions" or "attitudes toward the self" may be the most fruitful and valid approach to the study of personality change and stability over the life course. They favored the focus on the self-concept over other more abstract notions of personality. Bengtson et al. reviewed a vast literature on aging and self-concept change, most of which fails to meet the requirements of this review.[21] I return to the available research evidence on the stability of self-images subsequently.

The Stability of Identities. We can examine the question of the stability of political identities, using the synthetic cohort approach mentioned earlier. Drawing upon recent research in political socialization, in which self-identifications with respect to party loyalty were studied, we can assess the extent and patterns of stability of political party self-identification, while at the same time examine the question of the historical durability of such aspects of personality. These results are based upon analyses of the NES three-wave panels undertaken in 1956–1958–1960 and 1972–1974–1976 (Alwin et al., 1991). We can examine the extent to which the synthetic cohort data from the 1950s and 1970s studies tell a consistent story of life-cycle changes in the stability of attitudes over the entire life span. I present data on a measure of political party identification—measured over the three waves of each of the 1950s and 1970s panel studies.[22] Therefore we can compare estimates of 8-year stabilities both across cohort groups within the same panel study, as well as within the same cohort groups across time points (see Fig. 5). This latter intracohort comparison of levels of persistence represents the strongest evidence we have to date for the stability of identities.[23]

---

[21]One additional line of research on the stability of the self that is relevant and useful, although not reviewed here because the time period of measurement was months rather than years, was described by Serpe (1987) and Serpe and Stryker (1987).

[22]These results are drawn from Alwin et al. (1991).

[23]The question measuring political identity in the NES surveys is the following: "Generally speaking, do you usually think of yourself as a Republican, a Democrat, an Independent, or what? (If Republican or Democrat) Would you call yourself a strong (Republican/Democrat) or a not very strong (Republican/Democrat)? (If Independent, No Preference or Other) Do you think of yourself as closer to the Republican or to the Democratic party? This measure is used to assess the direction and intensity of political partisanship (see Converse & Pierce, 1987). In the following analysis I use this measure to estimate the stability of party identification using the full 7-point party identification scale, coded as follows: 1 = *Strong Democrat*, 2 = *Weak Democrat*, 3 = *Independent leaning Democrat*, 4 = *Independent*, 5 = *Independent leaning Republican*, 6 = *Weak Republican*, and 7 = *Strong Republican*. "Don't know," "Other," and "Uncertain" responses were omitted from the analysis.

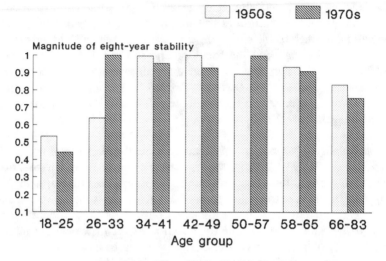

Fig. 5.   Stability of party identification.

The calculation of molar stabilities using these data permit us to obtain an estimate of the amount of stability in party identification experienced by each of the birth cohort categories, which each span a period of 8 years. These stability estimates (see Fig. 2) indicate strong support for the mid-life stability model of human stability (see Model E presented earlier in Fig. 1). The stabilities are lowest in young adulthood confirming the impressionable years thesis, and stabilities grow in magnitude to a very high level in midadulthood consistent with the aging-stability aspect of the model; however, after approximately age 67 years the level of stability declines systematically in a nontrivial fashion. This same pattern is confirmed for both the *directional* and *intensity* components of party identification (see Alwin et al., 1991), although the level of stability of intensity is generally significantly lower than for the direction of party support. The intensity of party loyalty reveals considerably lower stability in both youth and old age, but in all of these data there is fairly consistent support for the mid-life stability model.

In addition to these synthetic cohort results, there are two recent longitudinal cohort studies of political identities. One of these was conducted by Ronald Cohen, Theodore Newcomb, and myself (Alwin et al., 1991) in a 1984 follow-up of the women who participated in Newcomb's 1930s studies at Bennington College and his 1960s follow-up (Newcomb, 1943; Newcomb, Koenig, Flacks, & Warwick, 1967). We found that the political identities Newcomb had seen develop in young adulthood had gained considerable strength and continued with a rather high degree of stability into old age. Our results demonstrate that identities, once formed, can be incredibly stable structures. The molar stability estimates of a latent variable reflecting political orientations in the Bennington data are extremely high — in the range of .95. These results are based on three occasions of measurement over roughly 50 years in the life span. We attributed the high degree of stability in political orientations throughout the life span to two sets of factors: differential susceptibility to change, a tendency that among the Bennington women was demonstrably low, and differential opportunities for attitude change, which was reflected in the social support inherent in marital relationships and friendship ties of the Bennington women, and which among them created fewer opportunities for change (Alwin et al., 1991).

Sears and Funk (1990) reported a longitudinal study of the political attitudes held by a large sample of Americans originally recruited as children in the Terman Gifted Children Study begun in the 1920s to study the growth of intelligence (Terman & Oden, 1959). They studied two aspects of the self — political party identification and political ideology — measured at four time points between 1940 and 1977. They found a high level of stability across the 37-year period studies, with correlations averaging .69 for a composite attitude measure. They also found a high level of consistency between the measures. Both intermeasure consistency and overtime correlation increased with age. Unfortunately the Sears and Funk results leave several ambiguities, including the fact that they analyzed correlations uncorrected for unreliability of measurement, which means that their analysis does not consider the effects of age-related differences in measurement reliabilty.

The Stability of Self-Image.   Although some aspects of the self-concept, such as various aspects of identity, may be quite stable over most of the entire adult life span, it is not necessarily the case that other aspects of the self are equally stable. Mortimer et al. (1982) investigated the stability of this aspect of the self-concept in a panel study of Michigan college students, assessed over three time periods, during their first and fourth years in college and 10 years after graduation. The data were obtained from male graduates, who upon entry to the university in 1962 and 1963 joined a research project on the impact of college life, conducted by Theodore Newcomb and Gerald Gurin (see Mortimer et al., 1982; Mortimer & Lorence, 1981). Their measures of self-image were constituted from self-ratings of "Myself as a Person" using 29 semantic differential (bipolar) scales. An initial exploratory factor analysis of their 1976 data suggested four common factors in these ratings, referred to as "well-being," "sociability," "competence," and "unconventionality" (see Mortimer et al., 1982). Thus, it is possible to obtain some estimates of stability for an age-homogenous sample of men (although a somewhat biased sample, as indicated by Mortimer et al.), during their collegiate years and during the 10-year period following college graduation.

The procedures used by Mortimer et al. (1982) to analyze these data permit the extrapolation of molar stability estimates from their results that are free of contamination due to errors of measurement. These results—for the 18–21 years and 21–31 years age ranges—are presented in Fig. 6, extrapolated from the correlations of self-concept factors presented by Mortimer et al. These estimates reveal two important results. First, there is a clear tendency, as indicated by Mortimer et al. in their discussion of these results, for stability to increase with age. Thus, the development of the self-image appears to follow the same patterns found for aspects of political identity, with relatively lower levels of stability during the youngest adult years and increases in stability thereafter. Because of limitations of their data, Mortimer et al. were not able to specify a more complete trajectory of stabilities over the life span. The second important result stemming from the estimates of molar stability for these aspects of self-image, as shown in Fig. 6, is that they are only trivially lower in magnitude than the NES measures of political identity. The relatively lower estimated stability of self-images, as Mortimer et al. suggested, may reflect the fact that self-ratings such as these may be thought to depend to some extent on "specific roles, tasks, and the situational context," as well as on "idiosyncratic subjective processes" (p. 272). This, despite the fact that it was their

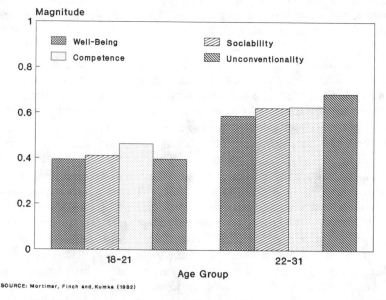

SOURCE: Mortimer, Finch and. Kumka (1982)

Fig. 6. Stability of self-image. From Mortimer, Finch, and Kumka (1982). Adapted by permission. Copyright 1982 by The Academic Press.

assumption that the stimuli involved would evoke more general, global self-evaluations. This presents somewhat of a dilemma in the interpretation of these findings. To the extent that these represent the *global self-concept*, they suggest that the self-concept may not be a highly stable phenomenon, at least through early adulthood.

We can only speculate on what the pattern of these results would be if they extended beyond age 31 years. But, if these results reflect self-images that are more situational and role-specific—and by implication less stable quantities than global self-concept—then one would be forced to conclude that global self-concepts would be relatively more stable aspects of personality than these results suggest. There is no way of resolving this dilemma, except through further interpretation and investigation. Something could perhaps be learned from an analysis in which the 29 items used by Mortimer et al. (1982) were analyzed separately, using simplex models such as those described earlier, and ordered according to whether they measure situation- and role-specific content versus more global content.

One set of possible insights on the issue of the stability of global versus role-specific stabilities is furnished by additional work by Mortimer and her colleagues. Employing two-wave panel data from the 1972–1973 and 1977 Michigan Quality of Employment surveys (Quinn, Mangione, & Seashore, 1975; Quinn & Staines, 1979), Lorence and Mortimer (1985) estimated stabilities for self-assessed job involvement for three age groups. Job involvement was assessed using a latent factor defined by items measuring "job involvement" and "effort expended at work." The three age groups were (a) under 30 years, (b) between 30 and 44 years, and (c) 45 to 64 years (in 1973). Using the same data, Mortimer et al. (1988) presented estimates of stability for a related concept—job satisfaction. Estimates of molar stability for the job involvement factor in Lorence and Mortimer's analysis and the job satisfaction factor from Mortimer et al. are presented in Fig. 7. These results provide some support for the model of mid-life stability in the case of the job involvement concept (contrary to the conclusions of Lorence and Mortimer who read this as support for aging-stability). Specifically, job involvement is almost entirely unstable in the youngest age group, growing more stable in midlife, but declining in stability in the oldest age group. In the case of job satisfaction the results do lend support to the aging-stability hypothesis—job satisfaction is seen to become increasingly stable with age. In neither case do the molar stabilities reach a very high magnitude, suggesting that these aspects of identity may be considerably less permanent than those discussed previously. This comparison suggests that role-specific self-concept is perhaps less stable that the more global aspects of the self. Lorence and Mortimer argued that job involvement grows increasingly stable with age because work experiences and work rewards change considerably less as persons age, suggesting that the age-related increases in

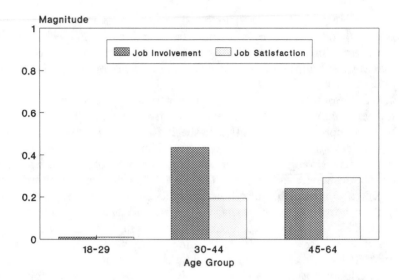

Fig. 7. Stability of job involvement and job satisfaction. From Lorence and Mortimer (1985) and Mortimer, Finch, and Maruyama (1988). Copyright 1985 by The American Sociological Association. Copyright 1988 by the American Association for the Advancement of Science.

the stability of job involvement occur in the context of an increasingly stable work environment. This conclusion is further articulated by Mortimer et al., who suggested that job satisfaction increases in stability either due to the increasing stability of social roles, or because of higher levels of susceptibility to change in early adulthood. These conclusions reinforce the importance of the distinction made in the previous discussion concerning personological versus environmental sources of stability and change.

D. THE STABILITY OF ATTITUDES

Attitudes are defined as latent, unobserved predispositions to respond along a positive or negative dimension (e.g., approval vs. disapproval, agree vs. disagree, approach vs. avoidance, etc.) toward an attitude object. The study of the stability of attitudes is important because of the distinctiveness of the attitude concept in modern social science and because of the difficulties presented in measuring a construct defined as a latent variable (see Alwin, 1973). Some researchers have concluded that there is little evidence that stable, underlying attitudes can be said to exist (e.g., Abelson, 1972; Wicker, 1969), but even among those who accept the theoretical legitimacy of the attitude concept, there is considerable skepticism that the concept applies to all members of the population (e.g., Converse, 1964,

1970). In any event, attitudes are often considered to be the least stable of all personality characteristics (Moss & Susman, 1980).[24]

There are several ways in which trajectories of individual-level stability in attitude orientations may be described (see Sears, 1981). One model—the persistence model—assumes a high level of stability in orientations from adolescence or early adulthood throughout the life span. For example, early discussions of the development of political orientations emphasized the stability of some aspects of the phenomenon from childhood. Based on high correlations between self-reports of party identification and retrospective reports about parents, Campbell, Converse, Miller, and Stokes (1960) suggested that persons might acquire their political orientations quite early and maintain them into adulthood. This view was supported by a number of researchers who argued that the family played a primary role in political socialization (e.g., Davies, 1965; Greenstein, 1965; Hess & Torney, 1967; Hyman, 1959).

Newcomb's (1943) classic research at Bennington College, however, demonstrated that political attitudes of young college-age adults can be quite malleable and open to change. Newcomb's research documented systematic and meaningful changes of attitudes over the collegiate years in a sample of women who confronted the growing popularity of the New Deal in the 1930s and 1940s in a setting providing information that was for the most part discrepant from their familial influences within the context of intensely supportive ties to faculty and the college community. Newcomb's research represented strong support for the notion that parental influence is attenuated as the child comes into contact with new reference groups through her pursuit of independence of thought and action (see Hyman, 1959). And this research gave way to the interpretation of early adulthood as particularly impressionable years (see Alwin et al., 1991; Alwin & Krosnick, 1991a; Kinder & Sears, 1985; Sears, 1981).

Although Newcomb's (1943) Bennington research provided some evidence for the suggestion that under certain conditions the divergence from parental orientations could be quite dramatic, what was less clear was the extent to which this kind of attitudinal flexibility or openness to change continued throughout life, or more specifically, how long it could last. One

---

[24]It is common in the literature on political socialization to find the terms *attitude persistence* and *attitude crystallization* used in conjunction, with authors frequently referring to the lack of attitude stability and crystallization in young adults, and the tendencies toward the growth of both attitude stability and attitude crystallization with age (see Sears, 1987). In fact, issues of attitude persistence and attitude crystallization are separate and separable questions. If we define attitude crystallization in terms of the constraint or cohesiveness of various indicators of latent attitude constructs, then it can easily be seen that the extent of stability in these latent attitudes is independent of the extent to which indicators of such a construct are interrelated (see Alwin et al., 1991).

view is that adult development is a process of continued change, and that social and historical experiences continue to stimulate change and the continued development of attitudes. The idea that there is a lifelong openness to change (see Kinder & Sears, 1985; Sears, 1981) suggests that such attitudinal flexibility continues throughout the life course, or that later periods of vulnerability to change reappear (see Gergen, 1980). However, the predominant view is that rather than continuity in openness to change, people's attitudes grow in strength, becoming more resistant to change with time. This view, which characterizes attitude development in terms of impressionable years followed by increased persistence with age, suggests that after some early period of vulnerability or openness to change, and once people establish important role commitments, through marriage and family formation, the transition to adulthood is considered accomplished, and the potential for continued openness to change is considerably diminished (see Ryder, 1965). Indeed, there is considerable support for these ideas in research on the stability of political attitudes (e.g., Alwin et al., 1991; Fendrich & Lovoy, 1988; Lang & Lang, 1978; Marwell, Aiken, & Demerath, 1987; Newcomb et al., 1967; Roberts & Lang, 1985; Sears, 1981, 1983; Sears & Funk, 1990).

Symbolic Versus Nonsymbolic Attitudes.   As predispositions to respond positively or negatively with respect to a particular object, attitudes may vary in their durability depending on the nature of that object (Sears, 1983). The attitude object can range from the abstract to the concrete, from quite diffuse content to very specific things like political institutions, political actors, or positions on sociopolitical issues. In addition to content, attitudes have a number of additional characteristics that refer to their nature and organization. For example, Sears used the term *symbolic attitudes* to refer to those attitudes that are developed early with relatively more affective than cognitive content, and that have an important influence on other attitudes and behaviors. This symbolic versus nonsymbolic distinction, thus, refers not simply to the nature of attitude object, but the degree of affective content, which is assumed to be more stable by virtue of its development through early socialization experiences. Although "cognitively barren," wrote Kinder and Sears (1985, p. 719), the early commitments of young children are clearly present. They cited a number of studies that indicate increasing likelihood of endorsement for a political party with increments of age. They concluded that, although young people are definitely capable of political choices, their commitment may be relatively weak, and "it is quite possible that these adolescent attitudes are potentially highly vulnerable to change" (p. 719). This suggests that even the most symbolic of attitudes may be quite malleable through childhood, adolescence, and early adulthood, a view that is increasingly coming to dominate current theoretical views on political socialization. Sears, for example, concluded that "as a crude baseline . . . some combination of a persistence and an impressionable years viewpoint best represents the course of basic symbolic predispositions over the life-span" (p. 108).[25]

According to Sears' (1983, 1988) reasoning, attitude objects can be ordered in terms of their expected degree of stability, from most to least symbolic, as follows: (a) political party identification and reactions to political candidates, (b) ideological orientations along a liberal/conservative dimension, (c) attitudes toward social groups, (d) attitudes on racial policy issues, (e) attitudes on nonracial policy issues, and (f) political efficacy. Using the NES data referred to earlier for 50 measures of attitudes, we tested Sears' formulation of the symbolic versus nonsymbolic attitude distinction (Alwin & Krosnick, 1991a). With the exception of political party identification (see previous discussion), we found very few systematic age-related differences in attitude stability were related to the nature of the attitude object, thus failing to support Sears' hypothesis of differences in age-related trajectories of symbolic versus nonsymbolic attitudes. We concluded that the theoretical linkage between aging and symbolic versus nonsymbolic attitude stabilities needs to be reconceived.

In an effort to reformulate Sears' (1983) framework for understanding the relationship between the nature of the attitude object and age-related trajectories of attitude stability, I have undertaken a reanalysis of the NES data, distinguishing between self-identifications (see earlier discussion) and symbolic attitudes (Alwin, 1992a). The category of symbolic attitudes includes: attitudes toward ideological labels (liberal and conservative), attitudes toward political parties, attitudes toward racial categories, and attitudes regarding racial policy issues. The category of nonsymbolic attitudes includes: attitudes toward politicabl institutions, attitudes regarding the role of government, attitudes toward public officials, attitudes toward political processes, attitudes toward political candidates, and attitudes toward social groups (excluding racial groups and political parties).

Molar stability estimates based on the NES data for 19 symbolic and 41 nonsymbolic attitudes by age group are given in Fig. 8. These results indicate that Sears' (1983) "crude baseline" for the definition of symbolic attitudes—the stabilities of which follow either a persistence or an impressionable years pattern—is not borne out. There is support in these results for the notion that attitude stabilities are low among the young, and that thereafter attitude stabilities increase in magnitude. However, the results presented in Fig. 8 indicate that after a peak stability in attitudes in mid-life

[25]I should note that Sears (1983) based his conclusions on normative stability estimates, and he did not have the benefit of the approach suggested here for examining life-course trajectories of attitudes (but see Sears, 1981).

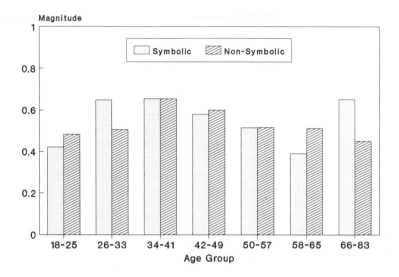

Fig. 8.   8-year stability of symbolic and nonsymbolic attitudes.

(ages 34 to 41 years) there is a return to earlier low levels of attitude stability. Indeed, the results for the nonsymbolic attitudes follow the predicted pattern of mid-life stability, and with the exception of an unusually high stability for the oldest group in the symbolic attitude domain, this pattern also holds for symbolic attitudes.

There are some additional conclusions to draw from these results. First, there is little support for the notion that attitudes are either nonexistent or highly unstable quantities, as some have suggested (see, e.g., Abelson, 1972; Converse, 1964, 1970; Wicker, 1969). Molar stabilities for most attitudes are remarkably high. Second, the distinction between symbolic and nonsymbolic attitudes seems not to be viable in predicting patterns of stability over the life-span attitude development. Few attitudes seem to follow the expected pattern of the persistence or impressionable years models, and those attitudes defined on theoretical grounds as symbolic in nature do not always follow either of these models. The exception to this are attitudes toward racial categories, although attitudes toward racial social policies do not appear symbolic with respect to life-span estimated trajectories of stability. Finally, the model that seems to be most often supported in this analysis of attitude stability is the mid-life stability model, which portrays a second impressionable period in older age similar in malleability to youth.

E. THE STABILITY OF LIFE-COURSE TRANSITIONS

Increasingly, human stability is of essence viewed as the result of the combination of two sets of factors—differential life-span susceptibilities to change and differential life-span opportunities for change. Thus, one important aspect of the linkage between human stability and opportunities for change is the extent of stability found in *positional* or *structural* aspects of an individual's life (see Stryker, 1980; Wells & Stryker, 1988). Ryder (1965) explicitly suggested that with the commitment to an occupational role, a residence, a family, and a way of life the individual experiences less potential for change as a result.

Indeed, there are a number of theoretical discussions that posit differential opportunities for change over the life span, rooted in life-cycle changes. Super et al. (1957), for example, suggested that there are stages in the development of the vocational career. The first is a *trial stage* (ages 22–30 years) in which young workers are trying out various options; the second is the *stabilization stage* (ages 31–44 years) in which the main vocational choices tend to form and stabilize; the third is the *maintenance stage* (ages 45–65 years) in which a great deal of stability inheres in the nature of the job. There is empirical support for these notions in the early status attainment research. Using a synthetic cohort aproach, Blau and Duncan (1967) simulated a life-cycle model of socioeconomic stability. They showed that occupational status increases gradually in stability over the life span, whereas the effects of parental background, and educational experiences decline systematically over the life span. The Blau–Duncan results suggest that some socioeconomic experiences increase in their stability, and achieve a great deal of stability over the life course, and because of this they are potential candidates for explaining the increased stability of personality and behavioral orientations. There is also evidence of this in the work of Mortimer and her colleagues (see Lorence & Mortimer, 1985; Mortimer et al., 1988).

Available evidence on the relative importance of personality versus environment in patterns of stability is relatively sparse. Our research on the Bennington College women provides considerable support, for example, that processes of social selection and social support linking the individual to the environment is strongly implicated (Alwin et al., 1991). We found that those women who were embedded in interpersonal environments that held political views consistent with their views were significantly less likely to experience attitude change than those women who inhabited less supportive settings (Alwin et al., 1991). Support also exists in the work of Caspi and Herbener (1990), who examined these issues in the Berkeley Guidance Study and the Oakland Growth Study. They found that marriage to similar others is a basic norm in society, and the extent of similarity was related to consistency in intraindividual organization of personality attributes across middle adulthood.

Thus, there is some support for what is commonly assumed to be a fundamental linkage between the individual and her environment, namely that as one becomes more tightly linked to particular positions, roles, activities, and commitments, individual personality also becomes more stable as a direct consequence. This conclusion is, however, only indirectly linked to existing data, reflecting a basic weakness of the available empirical record. Clearly more research is needed on this set of issues, the significance of which is fundamentally related to the basic question regarding the sources of patterns of individual stabilities, that is, whether they arise from personological or sociological processes, or both. Existing research suggests that the latter are much more important than the former, although more research is needed (see Alwin et al., 1991).

V. Conclusions

Processes of social and individual change are inexorably intertwined. People change because aspects of social experience change, and the ways in which people change influence the nature of society. Thus, the question of the life-span stability of human characteristics and orientations crosscuts the study of aging and the study of social change. Obviously, the extent of individual stability at different stages of the life span has important implications for models of human development and models of social change. If individuals are more or less vulnerable to the influences of social change at all stages of the life cycle, then the age distribution of the population expresses little about the potential for aggregate-level change. On the other hand, if cohorts experience differing historical circumstances during the process of personality formation, and if individuals tend to persist in their orientations after this early period of the life cycle, then the age distribution of the population may be relevant to the prediction of potential shifts in the population.

For purposes of verifying key assumptions about cohort stability and social change, the question seems to be, then, whether individuals tend to be more or less stable over their lives once they have experienced a "critical" stage of socialization, either early in their young lives or early in their adulthood. If so, the task of interpreting social trends is made easier. If not, the interpretative task is much more complex. In this chapter I have tried to cover the wide-ranging literature on the stability of individual differences in aspects of human personality. First I found that, with the exception of cognitive and intellective skills, personal self-identifications, and some attitudes, there is only a weak basis for the assumption of stability of human traits over the adult life span. I found further that the degree of stability is not uniform across the life span, nor does it necessarily follow the same course for all human traits. There is considerable evidence in support of the notion that youth is a particulary impressionable time in which the lowest levels of stability are experienced. Cognitive and intellective capacities and many aspects of the self seem to represent important exceptions to this, in that they experience high levels of stability from childhood and early adulthood or adolescence. Despite the highly impressionable character of most other personality attributes in young adulthood, most achieve relatively high stability soon after young adulthood, with mid-life typically being the apex of measured stability. By age 35 years most characteristics have reached their highest level of stability. After midlife, however, the trajectory of human stability is quite variable. Some traits continue to increase, whereas others decline in stability. Of course, it is important to realize that due to the limitations of the existing empirical record, molar stability estimates are not possible for many aspects of behavioral functioning, and in some instances the age range investigated was not a sufficient basis on which to draw a conclusion about life-span stability. This is particularly true in the area of personality ratings, because few estimates of molar stability are possible. For the data available, intellectual functioning and personality traits appear to stabilize relatively early and remain highly persistent over most of the adult life course. Identities also appear to be quite stable from early adulthood, although there is a noticeable lack of data on this topic. For political identities, the stability trajectory seems to follow a version of the mid-life stability model; other types of identities may be similarly volatile in both young and old age. This may make us want to revise Norman Ryder's (1965) contention that " . . . the potential for change is concentrated in the cohorts of young adults who are old enough to participate directly in the movements impelled by change, but not old enough to have become committed to an occupation, a residence, a family of procreation or a way of life" (p. 848). The mature age (sometimes called old age) is likely to be a time of change as well, however. One may become uncommitted to an occupation, a residence, a family of procreation, and a way of life. Thus, as Wilensky (1981) argued, the mature years may be a time of destabilization due to increases in significant life-cycle events. For attitudes as well, the mid-life stability pattern is one of the most common, suggesting that a second period of vulnerability to change occurs after midlife. This is consistent with the observation that although the experience of life-stage changes declines after youth, their likelihood increases again subsequent to midlife. These conclusions, it would be emphasized, stand in direct contradiction of the predominant aging-stability interpretations of the phenomenon of aging (e.g., Glenn, 1980; Lorence & Mortimer, 1985; Mortimer et al., 1982, 1988). Indeed, with the exceptions noted, most of the results presented earlier suggest support for the mid-life stability model, rather than the aging-stability model, a finding anticipated by Sears (1981).

It should be recognized that the estimated trajectories of human stability are "average" estimates in the sense that they describe the "typical" individual and represent a "normative" pattern of stability. Clearly there are individuals who exhibit highly stabilized patterns and others who exhibit relatively unstable tendencies over the life span. Although it may be tempting to find in these results some basis for a pattern that represents some kind of "normal" life-cycle development, or some types of normative stages in life, there is considerable risk in doing so. If there were something that could be said to be normal or normative, either in the sense that most people develop in certain ways in response to "typical" timing, duration, and sequences of events or that there is some kind of normal set of developmental processes that are "wired in" to the organism (e.g., the development of menses in virtually all women), it would then be possible to gauge departures from what is normal and focus on what is problematic or "deviant" with respect to development.

Although there is some support for the assumption that there are typical patterns of aging with respect to stability of human characteristics, as in the seeming generality of patterns of stability in political self-identifications, it is also clear that there are differences tied to the historical circumstances in which the observations are available (see Alwin et al., 1991). Furthermore, there is very little information available on this question, and a few transhistorical inferences that can be made with regard to patterns of stability (Alwin, 1993b). Thus, at this stage any search for normal patterns of aging, or even normal or typical happenings in people's lives, seems especially risky. In other words, it is extremely important that a search for "successful" patterns of aging take into consideration the vast realm of possible patterns of stability and change in individuals' lives. Not only are the historical circumstances that define and constrain opportunities for human development often quite variable within the same population, such opportunities may be immensely different within time and within cohorts. The implications of the previous analysis are that, although some human characteristics are capable of high degrees of stability, and some seem to reveal patterns of relatively high stability over some periods of the life cycle, given the degree of stability that is known to exist, it seems important that any inferences about expected patterns of change be made with considerable caution.

Acknowledgments

This work was supported in part by a grant from the National Institute on Aging (R01-AG04743-05). The author gratefully acknowledges the assistance of Abigail Alwin, Merilynn Dielman, Brian Labadie, Jessica Sansone, and Susan Sherry. Comments by Alexander von Eye, Avshalom Caspi, David Featherman, Jeylan Mortimer, and Sheldon Stryker were greatly appreciated.

References

Abelson, R. P. (1972). Are attitudes necessary? In B. T. King & E. McGinnies (Eds.), *Attitudes, conflict and social change* (pp. 19–32). New York: Academic.

Alwin, D. F. (1973). Making inferences from attitude-behavior correlations. *Sociometry, 36,* 253–278.

Alwin, D. F. (1988a). Measurement and the scaling of coefficients in structural equation models. In J. S. Long (Ed.), *Common problems/proper solutions: Avoiding error in quantitative social research* (pp. 15–45). Beverly Hills, CA: Sage.

Alwin, D. F. (1988b). Structural equation models in research on human development and aging. In T. W. Schaie et al. (Eds.), *Methodological advances in aging research* (pp. 71–170). New York: Springer-Verlag.

Alwin, D. F. (1989). Problems in the estimation and interpretation of the reliability of survey data. *Quality and Quantity, 23,* 277–331.

Alwin, D. F. (1991). Family of origin and cohort differences in verbal intelligence. *American Sociological Review, 56,* 625–638.

Alwin, D. F. (1993a). *The Life-span stability of symbolic vs. nonsymbolic attitudes.* Unpublished manuscript, Institute for Social Research, University of Michigan, Ann Arbor.

Alwin, D. F. (1993b). *Of time and human stability: aging, cohorts and social change.* Unpublished manuscript, University of Michigan, Institute for Social Research, Ann Arbor.

Alwin, D. F. (1993c). Socio-political attitude development in adulthood: The role of generational and life-cycle factors. In D. Krebs & P. Schmidt (Eds.), *New directions in attitude measurement* (pp. 61–93). Berlin & New York: Walter de Gruyter.

Alwin, D. F. (1993d). *The stability of personality in adolescence.* Unpublished manuscript, University of Michigan, Institute for Social Research, Ann Arbor.

Alwin, D. F., Cohen, R. L., & Newcomb, T. M. (1991). *Political attitudes over the life-span: The Bennington women after fifty years.* Madison: University of Wisconsin Press.

Alwin, D. F., & Krosnick, J. A. (1991a). Aging, cohorts and the stability of socio-political orientations over the life-span. *American Journal of Sociology, 97,* 169–195.

Alwin, D. F., & Krosnick, J. A. (1991b). The reliability of attitudinal survey measures: The influence of question and respondent attributes. *Sociological Methods and Research, 20,* 139–181.

Andrews, F. M., & Herzog, A. R.. (1986). Respondent age and survey measurement error. *Journal of the American Statistical Association, 81,* 403–410.

Asendorpf, J. B. (1992). Continuity and stability of personality traits and personality patterns. In J. B. Asendorpf & J. Valsiner (Eds.), *Stability and change in development* (pp. 116–154). Newbury Park, CA: Sage.

Baltes, P. B., & Nesselroade, J. R. (1973). The development analysis of individual differences on multiple measures. In J. R. Nessleroade & H. W. Reese (Eds.), *Life-span developmental psychology: Methodological issues* (pp. 219–251). New York: Academic.

Baltes, P. B., & Schaie, K. W. (1973). On life-span developmental research paradigms, retrospects and prospects. In P. B. Baltes & K. W. Schaie (Eds.), *Life-span developmental psychology: Personality and socialization* (pp. 365–395). New York: Adademic.

Baltes, P. B., & Schaie, K. W. (1976). On the plasticity of intelligence in adulthood and old age. *American Psychologist, 31,* 720–725.

Bengtson, V. L., Reedy, M. N., & Gordon, C. (1985). Aging and self-conceptions: Personality processes and social contexts. In J. E. Birren & K. W. Schaie (Eds.), *Handbook of the psychology of aging* (2nd ed., pp. 544–593). New York: Van Nostrand Reinhold.

Blau, P. M., & Duncan, O. D. (1967). *The American occupational structure.* New York: Wiley.

Block, J. (1971). *Lives through time*. Berkeley, CA: Bancroft.

Block, J. (1977). Advancing the science of personality: Paradigmatic shift or improving the quality of research. In D. Magnusson & N. S. Endler (Eds.), *Psychology at the crossroads: Current issues in interactional psychology* (pp. 37–63). Hillsdale, NJ: Lawrence Erlbaum Associates.

Block, J. (1981). Some enduring and consequential structures of personality. In A.I. Rabin, J. Aronoff, A. M. Barclay, & R. A. Zucker (Eds.), *Further explorations in personality* (pp. 27–43). New York: Wiley.

Bloom, B. (1964). *Stability and change in human characteristics*. New York: Wiley.

Botwinick, J. (1977). Intellectual abilities. In J. E. Birren & K. W. Schaie (Eds.), *Handbook of the psychology of aging* (pp. 580–605). New York: Van Nostrand Reinhold.

Brim, O. G., Jr., & Kagan, J. (1980). *Constancy and change in human development*. Cambridge, MA: Harvard University Press.

Campbell, A., Converse, P. E., Miller, W. E., & Stokes, D. E. (1960). *The American voter*. New York: Wiley.

Carlsson, G., & Karlsson, K. (1970). Age, cohorts and the generation of generations. *American Sociological Review, 35*, 710–718.

Caspi, A. (1987). Personality in the life course. *Journal of Personality and Social Psychology, 53*, 1203–1213.

Caspi, A., & Bem, D. J. (1990). Personality continuity and change across the life course. In L. Pervin (Ed.), *Handbook of personality theory and research* (pp. 549–575). New York: Guilford.

Caspi, A., Bem., D. J., & Elder, G. H., Jr. (1989). Continuities and consequences of interactional styles across the life course. *Journal of Personality,57*, 375–406.

Caspi, A., & Elder, G. H., Jr. (1988). Emergent family patterns: The intergenerational construction of problem behavior and relationships. In R. Hinde & J. Stevenson-Hinde (Eds.), *Relationships within families* (pp. 218–240). Oxford, England: Oxford University Press.

Caspi, A., Elder, G. H., Jr., & Bem, D. J. (1987). Moving against the world: Life-course patterns of explosive children. *Developmental Psychology, 23*, 308–313.

Caspi, A., Elder, G. H., Jr., & Bem, D. J. (1988). Moving against the world: Life-course patterns of shy children. *Developmental Psychology, 24*, 824–831.

Caspi, A., & Herbener, E. S. (1990). Continuity and change: Assortative marriage and the consistency of personality in adulthood. *Journal of Personality and Social Psychology, 58*, 250–258.

Converse, P. E. (1964). The nature of belief systems in the mass public. In D. E. Apter (Ed.), *Ideology and discontent* (pp. 206–261). New York: Free Press.

Converse, P. E. (1970). Attitudes and non-attitudes: Continuation of a dialogue. In E. R. Tufte (Ed.), *The quantitative analysis of social problems* (pp. 168–189). Reading, MA: Addison-Wesley.

Converse, P. E., & Markus, G. B. (1979). Plus ca change . . .: The new CPS election panel study. *American Political Science Review, 73*, 32–49.

Converse, P. E. & Pierce, R. (1987). Measuring partisanship. *Political Methodology, 11*, 143–166.

Costa, P. T., Jr., & McCrae, R. R. (1980). Still stable after all these years: Personality as a key to some issues in adulthood and old age. In P. B. Baltes & O. G. Brim, Jr. (Eds.), *Life-span development and behavior* (Vol. 3, pp. 65–102) New York: Academic.

Costa, P. T., Jr., McCrae, R. R., & Arenberg, D. (1983). Recent longitudinal research on personality and aging. In K. W. Schaie (Ed.), *Longitudinal studies of adult psychological development* (pp. 222–263). New York: Guilford.

Cunningham, W. R., & Owens, W. A., Jr. (1983). The Iowa state study of the adult development of intellectual abilities. In K. W. Schaie (Ed.), *Longitudinal studies of adult psychological development* (pp. 20–39). New York: Guilford Press.

Davies, J. C. (1965). The family's role in political socialization. *Annals of the American Academy of Political and Social Science, 361*, 10–19.

de Graaf, N. D., Hagenaars, J., & Luijkx, R. (1989). Intragenerational stability of postmaterialism in Germany, the Netherlands and the United States. *European Sociological Review, 5*, 183–201.

Duncan, G. J., & Kalton, G. (1987). Issues of design and analysis of surveys across time. *International Statistical Review, 55*, 97–117.

Elder, G. H., Jr., & Caspi, A. (1988). Human development and social change: An emerging perspective on the life course. In N. Bolger, A. Caspi, G. Downey, & M. Moorehouse (Eds.), *Persons in context: Developmental processes* (pp. 77–113). New York: Cambridge University Press.

Elder, G. H., & Caspi, A. (1990). Studying lives in a changing society: Sociological and personological explorations. In A. I. Rabin, R. A. Zucker, R. A. Emmons, & Frank, S. (Eds.), *Studying persons and lives* (pp. 201–247). New York: Springer.

Epstein, S., & O'Brien, E. J. (1985). The person-situation debate in historical and current perspective. *Psychological Bulletin, 98*, 513–537.

Feather, N. T. (1979). Value correlates of conservatism. *Journal of Personality and Social Psychology, 37*, 1617–1630.

Featherman, D. L., & Lerner, R. M. (1985). Ontogenesis and sociogenesis: Problematics for theory and research about development and socialization across the lifespan. *American Sociological Review, 50*, 659–676.

Fendrich, J. M., & Lovoy, K. L. (1988). Back to the future: Adult political behavior of former student activists. *American Sociological Review, 53*, 780–784.

Firebaugh, G. (1989). Methods for estimating cohort replacement effects. In C. C. Clogg (Ed.), *Sociological methodology 1989* (pp. 243–262). Oxford, England: Basil Blackwell.

Firebaugh, G., & Davis, K. E. (1988). Trends in anti-Black prejudice, 1972–1984: Region and cohort effects. *American Journal of Sociology, 94*, 251–272.

Gergen, K. J. (1973). Social psychology as history. *Journal of Personality and Social Psychology, 26*, 309–320.

Gergen, K. J. (1980). The emerging crisis in life-span developmental theory. In P. B. Baltes & O. G. Brim, Jr. (Ed.), *Life-span development and behavior* (pp. 32–65). New York: Academic.

Gergen, K. J., & Gergen, M. M. (1987). The self in temporal perspective. In R. P. Abeles (Ed.), *Life-span perspectives and social psychology* (pp. 124–137). Hillsdale, NJ: Lawrence Erlbaum Associates.

Gilligan, C., Brown, L. M., & Rogers, A. G. (1990). Psyche embedded: A place for body, relationships, and culture in personality theory. In A. I. Rabin, R. A. Zucker, R. A. Emmons, & Frank, S. (Eds.), *Studying persons and lives* (pp. 86–147). New York: Springer.

Glenn, N. D. (1980). Values, attitudes and beliefs. In O. G. Brim, Jr., & Kagan, J.(Eds.), *Constancy and change in human development* (pp. 596–640). Cambridge, MA: Harvard University Press.

Greenstein, F. I. (1965). *Children and politics*. New Haven, CT: Yale University Press.

Heise, D. R. (1969). Separating reliability and stability in test–retest correlation. *American Sociological Review, 34*, 93–101.

Hertzog, C. (1990). On the utility of structural equation models for developmental research. In P. B. Baltes, D. L. Featherman, & R. M. Lerner (Eds.), *Life-span development and behavior* (Vol. 10, pp. 257–290). Hillsdale, NJ: Lawrence Erlbaum Associates.

Hertzog, C., & Schaie, K. W. (1986). Stability and change in adult intelligence: 1. Analysis of longitudinal covariance structures. *Psychology and Aging, 1*, 159–171.

Hess, R. D., & Torney, J. V. (1967). *The development of political attitudes in children*. Chicago: Aldine.

Horn, J. L., & Donaldson, G. (1976). On the myth of intellectual decline in adulthood. *American Psychologist, 31*, 701–719.

Horn, J. L., & Donaldson, G. (1977). Faith is not enough: A response to the Baltes–Schaie claim that intelligence does not wane. *American Psychologist, 32*, 369–373.

Horn, J. L., & Donaldson, G. (1980). Cognitive development in adulthood. In O. G. Brim, Jr., & J. Kagan (Eds.), *Constancy and change in human development* (pp. 445–529). Cambridge, MA: Harvard University Press.

House, J.S. (1981). Social structure and personality. In M. Rosenberg & R. H. Turner, *Social psychology: Sociological perspectives* (pp. 525–561). New York: Basic Books.

Hyman, H. H. (1959). *Political socialization*. Glencoe, IL: Free Press.

Inglehart, R. (1985). Aggregate stability and individual-level flux in mass belief systems: The level of analysis paradox. *The American Political Science Review, 79*, 97–116.

Inglehart, R. (1990). *Cultural change: The impact of economic and political change on culture, and the impact of culture on economics, society and politics in advanced industrial society*. Princeton, NJ: Princeton University Press.

James, W. (1950). *The principles of psychology*. New York: Dover. (Original Work published 1890).

Jöreskog, K. G. (1974). Analyzing psychological data by structural analysis of covariance matrices. In D. H. Kranz et al. (Eds.), *Measurement, psychophysics, and neural information processing* (pp. 1–56). San Francisco: Freeman.

Jöreskog, K. G. (1979). Statistical estimation of structural models in longitudinal-development investigations. In J. R. Nesselroade & P. B. Baltes (Eds.), *Longitudinal research in the study of behavior and development* (pp. 303–351). New York: Academic.

Kagan, J. (1980). Perspectives on continuity. In O. G. Brim, Jr., & J. Kagan (Eds.), *Constancy and change in human development* (pp. 26–74). Cambridge, MA: Harvard University Press.

Kagan, J., & Moss, H. A. (1962). *Birth to maturity*. New York: Wiley.

Kessler, R. C., & Greenberg, D. F. (1981). *Linear panel models of quantitative change*. New York: Academic.

Kinder, D. R., & Sears, D. O. (1985). Public opinion and political action. In G. Lindzey & E. Aronson (Eds.), *The handbook of social psychology* (3rd ed., Vol. 2, pp. 659–741). New York: Random House.

Kohn, M. L., & Schooler, C. (with the collaboration of J., Miller, K. A., Schoenbach, C., & Schoenberg, R.). (1983). *Work and personality: An inquiry into the impact of social stratification*. Norwood, NJ: Ablex.

Kohn, M. L., & Slomczynski, K. M. (with the collaboration of Schoenbach, C.). (1990). *Social structure and self-direction: A comparative analysis of the United States and Poland*. Cambridge, MA: Basil Blackwell.

Krosnick, J. A. (1988). Attitude importance and attitude change. *Journal of Experimental Social Psychology, 24*, 240–255.

Lang, K., & Lang, G. E. (1978). Experiences and ideology: The influence of the sixties on an intellectual elite. In L. Kriesberg (Ed.), *Research in social movements, conflicts and change* (Vol. 1, pp. 197–230). Greenwich, CT: JAI.

Lerner, R. L. (1984). *On the nature of human plasticity*. New York: Cambridge University Press.

Looft, W. R. (1973). Socialization and personality throughout the life span: An examination of contemporary psychological approaches. In P. B. Baltes & K. W. Schaie (Eds.),

Life-span developmental psychology: Personality and socialization (pp. 25-69). New York: Academic.

Lorence, J., & Mortimer, J. T. (1985). Job involvement through the life course: A panel study of three age groups. *American Sociological Review, 50,* 618-638.

Mannheim, K. (1952). The problem of generations. In P. Kecskemeti (Ed.), *Essays on the sociology of knowledge* (pp. 276-320). London: Routledge & Kegan Paul.

Marwell, G., Aiken, M. T., & Demerath, N.J., III. (1987). The persistence of political attitudes among 1960s civil rights activists. *Public Opinion Quarterly, 51,* 359-375.

Mason, W. M., & Fienberg, S. E. (1985). *Cohort analysis in social research.* New York: Springer.

Mischel, W. (1969). Continuity and change in personality. *American Psychologist, 24,* 1012-1018.

Mortimer, J. T., Finch, M. D., & Kumka, D. (1982). Persistence and change in development: The multidimensional self-concept. In P. B. Baltes & O. G. Brim, Jr. (Eds.), *Life-span development and behavior* (Vol. 4, pp. 263-312). New York: Academic Press.

Mortimer, J. T., Finch, M. D., & Maruyama, G. (1988). In J. T. Mortimer & K. M. Borman (Eds.), *Work experience and psychological development through the life-span* (pp. 109-155). Boulder, CO: Westview.

Mortimer, J. T., & Lorence, J. (1981). Self-concept stability and change from late adolescence to early adulthood. In R. G. Simmons (Ed.), *Research in community and mental health* (Vol. 2, pp. 5-42). Greenwich, CT: JAI.

Moss, H. A., & Susman, E. J. (1980). Longitudinal study of personality development. In O. G. Brim, Jr., & J. Kagan (Eds.), *Constancy and change in human development* (pp. 530-595). Cambridge, MA: Harvard University Press.

Nesselroade, J. R. (1988a). Sampling and generalizability: Adult development and aging research issues examined within the general methodological framework of selection. In T. W. Schaie et al. (Eds.), *Methodological advances in aging research* (pp. 13-42). New York: Springer-Verlag.

Nesselroade, J. R. (1988b).Some implications of the trait-state distinction for the study of development over the life span: The case of personality. In P. B. Baltes, D. L. Featherman, & R. M. Lerner (Eds.), *Life-span development and behavior* (pp. 163-189). Hillsdale: NJ: Lawrence Erlbaum Associates.

Nesselroade, J. R. (1990). Adult personality development: Issues in assessing constancy and change. In A. I. Rabin, R. A. Zucker, R. A. Emmons, & S. Frank (Eds.), *Studying persons and lives* (pp. 41-85). New York: Springer.

Nesselroade, J. R., & Baltes, P. B. (1974). Adolescent personality development and historical change: 1970-1972. *Monographs of the Society for Research in Child Development, 39.* (No. 1, Serial No. 154).

Neugarten, B. L., & Peterson, W. A. (1957). A study of the American age-grade system. *Proceedings of the Fourth Congress of the International Association of Gerontology, 3,* 497-502.

Newcomb, T. M. (1943). *Personality and social change: Attitude formation in a student community.* New York: Dryden.

Newcomb, T. M., Koenig, K., Flacks, R., & Warwick, D. (1967). *Persistence and change: Bennington College and its students after 25 years.* New York: Wiley.

Quinn, R. P., Mangione, T. W., & Seashore, S. E. (1975). *The 1972-73 quality of employment survey.* Ann Arbor, MI: Survey Research Center, Institute for Social Research.

Quinn, R. P., & Staines, G. L. (1979). *The 1977 quality of employment survey.* Ann Arbor, MI: Survey Research Center, Institute for Social Research.

Riley, M. W. (1973). Aging and cohort succession: Interpretations and misinterpretations. *Public Opinion Quarterly, 37,* 774-787.

Riley, M. W. (1987). On the significance of age in sociology. *American Sociological Review*, *52*, 1-14.

Roberts, C. W., & Lang, K. (1985). Generations and ideological change: Some observations. *Public Opinion Quarterly, 49*, 460-473.

Rodgers, W. L. (1991). Interpreting the components of time trends. In P. V. Marsden (Ed.), *Sociological methodology 1991* (pp. 421-438). Oxford, England: Basil Blackwell.

Rogosa, D. (1988). Myths about longitudinal research. In K. W. Schaie, R. T. Campbell, W. M. Meredith, & S. C. Rawlings (Eds.), *Methodological issues in aging research* (pp. 171-209). New York: Springer.

Rokeach, M. (1960). *The open and closed mind: Investigations into the nature of belief systems and personality systems.* New York: Basic.

Rokeach, M. (1968). *Beliefs, attitudes and values: A theory of organization and change.* San Francisco: Jossey-Bass.

Rosenberg, M. (1981). The self-concept: Social product and social force. In M. Rosenberg & R. H. Turner (Eds.), *Social psychology: Sociological perspectives* (pp. 593-624). New York: Basic.

Ryder, N. B. (1965). The cohort as a concept in the study of social change. *American Sociological Review, 30*, 843-861.

Schaie, K. W. (1983). The Seattle longitudinal study: A 21-year exploration of psychometric intelligence in adulthood. In K. W. Schaie (Ed.), *Longitudinal studies of adult psychological development* (pp. 64-135). New York: Guilford.

Schooler, C. (1987). Psychological effects of complex environments during the life span: A review and theory. In C. Schooler & K. W. Schaie (Eds.), *Cognitive functioning and social structure over the lifecourse* (pp. 24-49). Norwood, NJ: Ablex.

Schooler, C., & Schaie, K. W. (Eds). (1987). *Cognitive functioning and social structure over the lifecourse.* Norwood, NJ: Ablex.

Searing, D. D., Wright, G., & Rabinowitz, G. (1976). The primacy principle: Attitude change and political socialization. *British Journal of Political Science, 6*, 83-113.

Sears, D. O. (1981). Life-stage effects on attitude change, especially among the elderly. In S. B. Kiesler, J. N. Morgan, & V. K. Oppenheimer (Eds.), *Aging and social change* (pp. 183-204). New York: Academic.

Sears, D. O. (1983). The persistence of early political predispositions: The roles of attitude object and life stage. *Review of Personality and Social Psychology, 4*, 79-116.

Sears, D. O. (1987). Implications of the life-span approach for research on attitudes and social cognition. In R. P. Abeles (Ed.), *Life-span perspectives and social psychology* (pp. 17-60). Hillsdale, NJ: Lawrence Erlbaum Associates.

Sears, D. O. (1988). Symbolic racism. In P. A. Katz & D. A. Taylor (Eds.), *Eliminating racism: Profiles in controversy* (pp. 53-84). New York: Plenum.

Sears, D. O. (1990). Whither political socialization research? The question of persistence. In O. Ichilov (Ed.), *Political socialization, citizenship education, and democracy* (pp. 69-97). New York: Teachers College Press.

Sears, D. O., & Funk, C. L. (1990). *The persistence and crystallization of political attitudes over the life-span: The Terman Gifted Children Panel.* Unpublished manuscript, University of California, Los Angeles.

Sears, D. O., & Weber, J. P. (1988, July). *Presidential campaigns as agents of preadult political socialization.* Paper presented at the 11th annual meeting of the International Society of Political Psychology, Meadowlands, NJ.

Serpe, R. (1987). Stability and change in self: A structural symbolic interactionist explanation. *Social Psychology Quarterly, 50*, 44-55.

Serpe, R., & Stryker, S. (1987). The construction of self and the reconstruction of social relationships.In E. Lawler & B. Markovsky (Eds.), *Advances in group processes* (Vol.4. pp. 41-66). Greenwich, CT: JAI.

Steckenrider, J. S., & Cutler, N. E. (1989). Aging and adult political socialization: The importance of roles and transitions. In R. Sigel (Ed.), *Political learning in adulthood: A sourcebook of theory and research* (pp. 56–88). Chicago: University of Chicago Press.

Stewart, A. J., & Healy, J. M., Jr. (1989). Linking individual development and social changes. *American Psychologist, 44*, 30–42

Stryker, S. (1980). *Symbolic interactionism: A social structural version*. Menlo Park, CA: Benjamin/Cummings.

Stryker, S. (1981). Symbolic interactionism: Themes and variations. In M. Rosenberg & R. H. Turner (Eds.), *Social psychology: Sociological perspectives* (pp. 3–29). New York: Basic.

Sullivan, H. S. (1953). *An interpersonal theory of psychiatry*. New York: Norton.

Super, D. E., Crites, J., Hummel, R., Moser, H., Overstreet, H., & Warnath, C. (1957). *Vocational development: A framework for research*. New York: Teachers College Press.

Terman, L. M., & Oden, M. H. (1959). *Genetic studies of genius: V. The gifted group at mid-life*. Stanford, CA: Stanford University Press.

Thurstone, L. L., & Thurstone, T. G. (1962). *SRA primary mental abilities*. Chicago: Science Research Associates.

Wells, L. E., & Stryker, S. (1988). Stability and change in self over the life course. In P. B. Baltes, D. L. Featherman, & R. M. Lerner (Eds.), *Life-span development and behavior* (pp. 191–229). Hillsdale, NJ: Lawrence Erlbaum Associates.

Werts, C. E., Jöreskog, K. G., & Linn, R. L. (1971). Comment on "The estimation of measurement error in panel data." *American Sociological Review, 36*, 110–13.

Wheaton, R. B., Muthén, B., Alwin, D. F., & Summers, G. F. (1977). Assessing reliability and stability in panel models. In D. R. Heise (Ed.), *Sociological methodology 1977* (pp. 85–136). San Francisco: Jossey-Bass.

Wicker, A. W. (1969). Attitudes vs. actions: The relationship of verbal and overt behavioral responses to attitude objects. *Journal of Social Issues, 25*, 41–78.

Wilensky, H. L. (1981). Family life cycle, work, and the quality of life: Reflection on the roots of happiness, despair, and indifference in modern society. In B. Gardell & G. Johansson (Eds.), *Working life* (pp. 235–265). New York: Wiley.

Wiley, D. E., & Wiley, J. A. (1970). The estimation of measurement error in panel data. *American Sociological Review, 35*, 112–117.

Wilson, G. D. (1973). *The psychology of conservatism*. New York: Academic.

Wohlwill, J. F. (1980). Cognitive development in childhood. In O. G. Brim, Jr., & J. Kagan (Eds.), *Constancy and change in human development* (pp. 359–444). Cambridge, MA: Harvard University Press.

Wholesome Knowledge: Concepts of Wisdom in a Historical and Cross-Cultural Perspective

Aleida Assmann

UNIVERSITY OF CONSTANCE

Abstract

Over the last decade, the focus of interest in developmental and life-span psychology has been extended from early infancy to later phases of life. This reorientaion has aroused renewed interest in cultural concepts of wisdom, which—it is hoped—may yield specific information concerning the cognitive and emotional potentials inherent in late adulthood. As wisdom is a value term embedded in cultural context, its content is highly variable. It ranges from pragmatic clues for problem solving and hints for social integration to ways toward cosmic adaptation and religious salvation. Wisdom is as historically various as it is polymorphous: Seven historical phases are briefly sketched and four aspects or "faces" of wisdom are outlined. Such effort at differentiation can hardly do justice to the complexity of the term but it may dispel the notion that wisdom can be treated as a continuous or unified concept. The last part brings the discussion back to some of the poignant questions of life-span research. Wisdom is habitually associated with age for two reasons: (a) its proximity to death, and (b) its capacity for retrospective evaluation of events. Wise judgments seem to be built on intuitions of order and balance. They are called "wise" when they transcend the rigid systems of social or moral norms and activate a more inclusive knowledge of man or women in the world, be it engendered in the body or the soul.

I. Introduction: The Return of Wisdom

Wisdom is a type of knowledge that is age-old and, for all we know, intimately connected with human aspirations and endeavors of all times and places. Yet it is also true that wisdom is only a recent discovery in many branches of the humanities. In psychology, the introduction of the deeply forgotten concept of wisdom is connected with the expectation of a new paradigm in the investigation of life-span development and behavior (Clayton & Birren, 1980; Sternberg, 1990). Psychology is not unique in having recently discovered wisdom. It has also returned to philosophy, from where (as some believe) it had been banned for more than 2,000 years (Oelmüller, 1989; Tenbruck, 1976). It has returned to ethics, which after a long period of preoccupation with universalistic norms has returned to situational causistry and the value of a good personal life (Krämer, 1976, 1983, 1985). It even touched the natural sciences as they shifted their focus from causal and mechanistic explanations to cybernetic and systemic structures (Schmidt,in A. Assmann, 1991). Principles such as homeostasis or autopoiesis hint at a hidden wisdom of nature.

Renewed scholarly attention to wisdom in the last quarter of this century could indeed be the symptom of a significant change in the climate of thinking, vaguely labeled, as *postmodernism*. I only mention two aspects of this epistemological change particularly relevant to the return of wisdom:

1. An acknowledgment of personal concerns, taking philosophical consideration for what had for a long time been disqualified as "accidental": the gendered body, the concrete circumstances of living, the importance of the social and natural environment.

2. An approximation between the humanities and the natural sciences. The gap between the two diverse branches of knowledge is far from being closed, but there are new concepts and methodologies that build bridges across the gulf. A concept such as wisdom hints at a lost nexus between the

two; wisdom transcends the clearly circumscribed worlds of philosophy, theology, or ethics in referring to possibilities of the acknowledging broader principles of life. We notice that where it is introduced as a concept, it "naturalizes" the domain of human values and "humanizes" the domain of natural laws (Ritschl, 1986).

My own approach to the study of wisdom has yet a different context. This is a history of literature that is stimulated by an interest in historical anthropology. Literary texts can be read according to the prevailing norms and swiftly changing fashions of literary criticism, but they can also yield valuable and more permanent information as to the historically changing nature of human beings, their aspirations and desires, their ideals and illusions, their problems and distresses, and their values and rules for behavior within different social frameworks. The opportunity to study the evolution of literature in a wider historical and cross-cultural perspective on wisdom was created by the informal cooperation of an interdisciplinary group of scholars who investigated common topics over the last decade. After the technology of media (orality/literacy) and the institutions of knowledge (canonization and censorship), the group concentrated on the concept of wisdom and the problem of its universality. This chapter proposes to present some of these discussions that so far are only available in a German collection of essays to an English-speaking audience (A. Assmann, 1991).

In psychology, the return of wisdom goes along with a new interest in the historical dimension of human behavior. Many recent studies on wisdom include historical surveys (Clayton & Birren, 1980; Sternberg, 1990). My own contribution responds to this new interest in the past as possible clues for the present. It tries, however, to considerably broaden the scope of material, parting from the canonical figures and topics. Plato, Aristotle, and Kant, important as they are for any history of thought, do not figure in our presentation as crucial representatives of wisdom. Nor does it come up with a unified, metahistorical and transcultural concept of wisdom. The aim is, rather, to revive some of the phenomenal wealth and paradoxical tensions associated with the topic of wisdom.

The second section offers an examination of tacit knowledge about wisdom, which is by nature intuitive and general. The third section presents a historical survey in seven steps. In reconstructing different historical scenarios, the assumption of a unified concept of wisdom gives way to a variety of concrete historical manifestations. The fourth section continues the segmentation of wisdom in a more systematic way. Four prototypes of the Sage are examined, blending evidence from literature (three of the types carry Shakespearean names) with material from different epochs and cultures. The last section addresses the crucial question of the relationship between wisdom and age, examining in detail some of the cultural factors that make such an alliance possible or call it into doubt.

I see a paradox in the fact that the concept of wisdom, which had been opposed to science, has now turned into a subject for scientific research. The fallacy lurking in this situation is to accommodate wisdom wholly to science by neatly dissecting it into parts and "objectifying" it as a clear-cut entity. As there is no sense in mystifying wisdom, there is no sense in totally anatomizing it. We have to remember that we are dealing not with objective facts but with a value term that has shaped minds and oriented actions. Wisdom is observable in that it is named and described in many documents, but it would not be wisdom were it not to leave ample room for ignorance, dissonance, and surprise.

In Western culture, the trace of wisdom, however archaic and universal it may be, was lost in the evolutionary process of civilization. It had to be "rediscovered" by psychologists as a specific anthropological resource, and it is being "reconstructed" by historians of culture. As usual, reflexivity and scientific research step in when live traditions vanish or undergo a profound change. This time, perhaps the interest of the various disciplines in wisdom may illuminate those elements in our modern world that have devalued it.

II. Tacit Knowledge About Wisdom

A. WHAT IS WISDOM?

It so happens that human beings are generally neither thoroughly foolish nor exclusively wise. They are odd, irrational mixtures of both. Wisdom together with its opposites — folly, stupidity, and vice — are terms to evaluate human behavior. These terms offer clear demarcation lines for the often blind and crooked ways of personal conduct. If it is generally agreed that people with a competence to act wisely are notoriously few, most of them are at least equipped with an intuition to identify a wise action. "This is wisdom!" is a common exclamation (Keppler & Luckman, 1989). To identify wisdom in a given situation is one thing; to provide an abstract definition for it is another. The question "What is Wisdom?" is an artificial, scientific question. It is problematic to treat wisdom as a general topic abstracted from the interpersonal context, where it is generated. If we have to provide a definition for wisdom, we may call it validated action, behavior, or attitude. It is in the eye of the beholder who estimates it rather than in that of the observer who measures it.

In other words, wisdom is an honorific predicate reserved for a specific form of knowledge. As it is a "common-sense-concept" (Sowarka, 1989), we may ask what are the aspects that are commonly invoked to qualify knowledge as wisdom? Let us examine four possibilities: extension, depth, difficult accessibility, and wholesomeness.

Extension: The Wise Person Knows More Than the Ordinary Person   In classical antiquity, wisdom was defined by Cicero as knowledge of divine and human affairs: *sapientia est rerum divinarum et humanarum scientia* (De Officiis, II,ii, 5). In the Renaissance, this became the most popular definition of wisdom: "The sentence can be found in Salutati and Bruni, in Reuchlin's *Breviloquus vocabularius* and in Elyot's *Governour*,in Erasmus, Cardanus, Pontus de Tyard, and Bodin, in every country of Europe and in virtually any year between the end of the fourteenth century and 1600" (Rice, 1958, p. 93). If knowledge (*scientia*) is total and inclusive, it turns into wisdom (*sapientia*). The drive toward unity of knowledge is typical of oral and encyclopedic societies. The wise person is the virtuoso of knowledge, the person with the largest memory and a vast stock of transmitted lore and experience. Cicero, who made the formula popular, was a great literary figure who like his admirers in the Renaissance adhered to the oral ideal of unity and comprehensiveness of knowledge. Extension, inclusiveness, and integration are marks of the kind of wisdom that is to be absorbed by memory. It is the opposite of specialized and fragmented knowledge, which is the fate of knowledge once it is systematically "excarnated" and given over to books. The truth of one book is challenged by that of another; literacy is a process of endless rivalry in the field of knowledge. The holistic quality of knowledge is "mnemophil," apt for memory, which demands order and shape. Quantity is a criterion for excellence only in relation to a frame that is confined by the natural limits and constraints of memory.

Depth: The Wise Person Knows Deeper Than Does The Ordinary Person
In oral and memory-directed societies, the wise person knows more than the others, whereas in a literate society, the wise person knows deeper than others. In a literate society, extension of knowledge no longer stands for wisdom but for meaningless accumulation of knowledge. Heraclitus was the first to draw a line between "knowing much" and "knowing deeply" (Hölscher, 1991). In a society where an abundance of specialized, fragmented, and, above all, controversial knowledge prevails, a new qualification of wisdom emerges. Wisdom is knowledge of what lies below the surface of tangible appearances. The Roman poet Virgil went not to the laboratories but to the Muses to learn about the hidden causes of life (*rerum cognoscere causas*). In his dark aphorisms, Heraclitus concealed hints to the hidden laws of existence: life as a flowing river, strife as father of all things, or the interdependence of polar tensions in the bow and the lyre. Such knowledge cannot be qualified as scientific because it is not the result of methodical abstraction and controlled progression. It does not lead on to

another step in the vast chain of knowledge. It is wisdom because it is ultimate insight gathered from long and deep meditation, tempered by personal feeling and experience.

Difficult Accessibility: The Wise Person Knows What is Beyond the Reach of the Ordinary Person.   Wisdom has often enough been shrouded in the veil of mystery. Tamino in Mozart's *Magic Flute* is warded off twice before he is admitted at the door of the temple of wisdom to undergo his initiation. There is an obvious affinity between wisdom, initiation, and esotericism. But it is not just the veil of esoteric exclusiveness that makes access to wisdom difficult. Confucius has frequently perplexed his disciples in privileging silence over verbal communication. He wanted to be without words and praised the way of the sky, who can speak in a nonverbal language (Wagner, 1991). Yet the unapproachable and unsayable wisdom of Confucius was verbalized by his disciples and canonized as a comprehensive curriculum to teach bureaucratic officials. Wisdom changes when it is transmitted through schools and books.

Wisdom also differs from ordinary knowledge in that it is not a competence that is safely at one's disposal. "Don't consider yourself to be wise," is the first maxim of the Egyptian Ptahhotep, the oldest wisdom-text preserved. Many texts repeat the warning that wisdom is hard to find, and seldom where one looks for it. According to Ptahhotep, wisdom can be discovered among the group of the population least associated with the prestigious education of the literati. It may be beyond the reach of the literate and dwell among the ordinary people:

> Wise speech is more concealed than malachite and yet it can be found among the maids at the grinding stones

Nor is wisdom a process that can ever be completed; it remains an open-ended venture:

> There is no artist who has reached perfection
> For the limits of this art are never to be reached.
>   (J. Assmann, 1991, p. 363; Lichtheim, 1973–1980 p. 63)

Wholesomeness: The Wise Person Knows What Is Good for Him or Herself or Another Person.   Wisdom is the knowledge of how to lead a good life. Such knowledge is — in the widest sense — practical. It has to stand the test; it is measured by the consequences of the action. The true test of wisdom is its regenerative power. It puts right what was crooked or marred; it releases what was blocked, remembers what was forgotten, checks what oppresses. In sum, wisdom restores a balance where it was lost. It may occur on the level of practical action, in which case it is a form of problem solving; it may have to do with the reflexive level of motivation, values, and the evaluation of the human condition, in which case it is soterological. The first axioms of Hebraic and Hellenic wisdom are soteriological and therapeutic, respectively:

- The fear of God is the beginning of wisdom.
- Know thyself.

Both derive the healing power of wisdom from self-limitation and self-recognition. Wisdom is imbued with a sense of the limitation of knowledge. Self-steering presupposes self-knowledge and self-limitation. In former times, such capacities were called virtues; today they are rediscovered in the realm of systemic biology and therapy. After God and the self, wisdom is linked with an awareness of the immanent laws of life, and it uses such knowledge to restore lost balance or promote reintegration.

B. HOW DOES WISDOM OPERATE?

It is suggestive to ponder this question by looking at wisdom within the frame of a story:

A father who felt his end approaching called his three sons to his deathbed. He said to them: "I shall not live much longer. This is the way I want you to distribute your legacy. I leave you 17 camels. The eldest shall receive one half, the middle one a third, and the youngest one a ninth." And he died. When trying to execute the father's will, the sons found themselves in great difficulties. As they stood perplexed, a stranger passed by on his camel. He asked them what their problem was. When he learned about the will, he added his own camel to the herd of the father and bid the sons to proceed in sharing the lot. The oldest received nine camels, the middle one six, and the youngest two. After the division was done, a solitary camel was left over. It was the camel of the stranger who mounted it and disappeared.

If we can for a moment abstract from that level of the story on which it is an ingenious solution of an arithmetical problem, we may consider it as an allegory on wisdom. The story revolves around two imperatives: that of the father and that of the stranger. The first creates a dilemma; the second resolves it. To overcome the perplexity, there is no need either to change the world or to introduce fixed principles.All that is needed is a new perspective. This perspective is the effect of cunning and imagination. In the light of a hypothetical "as if," the status quo can be transcended and the dilemma overcome. The course of life that had been interrupted can go on.

The story of the camels is used by P. Watzlawik to describe his work as a therapist. It brings out the affinity between therapy and wisdom. Both draw on the imagination, on hypothetical constructions and supporting fictions to open up new visions for reflection, new space for action, and a new stimulation for emotions. The achievement of wisdom is to suggest new options at a moment when life is paralyzed."Solomonic solutions" and "paradoxical interventions" break up the paralysis and restore lost balance. Like the advice of the stranger in the story, that of the wise person or the therapist has an occasional character; they do not lay out the general principles of how to deal with similar problems in the future. Wisdom, unlike the utopian spirit, is not driven by the question of how to change the world for the better. It abstains from the zealous hope of changing the fundamental conditions of life or of solving particular problems once and for all. It accepts the fact that there are no definite solutions and that the course of life remains always essentially unstable, threatened by dilemmas and crises. Under these circumstances, wisdom looks for strategic devices to make life more bearable and worthwhile. Such knowledge cannot be lifted from the specific situation nor can it be severed from the knower. It is rendered in the form of a story or a gnomic phrase and not in that of an abstract rule or a universal law.

C. WHERE DOES WISDOM FLOURISH?

Is wise thinking and acting based on more or less recognizable assumptions? What are the features of a world in which wisdom has a place; under what conditions is it rendered useless or discarded? Wisdom seems to flourish in an intermediary space between total order and total contingency. In a space that is rationally ordered and institutionally controlled, there is little room for wisdom. The fixation of positive laws, be it in the realm of science, law, or ethics, has made the world surely more rational and perhaps more safe, but hardly more apt for wisdom. What Max Weber has called "the disenchantment of the world," the process of a progressive rationalization of life-worlds, has devalued and repressed the age-old treasure of human experience collected and preserved under the label of wisdom.

Nor can wisdom flourish where the world is conceived as totally contingent. If there is no order at all, if every move is unexpected and erratic, if every next moment is the manifestation of the utterly new, wisdom has no chance. The special ingenuity of wisdom lies in the gift for recognitions. But recognition presupposes a pattern, however difficult it may be to detect. We may assume that wisdom flourishes in an intermediary space that is neither tightly structured by fixed rules nor totally given over to arbitrariness and confusion. It is expelled from a world in which order is firmly established; it belongs to a world in which order is to be discovered. Order is invisible but assumed to be there; it takes the sensitivity of wisdom to detect or restore it. A deeper *intuition of order* seems to be characteristic for wise attitudes in dealing with the world. This implicit order for which I propose the term *immanent providence* is not at all obvious; it is difficult to discern and requires continuous attention and awareness. Attention and distance, confidence and skepticism are mingled in this attitude to the world.

To say that wisdom depends on an intuition of order rather than an authoritative establishment of order, is to explain the marginalization of wisdom in the modern world as well as its positive reputation in the postmodern world. An intuition of order is not compatible with the utopian or revolutionary impetus. The Promethean spirit to liberate the world from the repressions of an envious god and to actively set it on the road to perfection is diametrically opposed to the principles of wisdom. Order is not to be brought about violently but to be discovered as already existing, because it is there before and independent from humankind. It is far from anthropocentric. In the perspective specific to wisdom, man is not the engineer of order but instead has to find his place in it. *Integration* and *adaption* rather than *change* and *innovation* are the modes of action normally associated with wisdom. Another story may illustrate what is meant by immanent providence and intuition of order. It comes from a Vedic collection of stories, the *Kathasaritsagara*, and is a satire on the concept of ascetic power (von Stietencron, 1991):

A powerful hermit once found a tiny mouse which had escaped from the claws of a buzzard. He took it home and transformed her into a young girl. When she had reached the right age, he wanted to wed her to an adequate partner. He asked the sun: Do marry this girl, I want to give her to a mighty one. The sun answered: the clouds are stronger than I am, they obscure me in the next moment. He asked the cloud who answered: the wind is stronger than I am, he pushes me in whatever direction he likes. The wind, when asked, replied: The mountain is stronger than I am, I cannot move him. The hermit asked the Himalaya, who replied: The mice are stronger, they dig holes into me. The hermit called a mouse and asked him: Do marry this girl! The mouse replied: With pleasure, but show me first how I can get her into my hole! The hermit considered the case. He gave her back her original shape and married her to the mouse.

The wise person abstains from the desire to change the world according to one's desires. For this reason, wisdom is rediscovered at the end of a century that has seen the most violent and most destructive schemes in the history of mankind. The impulse is no longer to change the world but to stabilize it and preserve the ecological balance. We should not forget, however, that there are situations when wisdom is morally questionable and cannot be considered the most valuable form of human behavior. This is the case when the overriding order is oppressive, bad, and brutal. To behave "wisely" in a totalitarian regime like that of the Nazis is to be quietistic, fatalistic, or opportunistic. It means to shun direct confrontation, to adapt to the circumstances, and to evade personal risks. Such behavior can help to solidify a perverse "order," to accept it as given and unchangeable. Under such conditions, a moral attitude may be more effective than a wise one. There are situations when impatience may be preferable to patience. Wisdom yields a deeper but not a counterfactual vision of an alternative world.

To sum up: Wisdom flourishes in an intermediary space between strict legality and utter contingency. Wisdom has a chance (a) when the space of personal action is not utterly defined by rules and obligations, (b) when problems arise for which there exist no specialized institutions and procedures; (c) when human action and existence are grounded on a confidence in an implicit order that supplies orientation; and (d) when truth is linked to human experience rather than scientific experiment, abstract rationality, or moral norms grounded in transcendence.

III. Metamorphoses of Wisdom — A Historical Survey

Wisdom is used here as a name for the kind of knowledge that is set apart as particularly valuable because it has an immediate bearing on the life of the individual and the community. This knowledge about how to survive and, more than that, to live well is as old as mankind and carefully guarded and transmitted from generation to generation. Early cultures have codified a rich stock of this type of knowledge, which was venerated and praised as the highest treasure. However uniform the prestige, the content of wisdom varies as the historical contexts vary. The wisdom of a nomadic tribe will differ from that of a village, the wisdom of the court will be different from that of an urban milieu, wisdom in a traditional society will be different from that in an industrial society. As "wholesome knowledge," it is defined largely by its practical efficiency that is specifically adapted to the respective environment. Let us now turn to those more specific contexts of wisdom and the ways it changes from one epoch to another and from one culture to another.

As we move from the level of intuitions to the level of texts, we find that what is praised as wisdom in one context may be denounced as worthless in another. We must be aware that wisdom is not a solid subject with clearly defined outlines. It is a value term that is mainly used as a pedagogical or polemical tool. The striking disparity in the material accounts for the fact that there are as yet no general studies of wisdom available. There is an abundance of specific monographs, to be sure, dealing with particular shapes of wisdom within a clearly defined genre of discourse, historical period, or cultural context. Only a cross-disciplinary collaboration can open up the possibility of a more integral, cross-cultural perspective.

A. WISDOM AS A SOCIAL VIRTUE IN ANCIENT CULTURES

Much of our still current proverbial wisdom has its roots in the ancient cultures of the Near East. A sentence like "man proposes, God disposes" is more than four thousand years old and can be traced back to the oldest Egyptian wisdom-text, the *Instruction of Ptahhotep*. Egyptian and Mesopotamian wisdom was transmitted to our modern Western culture through the *Book of Proverbs* in the Hebrew Bible. This collection of wisdom-texts is our link with the lost traditions of older cultures. Long before it entered the canon of the Bible, wisdom literature as a genre was developed and cherished in the third and second millennia B.C. Most of the maxims articulate the conservative and patriarchal ethos of the prudent housekeeper and the conscientious official. The proverbs are valued because they praise the social virtues that render communal life possible. At the same time, they denounce antisocial vices like greed, egotism, lust for revenge or power, as well as any form of unbridled passion. The ideal of man emanating from these texts is that of the fully domesticated, self-controlled, and efficient member of the community. (Women are less talked about; an important exception is the portrait of the good housewife in Prov. 31:10ff., the only example of an early wisdom-text attributed to a woman.) To be wise is not a superb or exclusive quality; it is to be moderate and behave according to the social norms. It is to live not according to the demands of the self but according to those of the community; it is to act not on the impulses but on the long-range consequences; it is to consider not only the present but also the future. Such behavior demands no outstanding capacities; it defines a standard that can be adopted by everyman. The gnomic wisdom is the textbook of this social education.

The themes of these texts are familiar. The problems invoked and the solutions offered are such as necessarily arise in smaller and larger communities, ancient and modern. Let us look more closely at an example that also testifies to the transcultural validity of this genre of texts. Although the Israelites looked at Egypt with disdain as their cultural other, they preserved Egyptian wisdom.

Take what is given to you, lying before your nose;
Don't mind what is yonder in the possession of another!

(Ptahhotep, 2500 B.C.)

Mind what is in front of you,
Don't desire the dainties of another one!

(Prov. 23:1b, 3a)

The composition of a proverb is usually two-fold, combining a positive and a negative half, a recommendation and a warning, a virtue and a vice.

These texts neatly sketch the world in white and black, in good and bad. They reduce the complexity of the world to a series of palpable "do's" and "don'ts." In fact, virtue is nothing else than the shunning of vice, and vice versa; in order to be wise, it is often enough to avoid what is harmful. Mundane wisdom is informed by a wealth of acute knowledge of what is detrimental for human relations. It is safe to stay content and mind one's own business; it is not safe to compare one's lot with that of others, to envy the neighbor or to compete with him.

Human nature being what it is, these age-old texts have hardly lost their immediate evidence and impact. This explains not only the perseverance of the wisdom-texts, it also accounts for their cross-cultural similarity. The virtues of listening, obedience, and silence, associated with cultural values like "whiteness," "slowness," or "coolness," are extolled from Africa (Sundermeier, 1991) through Egypt and Mesopotamia to China, and in cultures that are otherwise extremely different in their religious or political profiles. Although even today we can immediately grasp the point of these proverbs and appreciate their wisdom, we must note that their truth is not universal but strictly depends on the context. In traditional societies, discontent is considered a social danger, and any source of rivalry and competition is checked at the root. In societies built on the principle of evolution, however, strife and competition are hailed as dynamic forces keeping the motor of social life going. Discontent becomes a dynamo to transcend one's state and to promote general evolution. Hesiod speaks of the positive *eris*, recommending the productive quality of strife, competition, and discontent because such forces help to break up the stasis of a society.

The verbal gesture of these texts is authoritative, paradigmatically cast in the relation between teacher and student or father and son. There is no place for dialogue or dispute, only for listening, remembering, and obeying. These oral instructions, originally pronounced between father and son or master and disciple, are among the earliest themes to have penetrated into writing. In Egypt, some of the oldest papyri preserve wisdom texts as literature (c. 2000 B.C. J. Assmann, 1991). In the new kingdom (c. 1550–1100 B.C.E.), many parallel texts in often garbled writing show that wisdom texts were taught in schools for their verbal brilliance and pedagogical quality. Learning how to read and write was thus combined with instruction in the "fundamental pragmatics of life" (Baltes & Smith, 1990).

B. WISDOM AS A DIVINE GIFT IN THE HELLENISTIC PERIOD

The last 500 years B.C. suddenly explode with strikingly diverse concepts of wisdom (in Hebrew: *hokhma*; in Greek: *Sophia*). After Plato had removed wisdom from the mundane context to the transcendent heaven of the philosopher (Robinson, 1990), the Hellenistic world of the 4th century B.C. concentrated on a new manifestation of wisdom: Sophia or wisdom as a goddess. The sociocultural world in which the goddess of wisdom was born was no longer that of the early patriarchal cultures with their centralized bureaucracy, their monopoly of power, and their stratification of society. It was a multinational world with a heated intellectual climate. It was a context in which local traditions were in danger of being overrun by the Greek empire. In this situation, there were two options: either to fuse and assimilate or to dramatize the difference and to surpass the dominant culture. In such a heated cultural climate occurred the spiritualization of wisdom. Wisdom now meant soteriological knowledge as different groups competed and tried to emulate each other in pointing the way to spiritual elevation and salvation.

From a mundane and down to earth affair, wisdom had now been elevated to the heavens. Its new predicate is "divine." The search for wisdom was transferred from a human to a spiritual world. The female deity Sophia has left her traces in the wisdom-books of the Hebrew Bible, where she taints the strictly monotheistic and paternalistic character of Hebraic religion (Prov. 8:22-31). She is an embodiment of God's wisdom, "playing before God" and communicating with him, thus unfolding and dramatizing processes within God himself. Such externalization of divine wisdom was more than an allegorical or rhetorical device. It had profound consequences. Divine wisdom, which was hitherto perfectly unthinkable and beyond reach, had turned into a fascinating mystery. Although traditional wisdom adages like "man proposes, God disposes" had emphasized the abyss between human and divine knowledge, exhorting man to resign and trust in the latter, the new spirit of wisdom aspired to possess the very prerogative of God.

The gulf between divine and human wisdom was gradually closed as man claimed to become a shareholder in the fund of divine wisdom. Wisdom was both extolled as an attribute or playmate of God and at the same time it was placed within the reach of human aspirations. "Give me wisdom, the partner on your throne!" is the boldest claim in the Hellenistic *Sapientia Solomonis* (9:4), a source that was classified by the church fathers as apocryphal. Man lost sight of the more profane matters of life and aspired to become a partner of God's wisdom, including that which he had used as the creator of the world. Access to such knowledge was provided no longer through experience and memory but via prayer, faith, initiation, and vision. This spiritualization of wisdom has set the stage for neo-Platonic and Kabbalistic thinking in the Middle Ages and in the Renaissance, and it has returned full swing in the visionary philosophy of the 19th century where it was developed as an antidote to materialism and flourished in Russian sophiology (Groys, 1991).

C. CHRIST AS WISDOM IN MEDIEVAL THEOLOGY

For St. Augustine it was only a step from the Sophia as the female personification of divine wisdom to the son of God as the personification of the divine logos. The words of wisdom describing herself in the Proverbs: *When he established the heavens, I was there* (Prov. 8:27) were now related to Christ as the second person of the Trinity. In this way, Augustine cleared the theological concept of wisdom of its heretic connotations. The mysterious female goddess vanished from the scene. Augustine had converted to Christianity from Greco-Roman culture. To identify wisdom with Christ was to step out of a tradition in which wisdom had been defined as the knowledge of divine and human things. Augustine preserved only one half of the formula, confining wisdom to divine things and associating it with dogmatic theology. Paul had already polemically contrasted Greek wisdom (meaning foolishness) and Christian foolishness (meaning wisdom) and also hinted at the new identification of wisdom with Christ (1 Cor. 1:24). The Old Testament verse: *The fear of the Lord is the beginning of wisdom* (Ps. 111:10; Job 28:28) was condensed by Augustine into the formula: *Ecce pietas est sapienta.*

Theological wisdom is revelation. Man can neither search for it, nor learn it, or acquire it gradually through experience; the only way to receive it is through Grace. He is no longer the ambitious partner of God's secrets but the passive receiver of God's Grace. The role of the keeper of God's secrets is now reserved for Christ. He is the mediator of divine wisdom from Augustine to Dante (*Paradiso* 23, 37-39). It has been remarked that Augustine tied sapientia and Christianity together "with knots which held a thousand years" (Rice, 1958). Wisdom as relevant and wholesome knowledge was confined to the revelation of the scripture, dismissing intellectual curiosity as wayward and harmful speculation.

D. WISDOM AS THE CROWN OF MEDIEVAL LEARNING

Yet Augustine's deprecation of human wisdom was not accepted by the mainstream of medieval theology. Scholastic theology aimed at a harmonization of human and divine knowledge. There was the confidence that human knowledge, contained in the seven *artes liberales*, would find its completion and perfection in theology. At the core of this positive and inclusive estimation of wisdom lies the idea of the regenerative function of knowledge. God's image in man was defiled by the Fall, but it could be restored through learning. In his essay, *Of Education*, John Milton wrote:

"The end then of learning is to repair the ruins of our first parents by regaining to know God aright" (Milton, 1963, p. 146). With this sentence he echoed a received opinion of the Middle Ages: "Of all human acts or pursuits, then, governed as these are by Wisdom, the end and the intention ought to regard either the restoring of our nature's integrity, or the relieving of those weaknesses to which our present life lies subject" (Taylor, 1961, pp. 51f). The quotation is by Hugh of St. Victor at Paris dating from the 12th century. In a sermon, Hugh elaborated on the seven virtues as modes of healing or therapy of man's fundamental sickness, his fallen state:

> We want to speak about twelve things which have to do with healing humankind. There are sick persons, doctors, wounds, medicine, instruments, antidotes, diet, nurses, place, time, health and the rejoicing which follows on the recuperation of health. The antidotes are the seven gifts of the Holy Spirit, the spirits of wisdom and understanding, the spirits of counsel and fortitude, the spirits of knowledge and piety, the spirit of the fear of the Lord. . . .Fear expels pride, piety cruelty, knowledge indiscretion, fortitude weakness, counsel improvidence, understanding inconsiderateness, wisdom foolishness. Oh what good antidotes, by which such evil apostasies are cured!
>
> (Migne, 1844–1864, pp. 922–924)

In allegorical plays of the early Renaissance with titles such as *The Marriage of Wisdom and Wit* or *Wisdom and Science*, performed by students at the universities, wisdom appears as a bride who is promised to the student as a reward after persevering in his studies. She is the crown of the conscientious completion of his curriculum. In the happy ending, the successful student is married to wisdom who promises to stay with him all his life and cheer up his days.

E. THE WISDOM OF ACTION AND OF CONTEMPLATION IN THE RENAISSANCE

"Greatest scholars are not the wisest men" was a common saying in the early Renaissance, which signaled a profound break with the medieval tradition of wisdom. The knots that had tied together *sapientia* and theology were loosened and the encyclopedic ideal of scholastic philosophy broke apart. The system of knowledge based on Aristotle and the Bible was challenged by new empirical data that had no place in the grand scheme of a "summa." This crisis of knowledge became manifest in an abundance of reflections about wisdom. Wisdom still remained a common goal, whereas the content of the concept could no longer be taken for granted. Old certainties and institutions were called in doubt; new standards and their institutions were not yet established. In this productive state of fermentation, a plethora of new initiatives toward wisdom occurred. Wisdom had lost its unified shape. It no longer implied harmony and general consent but became controversial, polemical, critical, hypothetical, and also speculative, mystical, esoteric.

The Greek controversy about the priority of the contemplative ("bios theoretikos") or practical way of life ("bios praktikos") was transformed by Cicero into an acknowledgment of the respective excellence of each mode of wisdom (Luck, 1964). The famous Philosophia, a personification of wisdom, who consoled Boethius in prison wears a dress decorated with letters: in the upper part a θ standing for "bios theoretikos,": in the lower part a π signifying "bios praktikos." The multiplicity of approaches to wisdom in the Renaissance is centered around these two poles (Rice, 1958). The esoteric neo-Platonic wisdom of the Florentine academy (Ficino, Pico) or the negative transcendent Christian wisdom of Nicolaus Cusanus mark one end of the scale; the pragmatic strategies of successful worldly action (Machiavelli), the other end.

The thriving cities of upper Italy form the background of a new vogue of literature on the art of living. There was the rise of a new class of citizens who self-confidently claimed their rights against clerics and nobility. This class rediscovered the classical virtue of *prudentia* together with the practical philosophy of Aristotle. The wisdom of action resumed the old themes of a peaceful coexistence, worldly success, and a good life. It is notable how the leading virtues changed as modern man became more autonomous, more powerful, more resourceful, more selfish. In this context, the classical ideal of a "good life" was revived and stimulated a new, prolific discussion.

The proliferation of different concepts and visions of wisdom, so characteristic for the Renaissance, was due to the absence of authorities and institutions defining and controlling the norms of knowledge. The medieval church had guaranteed the harmony of natural science and theological wisdom. With the founding of the academies and the reshaping of the universities, the sciences found their new institutional frame. The Renaissance appears as an intermediate period that provided an open space for a centrifugal proliferation of voices in the age-old discussion of wisdom.

F. THE DECLINE OF WISDOM IN THE SCIENTIFIC AGE

If the Renaissance was characterized by an explosion of wisdom, a boom of multiple voices, early modernity witnessed an implosion of wisdom. The plurality and concreteness gave way to a homogeneous concept shrouded in mystery. The reason for this regress was the cultural construction of a new dichotomy. Wisdom was now defined as the opposite of science. Whereas science was being established epistemologically and institutionally, wisdom vanished and reappeared as an irrepressible shadow or uncanny ghost of science.

Why was wisdom more severely challenged in the modern era than in any other age? According to the new standards of reason, there was no longer room for the special mode of wisdom that Nietzsche had described as the mode of "nonlogical generalization" ("unlogisches Verallgemeinern"; Nietzsche, 1960, pp. 333). The reputation of this cognitive ability was destroyed with the advent of science and its mode of "logical generalization." Knowledge had to be curtailed and disciplined, accommodated to abstract laws or universal principles before it could claim any dignity. Kant set up new standards for knowledge, defining wisdom as the goal of science yet relentlessly submitting wisdom to the rule of science. Under these epistemological circumstances, wisdom became the shelter of debunked knowledge and forgotten lore. Among the aspects that were dropped in scientific discourse are: (a) the regenerative power of knowledge, the relation between knowledge and bodily or spiritual health, and, (b) the tie to the concrete demands of human existence. *De nobis silemus*: "We shall abstract from our personal selves" was Bacon's motto for the new scientific age.

Scientific discourse had been constituted by eliminating various elements such as religious revelation, mystical vision, knowledge of tradition, proverbial know-how, personal concerns, and subjective experience. Thus, a return to wisdom was also constantly open along any of these lines. Nietzsche followed Schopenhauer (who was the first to import Indian wisdom into Western philosophy) in renewing the claims of a deeply forgotten knowledge, pointing toward the bodily experience of cult and art. On a less emphatical and spectacular level, Nietzsche carried on the long wisdom tradition of the moralistic discourse, which has a quiet yet obstinate perseverance from Roman antiquity through authors like Montaigne and Chamfort up to Adorno and Cioran in the 20th century (Balmer, 1991). Over the centuries this essayistic discourse was a protected space for reflections on highly subjective experience, emphasizing a concrete and microscopic view of the world.

G. THE RETURN OF WISDOM IN POSTMODERNITY

One of the prominent features of postmodernity is the gradual dissolution of the barrier between science and wisdom. The accepted standards of rationality are in a state of revision. The ideal of purity that had marked the mainstream of theoretical knowledge in Western philosophy since Plato and Aristotle is being challenged, not only from without, but also from within the discourse of philosophy itself. It was perhaps to overdramatize the situation to speak of a transvaluation of values in the field of epistemology.

But wherever we find a growing recognition of the limits of knowledge, we see traces of wisdom. Modesty, as the primal virtue of the wise person, again appeals to the scientists whose skepticism was always methodological and never existential. Another aspect is the loss of an integrating perspective. World views, modes of thought, and forms of life are no longer bound under an obligatory and universally accepted set of values. In the postmodern condition of existential pluralism, the neglected figure of wisdom is summoned back from her exile and is restored as a respectable figure (Welsch, 1989).

After Wittgenstein had demonstrated the plurality of our speech games, philosophers are gradually coming to accept a plurality of rationalities. The present demand for wisdom may have something to do with the growing necessity to respond to plurality and to adapt to a world that is every day less unified and coherent. In such a situation, the first concern is to investigate the inherent logic of any respective system. In a time that has discovered the repressive and imperialistic implications of universalism, the respect for difference, deviance, and dissent—as well as for the unknowable, unreachable, and unsayable—has risen considerably. Wisdom has a long tradition of "coping" or adapting when the specific is revalued.

What exactly is this historic, adaptive resource of wisdom? The word *cope* hints at the role of wisdom in the postmodern scenario. The advantage of wisdom before science and theory lies in its pragmatic imagination. It is a type of knowledge that does not proceed inexorably along fixed lines. Instead, it flexibly adjusts to unexpected situations. The wise person has been defined as "the expert for the uncertain," as "the expert in problems for which no rules exist" (Welsch, 1989). In a world that is growing ever more complex and opaque, such a competence can become as important as ever. Wisdom, it seems, could again perform urgent social functions and regain cultural prestige in a world that is located on the borderline between order and chaos. In such a world, experts in the uncertain are more than welcome. Their competence is required "where diverse claims have to be met without the help of a rule from which to deduce the solution" (Welsch, 1989). In such situations, personal capacities once again become decisive: a sense for proportions, sensitivity, alertness, reflection, and judgment that is informed not only by knowledge, but also by intuition and personal experience.

IV. Four Types of the Sage

In my endeavor to reconstruct something of the diversity of the concept of wisdom, I now turn to a more synchronistic approach. After the historical metamorphoses I consider various types of wisdom. To be sure, there is no such thing as a unified stereotype of the wise person. However, there may be paradigmatic representatives or roles of the Sage, each of whom may highlight a different aspect. Such an approach isolates different segments of wisdom without losing touch with concrete phenomena. In our survey, the individual profiles of the different types have the status of tools that may help to map the complex topography of wisdom. But they are also more than that; they are social roles defined by the culture for individual human beings. I discuss four such roles or profiles: (a) *Solomon* representing judicial and political wisdom, (b) *Prospero* representing magical wisdom, (c) *Polonius* representing paternal wisdom, and (d) *Jaques* representing skeptical wisdom

A. THE WISDOM OF SOLOMON: JUDGMENT, DECISION, PREDICTION

Solomon is the wise king of the Hebrew legend. As texts of revelation and law were attributed to the name of Moses, texts of wisdom were attributed to Solomon. In this genre, his name became a mark of authenticity and quality. Here, we are not concerned with the texts that were transmitted under his name but with his image as a just ruler. This image shows similar features all over the world. Where leadership is not mediated through institutions but is populistic and personal as is the case of early and small societies, Solomon's qualifications are demanded of the ruler. The imminent dangers connected with personal rule are irrational selfishness and tyrannical abuse of power. The ideal ruler is praised as an incorporation of wisdom; he is the counterimage of the tyrant: He supports the weak like a father, is unbiased and just, knows himself, and respects the limits of his power.

His outstanding feature is the sharpness of his unbiased judgment, a judgment that immediately sets things straight and meets with broad consent. The ability to render a concise verdict when faced with a dilemma is esteemed as one of the highest qualities in oral (and verbally oriented) societies. And it is interesting to note that judicial wisdom of this kind still has its place in the English legal system, which is based on case law (Raible, 1991). Solomon's approach to a dilemma is very different from that of Alexander, who solved his problem in a rash act by impatiently and radically cutting through the Gordian knot. The "Solomonic solution" requires not a strong will but an alert mind, saturated with knowledge of the world and a rich store of human experience. In small societies where order is not rigidly defined by laws and controlled by institutions but is a matter of implicit presuppositions, order is maintained and restored through wisdom. It is the function of the ruler to maintain this order. In such a world, the irrational will and the greed for power are the great social dangers that have to be checked by wisdom.

The Arabic root "hkm" of "hakim" (the wise person) and "hokma" (wisdom) has the primary meaning of judgment, decision, and command (Biesterfeldt, 1991). The ability to discriminate between good and bad as between seeming and being is held to be the prerequisite of wise judgment. In the Islamic world, wisdom is a competence less of deeds than of words. To pronounce the right word at the right time, to coin a phrase that meets with the consent of opposing parties, to transcend a dilemma with a simple verbal image is valued as the highest form of knowledge.

The ideal of the wise ruler has its own history. The formula of praise applied to Roman emperors was that they were outstanding in combining what rarely goes together, namely *fortitudo et sapientia*, valor and wisdom. The kings of medieval legends took over this ideal image of the ruler (Haug, 1991). Medieval kings frequently represented themselves framed by allegorical representations of the four cardinal virtues: prudence (equals wisdom), justice, fortitude, and temperance. The image of the wise ruler changed between the medieval and the early modern period. The traditional qualities of the perfect ruler were the classical and Christian virtues. In the Renaissance, these qualities were replaced by a more specific competence, namely, preview (or circumspection). Titian has painted a famous allegory of prudence showing a triple head facing in three directions. We look into the face of a mature bearded man; his profile to the right shows (him as) a young man, that to his left shows the features of an aged man. The triple head is doubled by a substructure of three animal heads; a lion facing the spectator is placed in the middle, a fox looking to the right, a wolf looking to the left side. The three-dimensional head is a symbol for a combined knowledge of present, past, and future. This emblematic picture carries the inscription: EX PRAETERITO/PRAESENS PRUDENTER AGIT/NE FUTURU(M) ACTIONE(M) DETURPET (Out of the past/the present acts wisely/lest the future distort the action).

A new chapter in the history of Solomonic wisdom was opened with this step toward a temporalization of wisdom, with the demand of decisions to be made under the contingent pressures of time. Wisdom was dissociated from timeless virtues and timeless knowledge. It was no longer enough to consult the stock of exemplary collective experience. In the urban milieu of princes, merchants, and entrepreneurs it became more and more important to look closely into the empirical circumstances of a case and to consider the immediate past as well as the consequences in the future. "Truth is the daughter of time" (*veritas filia temporis*) was the Renaissance formula for the new liaison between wisdom and time. "Il faut savoir pour prévoir, et prévoir pour gouverner" (A. Comte) is a later version of the modern, temporal form of political wisdom.

B. THE WISDOM OF PROSPERO:
MAGIC, ALCHEMY, MYSTERY

Prospero is the exiled king in Shakespeare's *The Tempest*. He rules over an island and its few inhabitants. Under his rule, the island becomes an enchanted island, which means that he rules over it not with the wisdom of Solomon but with the wisdom of a magician. Prospero is the Merlin figure with the traditional insignia of a cloak, wand, and book. Solomon's knowledge is of the social world; Prospero's knowledge is of the cosmic world. He has a share in the secrets of the creator of the world, he knows the elements and energies, and is in contract with the spirits and essences.

Esoteric knowledge presupposes an enchanted cosmos animated by demonic forces. Prospero knows how to set in motion the spirits of the earth and the air, Caliban and Ariel. He is an expert in a kind of wisdom that was revived in the Renaissance under the name of alchemy (Debus, 1978). This wisdom is operative, experimental, and daring, surrounded by an aura of Faustian hybris and tragedy. As a magician, witch, or sorcerer, woman/man becomes God's or the devil's accomplice, performing in a smaller scale what the creator initially did in grand scale. In cultures that have not undergone the process of rationalization or "disenchantment of the world," magical knowledge is not tainted with the reproach of sinfulness and heresy. It is, rather, considered as highly exclusive knowledge, the carriers of which must be singled out and kept apart because they are endowed with special powers. The magi, shamans, and diviners carefully guard their knowledge and pass it on only to few and select successors.

With the emergence of the empirical sciences, the disenchantment of the world became an irreversible process that first excluded, then persecuted, and finally dried up the sources of magical and demonic wisdom. Scientists, engineers, inventors, and technicians took over what had formerly been a domain of wisdom. With breathtaking speed, Prometheus emulated Prospero in his art. The magical aspect of wisdom is usually dropped in recent studies on the subject: The reason is that the figure of Prospero, so impressive in former times and ancient cultures, was forgotten when science took over. One type of knowledge, however, is rarely replaced by another. What has lost its official social function can always reappear as occult knowledge. In this repressed condition, it merges with other bits and pieces of oblique or obsolete traditions. The result is the New-Age revival of "the alchemistic melting pot" of the pop culture of the 1970s with its fusion of Kabbalah and theosophy, swastica and Zarathustra, Blavatsky and Steiner, Vision of Christ and Anti-Christ (Dadelsen, 1984).

C. THE WISDOM OF POLONIUS:
EXPERIENCE, ADMONITION, ADVICE

Solomon and Prospero are outstanding figures. Their knowledge is excellent and singular. Polonius, on the other hand, is everyman (but not every woman). His knowledge can be as pedantic and trivial as that of the Shakespearean character in *Hamlet*, though it must not be. What is in this type of knowledge to deserve the name of wisdom?

The answer is: It is "relevant" (or pragmatic). In Shakespeare's play, Polonius is old and he has a son who is about to leave the country for a while. At the occasion of taking leave, the father condenses all relevant knowledge he can think of into seven exhortations which he introduces with the words: "Here, my blessing with thee! And these few precepts in thy memory!" (I, iii). There are two things a father can give to his son in parting from him: blessing and advice. The son is to receive both with the attitude of filial gratitude and duty. There is no time for dialogue or argument, no exchange of opinions and experiences. It is a scene of ritualized wisdom transfer, unilinear and apodictical. All that is asked of the son is his willingness to listen and remember.

In this paternal–filial scene we recognize a paradigmatic context for wisdom. In this context, wisdom means socialization. The son can become a full member of society only after the father has initiated him, as the father himself had been initiated by his father. The passing on of proverbial wisdom belongs to liminal situations such as leave-taking before a journey or at the deathbed. The words of wisdom are uttered at the threshold between the generations. The wisdom is "testamentary"; it passes on authority when the father withdraws from the life of action (J. Assmann, 1991). He can disappear when he has printed the maxims into his son's memory. The wisdom of Polonius is traditional and pragmatic; he is repeating the formula of age-old experience and by repeating them, memory solidifies experience and vice versa. The function of such wisdom is to bridge the gap from one generation to the next.

Looking more closely at the admonitions themselves, we discover that they are traditional but by no means universal. The continuity of gnomic and pragmatic wisdom is the backbone of life forms; it transmits and prolongs such attitudes and values that are selected to stabilize the identity of a group. Some of the maxims uttered by Polonius have an aristocratic touch (original citations in cursive print):

1. Be considerate, *give thy thoughts no tongue* (occurs twice).
2. Choose your friends carefully and stick to them; be aware of superficial acquaintances.
3. Don't get quickly involved in quarrels but be brave in combat.

4. Dress carefully but without extravagance.
5. *Neither a borrower, nor a lender be.*
6. *To thine own self be true.*

Polonius displays the concerns typical of conduct books that were in vogue in the early 17th century. B. Castilione provided the model for this genre with his *Il Cortegiano.* Here is a short sample of a much longer list of instructions contemporary with those of Polonius: "Learne but two partes of speeche, to speake good wordes, and to good purpose: goe cleanly but not gaily, and gaine honestly, and spend thriftilie: feede sparingly, drink moderately, sleepe soundly, but rise earely, so passing thy time merrily, thou shalt liue happily and die blessedlie" (Ustick, 1932, p. 426).

The general tenor of Maxims 1–5 is reluctance, the opposite of the wise act being the rash act. The golden mean, the principle of Aristotle's prudence, shines through the instructions. All over the world, wisdom is the wall that one has to erect against one's passions and impulses. Maxims 3 and 4 are connected with an aristocratic lifestyle, whereas the more general 1, 2, and 5 could also be applied in a bourgeois context. If we compare the instructions of Polonius with those of a father to his son in a pietistic family of the 18th century, some (concerning friends, exercise, and thrift) remain the same, some disappear (concerning battles and clothes), and a few new maxims emerge:

7. Divine wisdom transcends mundane wisdom.
8. Don't lose a day in studying the Bible.
9. Write a diary to scrutinize yourself and control your actions.

One could ask: Which maxims would be appropriate in our contemporary world? Here are a few suggestions.

10. Acknowledge the existence of your own body.
11. Don't waste natural resources.
12. Live with a responsibility for generations to come.
13. Respect the integrity of the other.

Among the maxims of practical wisdom, some are more specific than others. "Laugh when your superior laughs!" is a very specific rule (from an ancient Egyptian wisdom text); "Respect life!" is a very broad command. Proverbial wisdom oscillates between the palpably concrete case and the general ethos. Its productivity and longevity is due to the fact that concrete experience is never totally convertible into abstract norms. The last maxim in the speech of Polonius, *to thine own self be true*, is not only more general than the others, it also has a metahistorical validity (Trilling, 1972). It could serve as an existential motto or "implicit axiom" (Ritschl, 1986) in the year

100 B.C. as well as in the years 1600 or 1990. Other than the maxims that invoke the norms of social status, communal consent, and worldly or spiritual values, it confines all concerns to the individual self. The solipsistic stoic wisdom (Marc Aurel) and the ethics in pursuit of personal happiness (Krämer, 1976, 1983, 1985) are revived in a liberal, postmodern society. As the bonds between the individual and tradition or society are loosened, old/new demands concerning a good life are discovered. Group ethics and the norms of conscience are replaced by an ethics focused on the art of living.

The question, how to lead a good life?, has survived all its answers. Today, the answer is no longer provided by the authoritative voice of the father. This voice is replaced by that of the advisor or consultant. The linguistic mode of wisdom is no longer the imperative but the optative. Instead of do's and don'ts and claims being made on the memory, options are offered to be pondered. The new scenario for practical wisdom is the conciliatory situation. The figures of the advisor, the counselor, the therapist have no familial or official authority like the father, the teacher, or the preacher. Their authority is based purely on their expertise in having a more comprehensive view of life and a deeper insight into the nature of human motivations. What is offered as wisdom may no longer be free of charge; yet it is qualified as wisdom not by the bill but by free acceptance and acknowledgment. As in the time of the sophists, wisdom again flourishes in the marketplace, a matter of free and informal exchange.

D. THE WISDOM OF JAQUES: MELANCHOLY, IRONY, DOUBT

Jaques is the name of another Shakespearean character, this time taken from *As You Like it*. He is the professional fool of a king whom he entertains with cynical commentaries and paradoxical interventions. His wit and wisdom are tempered by the black bile of melancholy. The most famous of his orations describes the world as a stage (from which he has withdrawn to assume the role of the detached observer):

All the world's a stage,
And all the men and women merely players:
They have their exits and their entrances . . . (II, vii)

Distance is the first principle of this type of wisdom. The shift from the wisdom of Polonius to the wisdom of Jaques is that from a problem-solving to a problem-finding orientation (Arlin, 1975). The frame of orientation is now "the nonlogical, contradictory, impermanent nature of the universe" (Clayton & Birren, 1980, p.). In contrast to the wisdom of Polonius, the wisdom of Jaques is strictly nonnormative. It shares with

Eastern wisdom the quality that it cannot be put into precepts and exhortations. It has no immediate pedagogical value.

In Western culture, there are two traditions of the wisdom of Jaques, a more pessimistic and a more optimistic one. The pessimistic branch can be traced back to the ancient Near East and the Old Testament book of *Qohelet*. In contrast to the book of Proverbs, this text challenges the very idea of wisdom as virtue or wholesome knowledge. When facing the existential challenge of death, all knowledge and human aspirations come to naught. Wisdom can no longer be distinguished from foolishness:

> I look at everything,
> Everything that happens under the sun:
> Behold, all is nought
> And a catching of the wind. (Eccles. 1:14,17)

Under such auspices, wisdom is exchanged for something more valuable, which is either the spiritual way of faith or the sensual way of the flesh. To live well and enjoy life is the wisdom of an age that has lost its confidence in the past and in the future.

Jaques prefers to stay on the island as a hermit rather than return to a life at court. Shakespeare's contemporary, Michel de Montaigne, who also considered the social world a stage had chosen a similar destiny. He sold his office and withdrew into his library, leading a secluded life among his books and in the company of his dead friend La Boétie. In retreating from the active world and its demands, Montaigne entered into new relations with his environment and the cosmic order. Distance from worldly affairs brought him intimacy with the larger mysteries of the world. Typical of Montaigne is his fundamental critique of the will, the powers of intentionality and self-interest. Montaigne considered the general nexus of actions to be far too complex to decide with any amount of certainty what can safely be called good or bad, wise or foolish. Evaluation and judgment, traditional attributes of wisdom, were transcended in his radically skeptical perspective.

The new quality of a passive wisdom shines through this pessimistic attitude: a comprehensive and inclusive acceptance of what befalls, a flexibility to adjust to ever-changing conditions, and, most important, a sense for paradox and negativity. The pessimistic and skeptical touch of this wisdom matures into a cosmic piety. His noncommitted, unbiased gaze lingered on the *mores*, the multiple and contradictory ways of the world. Watching the inseparable interplay of good and bad, Montaigne became aware of a harmony evolving from paradox and apparent contradiction: "Like the harmony of the world, our life is composed of jarring elements, of diverse, long and short, high and low, soft and coarse tones. . . .

Without this mixture, life cannot subsist, and one string is as necessary as the other" (Montaigne, 1915, III, 13).

Montaigne is here echoing Plutarch, who himself echoed Heraclitus. Plutarch was convinced that it is impossible to purify life of its darker elements:

> The polar union of the universe similar to that of the lyre and the bow. Neither is there anything pure and simple in human life. In music we are used to high and low notes, in grammar to vowels and consonants? . . . As we carry the seeds of this polarity in us since our birth, the wise person, praying for the good, is also ready for the opposite and knows to use both without allowing for excess. (Plutarch, 1942, p. 23)

Montaigne explored this more optimistic tradition of wisdom, which is grounded not on a belief in divine providence, but, rather, on a belief in "immanent providence" and the systemic coherence of contrary impulses. Indifference, confidence, and the spirit of *laissez faire* are characteristic attitudes of the sage as the "confident skeptic": skeptic in relation to the ways of man, confident in relation to the ways of the universe. When Montaigne announced: *Mon mestier et mon art, c'est vivre* (II, 6), he reaffirmed the traditional bond between wisdom and the art of living. He translated it, however, into another dimension, considering the minute cycle of individual existence within the larger cosmic frame.

V. Wisdom and Age

How is wisdom related to age, as portrayed in the prototypes of the sages? Solomon as the ideal ruler is not distinguished by age; he is an outstanding mature person and the superior command of his cognitive faculties is a charismatic trait of his personality rather than the gift of older age. Nor does Prospero have a definite relation to age. If the legendary magicians are represented as old persons, it may be because they represent a type of knowledge that is as old as the creation of the world. In the figure of Polonius, however, age becomes an essential element of his wisdom. His wisdom is the wisdom of age, his words are those of the father, whose authority is based not only on the accumulated experience of life but also on the social status of the elderly. If Shakespeare poked fun at Polonius, this only shows that for him the honorable status of the elderly had ceased to be a social reality.

The wisdom of Jaques is also related to age, though in a very different way. If we think of the example of Montaigne, this position represents a cognitive structure that can be qualified as "mature relativism" (Schmidt, 1991). This position is not to be reached via learning and obedience. It is the effect of a shift in perspective, which may or may not occur on the basis of a rich mental and experiential development. It may be compared to L. Kohlberg's "seventh stage," the post-postconventional stage (Kohlberg, 1973). This stage is summed up by Clayton and Birren (1980) in the following way: "The individual shifts from seeing himself as the center of the universe to identifying with the universe and seeing himself from this perspective. What results is that the individual senses the unity of the universe in which he is but one element. The acquisition of this nondualistic, nonegoistic orientation signals resolution to these ontological questions" (p. 122).

In the case of Jaques, wisdom is related to age neither in a chronological nor in a sociocultural but in a developmental way. Age is a quality of wisdom rather than of the person; this "aged" or mature knowledge transcends all previous forms of cognition.

A. THE WISDOM OF OLD AGE OR THE PRINCIPLE OF BALANCE

There are two major perspectives on the relation of wisdom and age: One is the sociocultural, the other is the ontogenic.

The Sociocultural Perspective: Ascribed Wisdom. There seems to exist a universal presupposition that wisdom and age have to go together. Kant once remarked that wisdom cannot appear before the age of 60. But the advent of wisdom is not a question of calendar and dates. Every culture has its own implicit philosophy of the life cycle, investing every stage with a set of norms and values according to the specific risks, tasks, and potentials connected with the particular stage of the biography. The individual biographies are shaped in every stage by implicit cultural patterns. The association of wisdom and age belongs to such a normative pattern of the life cycle that is constructed by cultures to give shape and meaning to individual lives.

There is a well-known distinction among sociologists between ascribed and achieved status. We may transfer this terminology to our present question and distinguish between ascribed and achieved wisdom. In traditional societies, wisdom is ascribed and old age is evaluated as a positive norm. This stage is selected for the most important social functions. The role of a chieftain, for instance, cannot be assumed by an ever so skilled youngster. The patriarchs are figures of veneration; their old age assures them highest prestige in the community. Estimation of old age is a constitutive feature in traditional societies that are built on the principle of continuity. The older members represent this continuity because they guarantee the vital connection with the past and the dead.

If wisdom and age are conventionally associated in traditional societies, we may go one step further and ask what implicit wisdom is contained in such an association. An answer to this question could point to the principle of balance. The cultural linkage between wisdom and age counteracts a natural tendency to corruption built into the physical frame of the human being. The *genetic program* favoring the strong, fit, and healthy is thus balanced by a *cultural program* favoring the wise, creative, and intelligent. It is social wisdom to temper the "genes" with the "memes" (Csikszentimihalyi & Rathunde, 1990). There is wisdom in not *claiming sapientia et fortitudo*, for one and the same person, but to assign these to different age groups. The fusion of wisdom and valor builds up the image of a mega-man; the dissociation creates a network of mutual interdependence between body and mind, between younger and older generation. Modern societies are based on a different "wise" principle, the division of power. Traditional societies are built on the "wise" principle of balance, taming the physical power of the young by the insight and experience of the old.

There is a striking document that reflects upon the wisdom inherent in the fundamental combination of the potentials of son and father, body and mind. It is a late medieval text in which the allegory of wisdom interprets the mystery of the trinity (I leave out the verses on the third element, the holy spirit). In the divine realm, the order of corrupted nature is inverted; here, god the father is associated with might and power, god the son with wisdom:

> A fader is, thou wost, a name of age,
> Of impotence, and of debylite;
> A son a name is of youthe and courage,
> Of inscyence and instabylyte; . . .
> Wherfor the Fader in the Trynyte
> We clepe (equals call) "mighty," the Sonne, "full of all wyt," . . .
> To avoyde the vyce that in kynd (equals nature) is knyt
>
> (Harvey, 1984, p. 21ff)

What is achieved through inversion in the divine realm is achieved through the principle of balance in the human realm: a mitigation of the shortcomings of each age group through cultural institutions of interdependence.

The Ontogenetic Perspective: Achieved Wisdom.   To explore the potential for wisdom today, it is not enough to present a historical record of its complexity and longevity. We also have to look at the reasons for which it was obviated or has become obsolete. In posttraditional cultures that have a positive attitude to evolutionary change, history, and innovation, as well as to democracy, liberalism, and individuality, old age becomes socially dysfunctional. In modern civilizations old age has turned into a problem of care, attendance, protection, and charity. There is no implicit philosophy of the life cycle that invests old age with normative values, estimation, and prestige. The knowledge that was formerly sought from the elders was delegated to books and archives, which were considered much more reliable containers of knowledge. With the wide distribution of printed books, learning could be acquired by reading.

Gifted students no longer needed to sit at the feet of a given master. "Why should old men be preferred to their juniors now that it is possible for the young by diligent study to acquire the same knowledge?" asked an author of the 15th century (Eisenstein, 1979, p. 66). With such evolutionary changes, old age ceased to be a social norm and a cultural value. The task to give meaning to the last period of one's life was now delegated to the individual. Epicure had given the advice to timely study of philosophy in order to have something to rely on when the strength of the body vanished. In a similar way, the concept of wisdom suggests a precious resource to compensate for the decline of the physical capacities. But it is evident that such wisdom has ceased to be a social institution; it has to be achieved by the individual in the framework of his or her own development throughout life.

Psychological studies of wisdom and old age have concentrated on the ontogenetic and organismic perspective of wisdom. In this framework, the postreproductive years of retirement are associated with wisdom, which is defined as the integration of general cognitive, affective, and reflective components (Clayton & Birren, 1980). It is considered to be the result of an ongoing, progressive mental growth (Piaget, 1970) or a form of expertise achieved by continuous accumulation and optimizing of the cognitive faculties (Baltes & Smith, 1990). In the evolutionary perspective, wisdom is the ultimate stage in a teleology of immanent development.

We all know, however, that we do not grow wiser with the same irresistible and irreversible logic that we grow older. If wisdom is a quality that is no longer ascribed, neither through cultural nor through evolutionary norms, how is it generated? An important factor is life-event determinants, the specific yet generic biographical challenges that create the age-specific horizon of possibilities, tasks, and challenges (Baltes & Reese, 1984). The generic challenges of maturity are reproduction, upbringing and education of children, as well as an active occupational life and possibly the combination of both. The generic challenges of old age are the waning of influence and power, skills and strength. In a way different from any other stage of the life span, the last one is overshadowed by death. Whereas death is accidental in the other stages, it becomes existential in old age. In cultures all over the world, acknowledgment of death has been considered the prime generator of wisdom. If there is still justification is associating wisdom with age, it is perhaps less because we can count on some immanent organic progression or evolution, but because we have to face the limitation of our potentials and the necessity of death. Wisdom is generated through the challenge to process our lives and make decisions under the impact of this recognition. It is possible to put in a simple phrase what is most difficult to grasp: that death is the primal and permanent challenge to which wisdom is the response. This formula captures a universal feature of wisdom.

B. WISDOM AND DEATH

In a nonevolutionary perspective, we would favor an approach to wisdom that is related to discontinuity, crisis, and the existential challenge of death rather than relate wisdom to unimpeded continuous development. It is significant to note that death shares the fate of wisdom in having become something of a blind spot in Western culture. To stress the connection between wisdom and death is to point at a complex that was deeply forgotten under the premises and promises of progress. In a memorable lecture in Munich in 1919, shortly before his death, Max Weber (1973) touched upon this point of Western amnesia. For Weber, the collective project of science leaves little room for individual meaning. It has devalued death and drained life of its meaning. Science is the promise of a collective immortality; individuals die but humankind is eternal if it invests itself into the continuous growth and accumulation of knowledge. The obligations of science have taught human beings to abstract from the self and look beyond one's own death. The individuals' scientific endeavors can only contribute a tiny fragment of meaning to the overall investment, and it is the purpose of this fragment to be superseded in the infinite progress. In the light of this collective and transhistorical progress, the personal demands are obliterated, existential cares are not heeded, individual deaths have no meaning.

According to Weber, Tolstoi's central question was: Is there meaning in death or not? And his answer was: For members of Western cultures, no. The principle of progress undermines the lot of the individual, the meaningfulness of life and death. Abraham or any Russian peasant could die "old, having reached satiety of life"; they had a chance to achieve wisdom as the problems that moved them could still be answered within the scope of their experiences. For the members of Western civilization, however, there is no finitude in meaning, no resting point, and no satiety, only the suspense of meaning in the restless ongoing drive of transindividual progress.

Weber's reflections on Tolstoi's question point at a problem hidden in our modern scientific-technological world. The existential questions revolve around the essentially nonprogressive and, at the core, unchanging human nature. In a world that has opted for progress and change, they tend to lose their cultural significance. To be sure, there is the possibility of faith or of loyalty to a group as answers to existential questions. Wisdom, however, as has often been noted, is an art of problem finding rather than problem solving; it has a chance to thrive where change and uncertainty prevail and where definite and binding answers are missing or suspended.

C. EXPERIENCE AND AGE IN A WORLD OF CHANGE

Others have related the devaluation of wisdom in modern society to the dramatic changes in everyday experience. Modernity became possible when a fundamental break with tradition occurred. This break has led to a "dissociation of past and future" (J. Ritter), to a "gulf between experiences and expectations": (*Erfahrungsraum and Erwartunhgshorizont*, R. Koselleck, see Marquard, 1986, p. 86). In this time frame, which is adapted to evolution, the past ceases to be an integral dimension of life and is handed over to the care of custodians. Walter Benjamin, who was extremely sensitive to symptoms of a dramatically changing life world, observed that the art of oral narrative was on the decline. Something was lost that had once been the most reliable thing in the world: the capacity to convey, transmit, and exchange experiences. For Benjamin, the art of telling a story is intimately linked with the art of giving advice. Both make cognitive use of experience. Wisdom, according to Benjamin (1991), is the epic, or narrative shape of truth. But this kind of truth is dependent on reliable patterns and exemplary situations. To tell a story is to transform older experiences and to make them part of one's own stock. Other than the genre of the novel, which was developed together with the newspaper and is built on the principle of innovation, the art of story telling is dependent on a chain of generations, transmitting experiences, reflections, and values within a framework of recognizable circumstances.

The rupture between the past and the future, however, has shaken the foundation of this permanence. Experience lost its value in the 20th century. It could no longer be applied in a world that had changed beyond recognition. As mechanical production and ever new technologies of media took over, the accumulated fund of traditional wisdom became obsolete. What one had learned in youth was no longer usable when one had reached adulthood.

Benjamin's (1991) diagnosis of the waning of wisdom in the modern world has been confirmed from various points of view. The ancient logic of continuity was contained in the maxim: *ars longa, vita brevis.* Life is short, fleeting, fragmentary but knowledge and experience persevere. The discontinuity of human existence finds its remedy in the continuity of tradition. The conditions of modernity have inverted the logic. Now the values and patterns of life change even more rapidly than the individuals: *ars brevis, vita longa.* Today, we are witnessing within a life span a deeper change in the fundamental conditions and pragmatics of life than former generations have within centuries (Hahn, 1991).

The historian H. Kittsteiner (1991) illuminated another aspect in asking: What are favorable or unfavorable conditions for wisdom? He pointed at a fundamental difference between life in traditional and posttraditional societies. Traditional life is characterized by the instability of the foreground and the stability of the background of life. At every instant, life is exposed to violent and incalculable threats from the social and natural environment (wars, plagues, famines, or sickness). Although the actual conditions of life were radically contingent, the general conditions of human existence, however, remained stable: the way of life in the social and natural world. Under such conditions wisdom flourished; it could count on the repetition of recognizable situations and the validity of exemplary patterns of experience.

Modern times, on the other hand, are characterized by a stability of the foreground and a dramatic instability of the background. Laws, medicine, and technology have made everyday life so much more secure and expectable. But although we can count on the next day, we can no longer imagine what the world will be like for our children. We are not able to solve their problems with our answers. Wisdom loses its value in a world that has opted for change (Kittsteiner, 1991). This analysis is close to that which M. Weber presented earlier. In traditional societies, humankind has a chance of individual perfection through wisdom; one can grow wise as an individual whereas humankind stays essentially the same; in modern societies, individuals no longer grow wise, but humankind is considered to progress in knowledge. Wisdom (if that is still the word) is acquired by the species, not by the individuals.

The philosopher O. Marquard (1986) made an interesting contribution to the question of wisdom and aging in the modern world. According to Marquard, the accelerated change of our life worlds has engendered a profound alienation from reality (he called this syndrome *"tachogene Weltfremdheit,"* p. 82). For Marquard, growing old in our modern society no longer involves the prospect of a steady accumulation of knowledge and a confirmation of experience. According to him, factual and procedural knowledge vanishes rather than increases as one grows older in the present state of society. The situation of the elderly is now more like that of infants than that of the wise. For the very young, the world is in most instances strange, new, and opaque. So it is again for the elderly when experience loses its cultural and interpersonal validity. In an incomprehensible world, they are doomed to regress to a state of infantility.

Marquard's (1991) analysis of aging as loss of wisdom or a process of defamiliarization with the world can be summed up in five points: (a) devaluation of experience in a dramatically changing world, (b) a growing dependence on a kind of knowledge that is no longer related to experience, (c) a continuous compulsion to learn as a substitute for experience, (d) the derealization and half-fictionalization of the world, and (e) illusions and unrealistic expectations take the place of experience.

D. EFFEMINATE WISDOM AND VIRILE WISDOM

A thinker who praised wisdom but discarded the traditional nexus between wisdom and old age was Nietzsche. He called his own ideal of wisdom "the most *dangerous* thing in the world" (Welsch, 1989). "The sage in us dries up our elan" wrote Cioran, denouncing wisdom in a Nietzschean vein. Traditional wisdom was associated with quietism, self-restraint, balance, and continuity; Nietzsche's wisdom was to be associated with violence and rupture. Traditional wisdom was developed to abate the passions; Nietzsche's wisdom was to revive and strengthen them.

In the traditional framework of wisdom, the rational, reflective, and emotive faculties are cultivated as a compensation for the declining body and as a controller of the impulses of the will. The will is a dangerous force that has to be tamed in order to make a social and wholesome life possible. Nietzsche's transvaluation of wisdom asserts the powers of the will against the values of abstinence and self-restraints. Traditional wisdom, for him, was the philosophy of the sickly and toothless. He took it to be an abdication of life and opposed it to a wisdom that would be the expression of what he considered life, namely the will, vigor, and strong instincts.

This vitalistic attitude associates traditional concepts of wisdom with a decline of virility. This explains a gender difference in the attitude toward wisdom. For elder men, wisdom sometimes has this taste of effeminacy. Some of them are keen to dissociate themselves from the goal or reputation of wisdom. What for others may be an honorific term is for them tinged with boredom and senility. The title of the memoirs of a virile German actor, Curd Juergens, is meant as a statement of self-assertion and pride: *60 years and not a bit wise! (60 Jahre und kein bisschen weise)*.

E. THE WISDOM OF YOUTH

W. Benjamin's conclusion was that in a world of utter instability and complexity, in a world cut off from the past and exposed to the future, a new type of wisdom emerges. It is the wisdom of the child whose mind is exceptionally unbiased and alert because she or he is naturally equipped to cope with the unexpected and unexperienced, the utterly new. If the wisdom of the aged was based on a familiarity with the world, then it is the wisdom of the children to cope with an unfamiliar world. In Western tradition, the child is a symbolic figure with negative connotations (lack of culture, knowledge, and tradition) as well as positive ones (messianism, creativity, and the sudden breaking in of the new). After the long way to wisdom associated with maturity and old age had proved futile, the short way to wisdom associated with the child became fascinating (Zons, 1989). The type of wisdom that Benjamin considered appropriate for the modern industrial world with its permanent revolutions and transvaluations is epiphanic, sudden, immediate. The suggestive metaphor for this explosive kind of wisdom is the stroke of lightning. In a sudden illumination, the new is discovered with the evidence of a shock. It resists verbal communication and the formation of experience. It appears and disappears. Nothing remains.

F. WISDOM AND CONTINUITY

I have discussed various theories according to which wisdom is the last thing expected to flourish in our contemporary world. Yet what these views overlook is the essential continuity in human affairs underlying ever so drastic changes and revolutions. *The new meat is eaten with the old forks* was Brecht's version of the recognition. It is in itself a maxim of wisdom, dismissing total breaks and radical beginnings with a deeper sense of continuity.

One might as well invert the perspective and say: Wisdom disappears when the world is conceived in terms of radical change, and it reappears with the disposition to see a continuity in human impulses and actions, endeavors and experiences, problems and dilemmas. It is a perspective that contributes to make life more continuous, more recognizable, more familiar. The ever so intricate diagnosis of a world that has no place for wisdom ratifies such a situation. The insistence on continuities will make room for wisdom. The difference, however, between wisdom and traditionalism should not be overlooked. Wisdom does not praise continuity as a value in itself. It knows too well the continuity of foolishness, arrogance, and terror. The continuity of sanity, on the other hand, is much more precarious. Another line from Brecht highlights this obstinate continuity of wisdom, which is as improbable as it is irrepressible:

From the new antennae resounded the old stupidities,
wisdom was passed on from mouth to mouth. (Brecht, 1967, p. 856)

VI. Summary and Conclusions

Instead of presenting a neatly defined and theoretically unified concept of wisdom, I have tried to discover wisdom in concrete contexts and in the sometimes irritating multifariousness of its manifestations. The historical investigation has shown how wisdom has wavered between mundane and transcendent orientations. The more decisive changes of wisdom may be inferred from the partners with which it was yoked in opposition. Among the various contraries of wisdom were: vice and foolishness, technical skills, the human (as opposed to the divine) scope of experience, profane knowledge, disbelief, stupidity and, finally, science.

The four types of the sage highlighted different qualifications for wisdom: a sound judgment, a knowledge of how to wield the cosmic forces, practical and experiential knowledge related to a good life, and a mature relativism that considers the self within a larger perspective. The question about the relation between wisdom and age led into a discussion of the favorable and unfavorable conditions for the flourishing of wisdom. The suppression of death in Western culture combined with an ideology of progress and a rapidly changing life world are factors that have rendered the world less and less safe for wisdom.

I want to conclude with two suggestions. The first concerns *the cultural milieu and reputation of wisdom*. Perhaps the question about the favorable conditions for wisdom ought to be cast into a different form. The way to put the question should not be: "Is our world safe for wisdom?" but rather, "Which knowledge is indispensable for men and women to make their living and aging more worthwhile?" Wittgenstein who mapped the universe of scientific knowledge in his *Tractatus logicophilosophicus* conceded in this text: "We feel that even when all possible scientific questions are answered, the problems of our lives are not yet touched upon" (6.52).

Science may have been the great rival of wisdom in modernity, but it has become evident that however powerful this rival may be, it will never be able to replace wisdom. Science cannot address the problems that are raised within the scope of wisdom. The repression of wisdom by science has led into a dangerous impasse: "While being armed to the teeth with knowledge, we could end up with literally empty hands, perplexed and helplessly confronted with the challenges of life" (Guggenberger, 1987, p. 73).

Looking into the cultural history of humankind, however, one easily discovers the persistence of similar existential problems and is impressed by the many different ways in which these have received serious cultural attention. Cultural historians who recall and renew this evidence might help to promote the cultural rehabilitation of wisdom in our world — not as a mythical figure of ultimate knowledge, but as a specific response to pressing human demands. Such an acknowledgment of the age-old validity and irreplacability of wisdom might create better conditions for the growth of wisdom.

My second suggestion concerns *the interpersonal status of wisdom*. Empirical assessments by psychologists interested in the various concepts of wisdom in different cohorts have yielded an interesting result. Whereas younger people tend to associate wisdom with age, the elderly themselves are not prepared to do so (Clayton & Birren, 1980). They are far from confirming that in growing older they have moved closer toward wisdom. I would interpret this result as a confirmation of the interpersonal status of wisdom. I have distinguished between ascribed and achieved wisdom as a cultural predicate bestowed on a ruler or the elderly, on one hand, and wisdom as the unique acquisition of an individual during his or her individual life span, on the other. It is now time to qualify this distinction and maintain that in a minimal sense, all wisdom is ascribed. For wisdom to appear it takes at least two persons: the wise person and another one who identifies him or her as wise."I am wise" is not a well-formulated sentence in the cultural grammar of wisdom. Wisdom does not "belong" to the wise person. Which is to say, the evaluation of wisdom is part of the wisdom itself. To return to our starting point, wisdom is generated in the eye of the beholder and not in that of the observer. Of course this does not mean that there is no place for the observer, or that wisdom is of its very nature mysterious and defies empirical research. It only reminds the observer not to forget the beholder or ask him or herself, whether he or she is really the observer or rather the beholder, namely the person who is constituting wisdom by identifying it. Wisdom calls for a contextual approach that considers it not as emanating from one person but as generated between at least two persons. It may be true that in our contemporary society the wise person has not the clear profile or the accepted social quality that it had in other epochs and cultures. Yet as long as human problems prevail, a disposition also will prevail to exclaim from time to time: That is wisdom!

References

Arlin, P. K. (1975). Cognitive development in adulthood: A fifth stage? *Development Psychology, 19*, 602–606.

Assmann, A. (Ed.). (1991). Weisheit. *Archäologie der literarischen Kommunikation III*. München: Wilhelm Fink.

Assmann, J. (1991). *Weisheit, Schrift und Literatur im alten Ägypten*. In A. Assmann (Ed.), Weisheit. *Archäologie der literarischen Kommunikation III* (pp. 475–500). München: Wilhelm Fink.

Balmer, H. P. (1991). *Die Weisheit der untröstlichen Troester. Der moralistische Diskurs*. In A. Assmann (Ed.), Weisheit, *Archäologie der literarischen Kommunikation III* (pp. 525–536) München: Wilhelm Fink.

Baltes, P., & Reese, H. W. (1984). The life-span perspective in developmental psychology. In M. H. Bornstein & M. E. Lamb (Eds.), *Developmental psychology: An advanced textbook*. Hillsdale, NJ: Lawrence Erlbaum Associates.

Baltes, P. B., & Smith, J. (1990). Toward a psychology of wisdom and its ontogenesis. In R. J. Sternberg (Ed.), *Wisdom. Its nature, origins, and development*. New York: Cambridge University Press.

Benjamin, W. (1991). Der Erzähler. Betrachtungen zum Werk Nikolai Lesskows. In R. Tiedemann & H. Schweppenhäuser (Eds.), *Gesammelte Schriften* (Vol. 2, pp. 438–465). Frankfurt: Suhrkamp.

Biersterfeldt, H. H. (1991). *Weisheit als mot juste in der klassisch-arabischen Literatur.* In A. Assmann (Ed.), Weisheit, *Archäologie der literarischen Kommunikation III* (pp. 367–386). München: Wilhelm Fink.

Brecht, B. (1967). *Gesammelte Werke,* 10. Frankfurt: Suhrkamp.

Clayton, V. P., & Birren, J. E. (1980). The development of wisdom across the life span: A reexamination of an ancient topic. In (Ed.), *Life-span development and behavior* (Vol. 3, pp. 103–135). Hillsdale, NJ: Lawrence Erlbaum Associates.

Csikszentmihalyi, M., & Rathunde, K. (1990). The psychology of wisdom: An evolutionary interpretation. In R. J. Sternberg (Ed.), *Wisdom. Its nature, origins, and development* (pp. 25–51). New York: Cambridge University Press.

Dadelsen, H.- C. von. (1984). Bob Dylan oder die Umkehr von Bab-ylon, *Melos,* 4.

Debus, A. G. (1978). *Man and nature in the Renaissance.* Cambridge, England: Cambridge University Press.

Eisenstein, E. (1979). *The printing press as an agent of change. Communications and cultural transformations in early-modern Europe* (Vols. 1 & 2). Cambridge, England: Cambridge University Press.

Groys, B. (1991). *Die russische Sophiologie. Vladimir Solowjow und seine Schule.* In A. Assmann (Ed.), Weisheit, *Archäologie der literarischen Kommunikation III* (pp. 345–354). München: Wilhelm Fink.

Guggenberger, B. (1987). *Das Menschenrecht auf Irrtum.* Munich, Vienna: Hanser.

Hahn, A. (1991). *Zur Soziologie der Weisheit.* In A. Assmann (Ed), Weisheit, Archäologie der literarischen Kommunikation III (pp. 47–58). München: Wilhelm Fink.

Harvey, R. (Ed.). (1984). *The court of sapience* (Toronto Medieval Texts and Translations, 2). Toronto: University of Toronto Press.

Haug, W. (1991). *Vom Glanz der Weisheit zur Verzweiflung des Wissens.* In A. Assmann (Ed.), Weisheit, *Archäologie der literarischen Kommunikation III* (pp. 387–406). München: Wilhelm Fink.

Hölscher, U. (1991). *Heraklit über göttliche und menschliche Weisheit.* In A. Assmann (Ed), Weisheit, *Archäologie der literarischen Kommunikation III* (pp. 73–80). München: Wilhelm Fink.

Keppler, A., & Luckmann, T. (1989). Weisheits-vermittlung im Alltag. Wer in den Augen eines anderen weise ist, ist weise. *Oelmüller,* pp. 148–160.

Kittsteiner, H. D. (1991). *Über Weisheit, Kasuistik, Moralität und Geschichte.* In A. Assmann (Ed.), Weisheit, *Archäologie der literarischen Kommunikation III* (pp. 513–524). München: Wilhelm Fink.

Krämer, H. J. (1976). Prolegomena zu einer Kategorienlehre des richtigen Lebens. In *Philosophisches Jb. der Görres-Ges.* 83, 1. Halbband, 71–97.

Krämer, H. J. (1983). *Plädoyer für eine Rehabilitierung der Individualethik.* Amsterdam: Gruener.

Krämer, H. J. (1985). Neue Wege der philosophischen Ethik. *Salzburger Jb. für Philosophie,* 30, 87–96.

Lichtheim, M. (1973–1980). *Ancient egyptian literature* (Vols. 1–3), Berkeley: University of California Press.

Luck, G. (1964). Zur Geschichte des Begriffs "sapienta." In *Archiv für Begriffsgeschichte.*

Marquard, O. (1986). Zeitalter der Weltfremdheit? Beitrag zur Analyse der Gegenwart. In *Apologie des Zufälligen. Philosophische Studien* (pp. 76–97). Stuttgart: Ph. Reclam.

Migne, J. P. (1844–1864) *Patrologiae cursus completus . . . omnium sanctorum patrum* (Series Latina, Vols. 175–177). Paris.

Milton, J. (1963). Of education. In M. W. Wallace (Ed.), *Milton's prose. A selection* (pp. 145–158). London: Oxford University Press.

Montaigne, M. de (1915). *Essays*, III, 13, *Gesammelte Werke,übers.* v. Johann Joachim Bode, Otto Flake, und Wilhelm Weigan (Hg.). München: Georg Müller.

Nietzsche, F. (1960). Wissenschaft und Weisheit im Kampfe. In K. Schlechta (Ed.), *Friedrich Nietzsche. Werke in drei Bänden* (Vol. 3, pp. 333–348). Munich: Hanser.

Oelmüller, W. (Hg.) (1989). *Philosophie und Weisheit*, Kolloquien zur Gegenwartsphilosophie Bd.12. Paderborn: F. Schoeningh.

Piaget, J. (1970). *Genetic epistemology*. New York: Columbia University Press.

Plutarch. (1942). Von der Heiterkeit der Seele. In W. Ax (Ed.), *Plutarch. Moralia* (pp. 1–33). Leipzig: Diederich.

Raible, W. (1991). *Die Weisheit des (Fall-) Rechts*. In A. Assmann (Ed.), *Weisheit, Archäologie der literarischen Kommunikation III* (pp. 437–452). München: Wilhelm Fink.

Rice, E. F., Jr. (1958). *The renaissance idea of wisdom*. Cambridge, MA: Harvard University Press.

Ritschl, D. (1986). Die Erfahrung der Wahrheit. Die Steuerung von Denken und Handeln durch implizite Axiome. In *Konzepte. Ökumene, Medizin, Ethik. Gesammelte Aufsätze* (pp. 147–166). Munich: Chr. Kaiser Verlag.

Robinson, D. N. (1990). Wisdom through the ages. In R. J. Sternberg (Ed), *Wisdom. Its nature, origins, and development* (pp. 13–24). New York: Cambridge University Press.

Schmidt, S. J. (1991). *Weisheit, oder*. In A. Assmann (Ed.), *Weisheit, Archäologie der literarischen Kommunikation III* (pp. 555–564). München: Wilhelm Fink.

Sowarka, D. (1989). Weisheit und weise Personen: Common-sense-Konzepte älterer Menschen, *Zeitschrift für Entwicklungspsychologie und pädagogische Psychologie* 21.

Sternberg, R. J. (Ed.). (1990). *Wisdom. Its nature, origins, and development*. New York: Cambridge University Press.

Sundermeier, Th. (1991). *Der Mensch wird zum Menschen durch den Menschen. Weisheit in den afrikanischen Religionen*. In A. Assmann (Ed.), Weisheit, *Archäologie der literarischen kommunikation III* (pp. 117–130). München: Wilhelm Fink.

Taylor, J. (1961). *The didascalicon of Hugh of St. Victor*. New York: Columbia University Press.

Tenbruck, F. H. (1976). Zur soziologie der Sophistik, *Neue Hefte fur Philosophie. Moderne Sophistik, 10*, 51–77.

Trilling, L. (1972). *Sincerity and authenticity*. Cambridge, MA: Harvard University Press.

Ustick, L. W. (1932). Advice to a son: A type of seventeenth-century conduct book. *Studies in Philosophy, 29*, 409–441.

Von Stietencron, H. (1991). *Der Weise in Indien. Entsprechungen zur Weisheit in der indischen Tradition*. In A. Assmann (Ed.), Weisheit, *Archäologie der literarischen Kommunikation III* (pp. 271–288). München: Wilhelm Fink.

Wagner, R. (1991). *Die Unhandlichkeit des Konfuzius*. In A. Assmann (Ed.), Weisheit, *Archäologie der literarischen Kommunikation III* (pp. 455–464). München: Wilhelm Fink.

Weber, M. (1973). Vom inneren Beruf zur Wissenschaft. In J. Winckelmann (Ed.), *Max Weber. Soziologie, universalgeschichtliche Analysen, Politik* (pp. 311–339). Stuttgart: A. Kröner.

Welsch, W. (1989). Weisheit in einer Welt der Pluralität. In *Oelmüller*, pp. 214–249.

Zons, R. S. (1989). Die Weisheit der Alten und die Weisheit der Kinder. In *Oelmüller*, pp. 78–96.

Log-Linear Modeling of Categorical Data in Developmental Research

Alexander von Eye

MICHIGAN STATE UNIVERSITY

Kurt Kreppner

MAX PLANCK INSTITUTE FOR HUMAN DEVELOPMENT AND EDUCATION

Holger Weßels

FREIE UNIVERSITÄT BERLIN

INSTITUT FÜR SOZIALPÄDAGOGIK UND ERWACHSENENBILDUNG

Abstract

Developmental research often entails cross-sectional or longitudinal designs involving such categorical variables as early, on-time, or late maturation, family type, or problem status. In order to identify and extend data analytic methods useful in such studies, this article discusses the use of design matrices for log-linear analysis of developmental hypotheses in cross-sectional and longitudinal designs. The λ-parameters in log-linear models are introduced as weights for vectors of a design matrix, X. In exploratory or computer algorithm-controlled application of log-linear modeling, X is set up by the computer program, irrespective of the researcher's specific hypotheses concerning main effects and interactions. The chapter describes means to create design matrices to model hypotheses about development during any period of the life span. Data examples illustrate the analysis of cross-sectional designs, therapy outcome, and the testing of trends. The article also discusses strategies of log-linear modeling and problems with the interpretation of the parameter size.

I. Introduction

In research pertinent to any period within the life span, researchers frequently use statistical methods tailored for normally distributed, continuous data. Examples of normally distributed variables include spatial abilities (Petersen & Crockett, 1986) and memory performance (Schneider & Weinert, 1989). The most common methods for analyzing data sets in developmental research, causal modeling, or SEM (structural equation modeling), multiple regression analysis, or analysis of variance require outcome data of this type. However, many developmental studies produce data via direct observation and videotapes. In many of these cases, data do not meet the requirements for applying statistical methods from the general linear model (GLM).

Examples of categorical variables include classifications of events, behaviors, or communication acts. Examples of such classifications include the onset of menarche and the pattern of drug use (e.g., Tubman, Vicary, Von Eye, & Lerner, 1990). Categorical variables are often analyzed descriptively with researchers reporting the relative frequencies of categories. Categorical variables are also used as predictors for quantitative variables or as stratification variables. The method of log-linear analysis (Agresti, 1990; Bishop, Fienberg, & Holland, 1975; Fienberg, 1980; Haberman, 1978, 1979) is a method for analysis of cross-classifications.

Log-linear modeling allows one to analyze associations among nominal level categorical variables. In addition, extensions of log-linear modeling have been proposed that allow one to consider the ordinal character of variables (Agresti, 1984; Clogg, 1982; Goodman, 1979, 1985; Green, 1988). Examples of ordinal variables include SES, grades in school (e.g., Thoresen, 1991), adolescents' career interests (Schulenberg, Goldstein, & Vondracek, 1991), and many items in questionnaires (e.g., Radloff, 1977). In general, all changes that can be described by a bigger–smaller relationship belong to the class of ordinal variables.

In longitudinal research, categorical variables often remain unanalyzed for two reasons. First, researchers do not see a match between complex developmental hypotheses and statements resulting from standard application of, for instance, χ^2 measures. Second, interpretation of parameters of more complex multivariate methods such as log-linear modeling is not always easy (see Clogg & Eliason, 1987; Elliott, 1988; Holt, 1979; Page, 1977; Wilson, 1979).

This chapter discusses two types of applications not addressed in the recent literature (e.g., Green, 1988). The first is the custom-tailored testing of developmental hypotheses. The basic idea is to set up design matrices reflecting specific developmental hypotheses (Clogg, Eliason, & Grego, 1990; Hagenaars, 1990). The second application concerns the analysis of time series of events. Here, design matrices are created such that the shape of the time series is reflected or groups can be compared with respect to the frequency of behaviors over time. Both applications involve analyzing variables at the nominal or ordinal level. Both types of applications are important to developmental research.

II. Log-Linear Modeling of Cross-Classified Variables

Log-Linear modeling provides the researcher with the following options (cf. Goodman, 1984):

1. *Analysis of the joint frequency distribution of variables.* Results of these analyses are expressed typically in terms of a distribution type jointly displayed by the variables. For instance, two variables can be symmetrically distributed such that a square cross-tabulation is the same as its transpose, or $m_{ij} = m_{ji}$, where m_{ij} denotes the observed frequency in cell ij and m_{ji} denotes the observed frequency in cell ji.
2. *Analysis of the association pattern of response variables.* Results of these analyses are expressed typically in terms of first and higher order interactions between the variables constituting a contingency table. For instance, two variables can be either statistically independent or associated. In the latter case, states of one variable co-occur with certain states of the other variable more often than with other states.
3. *Assessment of the possible dependence of a response variable on explanatory or predictor variables.* Results of these analyses are expressed typically in terms of conditional probabilities of the states of the dependent or response variable, given the levels of the predictors. The most elementary model for two variables assumes that the criterion states are conditionally equiprobable, given the predictor state.

In order to adopt a log-linear model, the following three criteria must be met. First, a model must not be significantly discrepant from the relationships present in the data. In other words, the expected frequency distribution, estimated to meet the specifications of the model, must not be significantly different from the observed frequency distribution. Second, a model must be parsimonious. That is, it must contain as few main effect and interaction terms as possible and the latter must be of the lowest possible order. Third, the model should be in accordance with substantive assumptions. Comparisons of alternative models use statistical criteria to determine whether a less parsimonious model would provide a significantly better reproduction of the observed frequency distribution than a more parsimonious model.

Log-linear models are expressed typically in equation form such as in Equation 1 as follows. Each term of those equations expresses either a main effect or an interaction. The maximum number of main effects of d variables is, of course, d. The maximum number of interaction terms is $2^d - d - 1$. For instance, for $d = 2$ variables, the maximum number of interaction terms is $2^2 - 2 - 1 = 1$. For $d = 4$ variables, this number is $2^4 - 4 - 1 = 11$. Suppose we analyze the $d = 3$ variables A, B, and C. Then, the saturated model, or the model that contains all possible main effects and interactions, is

$$\log (m_{ijk}) = \lambda_0 + \lambda_i^A + \lambda_j^B + \lambda_k^C + \lambda_{ij}^{AB} + \lambda_{ik}^{AC} + \lambda_{jk}^{BC} + \lambda_{ijk}^{ABC}, \quad (1)$$

where λ_0 denotes the grand mean of the logarithm of the expected frequencies. The λ_1 denote the main effects, the λ_{12} denote the first-order interactions, and the λ_{123} denote the second-order interactions. (Later, we discuss the interpretation of interactions.)

In the pursuit of all three options, researchers attempt to fit models more parsimonious than the saturated model. This attempt involves four steps (Green, 1988). First, the researcher specifies models to be tested. In explanatory research, expectations concerning the pattern of relationships are derived from theory. For many theories more than one model can meaningfully be derived. These alternative models can differ, for instance, in the degree to which they are parsimonious. The usual approach to specifying log-linear models involves deleting terms from the saturated model. For instance, deleting the last term in Equation 1 and one of the terms describing the pairwise interactions leads to a model of conditional independence. Later, we show how to code interaction values in a special way. This allows the researcher to parameterize departures from independence (or other) models.

Second, the researcher estimates a log-linear model (e.g., see Fienberg, 1980; Green, 1988; Upton, 1978). This step involves calculating estimates of the values for the λ parameters and the expected frequencies. One of the main characteristics of expected frequencies is that they display a frequency distribution reflecting the model specifications.

Methods for estimating expected frequencies include weighted least squares and, far more common, maximum likelihood (ML) techniques (see Agresti, 1984; Bishop et al., 1975). Except for very simple models, which can be estimated by applying simple, one-step formulas, iterative computation is standard procedure.

Third, the researcher performs significance tests to determine if the differences between the observed and the expected frequency distributions are significant. The two most common tests are the likelihood ratio (LR) L^2,

$$L^2 = \Sigma_i \; m_i \; \log(m_i/\hat{m}_i) \tag{2}$$

and the Pearson X^2

$$X^2 = \Sigma_i \; (m_i - \hat{m}_i)^2/\hat{m}_i, \tag{3}$$

where $\hat{m}_i$ denotes the estimated expected frequencies and m_i the observed frequencies. In both formulas, the summation goes over all cells in the contingency table. The logarithm used in Equation 2 usually has base e = 2.71828 . . . ; that is, it is the natural logarithm. If the specified model is true, the two test statistics have the same asymptotic distribution. The differences between L^2 values are still distributed as χ^2 if the L^2 describe models from different hierarchical levels; in other words L^2 is preferable when one compares models. Pearson's χ^2 is defined even if the observed frequency is m = 0. (Notice that, although log 0 is not defined, one usually proceeds as if log 0 = 0.)

These test statistics typically are used to determine whether a model adequately represents an observed frequency distribution. If the difference between observed and expected frequencies is not significant, the model fit is good. We may then conclude that the model adequately represents the relationships present in the data. Otherwise, the model can be rejected.

These statistical tests may also be used to compare models from different hierarchical levels (nested models). The difference between two L^2 values is evaluated under the difference of the degrees of freedom of the two models. If the L^2 difference is significant, the more parsimonious model accounts for significantly less of the observed relationships than the more complex model.

The λ-values can be used to determine the significance of main effects and interactions. Divided by their standard errors, λ-values approximate standard normal z-values. The null hypothesis is that $\lambda = 0$.

Fourth, the researcher interprets the model. Log-linear models are interpreted using two types of information. The first is the pattern of main effects and interactions describing relationships among variables. Main effects tell us that univariate frequencies of variable categories differ significantly from their expected values. Interactions tell us that groups of two or more variables show a nonrandom pattern of co-occurrence. In other words, interactions tell us that lower order relationships are not constant across the levels of an additional variable. Notice, however, that when interactions exist, their lower order relatives, for example, main effects, do not refer to marginal distributions (cf. Holt, 1979; Page, 1977).

The λ-parameters are a second source of information. They provide information on the type of relationships. For instance, in two-way tables, positive λ-parameters for a row column-pair suggest that, considering the marginal frequencies, the probability for this pair is higher than for pairs with negative λ-parameters. Here, one must keep in mind that relatively high probabilities do not suggest high frequencies, because the marginal probabilities can be low.

The λ-parameters for three- and higher way interactions are more difficult to interpret. They indicate the amount by which lower order interaction parameters must be modified to depict the higher order interaction. Elliott (1988) introduced a method for expressing higher order interaction parameters directly rather than in terms of lower order interactions. Alba (1988) gave a description of how to interpret parameters in hierarchical log-linear models.

In the following sections we use the design matrix approach to log-linear models (Evers & Namboodiri, 1978). The design matrix approach has two major advantages (cf. Hagenaars, 1990 Rindskopf, 1990). First, it allows the researcher to specify models difficult or impossible to specify in terms of margins. These models include nonstandard models and many of Goodman's (1984) models of association. Second, the design matrix approach provides a framework that incorporates both standard and nonstandard log-linear models. We use a notation close to the standard notation of design matrices in the GLM (cf. Haber, 1985; Landis & Koch, 1979; McCullagh & Nelder, 1983). In the recent literature, this notation has been used to discuss models of change (Clogg et al., 1990), specifically transition models, Markov models with special effects, and symmetry models.

The Use of Design Matrices in Log-Linear Modeling.   In Equation 1, the λ-parameters for the main effect of variable A are indexed by variable i, the λ-parameters for the main effect of variable B are indexed by variable j, the λ-parameters for the interaction between A and B are indexed by the variable pair ij, and so forth. Now let $\vec{m}$ be the vector of the logarithms of the expected cell frequencies, $\vec{\lambda}$ the vector of parameters and X a design matrix parallel to a design matrix in the GLM. Then, any log-linear model can be represented as

$$\vec{m} = X\vec{\lambda} \tag{4}$$

The design matrix X contains vectors that specify the effects of interest. For the three variables A, B, and C, all main effects and interactions appear in Equation 1. Each column of X corresponds to one parameter.[1] The

---

[1] It is interesting to note that the likelihood equations also can be expressed in terms of the design matrix. We obtain $X'\vec{m} = X'm$. This implies that each column of X specifies the equality of a certain linear combination of the expected and the observed frequencies. For example, the vector in the design matrix in Table IV implies that the sum and the average of the differences of frequencies in the two cohorts across the change patterns 1 through 4 will be reproduced in the expected frequencies.

column vectors of X are constructed using the following rules (cf. Rindskopf, 1990):

1. Each column vector of X corresponds to only one local hypothesis. Hypotheses contrast groups of cells. Common methods for specifying vectors include dummy and effect coding. Both methods define groups of cells. Dummy coding assigns a 1 to all cells that belong to a group. All other cells are assigned a 0. Effect coding contrasts two groups in comparison to the mean. One group is assigned a 1, the other a -1. All other cells are assigned a 0. The present article focuses on effect coding. If two groups of cells are compared, the null hypothesis is that the frequencies in the two groups of cells do not differ from average. The number of cells in the two groups may differ. If one wants to force the expected frequency to equal the observed frequency for one cell, one defines a vector that contains a 1 for this cell and a 0 for all other cells.

2. Suppose a variable has c states. Then, the maximum number of independent main-effect λ-parameters for this variable is $c - 1$. In other words, the vectors for main effects are set up such that the cth vector would be a linear combination of the $c - 1$ independent vectors. In general, the columns of the design matrix X should be linearly independent to avoid singularities.

3. Vectors for first- and higher order interactions result from elementwise multiplication of main effect vectors from different main effects. Suppose variable A has c_A states and variable B has c_B states. Then, the number of nonredundant parameters for the A $\times$ B interaction is $(c_A - 1)(c_B - 1)$. Similarly, the number of parameters for an A $\times$ B $\times$ C interaction is $(c_A - 1)(c_B - 1)(c_C - 1)$. In nonhierarchical models, vectors for interactions may be specified without reference to vectors for main effects. (It should be noted that determining a variable category as a reference as is typical for logistic models [Alba, 1988] yields main effect vectors that are nonindependent. Therefore, interaction vectors will be nonindependent also. As a result, the design matrix may not be of full rank.)

4. Each cell in a comparison group is assigned the same value in a vector of X. Typically, cells in one group are assigned a 1, cells in the other group are assigned a -1. If variables have more than two categories, cells not involved in a comparison are assigned a 0. (Note that for weighting purposes or to model ordinal variables, values different from 1 or -1 may be chosen; see Agresti, 1984; Green, 1988.) In effect coding where parameters describe deviations from means, the sum of the elements of each vector is zero. Therefore, vector elements can be unequal if the number of cells in the two groups differ. In orthogonal polynomial coding (see later), the cross-product of each two vectors in X is also zero (see, e.g., Johnson, 1985).

Specifying a vector for the design matrix X means investing a degree of freedom. Thus, the number of degrees of freedom (df) for the log-linear model given in Equation 4 is

$$df = t - h \tag{5}$$

where t denotes the number of cells in the contingency table and h is the number of vectors in X, including the vector for λ_0.

Simple log-linear models estimate expected frequencies in a way similar to Pearson's chi-square test from the marginals. More complex models set up design matrices and estimate expected frequencies using iterative algorithms (Agresti, 1984; Clogg et al., 1990; Haberman, 1978). To analyze the matrices for the hypotheses discussed later in this chapter, one may apply Newton–Raphson algorithms for finding the location of the most likely parameter values (see Agresti, 1984). The module LOGLINEAR in the SPSS-X software package allows one to process design matrices of the kind discussed in this article. Other programs include SAS-CATMOD and GLIM. Programs for microcomputers include Rindskopf's (1987) BASIC and PASCAL programs. As alternatives to such maximum likelihood approaches as estimation using Newton–Raphson algorithms weighted least squares methods are often discussed where the weights are proportional to cell-wise standard errors (Dobson, 1990; Wickens, 1989).

For dichotomous variables, design matrices for the analysis of main effects and interactions have a simple form. Consider the three dichotomous variables A, B, and C. Crossed, these variables form a $2 \times 2 \times 2$ contingency table. The cells of this table have indices 111, 112, 121, 122, 211, 212, 221, and 222. For the analysis of the association pattern of these variables, programs routinely set up a design matrix. An example of such a design matrix appears in Table I.

Table I displays a design matrix for the saturated log-linear model for three dichotomous variables. It contains vectors for testing assumptions

TABLE I
Design Matrix for Saturated Log-Linear Model for a $2 \times 2 \times 2$ Table

Variables ABC	Coefficients of Design Matrix							
	λ_0	λ_A	λ_B	λ_C	λ_{AB}	λ_{AC}	λ_{BC}	λ_{ABC}
111	1	1	1	1	1	1	1	1
112	1	1	1	−1	1	−1	−1	−1
121	1	1	−1	1	−1	1	−1	−1
122	1	1	−1	−1	−1	−1	1	1
211	1	−1	1	1	−1	−1	1	−1
212	1	−1	1	−1	−1	1	−1	1
221	1	−1	−1	1	1	−1	−1	1
222	1	−1	−1	−1	1	1	1	−1

concerning the main effects and interactions of variables. The interpretation of these vectors is as follows. Column 1 corresponds to the constant term in Equation 1. A model involving only this term assumes that no effects are present in the table, or that the cell probabilities are equal. Some computer programs assume this vector. Thus, it must be omitted from model specifications for these programs (e.g., Rindskopf, 1987). The following examples do not include this vector, but assume it is there.

The second column represents the main effect for variable A. It contrasts the first and the second state of variable A. Column 3 contrasts the two states of variable B, and column 4 contrasts the two states of variable C. All three main effect vectors meet with the rules established earlier. They each correspond to only one hypothesis comparing the two levels of each variable. For each variable there is only one main effect vector, and cells in the same group are assigned either a 1 or a -1. For each vector, the sum of its elements is zero.

The vectors for the pairwise interactions result from element-wise multiplication of two main effect vectors. The fifth column or the vector corresponding to the interaction between A and B results from multiplying the elements of the second with the elements of the third column. Similarly, column 6, the vector corresponding to the interaction between A and C, results from multiplying elements of column 2 with those of column 4, and column 7 results from multiplying the elements of column 3 with those of column 4. The last column in Table I corresponds to the three-way interaction between A, B, and C. It results from multiplying the elements of the three main effect vectors with each other.

Computer programs such as Rindskopf's (1987) PASCAL programs routinely set up design matrices such as the one in Table I. For more complex designs or variables with more than two states the rules apply accordingly. (An example of a design matrix for a 3×3 table appears in Table II; cf. Agresti, 1984, p. 239.) A substantive example with interpretation of the vectors of the design matrix follows.

The example uses data from a project on family development (Kreppner & Lerner, 1989; Kreppner, Paulsen, & Schütze, 1982; von Eye & Kreppner, 1989). From the observational data collected in this project we use the variables "Affective Climate" (A) "Goal of Activity" (G), and "Target Activity" (T). We use two categories for each of these variables. A has categories neutral (1) and warm (2), G has categories continuation (1) and change (2), and T has categories mother (1) and father (2). Table II contains the cell frequencies for the $2 \times 2 \times 2$ table cross-classifying the A, G, and T variables.

We analyze Table II under a main effect, or independence model. This model assumes the variables A, G, and T are independent of each other. The following paragraphs interpret the design matrix generated to test this

TABLE II
Observed and Expected Frequencies and Design Matrix for the Main Effect Model
for the Cross-Tabulation of "Affective Climate" (A), "Goal of Activity" (G), and
"Target of Activity" (T)

Variables AGT	Frequencies		Standardized Residuals	Design Matrix Vectors		
	Observed	Expected				
111	3	4.38	− 0.661	1	1	1
112	19	17.24	0.424	− 1	1	1
121	7	5.75	0.520	1	− 1	1
122	21	22.63	− 0.342	− 1	− 1	1
211	2	2.10	− 0.072	1	1	− 1
212	8	8.27	− 0.095	− 1	1	− 1
221	3	2.76	0.144	1	− 1	− 1
222	11	10.86	0.042	− 1	− 1	− 1

model. The overall L^2 is $L^2 = 1.074$. For four degrees of freedom this value has a tail probability $p = .898$ suggesting that there is a good fit. (A comparative model is discussed later. It is statistically not inferior to this model; however, it is more parsimonious.)

The right-hand panel of Table II displays the design matrix for the model of independence between A, G, and T. The column with the constants is assumed. There is only one parameter per variable because they all are dichotomous. The first column represents the main effect for variable T. This effect suggests that neutral behaviors and affective warmth deviate from the column mean in opposite directions. The parameter estimate for λ_T is − .685, and its standard error is .145. In other words, this means that the marginal distribution is skewed, or that warmth is observed more often than affective climate. The ratio λ_T/s is $z = − 4.736$. This value exceeds in absolute value the critical value of $z = 1.96$ for alpha $= .05$. Thus we may conclude that the frequencies with which mother and father are targeted do differ from the column mean or, that mothers are more frequent targets than fathers.

Accordingly, the main effect for variable G implies that change- and continuation-oriented behaviors deviate from the column mean in opposite directions. The estimates for this hypothesis are $\lambda_G = − .136$, $s = .117$, and $z = − 1.159$. Thus, we can conclude that the differences from the column mean shown by the categories of variable G do not allow us to explain a significant portion of the frequency distribution in Table II.

For variable A we estimate $\lambda_A = 0.367$, $s = .124$, and $z = 2.956$. A more parsimonious model results if we eliminate the vector for the nonsignificant main effect. This model only contains the main effect terms for variables A and T. The overall L^2 is 2.430 with $p = .7870$ ($df = 5$). The difference between these two models is $L^2 = 1.356$. This value is not significant ($df = 1$, $p = .2442$). Thus, we may conclude that the more parsimonious model explains the frequency distribution in Table II as well as the model including all three main effects.

This example illustrates how one can use the design matrix approach for analysis of standard log-linear modeling and how one can interpret the vectors in the design matrix. The following sections apply the design matrix approach to designs pertinent to developmental research. The focus is on the translation of developmental hypotheses into design matrices. In addition, we discuss hypotheses that can be solved only with design matrices that contain vectors custom-tailored to reflect these hypotheses.

III. Modeling Hypotheses About Development

This section discusses the application of the design matrix approach to the testing of developmental hypotheses. First, examples of the custom-tailored analysis of developmental hypotheses in a cohort sequential design are given. Then we discuss repeated measurement designs. The focus is on relatively short time series.

The decision to focus on short time series has two reasons. First, for long time series with 20, 50, or 200 observation points there are well-known powerful methods such as factor analysis of time series or spectral analysis (see von Eye, 1990a, 1990b). Second, short time series are most frequent in developmental research in the social sciences.

A. ANALYSIS OF COHORT SEQUENTIAL DESIGNS

Cohort sequential developmental designs analyze variables that were repeatedly observed in two or more cohorts (e.g., Nesselroade & Baltes, 1974). In this section, we illustrate how to use the design matrix approach to analyze specific developmental hypotheses. The analysis of repeated observations is demonstrated in the next section.

The following example reanalyzes data discussed by Silbereisen, Noack, and von Eye (1992), reporting about the development of romantic friendships in early adolescence. A sample of $N = 606$ adolescents from two cohorts were observed on dating desire and success over a 1-year period. The example considers the following seven change patterns: (a) neither desire nor success on both occasions, (b) neither desire nor success on Occasion 1, desire but no success on Occasion 2, (c) desire but no success on Occasion 1, neither desire nor success on Occasion 2, (d) desire but no success on both occasions, (e) desire but no success on Occasion 1, desire and success on Occasion 2, (f) desire and success on Occasion 1, desire but no success on Occasion 2, and (g) desire and success on both occasions. The two cohorts were (a) early and (b) middle adolescents.

We analyze these variables under two models. The first is a standard main effect model. In the second we specify a hypothesis comparing the early with the middle adolescents. Table III contains the observed and the estimated expected frequencies, and the design matrix for the standard main effect model for the two variables dating behavior (D) and adolescent cohort (C).

Table III displays a design matrix that follows the aforementioned rules for effect coding. The elements in each vector sum up to zero. The vectors are not necessarily mutually orthogonal. For example, the inner product for vectors λ_{D1} and λ_{D2} is $+2$. (The inner product for orthogonal vectors is zero.) Overall, the independence model provides poor fit. The Pearson X^2 is 17.945 for which p ($df = 6$) $= .0064$ (for comparison, we obtain $L^2 = 18.6$).

In standard application of log-linear modeling, rejection of the model often terminates analysis. The model does not fit, and only one of the standardized residuals (Cell 22) indicated a significant deviation. Because of the poor fit, the model parameters cannot be interpreted. In the present context, however, we decide to invest one more degree of freedom for a test of the following hypothesis: Lack of dating success occurs more often than average in early adolescence. This hypothesis leads to the vector that appears in Table IV.

Table IV contains only one design matrix vector. However, this vector was added to the ones in Table III. Thus, the complete design matrix that yields the expected frequencies in Table IV contains all vectors from Table

TABLE III

Observed and Expected Frequencies and Design Matrix for Independence Model for the Variables Dating Behavior (D) and Adolescent Cohort (A)

Variables	Frequencies		Standard	Design Matrix						
DC	Observed	Expected	Residuals	λ_C	λ_{D1}	λ_{D2}	λ_{D3}	λ_{D4}	λ_{D5}	λ_{D6}
11	9	7.04	0.74	1	1	0	0	0	0	0
12	4	5.96	−0.80	−1	1	0	0	0	0	0
21	24	16.24	1.93	1	0	1	0	0	0	0
22	6	13.76	−2.09	−1	0	1	0	0	0	0
31	9	8.66	0.12	1	0	0	1	0	0	0
32	7	7.34	−0.13	−1	0	0	1	0	0	0
41	127	118.53	0.78	1	0	0	0	1	0	0
42	92	100.47	−0.85	−1	0	0	0	1	0	0
51	63	65.49	−0.31	1	0	0	0	0	1	0
52	58	55.51	0.33	−1	0	0	0	0	1	0
61	34	34.10	−0.02	1	0	0	0	0	0	1
62	29	28.90	0.02	−1	0	0	0	0	0	1
71	62	77.94	−1.81	1	−1	−1	−1	−1	−1	−1
72	82	66.06	1.96	−1	−1	−1	−1	−1	−1	−1

TABLE IV
Reanalysis of the Data from Table III Including a Vector for the Comparison of the Two Adolescent Cohorts

Variables DC	Frequencies		Standardized Residuals	Vector λ_H
	Observed	Expected		
11	9	7.90	0.39	1
12	4	5.10	− 0.49	− 1
21	24	18.24	1.35	1
22	6	11.76	− 1.68	− 1
31	9	9.73	− 0.23	1
32	7	6.27	0.29	− 1
41	127	133.13	− 0.53	1
42	92	85.87	0.66	− 1
51	63	58.66	0.57	0
52	58	62.34	− 0.55	0
61	34	30.54	0.63	0
62	29	32.46	− 0.61	0
71	62	69.80	− 0.93	0
72	82	74.20	0.91	0

III and the one from Table IV. Please notice that the first eight values of the design matrix vector in Table IV are identical to the ones in the first vector in Table III. Only the values for dating behavior categories 5, 6, and 7 are different.

The model that tests the hypothesis comparing the young and the middle adolescents in successful dating provides good fit. The Pearson X^2 is 8.971 ($L^2 = 9.4$), for which p ($df = 5$) $= .1102$. In addition, the added vector for the comparison is significant ($\lambda_H = .250$, $s_e = 0.083$, $z = 3.024$, $p = .0012$). Thus we conclude that the assumption that lack of dating success occurs more often in early adolescence than, on average, in late adolescence explains a significant portion of the deviations from independence. In other words, the association of low dating success and early adolescence allows one to explain the data in Table III when one also considers that the marginal sums are unequal.

B. ANALYSIS OF LONGITUDINAL DESIGNS

The analysis of longitudinal data with log-linear models proceeds under the constraint that designs must be set up so that each individual appears in the table only once. There are three main reasons for this constraint. The first reason is that counting individuals more than once leads to an artificial increase in the sample size and, thus, to an artificial increase in statistical power which, in turn, can lead to premature rejection of a model.

The second reason concerns independence observations. If an individual appears more than once in a table, the observations cannot be considered independent. Usually, one assumes that separate observations are probabilistically independent. This may not be the case if an individual is repeatedly observed at relatively short time intervals. Later, we discuss in more detail what can be done to deal with this problem.

The third reason is that one assumes that all observations are identically distributed. If this is not the case, data may be dissimilar and may not speak to the same effects. Under these conditions, data may form an amalgamation that has unknown properties and does not allow the researcher to identify a model that describes any of the effects present in the data.

In the methodological literature we find many examples of log-linear analyses of short time series (Agresti, 1990; Bishop et al., 1975; Clogg et al., 1990; Green, 1988; Upton, 1978). Two of these examples are taken up here and analyzed using the design matrix approach, thus demonstrating the general applicability of the approach. The examples include models for testing stability and therapy outcome hypotheses. Subsequently, we discuss curve fitting (for additional examples, see Clogg et al., 1990).

In all examples we apply the same principles for setting up the design matrix. First, we identify, on the basis of developmental theory, those cells for which we expect above - versus below-average frequencies. Second, we set up vectors for the design matrix following Rules 1 through 4 previously stated.

C. MODELS OF STABILITY

Some developmental models of stability assume that individuals display the same levels or states of variables across several points in time. For instance, trait theory of personality assumes that traits such as extraversion are enduring characteristics of individuals (Nesselroade, 1990). Stability models translate such assumptions into the hypothesis that, for instance, in univariate cross-tabulations the main diagonal cells contain more individuals than the off-diagonal cells. The following example expresses the assumption of stability in terms of a design matrix.

The example, taken from Lienert and von Eye (1984) (cf. Funke & Hussy, 1979; von Eye & Nesselroade, 1992), investigates the time needed to solve tasks in the "master mind" game. A sample of $N = 118$ high school students played master mind with a personal computer. Each subject was allowed eight trials. The subsample of $N = 98$ students who used all eight trials is included in the following analyses. Problem-solving time had categories $1 =$ less than 11 s and $2 =$ more than 11 s. The problem-solving times observed in Trials 6, 7, and 8 were crossed. A matrix with $2 \times 2 \times 2 = 8$ cells resulted.

For the following analyses we assume stability in problem-solving times. This assumption implies that the number of students displaying no change in problem-solving times is greater than the number of students decreasing or increasing their problem-solving times. In addition, because we allow changes, response time category frequencies may differ across the three trials. Therefore, we allow the response time variable to have a main effect at each of the trials. Table V gives the observed frequencies, the frequencies expected under this model, and the design matrix resulting for our assumptions.

The first three vectors in the design matrix in Table V correspond to the main effects of the three occasions. The last vector reflects the stability assumption. Each vector meets with the rule that the sum of its values be zero. However, the vectors in this matrix are not mutually orthogonal as, for example, in orthogonal polynomial coding. The L^2 shows that the assumption of stable response times in problem solving is tenable for those students who need all eight trials ($L^2 = 7.194$; $df = 3$; $p = .0660$). Notice that if one considers the differences in the marginal frequencies random and, therefore, does not include the main effect terms, the model no longer fits ($df = 6$; $L^2 = 25.664$; $p = .0003$).

D. THERAPY OUTCOME

Therapy outcome models often show clear patterns of interaction between independent and outcome variables. The design matrix approach allows the researcher to set up custom-tailored vectors that correspond to the hypotheses under study. This section discusses examples of design matrices for experiments on the effects of drugs or therapies. Here, vectors are specified that reflect the researchers' assumptions where the therapy has its strongest effect. An example of such an assumption is that the experimental group shows improvements more often than the control group.

TABLE V
Log-Linear Analysis of Stability Assumptions Concerning Three Trials of Problem Solving

Trial			Frequencies		Design Matrix			
6	7	8[a]	Observed	Expected	λ_1	λ_2	λ_3	λ_4
1	1	1	18	15.74	−1	−1	−1	1
1	1	2	4	4.86	−1	−1	1	−0.33
1	2	1	1	3.55	−1	1	−1	−0.33
1	2	2	6	4.85	−1	1	1	−0.33
2	1	1	4	7.36	1	−1	−1	−0.33
2	1	2	12	10.04	1	−1	1	−0.33
2	2	1	11	7.34	1	1	−1	−0.33
2	2	2	42	44.26	1	1	1	1

[a] 6 = problem-solving time in Trial 6; 7 = problem-solving time in Trial 7; 8 = problem-solving time in Trial 8.

The following example, adapted from Krauth and Kohnen (1981), analyzes the effects of client-centered psychotherapy on introverted neurotics. The experiment included experimental and control groups (random assignment). The patients in the experimental group immediately started therapy, whereas the control group started therapy later. The hypothesis of this investigation was that the frequency of changes from neurotic to normal behavior is higher in the therapy group than in the control group. Table VI gives the observed frequencies for the $2 \times 2 \times 2$ table of cross-classifying the variables G (group: 1 = experimental; 2 = control), B (status at pretest: 1 = critical symptom present; 2 = other symptoms present), and P (status at posttest: 1 = symptom cured; 2 = critical or other symptoms present).

The first vector of the design matrix in Table VI contains the main effect for variable B. This effect was considered because in both the experimental and the control groups the frequency of the critical symptom, neuroticism in introverts, was less frequent than other behavior patterns. The second vector contains the main effect for variable P. This effect was considered because the frequency of patients cured from the critical symptom was expected to be small if compared to the number of patients with other behavior patterns. The last vector corresponds to the hypothesis we tested. It implies that in Cell 111 there are more, and in Cell 211 there are fewer patients than average. Patients in Cell 111 are, at the posttest, free from the critical symptom. Patients in Cell 211 are also free from this symptom but did not participate in therapy. Thus, we contrast therapy effects against spontaneous recovery.

The L^2 shows that the three effects expressed in the three vectors clearly account for the observed frequency distribution ($L^2 = 4.232$; $df = 4$; $p = .3755$). The λ for the hypothesis concerning the therapy effect is significant ($z = 2.222$, $p = .0131$). Because the p for the overall test was so large, a more parsimonious model was tested also. To find out what we gained by adding the hypothesis test to the main effect tests, we dropped the

TABLE VI
Comparison of Experimental and Control Groups in Pretest — Posttest Experiment

Variables			Frequencies		Design Matrix		
G	B	P	Observed	Expected	λ_1	λ_2	λ_3
1	1	1	11	11.08	1	1	1
1	1	2	21	21.92	1	−1	0
1	2	1	22	16.42	−1	1	0
1	2	2	58	61.58	−1	−1	0
2	1	1	3	3.08	1	1	−1
2	1	2	23	21.92	1	−1	0
2	2	1	11	16.42	−1	1	0
2	2	2	65	61.58	−1	−1	0

last vector of the design matrix. As a result, L^2 increased to 9.304 ($df = 5$; $p = .0975$). From this, we may conclude that the second, more parsimonious model also explains the observed frequency distribution very well. However, a comparison of the two models showed that the hypothesis vector significantly improved the model fit ($L^2 = 5.072$; $df = 1$; $p = .0243$).

To show the effect of including the last vector in Table VI we compare the estimated expected frequencies of the model that only contains the two main effect vectors and the model tested in Table VI. For the first, the more parsimonious model, we obtain estimates (from Cell 111 to Cell 222): 6.37, 22.63, 17.13, 60.87, 6.37, 22.63, 17.13, 60.87. Although this model provides an overall good fit, it does not speak to the hypothesis under study at all. To the contrary, the estimated expected frequencies for Cells 111 and 211 are identical, thus contradicting the hypothesis. Adding the third vector in Table VI yields expected frequencies 11.08 and 3.08, respectively. Accordingly, the other estimates change so that the specifications set by the three vectors in the design matrix are met.

E. CURVE FITTING

This section deals with fitting univariate time series of categorical data. We still analyze short time series. The methods we discuss can become tedious for long series (methods for analysis of longer series are discussed, e.g., by Zeger, 1988; Zeger & Quaqish, 1988).

In the social sciences, researchers often assume that linear functions sufficiently describe the relationships between variables. In time series analysis, however, linear trends represent often just one component of a more complex, nonlinear function. Developmental theories often postulate trajectories that display nonlinear trends. Examples include stage theories that assume step functions (e.g., Fischer & Lamborn, 1989) or performance theories that assume an ability peak at a certain age and a leveling out or decline later (e.g., Hussy & von Eye, 1988).

Curve fitting using log-linear models involves as a first step the specification of the type of function expected to describe a time series. For many time series, functions can easily be given. If a researcher assumes, for instance, an increase in a behavior that peaks then decreases, a quadratic function may be appropriate. Processes that show an increase that approximates an asymptote can be described by exponential or logistic functions. Cyclic processes such as cyclical psychoses can sometimes be described using trigonometric functions.

In many instances, polynomials can be used to describe time series. Polynomials have the general form

$$y = a_0 x_0^0 + a_1 x_1^1 + a_2 x_2^2 + \ldots + a_i x_i^i + \ldots = \Sigma_i \, a_i \, x_i^i. \qquad (6)$$

For $i = 0$ one obtains $y = a_0 x_0^0 = $ constant. For $i = 1$ one obtains $y = a_0 x_0^0 + a_1 x_1^1$ which is the linear regression equation. In trend analysis of variance, one uses orthogonal polyomials. From the present perspective there are two advantages connected with the use of orthogonal polynomials. First, the coefficients of these polynomials meet the four criteria for vectors of design matrices formulated earlier. Therefore, the polynomial coefficients can be inserted directly as values of vectors of a design matrix. Second, for time series with up to 10 observation points, the polynomial coefficients are given in analysis of variance textbooks (e.g., Kirk, 1982, Table E12). Therefore they need to be calculated only for longer time series. Computer programs typically calculate polynomial coefficients automatically.

Orthogonal polynomials are used in analysis of variance with balanced designs where orthogonality is desirable so that the sums of squares can be decomposed uniquely. In the present context, orthogonality is confined to the relationships between vectors in the design matrix. For instance, their cross-products are zero. However, the estimators of two orthogonal vectors typically are correlated.

The following example again uses data from the project on family development (Kreppner et al., 1982). At seven occasions during the first 2 years of the second child's life, the number of times the mother attempted to exert control over the second child was observed. The number of control events counted at each occasion are analyzed for five families under the following assumptions:

1. The amount of control the mother exerts increases linearly over time.
2. Over time, the mother's attempts to exert control level out or even decrease.

These assumptions are analyzed using orthogonal polynomials. (Another option would have been to fit an exponential curve.) The first assumption implies an increase in the number of attempts to exert control over the increasingly active second child. There are many functions that meet with this assumption. Examples include exponential curves and step functions. In order to use a simple orthogonal polynomial we fit a linear function. For seven observation points, the coefficients of a linear orthogonal polynomial are -3, -2, -1, 0, 1, 2, 3 (see Kirk, 1982, Table E12). The second assumption implies a nonlinear time series. An initial increase is followed by a leveling out or a decrease. From the many functions that allow us to describe this pattern, we select the quadratic orthogonal polynomial. For seven observation points, it has coefficients 5, 0, -3, -4, -3, 0, 5.

It is important to note that these polynomial coefficients fulfill the criteria of orthogonal polynomial coding. First, the sum of the elements in each coefficient vector is zero. Second, the cross-product of the coding vectors for the two polynomials is also zero.

To test whether this operationalization of our assumption appropriately depicts the observed time series of event frequencies, we insert the vectors with the coefficients of the linear and quadratic polynomials in the design matrix and calculate a log-linear model. The results of the calculations and the design matrix appear in Table VII.

The estimated expected frequencies in Table VII are very close to the observed ones, and the L^2 is 4.797. For $df = 4$ this value indicates a very good fit ($p = .3088$). Thus, we may conclude that our assumptions, operationalized through orthogonal polynomials, meet with the relationships present in the observed data.

For reasons of comparison two additional models were tested. The first is less parsimonious than the one in Table VII. In order to take into account the fact that there is no increase in children's activity until they are able to crawl, the model adds a cubic polynomial to the model, thus assuming the curve is S-shaped. The resulting goodness of fit test does not indicate a significant improvement over the more parsimonious model ($L^2 = 3.244$, $df = 3$, $p, = .3555$). The second model is more parsimonious than the model in Table VII. It considers only the linear trend, assuming no leveling out toward the end of the second year. The goodness of fit test indicates that this model does not describe the observed time series appropriately ($L^2 = 20.475$, $df = 5$, $p = .0010$). Thus, we conclude the model in Table VII provides a statistically acceptable fit that is as good as the fit for less parsimonious models and is better than the fit for more parsimonious models.

One of the problems of fitting models for data from repeated observations is that one of the three major assumptions of chi-squared testing is violated. The assumptions concern the independence of the observations, the similarity of their distribution, and the sample size (Wickens, 1989).

TABLE VII
Approximation of Univariate Time Series Using Log-Linear Model

Point in Time	Frequencies		Design Matrix	
	Observed	Expected	λ_1	λ_2
1	7	3.99	−3	5
2	6	9.56	−2	0
3	15	18.70	−1	−3
4	33	29.83	0	−4
5	42	38.84	1	−3
6	40	41.28	2	0
7	35	35.80	3	5

Obviously, repeated observations violate the first of these assumptions. Although repeated measurement analysis of variance adjustments of the F tests are available, for example, via the Greenhouse–Geisser and the Huynh–Feldt epsilon parameters, there is no such standard correction in log-linear modeling. Two solutions have been discussed. The first generates a higher dimensional contingency table cross-classifying observations from different occasions. Table V gives an example of this solution. However, often the sample size limits this approach.

The second solution used modified test statistics (Altham, 1979; Wickens, 1989). When observations are time series they often are positively associated with the previous K observations. A modified statistic for this situation was proposed by Altham:

$$X^2_{mod} = X^2/(2k + 1). \tag{7}$$

This test statistic is distributed as chi-square. It is safe in the sense that one operates under a Type I error probability that does not exceed the nominal level alpha. However, this test statistic may be very conservative; that is, it requires large discrepancies to reject the null hypothesis of no differences between observed and expected frequency distributions.

Applied to our example we obtain $K = 6$, and $X^2_{mod} = X^2/13$. For the model tested in Table VII we obtain $X^2_{mod} = 4.797/13 = 0.37$. Thus, our conclusion does not need to be modified, in spite of the dependence. However, more parsimonious models may provide a good fit also. For instance, the model that considers only the linear trend cannot be rejected either.

IV. Discussion

This chapter uses the design matrix approach to show how custom-tailored log-linear modeling of changes in categorical variables is possible in developmental research. This approach has several characteristics that make it attractive for use in longitudinal and cross-sectional research. First, the researcher has a tool for expressing hypotheses in a very detailed fashion. This includes hypotheses in nonstandard or association models that otherwise are hard or impossible to test. Rather than leaving the construction of the design matrix with program default specifications, the researcher determines the type of effects to be tested. It follows that the effects the researcher is interested in do not need to be inferred. Rather, they are tested directly.

For instance, suppose a researcher analyzes a 3×3 table under the assumption that main effects allow one to describe the data satisfactorily. Computer programs typically generate effects such that for the first variable the first and the third categories are contrasted in a first coding vector. Then, in a second coding vector, the second category is substituted for the first. The same procedure is applied to the second variable (e.g., see Agresti, 1984; Hagenaars, 1990). In general, for the c states of a variable, c − 1 coding vectors are generated. Of these effects, none might be of interest to the researcher. Of course, from the effects generated by the programs, others can be inferred. However, this is an unnecessary step if the researcher specifies the design matrix vectors.

Suppose, furthermore, the researcher wants to parameterize deviations from independence in this 3 × 3 table. Then, the design matrix approach proves to be an easy to use tool for the specification of hypotheses.

The second characteristic of the design matrix is closely related to the first. It concerns parameter evaluation. Parameters can be evaluated with respect to two characteristics. The first is statistical significance. The second argument in the parameter evaluation involves their magnitude. Unfortunately, the magnitude of λ-parameters is not always as easy to interpret as regression coefficients that indicate how many steps on the y-axis go hand in hand with one step on the x-axis. Main effect parameters, that is parameters that deal with categories of only one variable, can be interpreted as measures of deviations of row and column means from the grand mean. Special hypotheses are expressed in terms of positive and negative values in coding vectors. These values also indicate deviations from the column mean. Interpretation of effects uses the pattern of these values. (For technical details concerning parameter interpretation in nonhierarchical models, see Rindskopf, 1990.)

The parameters of the design matrix approach are generally closer to researchers' hypotheses than parameters from routine application of software programs. This results from the way the coding vectors for the interactions are constructed. Most computer programs calculate these vectors using the methods described earlier (see Table I). Thus, the estimated parameters may not speak to the researcher's hypotheses. In the design matrix approach, vectors, especially vectors reflecting interaction terms, are included only as far as they reflect substantive hypotheses. Therefore, there may be fewer λ-parameters to interpret, and they may speak directly to the researcher's hypotheses.

The design matrix approach does not necessarily lead to hierarchical log-linear models. Hierarchical models' higher order interaction terms imply all lower order terms. For instance, the triplet interaction between the variables A, B, and C, or ABC, implies the first-order interactions AB, AC, and BC, and the main effects A, B, and C. One can include all these effects in the design matrix, thus constructing hierarchical models. However, if the substantive assumptions do not imply hypotheses corresponding to hierarchical models, there is no need to formulate these. From this characteristic follows greater flexibility of the design matrix approach. However, one has to construct the design matrix by hand, which can be tedious if the matrix under study is large.

In this chapter we used the design matrix approach for analysis of hypotheses in developmental research (cf. Clogg et al., 1990). It is obvious that this approach can be applied also to problems in other areas of social science research. Examples include the testing of hypotheses in clinical, educational, and sociological research. In addition, the design matrix approach is not confined to nominal level variables. The ordinal character of variables (cf. Agresti, 1984; Green, 1988) can be considered as well. It is also possible to include variables that have categories reflecting interval or ratio scale levels, and to test hypotheses utilizing this information.

In developmental research, investigators often collect variables of different types. For instance, categorical variables such as communication styles, ordinal variables such as the Tanner stages, and interval level variables such as intelligence measures are collected. The methods presented in this chapter allow one to analyze custom hypotheses involving all types of variables.

Acknowledgments

Preparation of this article was supported in part by NIA Grant #5T32 AG00110-07, "Training in Aging Research Methodology."

References

Agresti, A. (1984). *Analysis of ordinal categorical data.* New York: Wiley.

Agresti, A. (1990). *Categorical data analysis.* New York: Wiley.

Alba, R. D. (1988). Interpreting the parameters of log-linear models. In J. S. Long (Ed.), *Common problems/proper solutions. Avoiding error in quantitative research* (pp. 258–287). Newbury Park, CA: Sage.

Altham, P. M. E. (1979). Detecting relationships between categorical variables observed over time: A problem of deflating a chi-squared statistic. *Applied Statistics, 28,* 115–125.

Bishop, Y. M. M., Fienberg, S. E., & Holland, P. W. (1975). *Discrete multivariate analysis.* Cambridge, MA: MIT Press.

Clogg, C. C. (1982). Some models for the analysis of association in multi-way tables having ordered categories. *Journal of the American Statistical Association, 77,* 803–815.

Clogg, C. C., & Eliason, S. R. (1987). Some common problems in log-linear analysis. *Statistical Methods and Research, 16,* 8–44.

Clogg, C. C., Eliason, S. R., & Grego, J. (1990). Models for the analysis of change in discrete variables. In A. von Eye (Ed.), *New statistical methods for longitudinal research* (pp. 409–441). New York: Academic Press.

Dobson, A. (1990). *An introduction to generalized linear models.* London: Chapman & Hall.

Elliott, G. C. (1988). Interpreting higher order interactions in log-linear analysis. *Psychological Bulletin, 103,* 121–130.

Evers, M., & Namboodiri, N. K. (1978). On the design matrix strategy in the analysis of categorical data. In K. F. Schuessler (Ed.), *Sociological methodology* (pp. 86–111). San Francisco: Jossey-Bass.

Fienberg, S. E. (1980). *The analysis of cross-classified categorical data* (2nd ed.). Cambridge, MA: MIT Press.

Fischer, K. W., & Lamborn, S. D. (1989). Mechanisms of variation in developmental levels: Cognitive and emotional transitions during adolescence. In A. de Ribaupierre (Ed.), *Transition mechanisms in child development, the longitudinal perspective* (pp. 33–67). Cambridge England: Cambridge University Press.

Funke, J., & Hussy, W. (1979). Informationsverarbeitende Strukturen und Prozesse. Analysemöglichkeiten durch Problemlöseparadigmen. *Trierer Psychologische Berichte, 6,* (8).

Goodman, L. A. (1979). Simple models for the analysis of association in cross-classifications having ordered categories. *Journal of the American Statistical Association, 74,* 537–552.

Goodman, L. A. (1984). *The analysis of cross-classified data having ordered categories.* Cambridge, MA: Harvard University Press.

Goodman, L. A. (1985). The analysis of cross-classified data having ordered categories: Association models, correlation models, and asymmetry models for contingency tables with and without missing entries. *Annals of Statistics, 13,* 10–69.

Green, J. A. (1988). Log-linear analysis of cross-classified ordinal data: Applications in developmental research. *Child Development, 59,* 1–25.

Haber, M. (1985). Maximum likelihood methods for linear and log-linear models in categorical data. *Computational Statistics and Data Analysis, 3,* 1–10.

Haberman, S. J. (1978). *Analysis of qualitative data: Vol. 1. Introductory topics.* New York: Academic Press.

Haberman, S. J. (1979). *Analysis of qualitative data: Vol. 2. New developments.* New York: Academic Press.

Hagenaars, J. A. (1990). *Categorical longitudinal data.* Newbury Park, CA: Sage.

Holt, D. (1979). Log-linear models for contingency table analysis. On the interpretation of parameters. *Sociological Methods & Research, 7,* 330–336.

Hussy, W., & von Eye, A. (1988). On cognitive operators in information processing and their effects on memory in different age groups. In F. E. Weinert & M. Perlmutter (Eds.), *Memory development: Universal changes and individual differences* (pp. 275–291). Hillsdale, NJ: Lawrence Erlbaum Associates.

Johnson, R. A. (1985). Analysis of age, period, and cohort effects in marital fertility. In W. M. Mason & S. E. Fienberg (Eds.), *Cohort analysis in social research* (pp. 229–257). New York: Springer.

Kirk, R. E. (1982). *Experimental design.* Belmont, CA: Brooks/Cole.

Krauth, J., & Kohnen, R. (1981). KFA XIVb. Behandlungsinduzierte Symptommusterabfolgen im Therapie-Wartegruppen Vergleich. *Zeitschrift für Klinische Psychologie und Psychotherapie, 29,* 307–314.

Kreppner, K., & Lerner, R. M. (Eds.). (1989). *Family systems and life-span development.* Hillsdale, NJ: Lawrence Erlbaum Associates.

Kreppner, K., Paulsen, S., & Schütze, Y. (1982). Infant and family development: From triads to tetrads. *Human Development, 25,* 373–391.

Landis, J. R., & Koch, A. A. (1979). The analysis of categorical data in longitudinal studies of behavioral development. In J. R. Nesselroade & P. B. Baltes (Eds.), *Longitudinal research in the study of behavior and development* (pp. 233–261). New York: Academic.

Lienert, G. A., & von Eye, A. (1984). Testing for stability and change in multivariate t-point observations by longitudinal configural frequency analysis. *Psychologische Beiträge, 26,* 298–308.

McCullagh, P., & Nelder, J. A. (1983). *Generalized linear models*. London: Chapman & Hall.

Nesselroade, J. R. (1990). Adult personality development: Issues in assessing constancy and change. In A. I. Rabin, R. A. Zucker, R. A. Emmons, & S. Frank (Eds.), *Studying persons and lives*, (pp. 41-85). New York: Springer.

Nesselroade, J. R., & Baltes, P. B. (1974). Adolescent personality development and historical change: 1970-72. *Monographs of the Society for Research in Child Development, 39*(1, Whole No. 154).

Page, W. F. (1977). Interpretation of Goodman's log-linear model effects: An odds ratio approach. *Sociological Methods & Research, 5*, 419-435.

Petersen, A. C., & Crockett, L. (1986). Pubertal development and its relation to cognitive and psychosocial development in adolescent girls: Implications for parenting. In J. B. Lancaster & B. A. Hamburg (Eds.), *School-age pregnancy and parenthood: Biosocial dimensions* (pp. 147-175). New York: Aldine.

Radloff, L. S. (1977). The CES-D scale: A self-report depression scale for research in the general population. *Applied Psychological Measurement, 3*, 385-401.

Rindskopf, D. (1987). A compact basic program for log-linear models. In R. M. Heiberger (Ed.), *Computer science and statistics. Proceedings of the 19th symposium on the interface* (pp. 381-385). Alexandria, VA: American Statistical Association.

Rindskopf, D. (1990). Nonstandard log-linear models. *Psychological Bulletin, 108*, 150-162.

Schneider, W., & Weinert, F. E. (1989). Universal trends and individual differences in memory development. In A. de Ribaupierre (Ed.), *Transition mechanisms in child development, the longitudinal perspective* (pp. 68-106). Cambridge, England: Cambridge University Press.

Schulenberg, J., Goldstein, A. E., & Vondracek, F. W. (1991). Gender differences in adolescents' career interests: Beyond main effects. *Journal of Research on Adolescence, 1*, 37-61.

Silbereisen, R. K., Noack, P., & von Eye, A. (1992). Transition in adolescents' friendship development and change in favorite leisure contexts. *Journal of Adolescent Research, 7*, 80-93.

Thoresen, C. E. (1991). Type A and teenagers. In R. M. Lerner, A. C. Petersen, & J. Brooks-Gunn (Eds.), *Encyclopedia of adolescence* (pp. 1168-1180). New York: Garland.

Tubman, J. T., Vicary, J. R., von Eye, A., & Lerner, J. V. (1990). Longitudinal substance use and adult adjustment. *Journal of Substance Abuse, 2*, 317-334.

Upton, G. J. G. (1978). *The analysis of cross-classified data*. New York: Wiley.

Von Eye, A. (Ed.). (1990a). *Statistical methods in longitudinal research* (Vol. 1) Boston: Academic Press.

Von Eye, A. (Ed.). (1990b). *Statistical methods in longitudinal research* (Vol. 2). Boston: Academic Press.

Von Eye, A., & Kreppner, K. (1989). Family systems and family development: The selection of analytical units. In K. Kreppner & R. M. Lerner (Eds.), *Family systems and life-span development* (pp. 247-269). Hillsdale, NJ: Lawrence Erlbaum Associates.

Von Eye, A., & Nesselroade, J. R. (1992). Types of change: Application of configural frequency analysis in repeated measurement designs. *Experimental Aging Research*.

Wickens, T. D. (1989). *Multiway contingency tables analysis for the social sciences*. Hillsdale, NJ: Lawrence Erlbaum Associates.

Wilson, T. P. (1979). On not interpreting coefficients. Comments on Holt. *Sociological Methods & Research, 8*, 233-240.

Zeger, S. L. (1988). A regression model for time series of counts. *Biometrika, 75*, 621-629.

Zeger, S. L., & Quaqish, B. (1988). Markov regression models for time series: A quasi-likelihood approach. *Biometrics, 44*, 1019-1031.

Integrating Scholarship and Outreach in Human Development Research, Policy, and Service: A Developmental Contextual Perspective

Richard M. Lerner, Julia R. Miller, Jack H. Knott,
Kenneth E. Corey, Timothy S. Bynum, Leah Cox Hoopfer,
Marvin H. McKinney, L. Annette Abrams,
Richard C. Hula, and Patterson A. Terry

MICHIGAN STATE UNIVERSITY

Abstract

Societal changes affecting higher education stress the importance of better integrating scholarship with the needs of the communities and constituencies within which the academy is embedded. The pressures for this integration may be most pronounced in those areas of scholarship pertinent to human behavior and development. At the same time, historical trends and conceptual developments within the field of human development are associated with a theory of development, developmental contextualism, that promotes this synthesis of research about "basic" processes and about "applied" problems of human behavior and development. Developmental contextualism stresses that the basic process of human development involves changing relations between individually distinct people and the actual, multilevel contexts within which they live (e.g., families, schools, and communities). To explain how variations in these person-context relations may influence individuals' developmental trajectories, researchers may introduce policies or programs as "experimental manipulations" of the natural ecology. Such basic, explanatory investigations constitute intervention research, and the evaluation of the outcomes of such research both informs scholars, policymakers, and interventionists about the efficacy of policies and programs and brings data to bear on the plasticity of human development that may exist or that may be capitalized on to enhance human life. We discuss the implications of this vision of research for the design and delivery of human development policies and interventions and for future scholarly and service themes. We conclude that multiple disciplines and multiple professions should work toward integrating research, policies, and programs, focusing on human diversity and contextual variation. Moreover, we argue that a community-collaborative orientation to this integration is necessary to advance understanding of, and service to, people's developing relations to their social world.

I. Introduction

The 1990s may be a period of profound challenge for the scholars and practitioners involved in the field of human development. Financial problems confronting institutions of higher education and the communities they serve may lead the academy to reorganize internally in order to foster better fiscal health and to reorient externally in order to promote greater community accountability (Bok, 1992; Boyer, 1990; Lynton & Elman, 1987). Moreover, economic and societal pressures converge. Government, business, and "grass roots" constituents demand that the resources society allocates to both "public" and "private" universities be spent on activities that are relevant to the needs of the constituents—as the constituents, and not the professorate, conceive of and define these needs (Boyer, 1990; Lynton & Elman, 1987). Accordingly, internal reorganization and external reorientation will be produced by a recognition that a revised approach to the knowledge "functions" of the academy—that is, knowledge generation, knowledge transmission, knowledge preservation, and knowledge application—will be required if scholarship is to be used to address key and pervasive problems confronting society (e.g., economic development, environmental quality, health care, and the quality of life of children and families).

Integrative responses by universities to these economic and societal pressures may be especially important at this point in our nation's history. Indeed, providing a frame for such integration may be a special contribution that universities can make to society. This role for universities is brought to the fore because the issues associated with the key problems confronting society cross domains of scholarship, involve the public, business, and private sectors of society, and occur in distinct ways in different community settings. Accordingly, to address these problems academics must join in both multidisciplinary and multiprofessional collaborations, associations that require knowledge of and the participation by the members of the specific communities one is attempting both to understand and to serve (Lerner & Miller, 1993; Miller & Lerner, in press).[1]

[1]One should not underestimate the complexity of the details of this university-community collaboration. For instance, communities are not monolithic, there may be disparity in their "needs" and their "wants," and scholars may have to employ different techniques both to understand these aspects of community variation and to integrate it with their own knowledge base.

Arguably, this pressure to collaboratively link the knowledge functions of the academy with the needs of the community—an activity we label as *outreach*—is greatest within the areas of scholarship associated with the study of human behavior and development. Similarly, it may be argued that there is no arena of study better able to illustrate what may be gained by the academy and by society when scholarship and outreach are merged. On the one hand, the impetus for outreach may be most salient among scholars of human behavior and development because, ultimately, all problems of society involve behavior and development. Individuals and social groups may be either producers of the instances of these problems and/or agents of the policies and programs aimed at addressing them. On the other hand, historical changes in the multiple disciplines involved in the fields of study dealing with human behavior and development have resulted in an emphasis on knowledge application, on *applied developmental science* (Fisher et al., 1993; Fisher & Lerner, in press).

Moreover, this emphasis has been both legitimated and extended by the articulation of a theory of human development—*developmental contextualism* (Lerner, 1986, 1991, 1992; Lerner & Kauffman, 1985)—that has become prominent in psychology and sociology over the course of the last two decades (Baltes, 1987; Featherman, 1983). As we explain later, this view conceptually frames what are perhaps the two major developmental perspectives of this period: the life-span view of human development (e.g., Baltes, 1968, 1979, 1983, 1987; Baltes & Schaie, 1973; Brim & Kagan, 1980; Elder, 1979, 1980; Featherman, 1983, 1985; Featherman & Lerner, 1985; Lerner, 1984; Lerner & Busch-Rossnagel, 1981; Lerner & Spanier, 1978; Nesselroade & Baltes, 1979; Schaie, 1965), and the ecological view of human development (Bronfenbrenner, 1977, 1979; Bronfenbrenner & Crouter, 1983).

Developmental contextualism provides a view of the basic process in human development, of causality, and of the means through which explanations of human development may be tested; these features of developmental contextualism result in a revised (and, admittedly, perhaps even a radical) conceptualization of the relation between basic and applied research. This notion is that intervention research is basic research in human development.

We believe that, to the extent that developmental contextualism, and this conceptualization of the link between basic research and intervention research, are intellectually sound and are empirically and societally useful perspectives, a productive means may exist for the academy and the community to collaborate around issues of scholarship and outreach pertaining to human behavior and development. Accordingly, we review the conceptual foundations of developmental contextualism and its approach to the topics of *basic process* and *explanation*. In turn, we discuss the implications for scholarship and outreach that derive from the manner in which these topics are treated within developmental contextualism.

II. On the Distinction Between Basic and Applied Research

Education and training in the disciplines involved in the study of human development have traditionally involved a distinction between basic and applied research. As is the case with other areas of behavioral and social science, this division rests on the view that the basic researcher pursues "pure" problems; that is, he or she studies the variables involved in the core processes of behavior and development. These processes are seen to account for the structure and/or function of target phenomena and, as such, understanding their character allows one to go beyond description and attain an appreciation of the causes, the explanations, of development. In short, the basic researcher explains how development works in the world of the experimental, or at least the controlled, situation.

In turn, applied research has been seen as involving study of the functioning of one or more basic processes as they are embedded in their "natural state," that is, in the actual ecology of human life; the goal of such research has been seen to be the identification of the ways in which basic knowledge can be used, or must be modified, to design and deliver interventions. The applied researcher, then, studies how development actually happens in the ecology of human life. In other words, then, the distinction between basic and applied research is that the former endeavor may be cast as the pursuing of "knowledge for its own sake." Within such a view applications from basic research arise from serendipity, whereas in applied research intervention is the core focus.

It is fair to say that a status hierarchy has existed in academe regarding the distinctions between basic research and applied (or intervention) research. Ascriptions of "pure scientists" and positions of higher academic standing have been typically afforded colleagues engaged in endeavors labeled basic research. Whatever the history, or current standing, of such appraisals in academe in general, in regard to the study of human development the rationale for distinctions between basic and applied research are quite fuzzy and rapidly eroding (Fisher & Lerner, in press; Lerner, 1991; Lerner & Tubman, 1990). The bases of this dissolution of divisions between research aimed at understanding basic processes, on the one hand, and research studying development in the ecologically valid settings of human life, on the other, have arisen in the theoretical and empirical literatures associated with the study of development across the life span (e.g., Baltes, 1987; Featherman, 1983; Lerner, 1984, 1986).

Over the last two decades the study of humans and their contexts—for example, their families, schools, and communities — has evolved in at least three significant directions. These trends involve changes in the conceptualization of the nature of the person, the emergence of a life-span perspective about human development, and a stress on the contexts of development. These trends were products and producers of a superordinate theoretical perspective, one termed developmental contextualism (Lerner, 1986, 1991; Lerner & Kauffman, 1985). It is this perspective that has promoted a framework for synthesizing basic and applied research endeavors.

Features of Developmental Contextualism: Implications for Applied Science. Developmental contextualism stresses that reciprocal relations, or "dynamic" (Lerner, 1978) interactions, exist among variables from multiple levels of organization (e.g., biology, psychology, social groups, and culture). These dynamic relations structure human behavior. In addition, this system of integrated, or "fused," levels of organization is itself embedded in, and dynamically interactive with, history (Schneirla, 1957; Tobach, 1981; Tobach & Greenberg, 1984); this temporality provides a change component to the multiple, integrated levels comprising human life. In other words, within developmental contextualism a changing configuration of interrelations among multiple levels of organization constitutes the basis of human life — of behavior and development (Ford & Lerner, 1992). It is for this reason that *applied science*, when seen from a developmental contextual perspective, that is, from a perspective that stresses multilevel, integrated, systematic, and successive change, is aptly termed *applied developmental science* (Fisher & Lerner, in press).

It is possible to characterize much of the history of the study of human development prior to the mid-1970s as involving theory and research predicated on either organismic or mechanistic models of development (Lerner, 1986; Overton & Reese, 1973; Reese & Overton, 1970). In turn, it is accurate to say that since the 1970s developmental contextual conceptions have been increasingly prominent bases of scholarly activity (Dixon & Lerner, 1992; Dixon, Lerner, & Hultsch, 1991; Lerner, Hultsch, & Dixon, 1983). Indeed, the three aforementioned directions involved in the study of human development exemplify this role of developmental contextualism.

III. Contemporary Trends in the Study of Human Development

Developmental contextualism stresses that people interact dynamically with the more molecular (e.g., biological) and the more molar (e.g., familial) levels of organization involved in their behavior and development. Because of these relations, individuals have come to be understood as active producers of their own development (Lerner & Busch-Rossnagel, 1981;

Lerner & Spanier, 1978; Lewis & Rosenblum, 1974). In human life, these contributions primarily occur through the reciprocal relations individuals have with other significant people in their context, for example, children with family members, caregivers, teachers, and peers.

Moreover, the content and functional significance of these effects people have on others and, in turn, on themselves occur as a consequence of individual's characteristics of organismic and/or behavioral individuality (cf. Schneirla, 1957). Individual differences in people evoke differential reactions in others, reactions that provide feedback to people and influence the further, individual character of their development (Lerner, 1982). Accordingly, individuality—diversity—is substantively central in understanding the way in which the person is an active agent in his or her own development. That is, the unique fusion of biological, psychological, and sociocultural levels makes the person individually distinct; this individuality provides the basis of further, distinct interactions with the context and promotes the continued development of an individual developmental trajectory.

The second trend that arose in the 1970s in relation to developmental contextualism promoted as well a concern with individual differences, and with diversity of human developmental pathways across life. The emergence of interest during the 1970s and 1980s in a life-span perspective about human development (e.g., Baltes, 1987; Baltes, Reese, & Lipsitt, 1980; Lerner, 1984; Lerner & Spanier, 1980) led to the understanding that development occurs in more than the childhood or adolescent years. Parents as well as children develop as distinct individuals across life.

Parents develop both as adults in general and, more specifically, in regard to their familial and extrafamilial roles (e.g., their vocations or careers). Indeed, the influence of a child on his or her parents will depend in part on the prior experience the adult has had with the parental role and on the other roles in which the parent is engaged (e.g., worker and/or adult–child and—with increasing frequency in our society—caregiver for an aged parent). Thus, a person's unique history of experiences and roles, as well as his or her singular biological (e.g., genetic) characteristics (McClearn, 1981), combine to make him or her unique—and with time, given the accumulation of the influences of distinct roles and experiences, increasingly different from others of his or her age group over the course of life (Lerner, 1988; Lerner & Tubman, 1989; Schaie, 1979).

The life-span perspective underscores, then, the developmental contextual idea that changing relations between the person and his or her context provide the basis, across life, of the individual's specific and singular repertoire of physical, psychological, and behavioral characteristics. This link between person and context was a product and a producer of the third trend emerging in the study of human development since the 1970s.

The study of children and their parents became increasingly "contextualized" (Lerner & Kauffman, 1985), or placed within the broader "ecology of human development" (Bronfenbrenner, 1979), during this period. This focus has involved a concern with the "real-life" situations within which children and families exist, and with the study of the bidirectional relations between the family and the other social settings within which children and parents function, for instance, the workplace, the day-care, and the formal and the nonformal educational and recreational settings present in a neighborhood or a community (e.g., see Kreppner & Lerner, 1989). The contributions of Bronfenbrenner (1979) and his colleagues (e.g., Bronfenbrenner & Crouter, 1983) have been a major catalyst in moving the study of human development beyond its status into the 1970s, as *"the science of the strange behavior of children in strange situations with strange adults for the briefest possible periods of time"* (Bronfenbrenner, 1977, p. 513).

In essence, then, within the contemporary study of human development there has been an increasing focus on the connections across life between the active, developing individual and the changing, multiple contexts within which he or she is embedded. Indeed, within the field of human development this focus is legitimated through subscription to the developmental contextual notion that the basic process of development is one of changing person-context *relations* (Gottlieb, 1991, 1992; Lerner, 1991). This understanding of basic process results, then, in an emphasis in research on the appraisal of the relations between an individual's development and the changing familial, community, societal, and cultural contexts within which the person is embedded. Accordingly, developmental contextualism leads to a focus, across the course of life, on individual differences — of people and of settings. These foci have important implications for research and for the policies and programs, aimed at understanding and optimizing, respectively, the course of human development.

IV. A Revised Vision of the Research Agenda for Human Development

The emphasis in developmental contextualism on the bidirectional connections between the individual and the actual ("ecologically valid") settings within which he or she lives has brought to the fore of concern in the social and behavioral sciences an emphasis on *diversity* (individual differences) and *context* (of peoples and their sociocultural institutions). In addition, the developmental contextual stress on the relation between the individual and his or her context has resulted in the recognition that a synthesis of perspectives from multiple disciplines is needed to understand the multilevel (e.g., person, family, and community) integrations involved in human development. Furthermore, there has been a recognition that to understand the basic process of human development—the process involved in the changing relations between individuals and contexts—both descriptive and explanatory research must be conducted within the actual ecology of people's lives.

Descriptive research involves the depiction, or representation, of development as it exists for a given person or group, in one or more contexts, at one or more points in time. Explanatory research involves the introduction (through manipulation or modeling) of variation into such person-context relations. These planned variations in the course of human life are predicated on (a) theoretical ideas about the source of particular developmental phenomena (for specific combinations of people and contexts), or on (b) theoretically guided interests about the extent to which a particular developmental phenomenon (e.g., cognitive development in the aged years) may show systematic change in structure and/or function, that is, *plasticity*, across the life span (Baltes, 1987; Lerner, 1984). In the case of either of these predications, such researcher-introduced variation is an attempt to simulate the "natural" variation of life; if theoretical expectations are confirmed, the outcomes of such investigations provide an explanation of how developmental change occurs within a person or group.

Given the developmental contextual focus on studying person-context relations within the actual ecology of human development, explanatory investigations by their very nature constitute intervention research. In other words, the goal of developmental contextual explanatory research is to understand the ways in which variations in ecologically "valid" person-context relations account for the character of actual or potential trajectories of human development, that is, life paths enacted in the "natural laboratory" of the "real world." Therefore, to gain understanding of how theoretically relevant variations in such person-context relations may influence actual or to-be-actualized developmental trajectories, the researcher may introduce policies and/or programs as, if you will, "experimental manipulations" of the proximal and/or distal natural ecology. Evaluations of the outcomes of such interventions become, then, a means to bring data to bear on theoretical issues pertinent to changing person-context relations and, more specifically, to the plasticity in human development that may exist, or that may be capitalized on, to enhance human life (Lerner, 1988). In other words, a key theoretical issue for explanatory research in human development is the extent to which changes—in the multiple, fused levels of organization comprising human life—can alter the structure and/or function of behavior and development.[2]

---

[2]It is also of theoretical interest to determine the level of organization, or combination of levels, that has the most impact. Is it a person's neighborhood, business associates or

Of course, independent of any researcher-imposed attempts to intervene in the course of human development, the naturally occurring events experienced by people constantly shape, texture, and help direct the course of their lives. That is, the accumulation of the specific roles and events a person experiences across life—involving normative age-graded events, normative history-graded events, and nonnormative events (Baltes et al., 1980)—alters each person's developmental trajectory in a manner that would not have occurred had another set of roles and events been experienced. The between-person differences in within-person change that exist as a consequence of these naturally occurring experiences attest to the magnitude of the systematic changes in structure and function—the plasticity—that characterizes human life.

Explanatory research is necessary, however, to understand what variables, from what levels of organization, are involved in particular instances of plasticity that have been seen to exist. In addition, such research is necessary to determine what instances of plasticity may be created by science or society. In other words, explanatory research is needed to ascertain the extent of human plasticity or, in turn, the limits of plasticity (Lerner, 1984). From a developmental contextual perspective, the conduct of such research requires the scientist to alter the natural ecology of the person or group he or she is studying. Such research may involve either proximal and/or distal variations in the context of human development (Lerner & Ryff, 1978); but, in any case, these manipulations constitute theoretically guided alterations of the roles and events a person or group experiences at, or over, a portion of the life span.

These alterations are indeed, then, interventions: They are planned attempts to alter the system of person-context relations, constituting the basic process of change; they are conducted in order to ascertain the specific bases of, or to test the limits of, particular instances of human plasticity (Baltes, Dittmann-Kohli, & Dixon, 1984; Baltes, Smith, & Staudinger, 1992). These interventions are a researcher's attempt to substitute designed person-context relations for naturally occurring ones in an attempt to understand the process of changing person-context relations providing the basis of human development. In short, then, basic research in human development is intervention research.

Accordingly, the cutting-edge of theory and research in human development lies in the application of the conceptual and methodological expertise of human development scientists to the "natural ontogenetic laboratory" of the real world. Multilevel, and hence, qualitatively and quantitatively multivariate, and longitudinal research methods must be used by scholars

professional colleagues, family, or broader social and political structure that plays a more prominent role in the development of a given behavior?

from multiple disciplines to derive, from theoretical models of person-context relations, programs of research that involve the design, delivery, and evaluation of interventions aimed at enhancing—through scientist-introduced variation—the course of human development.

A similar argument was made by Lanier (1990) in regard to how past approaches to educational research must be altered in order to improve teaching and the educational development of youth. Calling for what she termed "interventionist inquiry," Lanier argued for:

> educational research on teaching that is comparable to that which Dewey supported in his Chicago years—i.e., (1) experimentation within a naturalistic setting, notably the laboratory school; (2) a testing ground and link between scientific and social innovation; and (3) a means to increase educational efficiency by creating a more cohesive, interrelated social system, education being an interactive process among schools and various other social institutions . . . In order to have the best chance of improving practice, scholarly inquiry needs to occur in conjunction with substantial ongoing development and responsible experimentation in schools . . . This is why it is essential to combine rigorous inquiry with intervention on a systemic basis. (pp. 1–2)

In sum, in developmental contextualism there is a stress on ontological (and on epistemological, we would add) relationism and contextualization. These emphases have brought to the fore of scientific, intervention, and policy concerns issues pertinent to the functional import of diverse instances of person-context interactions. Examples are studies of the effects of variations in maternal employment on infant, child, and young adolescent development; the importance of differences in quality day care for the immediate and long-term development in children of healthy physical, psychological, and social characteristics; and the effects of variations in marital role strain and in marital stability-instability on the healthy development of children and youth.

Accordingly, as greater study has been made of the actual contexts within which people live, behavioral and social scientists have shown increasing appreciation of the *diversity* of patterns of individual and family development that exist, and that comprise the range of human structural and functional characteristics. Such diversity—involving racial, ethnic, gender, physical handicaps, national, and cultural variation—has, to the detriment of the knowledge base in human development, not been a prime concern of empirical analysis (Fisher & Brennan, 1992; Hagen, Paul, Gibb, & Wolters, 1990).

Yet, from a developmental contextual perspective, there are several reasons why this diversity should become a key focus of concern in the study of human development (Lerner, 1991, in press-a, in press-b). Diversity of people and their settings means that one cannot assume that general rules of development either exist for or apply in the same way to all children and families. Moreover, one cannot assume, even if only small portions of the total variance in human behavior and development reflect variance that is unique to an individual or group, that this nonshared variance is not the most salient information we have when attempting to understand or enhance the quality of the lives for the person or group. Accordingly, a new research agenda is promoted. This agenda would focus on diversity and context while at the same time attending to individual development, family changes, and the mutual influences between the two.

Simply stated, from this perspective integrated multidisciplinary and developmental research devoted to the study of diversity and context would be moved to the fore of scholarly concern. In addition, however, scholars involved in such research would have at least two other concerns, ones deriving from the view that basic, explanatory research in human development is, in its essence, intervention research.

V. Implications for Policies and Programs

In order to be complete, the integrative research promoted by a developmental contextual view of human development must be synthesized with two other foci. Research in human development that is concerned with one or even a few instances of individual and contextual diversity cannot be assumed to be useful for understanding the life course of all people. Similarly, policies and programs derived from such research, or associated with it in the context of a researcher's tests of ideas pertinent to human plasticity, cannot be assumed to be applicable, or equally appropriate and useful, in all contexts or for all individuals. Accordingly, developmental and individual differences-oriented policy development and program (intervention) design and delivery would need to be integrated fully with the new research base for which we are calling.

As emphasized in developmental contextualism, the variation in settings within which people live means that studying development in a standard (e.g., a "controlled") environment does not provide information pertinent to the actual (ecologically valid), developing relations between individually distinct people and their specific contexts (e.g., their particular families, schools, or communities). This point underscores the need to conduct research in real-world settings, and highlights the ideas that: (a) Policies and programs constitute natural experiments, that is, planned interventions for people and institutions; and (b) the evaluation of such activities becomes a central focus in the developmental contextual research agenda we have described.

In this view, then, policy and program endeavors do not constitute secondary work, or derivative applications, conducted after research evidence has been compiled. Quite to the contrary, and consistent with Lanier's (1990) concept of interventionist inquiry, policy development and implementation, and program design and delivery, become integral components of our vision for research; the evaluation component of such policy and intervention work provides critical feedback about the adequacy of the conceptual frame from which this research agenda should derive (cf. Lanier, 1990).[3] This conception of the integration of multidisciplinary research, endeavors centrally aimed at diversity and context, with policies, programs (interventions), and evaluations is illustrated in Fig. 1.

To be successful, this developmental, individual differences and contextual view of research, policy, and programs for human development requires not only collaboration across disciplines. In addition, two other types of collaboration are required. First, multiprofessional collaboration is essential. Colleagues in the research, policy, and intervention communities need to plan and implement their activities in a synthesized manner in order to successfully develop and extend this vision. All components of this collaboration should be understood as equally valuable, indeed, as equally essential. The collaborative activities of colleagues in university extension and outreach, in service design and delivery, in schools, in policy development and analysis, and in academic research are vital to the success of this new agenda for science and service for children, youth, parents, and their contexts, for example, families, schools, and communities.

Moreover, given the contextual embeddedness of these synthetic research and service activities, collaboration should occur with the people we are trying both to understand and to serve. Without incorporation of the perspective of the community into our work, without the community's sense of ownership and of assigned value and meaning, research and service activities cannot be adequately integrated into the lives we are studying. Our viewpoints about collaboration lead to some observations about directive themes that might organize the future activities of the professionals involved in studying and enhancing human development.

VI. Potential Scholarly and Service Themes

Together, the aforementioned facets of developmental contextual-oriented scholarship in the study of human development suggest several important themes for research, training, and service. First, a developmental, individual differences perspective is required to understand both developing people and their contexts. This perspective must focus on the

---

[3]The research itself can be more or less interventionist, depending on what research questions guide implementation strategies, data collection, or program design.

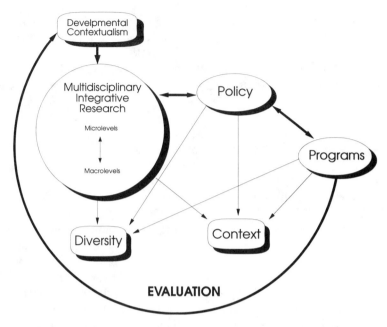

Fig. 1. A developmental contextual model of the integration of multilevel, multidisciplinary research, aimed at diversity and context, with policies, programs, and evaluations.

relations within a setting (e.g., relations within the family, between parents and children) and, as well, on the relations between each (family) member and the other settings within which he or she functions (e.g., children and day-care settings and parents and the workplace). In addition, the relations among settings must become a focus of developmental analysis as well (Bronfenbrenner, 1977, 1979). The compilation of such information will afford a profile of the individual people and relations that comprise a specific social context such as a family (Bronfenbrenner & Crouter, 1983).

Second, the study of human development must become broadly contextualized. Variables from multiple levels of organization—ranging from biology and health through social institutions involving education, politics, and the economy—affect people across their lives. It is the array of these variables as they extend across life that can make each person increasingly individually distinct from others in his or her family, social group, cohort, or society (Lerner, 1988; Lerner & Tubman, 1989).

Moreover, as we have stressed, the contextual and developmental approach to the study of human development must emphasize diversity. There is no one developmental path that is ideal for all people. As such, a key scientific concern of scholars of human development is the understanding of the richness of human life reflected in racial, ethnic, gender, physical handicap, national, and cultural variation. Education, intervention, outreach, and policy endeavors similarly should emphasize the specific patterns of contextual variation associated with the diverse peoples of concern to scholars.

Third, then, because no one discipline or professional area has an experiential or a knowledge base (or a repertoire of methodologies) sufficient to understand this diversity, or the interrelated influences of multiple levels of organization on human development, a multidisciplinary and multiprofessional approach to training, research, and service is needed. In other words, to study the phenomena and problems of children, youth, and families, as they function and develop in their real-life settings, and to provide effective health, family, and human policies and services, interdisciplinary conceptualizations and multiprofessional collaborations are required.

For example, there is a growing recognition that major familial problems, such as patterns of family instability and family violence, involve the interaction of psychological, social, economic, historical, and environmental factors. Moreover, there is a renewed and growing recognition that policies and programs that promote individualized, developmental, and preventive approaches to such concerns are more effective, more humane, and less expensive than is the sole reliance on remedial strategies (e.g., Dryfoos, 1990; Huston, 1992; McKinney, Abrams, Terry, & Lerner, in press; Schorr, 1988, 1992).

The results of evaluations of such programs suggest that effective means may be found to enhance the lives of children and parents from numerous sectors of our society (Dryfoos, 1990; Schorr, 1988). The importance of such enhancement may, we sense, be a concern moving to the forefront of the American political agenda. Over the course of the last several years we believe that the important national emphasis on geopolitical and international trade concerns has become interrelated with a focus on social issues germane to the other basic and applied concerns of behavioral and social scientists. Such issues as homelessness among American families, teenage pregnancy and childbearing, hunger, a weakened educational system, a shortage of quality day care, and deteriorating living and economic conditions among children and families near or below the poverty line are competing for a place on the ever more crowded "front burner" of the American political agenda (Anderson & Hula, 1989; Huston, 1992; McKinney et al., in press).

Clearly, these are issues that a field devoted to the study of human development should be especially well suited to address. They are problems involving how children and their parents behave: how they eat, or in fact whether they do; how they plan for and attempt to actualize their economic, social, and personal goals; how they design their environments to live enjoyable, efficient, and safe lives; how they relate to each other, both positively and negatively, within the family and within the community; and whether society's policies and services allow them to attain lives of quality and enrichment, to maintain a life marked by health, spiritual well-being, and financial security, and to develop successfully with dignity and respect.

However, these child and familial problems are not clustered in the ways that academic disciplines, professions, or services are divided. To address these problems we need, of course, to break them down into manageable elements, and here certainly disciplinary research is relevant and useful. But, related to the ideas of dynamic interaction, or multilevel fusion, emphasized in developmental contextualism, we believe that, in order to deal adequately with the problems as they really exist in our world, scholars, policy makers, and interventionists involved in human development study and service must be committed to putting the elements of the problems together.

This integration should be a key facet of the mission of academic fields or professions aimed at advancing science and service for human development. The knowledge base that may be generated in activities associated with such a mission may be extended into policies, programs, and services for the children, youth, and families of the state, of the nation, and — given the proper collaborative arrangements — the world.

In sum, we believe that research should be conducted with an appreciation of the individual differences in human development, differences that arise as a consequence of diverse people's development in distinct families, communities, and sociocultural settings. In turn, policies and programs should be similarly attuned to the diversity of people and context in order to maximize the chances of meeting the specific needs of particular groups of children and youth. Such programs and policies should be derived appropriately from research predicated on an integrative multidisciplinary view of human development. The evaluation of such activities should provide both societally important information about the success of endeavors aimed at human enhancement, and theoretically invaluable data about the validity of the synthetic, multilevel processes posited in developmental contextualism to characterize human developmnt.

VII. Challenges and Opportunities of a Developmental Contextual Approach to Research, Policy, and Programs

Meeting the challenge represented by the need to merge research with policy, and with intervention design, delivery, and evaluation, will bring the study of human development to the threshold of a new intellectual era. The linkage between research, policy, and intervention we have envisioned will demonstrate to scientists, policymakers, and interventionists that the basic processes of human behavior are ones involving the development of relations between individually distinct people and the specific social institutions they encounter in their particular ecological setting (Anderson & Hula, 1989).

This demonstration will be a matter, then, of bringing data to bear on the validity of the developmental contextual conception of basic process and of basic research (Lerner, 1991). Simply put, studying changing relations between diverse peoples and contexts alters the core analytic frame in investigations of human development from a "personological" one to a person-context relational one (Lerner, 1988, 1991); this alteration makes the evaluation of the programs and policies aimed at changing developmental patterns of youth a theoretically vital activity, one providing critical empirical feedback about the conceptual usefulness of the ideas of multi-level integration from which the policies and programs should have been derived.

It is for these reasons then, that we have argued that policy and program design, delivery, and evaluation are not "second-class citizens" to basic research. Within the frame of the fused levels of organization that comprise human behavior and development, they constitute necessary and basic empirical tests of the core, relational process of life. Accordingly, if we wish to meet the challenge of human development, the activities of colleagues whose expertise lies in policy and program design, delivery, and evaluation are not to be set apart from "basic" scientific activity. The expertise of policy and program professionals must be integrated with that of the researcher, in a fully collaborative enterprise, if we are to make continued progress in the understanding and enhancement of people across the entire span of their lives (Knott, 1986; Knott & Wildavsky, 1980).

In other words, the knowledge generation-application avenue is not a one-way street. Indeed, just as the practicing physician is often a source of issues that medical scientists then address, colleagues in the policy and program delivery arenas — whose roles emphasize the interface with specific individuals, families, schools, and communities — can provide invaluable feedback both about how the fruits of scholarship are being received and used and about new concerns that might be addressed with this scholarship (Knott, 1986; Knott & Wildavsky, 1980).

In sum, then, the burgeoning high-quality scientific activity in the developmental contextual study of human development has involved: first, the recognition of the importance of theory and research aimed at eluci-dating the relations between individually different, developing people and their diverse and changing contexts; and, second, the growing appreciation of the necessary linkage among research, policy, and intervention that must exist for the nature of human development — and, more specifically, its individuality and plasticity—to be understood and for the challenges of each period of the life span to be best met.

However, we should note here that there is a "double-edged sword" within the literature. As scholars have increased their understanding of the centrality of individual differences, of context, and of research-application linkages, an important limitation of the contemporary scientific literature has become apparent. Despite the value of the extant knowledge base about human development, and of the numerous examples of successful prevention programs for children, adults, and families living in "risk" conditions (Dryfoos, 1990; Schorr, 1988), most research investigations in the developmental literature have involved the study of U.S., White, middle-class samples (Fisher & Brennan, 1992; Hagen et al., 1990). There are, of course, some prominent, high-quality investigations of human development that have studied either other than White or middle-class U.S. samples, or individuals and families from national or cultural settings other than the United States (e.g., Baltes et al., 1984, in press; Brookins, 1991; Mead, 1928, 1930, 1935; Reid, 1991; Spencer, 1990, 1991; Spencer & Dornbusch, 1990; Spencer & Markstrom-Adams, 1990; Stattin & Magnusson, 1990; Whiting & Whiting, 1991). Nevertheless, as a consequence of the sampling that has characterized most of the studies in the literature, scientific generalizations about the nature of human development must be tentative. Perhaps more important, policies and interventions formulated on the basis of this information are also limited in important ways.

We illustrate these points by reference to the history of the field of developmental psychology. Within this field it is a fair but unfortunate conclusion that neither human diversity nor contextual variation have been adequately appreciated or understood. Indeed, one might infer from reading the pages of the leading research journals in the field (e.g., *Child Development* or *Developmental Psychology*) that to understand development it suffices to study, almost exclusively in laboratory-experimental situations, White, middle-class, school-age, U.S. children. In fact, in an analysis of randomly sampled articles published in *Child Development* over the course of more than 50 years, Hagen et al. (1990) found that, among the studies that informed readers of the demographic characteristics of the children sampled, the preponderant majority of the investigations did indeed appraise groups having these characteristics. However, Hagen et al. also reported that most of the *Child Development* articles in their sample reported neither the race nor the socioeconomic status of the children. Fisher and Brennan (1992), in an analysis of *Child Development* as well as of other prominent developmental journals, confirmed the findings of Hagen et al.

Thus, scholars publishing in the best journals in the field of developmental psychology have, as a group, acted either (a) as if they were studying the "generic child," a child whose context was of such little importance that even mention of some of its general characteristics (e.g., socioeconomic status) was not necessary, or (b) as if the only demographics worth mentioning were White, middle-class ones.

It may be deemed by some as impolite or impolitic to point to this shortcoming. However, such lack of sensitivity to human diversity and contextual variation cannot continue. Obviously, the absence of this sensitivity is morally repugnant to many people. In addition, however, such lack of sensitivity is simply bad science. Even before we reach the next century we will be a nation wherein "minority" children constitute the majority of the youth of our country. Only by assessing these children and youth can we gain understanding of diversity, of context, and of the plasticity of human life that is manifested by the changing relations between individually distinct people and their changing contexts. This observation leads to some concluding points.

VIII. Conclusions

The developmental contextual view of the basic process of human development brings to the fore the cutting-edge importance of continued empirical focus on individual differences, on contextual variations, and on changing person-context relations. Nothing short of these emphases can be regarded as involving a scientifically adequate developmental analysis of human life. And nothing short of data involving these emphases should be used for policies and programs suitable for individually different children and youth developing in relation to their specific contexts. Simply put, policies and programs that are derived from research on contextualized and homogenized groups of people will be too global and too undifferentiated to be of value for today's children, youth, or adults, or for the people who will populate our nation tomorrow (Anderson & Hula, 1989).

Accordingly, the specific challenge that now is before us is at least threefold. First, we should focus our multidisciplinary research efforts on the diverse people and settings about which we must learn if we are to obtain an adequate understanding of the range of developmental patterns, and of the richness and potential, of human life. Our research efforts should not only involve the implementation of a synthesis of ideas and methods from multiple disciplines; in addition, this integration should be employed in research with people of as wide a range of ethnic, racial, family, community, and sociocultural backgrounds as possible.

Second, it is clear that such research will not succeed unless the people from within these diverse settings are engaged cooperatively in the endeavor. As emphasized in developmental contextualism, individuals are active producers of their own development (Lerner, 1982). Thus, as we have argued, such research must be seen as relevant and important by the individuals, families, and communities about whom we wish to learn; such research, then, should be seen as returning, or providing, something of value to these groups. Simply stated, the people we seek to understand and serve must become our collaborators in our research; it is they who define what is of value, of importance, to their lives.

Accordingly, techniques that give voice to the community need to be employed in order to activate this university-community collaboration. One example of how this interaction may occur exists in the sociological literature. Burton (1990) used focus group methodology to elucidate the perspective of members of African-American communities about parenting and intergenerational relations. Another example exists within the political science literature. Hula (1990) used community empowerment techniques to engage tenants of public housing projects in the management of their housing.

In offering such service, the policies implemented, and programs delivered, by colleagues working within these settings become central. Accordingly, the knowledge and expertise of these professionals are necessary not only for the critical conceptual reasons noted previously. In addition, collaboration is vital for reasons relating to the practical issues involved in attempting to actually do the research we see as requisite for advancing knowledge of developmental diversity in human development across the life span.

Finally, a third challenge, one that brings us full circle to the issues confronting higher education in the 1990s, is to treat the implications of the developmental contextual model for change in the behavior of scholars studying the model and for change in institutions within which these scholars work. The integrations among levels that are specified in the model do not preclude the people, roles, and social institutions involved in higher education and social science. We, as scholars, are not disconnected from the people and society we study and serve. As parts of the same system it is entirely appropriate that we discuss — within the frame of the model — what changes need to be developed in scholars and scholarly institutions in order to best implement or test the model.

Established scholars should begin to reorient their own work. In addition, educators in each of the disciplines involved in the study of human development should begin to train their students differently (Birkel, Lerner, & Smyer, 1989; Fisher et al., 1993). An appreciation of systematic change, context, and human relationships should be the cornerstone of future graduate education. This is a central point stressed in the growing attention being paid among scholarly societies and universities to the importance of

training in applied developmental science for future scholars and professionals in fields associated with human development and education (Fisher
et al., 1993). We should instill in these future scholars and professionals a
greater appreciation of the importance of interindividual differences in the
timing of causal, dynamic interactions—for the development of human
diversity and for the contextual variation that is both a product and a
producer of it (Lerner, 1982; Lerner & Busch-Rossnagel, 1981).

Furthermore, it is important to add that university tenure and promotion
committees evaluating scientists studying development must be urged to
begin to consider the relative value of multidisciplinary collaborative, and
hence multiauthored, publications, in comparison to within-discipline,
single-authored products. We must also consider the nature of the reception
given by university review committees to the sort of contextual and
collaborative research we are furthering. The issue to be debated here is
whether we can train future cohorts of applied developmental scientists to
engage productively in the multidisciplinary, multiprofessional, and community collaborations requisite for advancing understanding of the basic
process of development and then not reward and value them for successfully doing so. In essence, we must engage in a debate about changing the
reward system within our universities. If we follow a developmental
contextual perspective that leads to the synthesis of science and service, then
it would seem that we must devise means to assign value to, and reward, an
array of collaborative, multidisciplinary, and multiprofessional activities.
Similarly, if we are to take seriously the need for change-oriented (and
hence longitudinal), multilevel (and hence multivariate), and multidisciplinary research, we must recognize the need to educate government agencies
and private foundations about the time and financial resources that should
be given to such collaborative activities.

In sum, then, the challenge in the study and enhancement of human
development is to integrate multiple academic disciplines and multiple
professional activities with the community. The result of such efforts will
be, first, a better understanding of the multilevel processes that relate the
individually distinct, developing person to his or her specific setting.
Second, this integration will afford better tests of the developmental
contextual theoretical integrations legitimating this multidisciplinary and
multiprofessional collaboration. Third, then, a more adequate database will
be available for the design, delivery, and evaluation of policies and
programs aimed at the enhancement of our nation's only truly invaluable
resource, our people.

Our task, then, is not just to do more or to do better. If we are to
significantly advance science and service for the people of our nation, we
must engage in new activities. This is the challenge before us as we approach
the next century. And this is the path upon which we, as scientists, policy
makers, interventionists and, most basically, citizens, must embark.

Acknowledgments

The preparation of this chapter was supported in part by grants from the W. K. Kellogg Foundation, the C. S. Mott Foundation, and by NICHD Grant HD23229. Reflecting the multidisciplinary, multiprofessional, and community integration for which we call, this chapter involves a collaboration among authors with backgrounds in developmental psychology, home economics, human ecology, political science, urban planning, geography, criminology, community-based youth and family programming, federal government service, education, state government service, policy analysis, and sociology.

References

Anderson, E., & Hula, R. C. (1989). Symposium: Family policy. *Policy Studies Review, 8,* 573–736.

Baltes, P. B. (1968). Longitudinal and cross-sectional sequences in the study of age and generation effects. *Human Development, 11,* 145–171.

Baltes, P. B. (1979). Life-span developmental psychology: Some converging observations on history and theory. In P. B. Baltes & O. G. Brim, Jr. (Eds.), *Life-span development and behavior* (Vol. 2, pp. 255–279). New York: Academic.

Baltes, P. B. (1983). Life-span developmental psychology. Observations on history and theory revisited. In R. M. Lerner (Ed.), *Developmental psychology: Historical and philosophical perspectives* (pp. 79–111). Hillsdale, NJ: Lawrence Erlbaum Associates.

Baltes, P. B. (1987). Theoretical propositions of life-span developmental psychology: On the dynamics between growth and decline. *Development Psychology, 23,* 611–626.

Baltes, P. B., Dittmann-Kohli, F., & Dixon, R. A. (1984). New perspectives on the development of intelligence in adulthood: Toward a dual-process conception and a model of selective optimization with compensation. In P. B. Baltes & O. G. Brim, Jr. (Eds.), *Life-span development and behavior* (Vol. 6, pp. 33–76). New York: Academic.

Baltes, P. B., Reese, H. W., & Lipsitt, L. P. (1980). Life-span developmental psychology. *Annual Review of Psychology, 31,* 65–110.

Baltes, P. B., & Schaie, K. W. (1973). On life-span developmental research paradigms. Retrospects and prospects. In P. B. Baltes & K. W. Schaie (Eds.), *Life-span developmental psychology: Personality and socialization* (pp. 365–395). New York: Academic.

Baltes, P. B., Smith, J., & Staudinger, U. M. (1992). Wisdom and successful aging. In T. B. Sonderegger (Ed.), *Nebraska symposium on motivation* (Vol. 39, pp. 123–167). Lincoln: University of Nebraska Press.

Birkel, R., Lerner, R. M., & Smyer, M. A. (1989). Applied developmental psychology as an implementation of a life-span view of human development. *Journal of Applied Developmental Psychology, 10,* 425–445.

Bok, D. (1992). Reclaiming the public trust. *Change,* pp. 13–19.

Boyer, E. L. (1990). *Scholarship reconsidered: Priorities of the professoriate.* Princeton, NJ: The Carnegie Foundation for the Advancement of Teaching.

Brim, O. G., & Kagan, J. (Eds.). (1980). *Constancy and change in human development.* Cambridge, MA: Harvard University Press.

Bronfenbrenner, U. (1977). Toward an experimental ecology of human development. *American Psychologist, 32,* 513–531.

Bronfenbrenner, U. (1979). *The ecology of human development.* Cambridge, MA: Harvard University Press.

Bronfenbrenner, U., & Crouter, A. C. (1983). The evolution of environmental models in developmental research. In W. Kessen (Ed.), *Handbook of child psychology: Vol. 1. History, theories, and methods* (pp. 39–83). New York: Wiley.

Brookins, G. K. (1991). Socialization of African-American adolescents. In R. M. Lerner, A.

C. Petersen, & J. Brooks-Gunn (Eds.), *Encyclopedia of adolescence* (pp. 1072–1076). New York: Garland.

Burton, L. M. (1990). Teenage childbearing as an alternative life-course strategy in multi-generation Black families. *Human Nature, 1*(2), 123–143.

Dixon, R. A., & Lerner, R. M. (1992). A history of systems in developmental psychology. In M. H. Bornstein & M. E. Lamb (Eds.), *Developmental psychology: An advanced textbook* (3rd ed., pp. 3–58). Hillsdale, NJ: Lawrence Erlbaum Associates.

Dixon, R. A., Lerner, R. M., & Hultsch, D. E. (1991). The concept of development in individual and social change. In P. Van Geert & L. P. Mos (Eds.), *Annals of theoretical psychology* (Vol. 7, pp. 279–323). New York: Plenum.

Dryfoos, J. G. (1990). *Adolescents at risk: Prevalence and prevention.* New York: Oxford University Press.

Elder, G. H., Jr. (1979). Historical change in life patterns and personality. In P. B. Baltes & O. G. Brim, Jr. (Eds.), *Life-span development and behavior* (Vol. 2, pp. 117–159). New York: Academic.

Elder, G. H., Jr. (1980). Adolescence in historical perspective. In J. Adelson (Ed.), *Handbook of adolescent psychology* (pp. 3–46). New York: Wiley.

Featherman, D. L. (1983). Life-span perspectives in social science research. In P. B. Baltes & O. G. Brim, Jr. (Eds.), *Life-span development and behavior* (Vol. 5, pp. 1–57). New York: Academic.

Featherman, D. L. (1985). Individual development and aging as a population process. In J. R. Nesselroade & A. von Eye (Eds.), *Individual development and social change: Explanatory analyses* (pp. 213–241). New York: Academic.

Featherman, D. L., & Lerner, R. M. (1985). Ontogenesis and sociogenesis: Problematics for theory about development across the lifespan. *American Sociological Review, 50,* 659–676.

Fisher, C. B., & Brennan, M. (1992). Application and ethics in developmental psychology. In D. L. Featherman, R. M. Lerner, & M. Perlmutter (Eds.), *Life-span development and behavior* (Vol. 11, pp. 189–215). Hillsdale, NJ: Lawrence Erlbaum Associates.

Fisher, C. B., & Lerner, R. M. (Eds.). (in press). *Applied developmental psychology.* Cambridge, MA: McGraw-Hill.

Fisher, C. B., Murray, J. P., Dill, J. R. Hagen, J. W., Hogan, M. J., Lerner, R. M., Rebok, G. W., Sigel, I., Sostek, A. M., Smyer, M. A., Spencer, M. B., & Wilcox, B. (1993). The national conference on graduate education in the applications of developmental science across the life span. *Journal of Applied Developmental Psychology, 14,* 1–10.

Ford, D. L., & Lerner, R. M. (1992). *Developmental systems theory: An integrative approach.* Newbury Park, CA: Sage.

Gottlieb, G. (1991). Experiential canalization of behavioral development: Theory. *Developmental Psychology, 27,* 4–13.

Gottlieb, G. (1992). *Individual development and evolution: The genesis of novel behavior.* New York: Oxford University Press.

Hagen, J. W., Paul, B., Gibb, S., & Wolters, C. (1990, March). *Trends in research as reflected by publications in Child Development: 1930–1989.* Paper presented at the biennial meeting of the Society for Research on Adolescence, Atlanta.

Hula, R. (1990). Alternative management strategies for public housing. In W. Gromley (Ed.), *Privatization and its alternatives* (pp. 134–162). Madison: University of Wisconsin Press.

Huston, A. C. (Ed.). (1992). *Children in poverty: Child development and public policy.* Cambridge, England: Cambridge University Press.

Knott, J. H. (1986). The multiple and ambiguous roles of professionals in public policy making. *Knowledge: Creation, Diffusion, Utilization, 8,* 131–153.

Knott, J. H., & Wildavsky, A. (1980). If dissemination is the solution, what is the problem? *Knowledge: Creation, Diffusion, Utilization, 4,* 537–578.

Kreppner, K., & Lerner, R. M. (Eds.). (1989). *Family systems and life-span development.* Hillsdale, NJ: Lawrence Erlbaum Associates.

Lanier, J. E. (1990). *Report to focus group colleagues on "teaching," National Academy of Education study on the future of educational research.* East Lansing: Michigan State University, College of Education.

Lerner, R. M. (1978). Nature, nurture and dynamic interactionism. *Human Development, 21,* 1-20.

Lerner, R. M. (1982). Children and adolescents as producers of their own development. *Developmental Review, 2,* 342-370.

Lerner, R. M. (1984). *On the nature of human plasticity.* New York: Cambridge University Press.

Lerner, R. M. (1986). *Concepts and theories of human development* (2nd ed.). New York: Random House.

Lerner, R. M. (1988). Personality development: A life-span perspective. In E. M. Hetherington, R. M. Lerner, & M. Perlmutter (Eds.), *Child development in life-span perspective* (pp. 21-46). Hillsdale, NJ: Lawrence Erlbaum Associates.

Lerner, R. M. (1991). Changing organism-context relations as the basic process of development: A developmental contextual perspective. *Developmental Psychology, 27,* 27-32.

Lerner, R. M. (1992). *Final solutions: Biology, prejudice, and genocide.* University Park: Penn State Press.

Lerner, R. M. (in press-a). Diversity and context in research, policy, and programs for children and adolescents: A developmental contextual perspective. In G. K. Brookins & M. B. Spencer (Eds.), *Ethnicity and diversity: Implications for research and policies.* Hillsdale, NJ: Lawrence Erlbaum Associates.

Lerner, R. M. (in press-b). The integration of levels and human development: A developmental contextual view of the synthesis of science and outreach in the enhancement of human lives. In K. Hood, G. Greenberg, & E. Tobach (Eds.), *Approach withdraw theory and behavioral development.* New York: Garland.

Lerner, R. M., & Busch-Rossnagel, N. A. (Eds.). (1981). *Individuals as producers of their development: A life-span perspective.* New York: Academic.

Lerner, R. M., Hultsch, D. F., & Dixon, R. A. (1983). Contextualism and the character of developmental psychology in the 1970s. *Annals of the New York Academy of Sciences, 412,* 101-128.

Lerner, R. M., & Kauffman, M. B. (1985). The concept of development in contextualism. *Developmental Review, 5,* 309-333.

Lerner, R. M., & Miller, J. R. (1993). Integrating human development research and intervention for America's children: The Michigan State University model. *Journal of Applied Developmental Psychology, 14,* 347-364.

Lerner, R. M., & Ryff, C. (1978). Implementation of the life-span view of human development: The sample case of attachment. In P. B. Baltes (Ed.), *Life-span development and behavior* (Vol. 1, pp. 1-44). New York: Academic.

Lerner, R. M., & Spanier, G. B. (Eds.). 1978). *Child influences on marital and family interaction: A life-span perspective.* New York: Academic.

Lerner, R. M., & Spanier, G. B. (1980). *Adolescent development: A life-span perspective.* New York: McGraw-Hill.

Lerner, R. M., & Tubman, J. (1989). Conceptual issues in studying continuity and discontinuity in personality development across life. *Journal of Personality, 57,* 343-373.

Lerner, R. M., & Tubman, J. (1990). Plasticity in development: Ethical implications. In C. B. Fisher & W. W. Tryon (Eds.), *Ethics in applied developmental psychology* (pp. 113-131). Norwood, NJ: Ablex.

Lewis, M., & Rosenblum, L. A. (Eds.). (1974). *The effect of the infant on its caregiver.* New York: Wiley.

Lynton, E. A., & Elman, S. E. (1987). *New priorities for the university: Meeting society's needs for applied knowledge and competent individuals.* San Francisco: Jossey-Bass.

McClearn, G. E. (1981). Evolution and genetic variability. In E. S. Gollin (Ed.), *Developmental plasticity: Behavioral and biological aspects of variations in development* (pp. 3–31). New York: Academic.

McKinney, M., Abrams, L. A., Terry, P. A., & Lerner, R. M. (in press). Child development research and the poor children of America: A call for a developmental contextual approach to research and outreach. *Home Economics Research Journal.*

Mead, M. 1928). *Coming of age in Samoa: A psychological study of primitive youth for Western civilization.* New York: Morrow.

Mead, M. (1930). *Growing up in New Guinea.* New York: Morrow.

Mead, M. (1935). *Sex and temperament in three primitive societies..* New York: Morrow.

Miller, J. R., & Lerner, R. M. (in press). Integrating research and outreach: Developmental contextualism and the human ecological perspective. *Human Ecology Forum.*

Nesselroade, J. R., & Baltes, P. B. (Eds.). (1979). *Longitudinal research in the study of behavior and development.* New York: Academic.

Overton, W. F., & Reese, H. W. (1973). Models of development: Methodological implications. In J. R. Nesselroade & H. W. Reese (Eds.), *Life-span developmental psychology: Methodological issues* (pp. 65–86). New York: Academic.

Reese, H. W., & Overton, W. F. (1970). Models of development and theories of development. In L. R. Goulet & P. B. Baltes (Eds.), *Life-span developmental psychology: Research and theory* (pp. 115–145). New York: Academic.

Reid, P. T. (1991). Black female adolescents, socialization of. In R. M. Lerner, A. C. Petersen, & J. Brooks-Gunn (Eds.), *Encyclopedia of adolescence* (pp. 85–87). New York: Garland.

Schaie, K. W. (1965). A general model for the study of developmental problems. *Psychological Bulletin, 64,* 92–107.

Schaie, K. W. (1979). The primary mental abilities in adulthood: An exploration in the development of psychometric intelligence. In P. B. Baltes & O. G. Brim, Jr. (Eds.), *Life-span development and behavior* (Vol. 2, pp. 67–115). New York: Academic.

Schneirla, T. C. (1957). The concept of development in comparative psychology. In D. B. Harris (Ed.), *The concept of development* (pp. 78–108). Minneapolis: University of Minnesota.

Schorr, L. B. (1988). *Within our reach: Breaking the cycle of disadvantage.* New York: Doubleday.

Schorr, L. B. (1992). Effective programs for children growing up in concentrated poverty. In A. C. Huston (Ed.), *Children in poverty: Child development and public policy* (pp. 260–281). Cambridge, England: Cambridge University Press.

Spencer, M. B. (1990). Parental values transmission: Implications for Black child development. In J. B. Stewart & H. Cheatham (Eds.), *Black families: Interdisciplinary perspectives* (pp. 111–130). Atlanta: Transactions.

Spencer, M. B. (1991). Identity, minority development of. In R. M. Lerner, A. C. Petersen, & J. Brooks-Gunn (Eds.), *Encyclopedia of adolescence* (pp. 525–528). New York: Garland.

Spencer, M. B., & Dornbusch, S. (1990). Challenges in studying minority adolescents. In S. Feldman & G. Elliott (Eds.), *At the threshold: The developing adolescent* (pp. 123–146). Cambridge, MA: Harvard University Press.

Spencer, M. B., & Markstrom-Adams, C. (1990). Identity processes among racial and ethnic minority children in America. *Child Development, 61,* 290–310.

Stattin, H., & Magnusson, D. (1990). *Pubertal maturation in female development.* Hillsdale, NJ: Lawrence Erlbaum Associates.

Tobach, E. (1981). Evolutionary aspects of the activity of the organism and its development.

In R. M. Lerner & N. A. Busch-Rossnagel (Eds.), *Individuals as producers of their own development: A lifespan perspective.* New York: Academic.

Tobach, E., & Greenberg, G. (1984). The significance of T. C. Schneirla's contribution to the concept of levels of integration. In G. Greenberg & E. Tobach (Eds.), *Behavioral evolution and integrative levels* (pp. 1–7). Hillsdale, NJ: Lawrence Erlbaum Associates.

Whiting, B. B., & Whiting, J. W. M. (1991). Preindustrial world, adolescence in. In R. M. Lerner, A. C. Petersen, & J. Brooks-Gunn (Eds.), *Encyclopedia of adolescence* (pp. 814–829). New York: Garland.

Author Index

Subject Index